Tracing My African Routes

Out and Back to Africa in a 1929 Morris

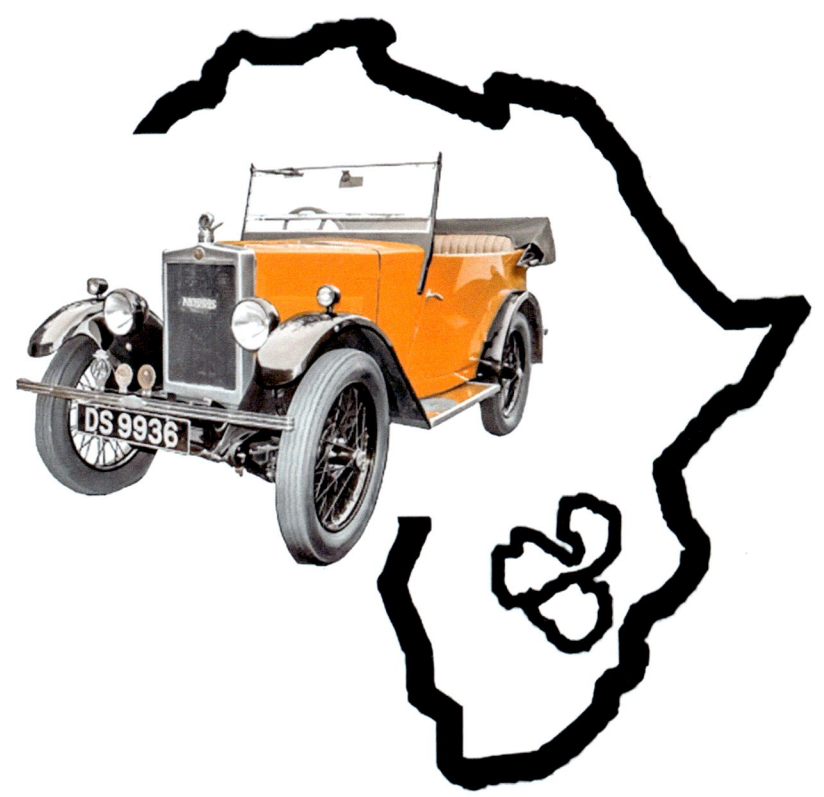

Four elderly men on a crazy adventure around Zimbabwe
and Zambia in a baby vintage car

Peter W. Hills

Helion & Company

Helion & Company Limited
Unit 8 Amherst Business Centre
Budbrooke Road
Warwick
CV34 5WE
England
Tel. 01926 499619
Email: info@helion.co.uk
Website: www.helion.co.uk
X (formerly Twitter): @Helionbooks
Facebook: @HelionBooks
Visit our blog at helionbooks.wordpress.com

Published by Helion & Company 2024
Designed and typeset by Mach 3 Solutions (www.mach3solutions.co.uk)
Cover designed by Paul Hewitt, Battlefield Design (www.battlefield-design.co.uk)

ISBN 978-1-804517-41-3

British Library Cataloguing-in-Publication Data.
A catalogue record for this book is available from the British Library.

For details of other military history titles published by Helion & Company Limited, contact the above address, or visit our website: http://www.helion.co.uk

We always welcome receiving book proposals from prospective authors.

Dedicated to my Dad, Chilupala

(the one with no hair – Chibemba)

Contents

Tracing My African Routes

Out and Back to Africa in a 1929 Morris

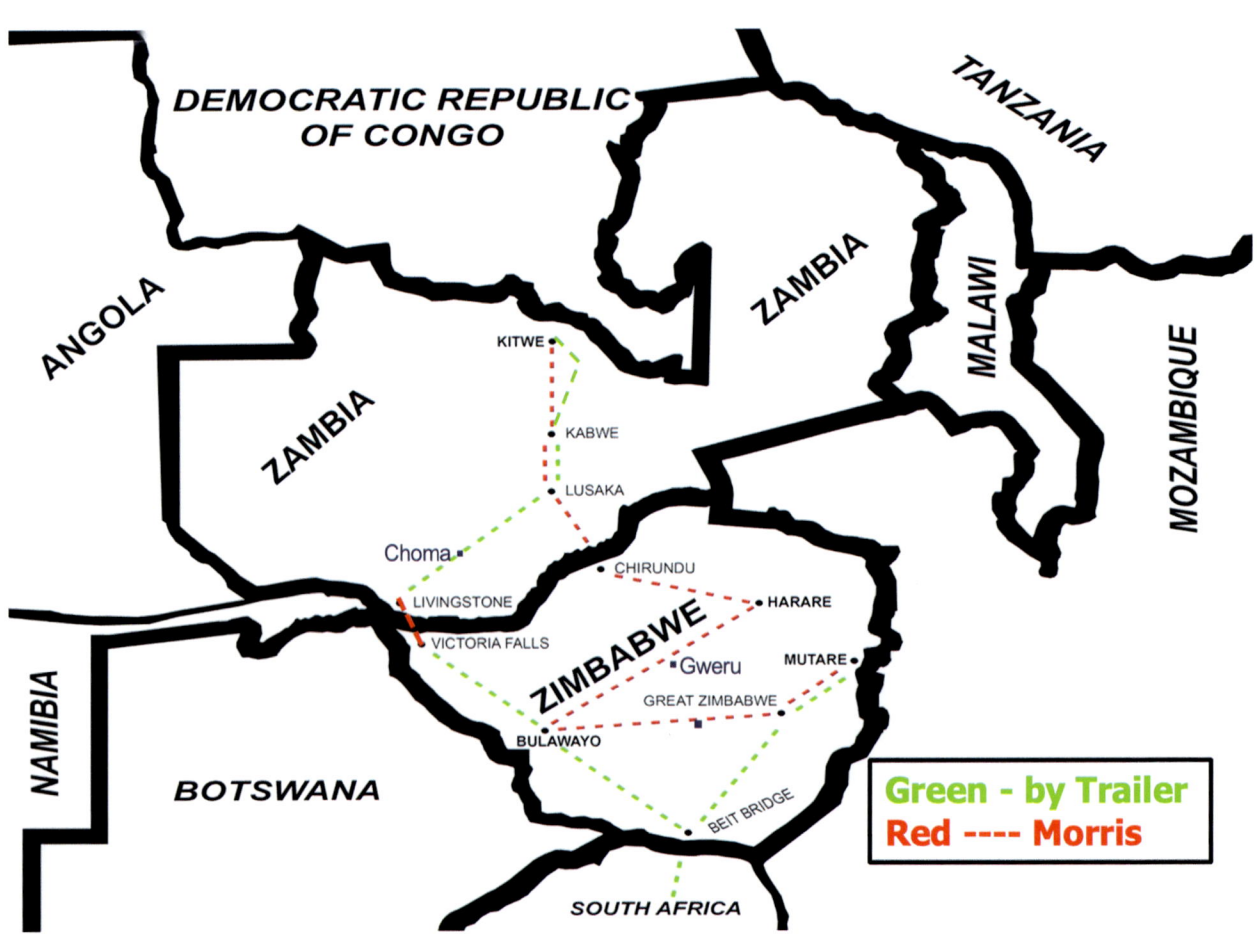

Planned Tour Map of Zimbabwe and Zambia

Technical Guides

To serve the owners of vintage and pre-war cars, this book includes a consolidated section of Technical Guides. These were initially written for my various car club magazines but now I have updated and improved them as further experience was gained. It is hoped that the detailed photos, descriptions and methods will be of interest and of use to those maintaining and restoring similar vehicles. Perhaps future custodians unfamiliar with the engineering skills of the past will find these guides a useful reference.

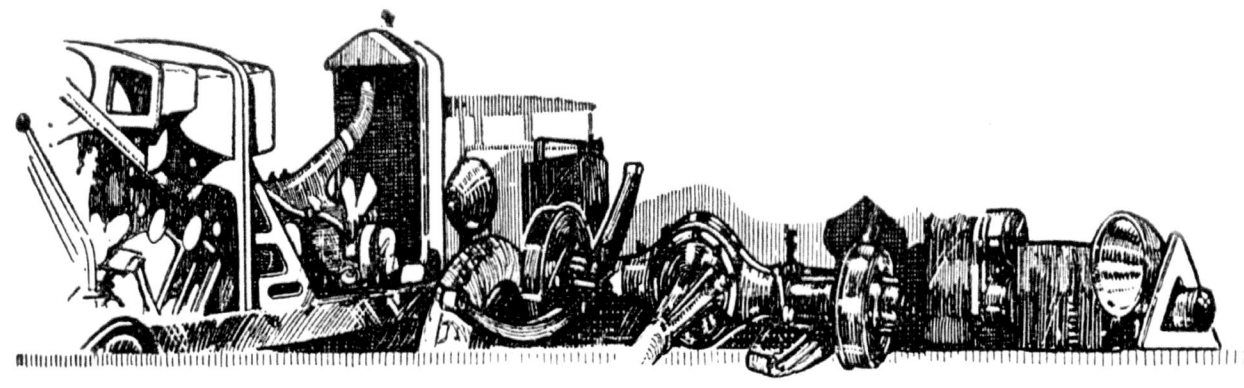

Fig. 3: Morris Technical Guide List (Refer to Chapter 13)

Acknowledgements

My wife Sandy Hills, without her constant support none of this would have been possible.

The BTA Team: Wayne Taylor, David Forgus and Graham Pringle (my diarist who spent many hours after the trip writing up the daily diary and subsequently typing up his notes). Graham Lowden, my brother-in-law, who was on hand at every turn especially while repairing the Morris in Cape Town, and his sage advice. John Ryall for arranging to transport the Morris in his container from London to Cape Town and its return. Feliciano Martins for the replacement crankshaft system in my time of need. Aubrey Springer who machined many parts and fitted the new crankshaft to meet my deadline. Ronnie McFarland of Basticks Engine Reconditioners who pulled out all stops to machine engine parts. Steve Martin who supplied the banners and decals at no expense. Peter Price of Priclo Trailers who provided a reconditioned trailer with comprehensive spares at a discounted price. Jack and Shirley Downsborough for accommodation in Johannesburg. Kevin Woodward of Hillside Golf Club who researched records of the first owner and arranged the farewell with club members. Dr Eng. Mutezo, Birchenough Hotel. Bruce Beckley – Bulawayo arrangements. Bryan Christie's garage facilities and assistance (Bulawayo). Tim McAlastair for the differential spares. Dudley and Prue Searle, Harare accommodation, and arranging the VCCZ meeting at their Pangoula Farm. Maurice Diamond's generous accommodation at Siavonga, Kariba. Rodney Wayland-Green – organising the DHL of replacement spider gears for the Diff. Theo Pieterse for giving us a lake trip and driven tour around Kariba. Lynn Quarmby (Casson) and Dimitri and Charlotte Klironomos (Lynne's stepdaughter) and George and Tonia Klironomos at Kamushi Farm Kitwe for accommodation and engineering support. The Lusaka team: Ken and Mairi Cummins (accommodation), Bobby van der Merwe, Gerard Fagan, René Lourens, Hans and Gea Sportel (emergency accommodation). Rory and Dori McDougall for a wonderful stay at Masuku Lodge Choma. Joyce M. Maycock for reviewing the draft of this book and the technical section. Rose Malinaric for initial and ongoing editing of this book and guidance towards publication. Duncan Rogers of Helion and Co for his help throughout and Stephen Ede-Borrett for his assistance in the editing process.

Past preparation and research over the years:
Roy Rodney Scott who was with me when we found the Morris in the bushes. The contributors in Zambia for the early restoration as engraved on the Morris's name plate. Mrs Rene Lang for formally transferring ownership and providing key records. My father Douglas Hills for getting the engine started. Harry Edwards the Morris Register Historian. Donna and Ian Trott for family photos of her tjorrie and constant encouragement. Ken Hall for the bodywork. John Cartlidge, upholstery. John D. Nagle – *The Complete Morris Minor*, and my family who were involved from time to time to completion.

Introduction

It was during 1970 that my school pal Roy Scott and I found the wreck of a 1929 Morris Minor Four-Seat Tourer in the bushes at Itimpi, a deserted smallholding outside Kitwe in Zambia, formerly Northern Rhodesia (Fig.1). Aged 26, with blind enthusiasm I took the wreck home and immediately commenced to restore it. Over the next 22 years, despite changing homes several times as well as moving to England, by 1992 this little car was brought to Concours condition (Fig.2). Through much research during this period, with considerable luck, I managed to identify all the car's previous owners and learned much of its early history.

Fig.1: Chassis M10228 as found in Zambia,1970

Fig.2: Chassis M10228 restored in the UK, 1992

In 2019, 49 years after finding the car, I shipped the Morris to Cape Town with the intention of touring Zimbabwe and Zambia to visit the addresses and cover the route its 10 previous owners might have taken. It did not occur to me that, while Cameron Gilg undertook his 1933 trans-Africa journey at the age of 23, I was in my late seventies, some 55 years older! Soon after the car arrived in South Africa Covid-19 intervened; so the trip finally took place in 2023. This is my story.

The prospect of driving a 1929 Morris Minor around Central Africa seems quite crazy – some said foolish! Surely such a journey in 2023 would be quite tame compared to Gilg and Kay's journey in a similar car from Liverpool to Cape Town in 1933 (Ref.1). At that time many roads were undeveloped or nonexistent, few support services were available, let alone the availability of fuel. Had the infrastructure of independent Africa improved by 2023 (see Appendix V: Politics). I would soon find out: like the curate's egg – good in parts!

Stage 1 of the plan was to transport the Morris in a box trailer from Cape Town to Mutare Zimbabwe where the first owner had registered it. Then we would visit the addresses of the next nine owners and finally return with the car back to the jungle where I found it in 1970. This would require driving some 1,500 miles. To achieve this crazy goal, I needed a back-up team of three with specific skills. After completing the mission, we would then transport the car in the box trailer back to Cape Town before returning it to the UK, as required by the conditions of the *Carnet de Passages en Douane*.

I had grown up in Northern Rhodesia (now Zambia) while team member Graham Pringle was born in Southern Rhodesia (now Zimbabwe): the visit would be a nostalgic return to the haunts of our youth, our towns, our schools. Apart from touring the familiar and changing countryside, we had been brought up in the local culture and understood the people. The lush tropical rainforests, mountains, escarpments, balancing rocks, deserts, the *Acacia* and *Miombo* trees, the familiar smell of the grassland would be a fond reminder of happy days when life was simpler – spent mainly outdoors fishing and birding.

From the time the Morris arrived in Cape Town I faced several major obstacles: it seemed as if someone was saying "stop this foolish idea". The global pandemic postponed the trip year after year – 2020, 2021 and 2022 – but finally we set the date for departure at 23 March 2023.

Assembling a committed support team further challenged me, virtually to the last minute. And then, when all was prepared, on 5 March the Morris's crankshaft failed catastrophically. Amazingly, I obtained a replacement and its associated elements the very next day. A Herculean engineering effort was required to customise, assemble and install the repaired engine. To the astonishment of many, the car was back on the road just 13 days later. During the trip we experienced further challenges with both the Morris and the back-up vehicle as well as the box trailer. The resourcefulness of the team, friends, strangers and lots of good fortune culminated in our achieving all objectives of the tour and a safe return to Cape Town on 10 May 2023. We had been away exactly 49 days, covering 9,767 kilometres, tired but exhilarated.

This book details the car's day-to-day journey around Zimbabwe and Zambia, the iconic sites, its unique history and that of the car's past owners, and aspects of the two countries it resided in. The people we met, travel statistics, as well as a technical section are all part of the mix.

Our tour was not only about a little car's actual 1,509 mile journey around Central Africa but also to raise funds for a charity supporting and educating Aids orphans in Zambia (Ref.2). UK Charity number: 1071660.

Please consider making a donation to support the life-changing work we do helping young Zambians into education to help break the cycle of poverty.

You can donate here. Thank you!

I am very proud of the Out and Back-to-Africa (BTA) Team and indebted to them; without their commitment, cooperation and comradeship the trip would not have been possible or have been enjoyable. All agreed it was the experience of a lifetime "Tracing My African Routes".

Chapter 1

The Morris Minor 1929 and 1933: Trip Objectives

History of the 1929 Morris Minor

The first Morris Minor was developed to compete and catch up with sales of the very successful Austin 7. It was a larger and far better quality of build than the Austin but it never matched Austin's production numbers. The Morris Minor was launched late in 1928 for the 1929 season with William Morris posing with a prototype late in 1928 quoting the popular song "Yes Sir, That's My Baby".

Most people are more familiar with the famous (bubble shape) Morris Minor that was launched in 1948 at the British Motor Show in London. This popular car was exported around the world; many are still in regular use. My first Morris Minor model 1000, was a *c.* 1959 that I reconditioned at Kitwe Zambia. In February 1965 I drove it to Johannesburg and back for my pal Frank Jenkins's 21st birthday without any issue, covering 4,200 kilometres.

The 1929 Morris Minor Tourer Specifications: Coach built, two-door body. Adjustable bucket type seats (near-side seat folds and tips). Complete all-weather equipment of metal framed hood and rigid side screens with signalling flaps. Double-pane adjustable windscreen. Coachwork finished in blue or brown cellulose to choose, with Rexine upholstery to match. Price with Triplex windscreen: £127.

Fig.4: The First Morris Minor

Fig.5: My Morris 1000 and BSA bike

Table 1: Morris Minor Production Records by Body Type and Season

Season	1929	Percent	1930	Percent	1931	percent	Totals by Model	Total percent
Saloon	8,925	73.2	11,343	77.2	5,557	72.3	25,825	74.7
Tourer	2,067	17.0	1,386	9.4	389	5.1	3,842	11.1
Van			1,243	8.5	865	11.2	2,108	6.1
Semi-sports					744	9.7	744	2.2
Chassis	1,200	9.8	725	4.9	136	1.8	2,061	6.0
Totals by season	12,192		14,697		7,691		34,580	

(Source: Vintage Minor Register)

Details of my 1929 Morris Minors were confirmed against the original Rhodesian Registration numbers by the British Motor Heritage Trust Certificate issued 29 October 1991 as follows:

Chassis VIN: M/10228
Engine Number: 9668
Body Number:10707
Manufactured 5–10 July 1929
Dispatched 17 July 1929
Cowley, Oxford, England 17 July
Exported (to Southern Rhodesia)

Fig.6: BHT Confirming M10228 was exported

This was "golden" information that the certificate confirmed that Chassis 10228 had been exported from the Morris factory to Southern Rhodesia (Zimbabwe). It was first registered in Umtali (Mutare) as U750, the chassis and engine numbers match the certificate.

Gilg and Kay 1933 Liverpool to Cape Town

Alan Cameron Gilg (aged 23) and Walter Kay drove a 1933 Morris Minor Tourer (SV) from Liverpool to Cape Town.

The book *Turn Left – The Riffs Have Risen* (Ref.1) was written a long time after Alan Gilg's death by Barry Cockcroft who published it through the RAC in 1981. Fortunately, Gilg left a meticulous log detailing each day of their trip. He also carried a 16mm cine camera, producing many feet of stills and movies that lay in a cupboard for 40 years. Their incredible journey across the Sahara and down Africa took them five months. The map (Fig.8) illustrates the amazing route they took.

In the 1970s Yorkshire Television used the data from the RAC book and Gilg's footage to create a documentary that was transmitted to a TV audience of many millions in the UK. Throughout our 2023 Back-to-Africa venture we recorded as much footage as possible but hope it won't take 40 years to publication! The 2023 trip was an endeavour to visit some of the locations that the Gilg–Kay trip had stayed at – principally the Broken Hill Boon Hotel (Kabwe, Zambia), repeat crossing the Victoria Falls staying overnight at the Winburg Hotel (Free State, South Africa). One similarity of our trip is that they carried many spares that they did not use but not the ones they needed; the BTA trip experienced the same!

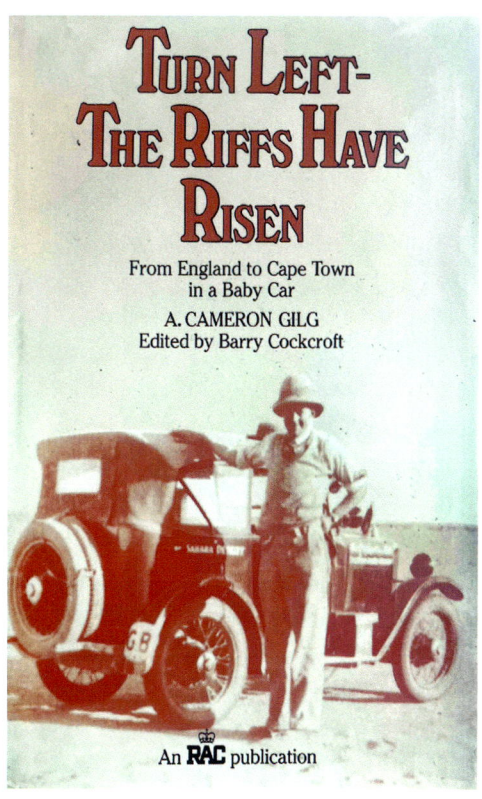

Fig.7: Published by RAC

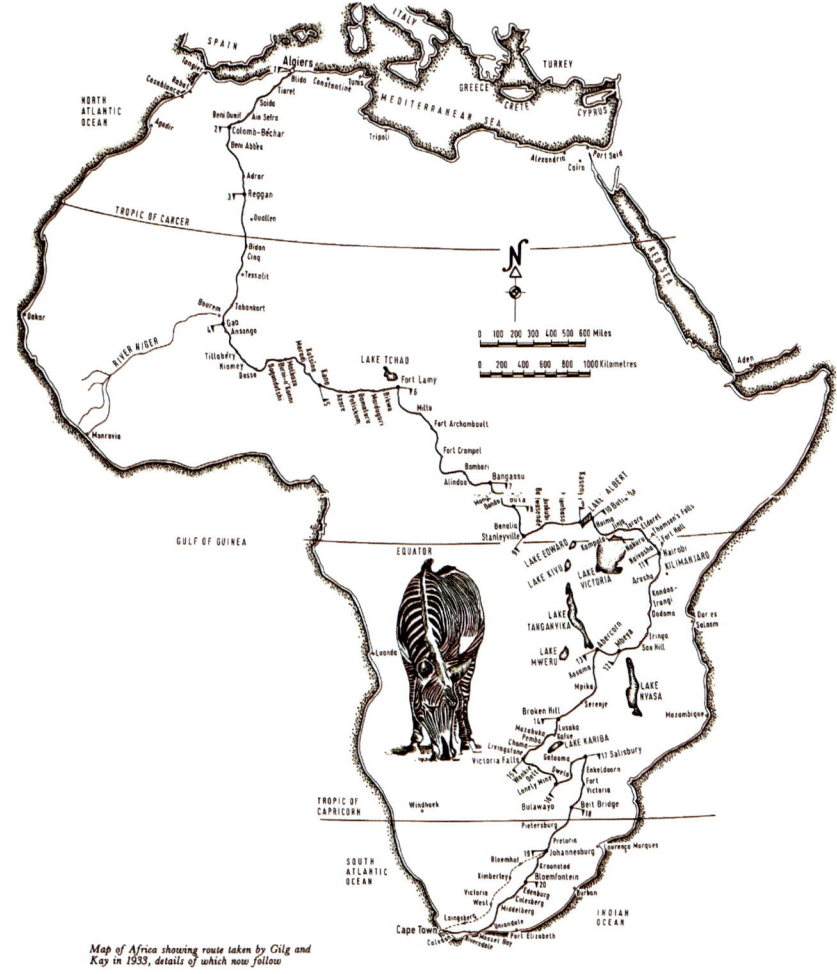

Fig.8: Gilg and Kay – Map
Liverpool to Cape Town, 1933

My 1929 new Morris Minor was shipped to Beira in Mozambique, then to Umtali (Mutare) where it was sold by F.R. Lark & Co of Umtali, the Morris agent. The car must have travelled some 13,055 kilometres by sea, add to that the estimated 60,000 kilometres by the 10 owners over 25 years. In 1984 we airfreighted the car from Zambia to Manchester, England. This would have added approximately 7,822 kilometres, then to Cape Town and back to the UK – in total the car has probably covered some 112,877 kilometres or 70,138 miles in its lifetime. Perhaps this is a record for such a baby car 95 years old in 2024? The Morris odometer and speedometer (Fig.9) resets after only 10,000 miles; so a high mileage was not expected

1929 Morris Minor 4 Seat Tourer - M10228

Fig.9: Morris odometer in Miles/Kilometres

with this little runabout. It is possible that the car has been around the clock at least five times. Note that even in 1929 it catered for countries using kilometres – no excuse for UK visitors speeding around the Continent of Europe!

Objectives to Tracing My African Routes

The Gilg and Kay 1933 Morris Minor Tourer trip from Liverpool, England to Cape Town, South Africa in 1933 had already proved the capability of this baby car; so there was no point in repeating that exercise. The 1933 model had the simpler and perhaps more reliable side-valve engine whereas the 1929 model has an overhead cam engine that is sportier but more complex.

The prime objective of the 2023 "Tracing My African Routes in a 1929 Morris Minor" trip was to visit the addresses of the car's 10 past owners in the now Zimbabwe and Zambia. The pinnacle of the tour would be to place the car at the same spot outside Kitwe in Zambia where I found it as a wreck in 1970. Achieving this 53 years later would probably be a unique accomplishment in the annals of motoring but would also be a nostalgic day for me and fun for the BTA Team.

A secondary objective was to raise funds for the Cecily's Fund Charity to support and educate Aids orphans in Zambia (Ref.2).

The logistics to achieve these objectives seemed insurmountable since the Morris was in the UK and of course would need to return to Africa. As events developed, after nine years of working in India, in 2014 we decided that we would spend our retirement chasing the sun with residences in both the UK and South Africa. Since my wife, Sandy, had spent her early life in Cape Town and she has family there, and I have several close school friends in the area, settling in was quite easy for us.

Once established in Cape Town we joined the renowned Crankhandle Club (CHC) where members operate cars from a 1901 Benz to just about every model you can imagine (Ferraris, Jaguars and many more rare cars in superb condition). The knowledge, technical skills and traditional engineering facilities in the Western Cape are excellent – as is the camaraderie of the CHC members – and these enhanced our way of life there.

Now settled in South Africa it seemed possible that the Morris could come to the Cape and make the long-dreamed-of journey back to Kitwe. In 2019 I arranged for the car to be shipped to Cape Town to make the trip in 2020 but global events postponed everything. Despite this the objective remained alive.

Achieving my goal required the Morris travelling 33 days, covering 1,509 miles around two developing African countries. In reality it entailed so much more as it required shipping the car in a container from the UK to South Africa and returning – that would total some 32,000 kilometres or 19,737 miles.

Chapter 2

Selected Past Owners

List of Past Owners

Returning a wrecked and rusty vintage car to Concours condition is both challenging and demanding – never mind the determination and focus it requires to complete the task. Few well-intentioned planned restorations go to term but when they do the result can be stunning and very satisfying. During the restoration process it is rare that data becomes available on the users of the vehicle – especially when attempting to trace its history. The 1929 Morris Minor Four-Seat Tourer chassis M10228 is a rare car, not because of its unique features or great quality. It was often scrapped as spares for the more popular MG sports car "J" series that used the same front axle and engine block. By 1992 when my car launched there were only eight other 1929 tourers listed on the *Vintage Minor Register* as being on the road.

From the start of the restoration project, to obtaining the car's registration documents, I have been able to research the past owners and by luck the process gained momentum over the years. I am told that the detailed data I have acquired on the Morris's past owners is unique in the annals of car restoration. As more information became available excitement spurred me on to share it globally via magazine publications and social media in the hope that more of the car's history would be revealed. This certainly proved to be the case: in addition to data from Donna Trott (née Lang), Bruce Beckley (Bulawayo) and Ken Moore, (Australia). I hope more links will arise from this publication. We registered at the British Library to search through newspapers and gazettes of Southern Rhodesia and found adverts of the Morris Minor.

This section covers the research into each owner of the Morris based on fact and hearsay. Over time it is hoped that more facts will emerge from the wider publication of this book. The research started in 1970 by following up the number plate NK3177 (Northern Rhodesia, Kitwe) and the Southern Rhodesia number U750 (Umtali).

The list of past owners was provided by the Central Vehicle Register in Salisbury (Rhodesia) on 17 March 1971. Unfortunately, the Register's archives on U750 only went back to October 1936. When in the UK I was able to obtain details of the four RAF owners. Their serial numbers were researched at RAF Innsworth, Gloucester, HR HQ England. The RAF would not reveal the past owner's addresses but forwarded letters that I had provided. Much later the letters were returned to me from the current residents, thus identifying the officers' last known addresses.

- 1936. The earliest record of registration as U750. First owner, Arthur Ward, c/o Hillside Golf Club, P.O. Box 469, Umtali, Southern Rhodesia. Ward founded the Tanganda Tea Estate Company. Mr Ward's nephew lived in Nottingham as of 2000. If Mr Ward was the first owner in 1929 then why was it reported only in 1936?
- 1940, 7 July. Second owner, Mary O'Gorman, c/o Isolation Hospital, Bulawayo, Southern Rhodesia. (364 miles from Umtali). "Sister Gorman was the Matron at Ingutsheni Hospital and was a friend of my mother's." Ken Moore, Australia, 25 March 2002.

- 1941, 17 December. Third owner, Corporal Sydney John Hammond (SN770457), c/o 63 Married Quarters, RAF Cranborne, Salisbury, Southern Rhodesia.
- 1942, 26 November. Fourth owner, Flight Sergeant William Owens (SN 560841), c/o RAF Cranborne, Salisbury, Southern Rhodesia. Owens served from 19 September 1942 to 3 September 1944. Died 1980 on RAF pension.
- 1943, 30 June. Fifth owner, Corporal Charles Edward Haines (SN 640521), c/o Belvedere RAF Salisbury. Haines served in Southern Rhodesia from June 1940 and was discharged on 31 August 1941. His last known address was The Cottage, Frisby-on-the-Wreake, Melton Mowbray, Leicestershire, England. Yet he owned the Morris in 1943. What did he do between August 1941 and March 1943? He must have stayed on in Southern Rhodesia for some time.
- 1944, 23 March. Sixth owner, Flight Lieutenant Graham Willy Bates (SN 774082), c/o RAF Belvedere, Salisbury. Born 22 September 1914, Johannesburg. Bates served in the RAF from June 1940 to May 1941. His last known address was Collingwood Farm, P.O. Box 44, Concession, Southern Rhodesia.
- 1944, 23 November. Seventh owner, Mary Sims, Hunyani, P.O, Glen Atholl Estate, Banket, Southern Rhodesia.
- 1945, 7 March. Eighth owner, Donald Lewis Mayor, Plot 1, Frazer Road, Parktown, Salisbury, Southern Rhodesia.
- 1946, 24 April. Ninth owner, Rene Lang, listed as Parkview, P.O. Grand Hotel. Registration book states 154 Park Street, Parkview, Salisbury, Southern Rhodesia.
- 1948, 14 July: Tenth owner, Nicholas Johannes Oosterhuisen, Ngoro Farm, Headlands, Southern Rhodesia.
- 1953. The Morris was driven to Northern Rhodesia by Rene Lang, P.O. Box 155, Kitwe and registered as NK3177. The car crashed and was abandoned in the same year at Garneton (Itimpi), 6 miles outside Kitwe.
- 1970, 1 June. Eleventh owner, Peter William Hills, 12 Stanley Street, Kitwe, Zambia. Recovered the wreck from Itimpi. It had a side-valve engine, M8 wheels and Model-T Ford headlamps. It was partially restored in Zambia as a running chassis.
- 1984, March. Airfreighted to Meadow House. Ashton Lane, Ashton, Chester, England.
- 1992. Restored and on the road in Concours condition. Registered as DS9936 (an age-related plate from Peebles, Scotland). Now at 6 Somerset Lodge, 1 Briar Walk, Putney, London SW15 6UE UK. Won best vintage car, National Morris Register Rally 1992, 2018 and many subsequent awards.

A puzzle: Mrs Lang drove the car into Northern Rhodesia and registered it on 13 January 1954 as NK3177. The Salisbury Vehicle Register lists Nicholas Johannes Oosterhuisen, as the owner after Mrs Lang in 1948 and Mr Oosterhuisen's address, Headlands, is some 140km (91 miles) south-east of Salisbury towards Umtali.

I have come to the conclusion that the record is unreliable. This would mean that the car had made its way halfway to Umtali and then returned to Salisbury for the next owner. This seems unlikely.

Photographic evidence indicates that Mrs Lang owned the car in the first quarter of 1949. Somehow the Central Vehicle Records must have got it wrong.

The following comments of past owners is based on information gathered – which appears to be reliable data. The other addresses we visited are covered in the day-to-day travel reports.

First Owner – Arthur Ward listed as 1936

In 1929 the Morris agent in Umtali was F.H. Lark as listed on the 1929 advert. It is likely they imported and supplied the Morris Minor to the first owner Arthur Ward (Fig.10). What is curious is that the registration date of U750 was 1936 and not 1929. It is understood that car registrations were established in the Colony of Southern Rhodesia in 1926. Once a vehicle had a registration number, it would remain throughout the car's life irrespective of its location in the colony.

Fig.10: Arthur Ward, first owner

Perhaps the car stayed at Mr Ward's private farm property Chipinga as there would be no need for registration and road tax on a large private farm. Later it may have been used in the growing city of Umtali (Mutare) and only registered 6 years after its initial purchase. Alternatively, it may have been previously owned but the Salisbury (Harare) Central Vehicle Records did not have any earlier records since Umtali was quite remote.

It seems curious that the first owner, Arthur Ward, an established tea farmer living in Chipinga about 80 miles from Umtali, registered the address of the car at the Umtali Club. By 1936 Mr Ward may have been semi-retired (at age 54?) and living in Umtali (now Mutare) or perhaps he was more focused on running the tea production factory than living at the farm.

There was no railway line from the farm to Umtali and the terrain is very hilly. The best transport was by horse, but 80 miles is hard going for horse and rider and the Morris would be unsuited to the dirt tracks; it is likely he would have used a more robust large American car. However, when in the town having an inexpensive runabout car would be quite practical to do shopping, play golf, and have drinks with the boys at the Umtali Club.

Arthur Ward helped develop the Tanganda Tea Estate Company. In 2000 I located his nephew, living in Nottingham, who provided an outline history of the Tanganda Tea Company (Ref.5). Contrary to what is printed in the 2022 Tanganda Tea Company's Annual Report that I was handed when visiting, Arthur was not simply a retired tea planter. He was trained as an electrical engineer at Westinghouse in Manchester, England.

In 1907 Arthur and his brother emigrated to Southern Rhodesia where they purchased land in the Chipinga area and attempted to farm. Not being experienced in farming they struggled to grow much as the land was unsuitable for cash crops or livestock.

By 1914, with Europe at war, the two brothers travelled by tramp steamship back to England where they signed up to serve King and Country. The recruiting officer took note of Arthur's training and he was immediately sent to Assam in India to electrify the tea-making industry for the war effort.

After the armistice of World War 1 in 1918, Arthur returned to Southern Rhodesia where he realised that his land was ideal for growing tea. The rest is history: the Tanganda Tea Company (Fig.11) grew to be a publicly listed organisation that thrives to this day. I visited the factory and was assisted by the friendly and well-spoken company secretary.

Fig.11: U750 at the Tanganda Tea Company in Mutare – 2 April 2023

By kind invitation of Kevin Woodward (secretary of the Hillside Golf Club) we were invited to the Umtali (Mutare) Club for tea and sandwiches. The building was originally constructed as a hotel in the late 1890s but Cecil John Rhodes persuaded investors that it should become a gentlemen's club with residential rooms (Fig.12).

Fig.12: The Mutare Club over 126 years later with Morris and postbox, 2023

We had a fascinating and informative tour of the Club that has many pictures of the town's pioneering days at the turn of the century. By 1898 the first tramway was established in the country but by 1920 it was discontinued (Figs.13, 14).

Fig.13: Umtali Club far distant left, 1898

Fig.14: Umtali Club on Main Street with tramlines

Prior to our arrival, Kevin Woodward had searched the Club's records and found Arthur Ward's name listed in the Register of Candidates for Election in 1926 as a farmer along with four dentists (Fig.15).

Fig.15: Arthur Ward's name listed in Umtali Club's Register, 1926

The local Morris agent in Umtali was F.H. Lark and Co. The main Morris agent in the colony of Southern Rhodesia was Fath & Co. based in Bulawayo and established there in 1905 as Wagon Builders, Farriers and Blacksmiths.

Many companies could see that motor vehicles would soon replace horses; so they needed to evolve their business with the changing times and market. We found several newspaper adverts of the latter company in the British Library extolling the imaginative performance of the Morris Minor in 1929! Fath & Co probably serviced the Morris Minor when it was owned by Mary O'Gorman, the second owner in Bulawayo (Figs.16, 17).

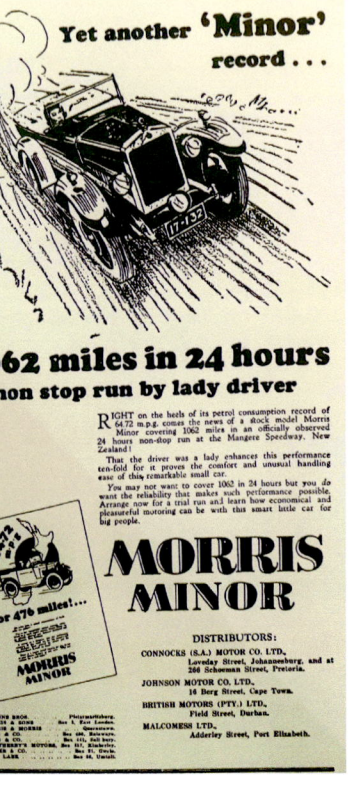

Fig.16: Adverts for the Morris Minor in Southern Africa in 1929

Fig.17: Fath & Co. became Morris agents in Bulawayo

Leaving Mutare for Bulawayo the prime objective was to visit the Isolation Hospital where Mary O'Gorman was Matron, the second owner of the Morris in 1940. The original hospital has been replaced by the Ingutsheni Hospital (Fig.217).

Royal Air Force Owners in Southern Rhodesia during WW2

Based on the Southern Rhodesia Central Vehicle Registration Office, the third to sixth owners of the Morris are recorded and then identified in detail by RAF Innsworth, Gloucester the HR headquarters in England. Full details are listed on page 16 of this book:

- 1941, 17 December. Third owner, Corporal Sydney John Hammond (SN770457)
- 1942, 26 November. Fourth owner, Flight Sergeant William Owens (SN 560841)
- 1943, 30 June. Fifth owner, Corporal Charles Edward Haines (SN 640521)
- 1944, 23 March. Sixth owner, Flight Lieutenant Graham Willy Bates (SN 774082)

Fourth Owner – William Owens listed as 1942, RAF Cranborne

1942, 26 November. Fourth owner, Flight Sergeant William Owens (SN 560841), was based at Cranborne, Salisbury (Harare). The site was originally known as Hillside, but renamed Cranbourne in 1939, with the spelling later revised to Cranborne. It is located 3 miles south-east of Salisbury. On the other side of the city was Belvedere Airport built in 1937. A flying school was set up here in 1937 for the Southern Rhodesia Air Force. A Service Flying Training School was opened there in July 1940, as part of the Rhodesia Air Training Group. From 28 November 1947 it acted as the main Southern Rhodesia Air Force base – including the Spitfire squadrons. The rapid post-war expansion of the city of Salisbury forced its closure in 1952, when New Sarum opened. The area was built over and Cranborne Barracks now occupies part of the site.

Owens, William ("Spike") received DMM 1973 499; for the restoration of SR64 596 a Provost to flying condition 1979, he is mentioned in the book: *A Pride of Eagles: The Definitive History of the Rhodesian Air Force 1920–1980* by Beryl Salt (Ref.6), (Fig.18).

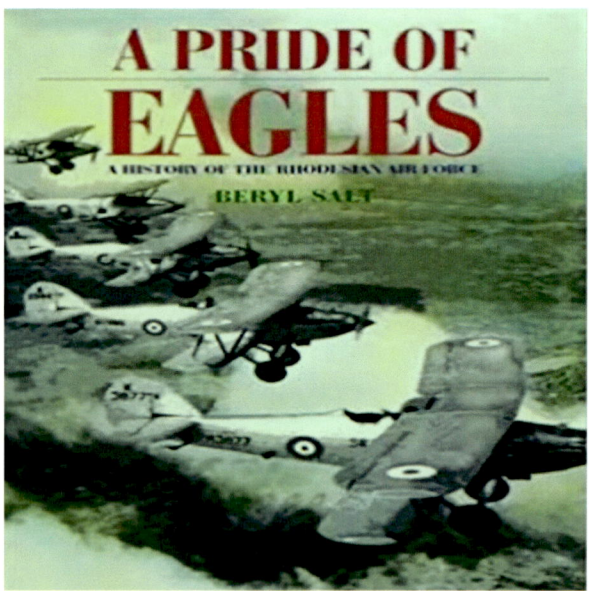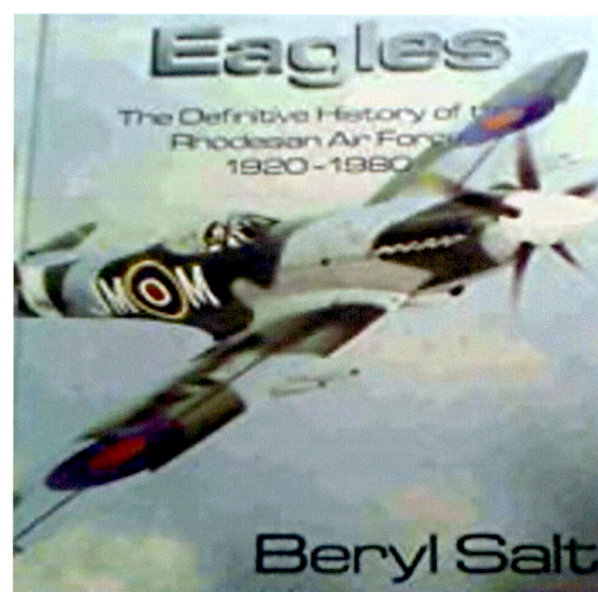

Fig.18: Books *A Pride of Eagles* – Rhodesian Air Force

The books chronicle the story of military aviation in Rhodesia from the early romantic days of "bush" flying in the Twenties and Thirties when aircraft were refuelled from jerry cans and landing grounds were often the local golf course. In 1939, before the outbreak of World War II, the tiny Rhodesian Air Force became the first to take up battle stations. The three Rhodesian squadrons served in East Africa, the Western Desert, Italy and Western Europe. A famous Rhodesian RAF Fighter Pilot was Ian Douglas Smith, Prime Minister 1964–79 (Ref.7). He served as a Flight Lieutenant in RAF squadron 237 from 1941–45. A Hurricane crash in Egypt caused severe facial and body wounds that remained conspicuous for the rest of his life. Following his recovery, he served in Europe, where he was shot down in a Spitfire and then fought alongside Italian partisans. In 1945 he flew over Germany.

After the war, Rhodesia, on a negligible budget, rebuilt its air force, equipping it with Ansons, Spitfires, Vampires, Canberras, Hawker-Hunters and Alouettes. Following UDI, the Unilateral Declaration of Independence from Britain in 1965, international sanctions were imposed, resulting in many remarkable and groundbreaking innovations, particularly in the way of ordnance. The bitter "bush war" followed in the late Sixties and Seventies, with the RhAF in the vanguard of local counter-insurgency operations and audacious pre-emptive strikes against vast guerrilla bases in neighbouring Mozambique, Zambia and Botswana and as far afield as Angola and Tanzania. With its ageing fleet, including C-47 Dakotas that had been at Arnhem, the RhAF was able to wreak untold havoc on the enemy, Mugabe's ZANLA and Nkomo's ZIPRA. The late author (Beryl Salt) took over 30 years in writing this book; the result is a comprehensive record that reflects the pride, professionalism and dedication of what were some of the world's finest airmen of their time. This colourful look at the Rhodesian Air Force is sure to be of interest to military historians everywhere.

Belvedere Airport (ICAO)

The fifth and sixth owners of the Morris served at the Belvedere Airport that today has given way to a housing and industrial estate. The original civil airport for Salisbury opened in the 1930s and was used by the Southern Rhodesia Air Unit from November 1935. Number 25 EFTS was opened here on 24 May 1940, as part of the RATG. After WW2 it was converted to civil use. Located on the other side of the city from Cranborne, it was presumably closed in 1956 when the new Salisbury Airport opened.

Seventh owner – Mary Simms 1944

Her farm was the Glen Atholl Estate, Banket, Southern Rhodesia. See Day 22: 13 April where we learned from Dirk Kriel that after her family were evicted from the farm by the Zimbabwe "veterans", they discovered that the whole area was rich in alluvial gold.

Ninth or Tenth Owner – Mrs Rene Lang 1946

The ninth or tenth owner's address was listed as: Mrs Rene Lang, Parkview, P.O. Grand Hotel, Salisbury. The hotel no longer exists but we did visit the original site located at Speke and First Avenue in Salisbury city centre. Only later did I notice Mrs Lang's physical address listed in the Southern Rhodesia car registration document as 157 Park Street, Parkview, Salisbury. We attempted to locate this property, but roads and names have changed and Park Street no longer exists.

Mrs Lang was known to me when I was around 16 years of age. As a Senior Scout, we used to meet on a Friday evening in the Kitwe town centre around the corner from St Michael's Church. After our meeting some of us would change out of our scout uniforms into jeans and casual shirts and make our way to the Church Hall (Fig.389) to dance. Mrs Lang used to organise "sessions", mainly gramophone records but occasionally the odd skiffle group. Entrance was a shilling (5p) – a lot to us in those days – but coming late and with cunning tactics we managed to sneak into the hall where we enjoyed bopping to Elvis Presley and the like. Mrs Lang organised these sessions to raise funds for her girls' softball club. She was known to many young girls as Ma Lang as she would often save some of the wilder ones from a wasted life. Unkindly, we regarded her as "the old bat at the door" who would attempt to keep us wild things in some sort of control.

When I recovered the Morris, I noticed that it still had its registration plate NK3177 (N- Northern Rhodesia K-Kitwe) attached. Having made good restoration progress by sand blasting and painting the chassis I decided to check with the Kitwe Town Council offices to find out if they might have a record of the car and its owner. They produced a record card that the car was imported into Northern Rhodesia by Mrs Rene Lang in 1953 and was issued Customs Certificate Number 7390. It was first taxed on 13 Jan 1954; no subsequent taxes had been paid. Interestingly, by 1953 the Federation of Rhodesia and Nyasaland had come into being. There was a common customs union: I wondered why a customs certificate was issued at that time.

Sometime later I visited my friend Roy Scott, a trainee at a curtain shop in Kitwe town centre. He asked about the car's progress. When I mentioned that the last registered owner was a Mrs Rene Lang, an elderly lady buying curtains overheard the conversation and said, "I know Mrs Lang, she works at Zambolts." Without delay I visited Mrs Lang at her office and she had a lot to say: "You have no right to take my car – that drunken Mr Heath has been selling scrapped vehicles on our property to fund his tipple!" Heath was living on their land on a grace and favour basis. Mrs Lang told me that her husband planned to repair the car some day! After further discussion Mrs Lang conceded that the car would probably never be repaired and, since I had already started work on it, she agreed to a free transfer of ownership.

Mrs Lang then invited me to her farm on the other side of town near the TanZam depot on the road to Ndola. Amazingly, she had kept the car's Northern Rhodesia logbook (locally known as the Blue Book) (Figs.25, 26), folded inside was the Southern Rhodesian Registration card (Figs.19, 20) that stated its past registration as U750 (U-Umtali). She had also stored the two missing rear Morris magna wheels that she gave me. Then she produced the rare period Joseph Lucas ignition sports coil (with a brass name plate) that is still functioning in the car 54 years later. These items were gratefully received.

I noted that the NR logbook described the car as a 1926 Morris – probably a guess at the time of registration in Kitwe. Both the NR and SR registration documents gave the same chassis and engine number and much later these numbers were verified by the British Motor Heritage Trust vehicle tracing service. The Morris was manufactured between 5 and 10 July 1929 and despatched for export on 17 July 1929. The fact that the car was exported and never registered in England suggests that the first registered owner, Arthur Ward, had the car between 1929 and 1940. After the outbreak of WW2 in 1939 automotive companies like Morris started manufacturing aircraft and ceased making cars. During that period new cars became rare and people kept their vehicles running as long as possible. When I started the car's restoration, I found the car's shackle pins were worn down by 50 percent and the main suspension springs were severely worn oval – indicative of a long operating life.

Mrs Lang purchased U750 in April 1946. She informed me that one day in Salisbury the Morris collided with a small bus full of African workers. The bus was coming round a corner slightly off balance, it hit the Morris's dumb iron causing the bus to tip onto its side. Fortunately, no one was injured and there was little damage to the Morris. After that incident the car was known locally as "Piccaninny Danger". Apparently, it took part in hill climbing events and racing at the Hunyani Race Track, Salisbury. U750 was last taxed in Southern Rhodesia in Mrs Lang's name on 24 October 1953.

Mrs Lang drove U750 to Kitwe, Northern Rhodesia 822 miles from Salisbury. A remarkable achievement considering that the road was mainly dirt and went across the Zambezi River, down and up the Chirundu escarpment climbing to the Copperbelt plateau at 4,100 feet. Mrs Lang stated that by 1953 the soft top had rotted – so some Africans thatched it with elephant grass to protect her from the fierce tropical sun that can exceed 40° C in the wild Zambezi Valley. She said that she had been too frightened to stop the car because of the numerous wild animals that roam the area. Elephants, antelope, baboons and warthog are still in evidence today despite the poaching in the valley.

On 13 January 1954 U750 was re-registered NK3177 at Kitwe, the largest of the Copperbelt mining towns. During 1954 a "friend" of the Langs crashed the Morris and it was dumped in the bush at Mrs Lang's property at Itimpi, 5 miles from Kitwe. Itimpi was a new area of smallholdings of around 5 acres occupied by those who wished to live out of the main town and become almost self-sufficient. Mr Garnet Richards, the father of a school friend, Bryan Richards, was a great horseman and polo player who kept his horses there. I slept over at their "farm" several times. Mr Garnet Richards was an assay chemist at Rhokana Mine but also a competent photographer who had his own studio in Kitwe town centre. Later it became Andrew Hayward's photo shop and he took our wedding photos in 1967. Mr Richards did a lot to develop the Itimpi area as it grew. He was instrumental in setting up the local management council that later renamed Itimpi as Garneton in honour of Mr Garnet Richards. His son Bryan visited me in Chester, UK in the mid-1990s but sadly I heard later that he had passed away. Zambia is on a plateau at an altitude of 1,200–1,300 metres with low humidity. The rainy season is between November and April and for the rest of the year it is dry and hot, reaching around 37° C in October, the "suicide month." Fortunately, the environment is such that metal corrosion is reduced but the annual bush fires and termites had taken their toll on the Morris, leaving little of the original wood frame remaining. Damage was also caused by vandals who hammered in the radiator core which exacerbated the severe condition as found.

The car was formally identified by the *Morris Register* in the UK from its chassis number M/10228 as a 1929 Morris Minor Four-Seat Tourer. It was originally fitted with an 875cc overhead camshaft engine. The OHC engine (Number 9668) had been replaced with a side-valve engine (Number 24616 made in November 1932). This was probably due to wear and tear of the original engine but also the perennial problem of oil leaking from the overhead camshaft drive into the vertical dynamo.

Several other parts of the car as found were not original. In particular, the headlamps were Model-T Ford and the wheels were *c.* 1936 Morris "magna" (large) hubs. Bruce Beckley of Bulawayo reports that his grandfather fitted these items (Fig.226).

During a business visit to Zambia in 1994 I discovered that Mrs Lang had died but that a daughter Donna had come up from Cape Town to attend the funeral in Kitwe. With only the name Donna but knowing that she could be a softball player, I contacted a family friend, Tony Rauch. He was a national softball coach and in two days found Donna Trott (née Lang) working at Varsity Sports, a shop she owned with her husband Ian. A year later, on a business visit to Cape Town I surprised Donna and Ian with my story of the Morris that she fondly refers to as "Tjorrie", a local name for a car. This was the start of an ongoing deep friendship with Donna and Ian: he is an international cricket coach, and they often stay with us when they are in London. Their son Jonathan Trott (Fig.29) played Number 3 bat for England and is currently the coach for Afghanistan's cricket team. One year I received a Christmas card from Donna enclosing a photo of her mother with the Morris *c.* 1950 (Fig.24). Wow! Was I excited? Later she found more pictures taken between 1949 and 1960 (Figs.21, 23). The photo taken in 1960 of Donna on the Morris in Zambia (Fig.27) was replicated with her in London in 2016 (Fig.28). What is of particular interest from these photos is that the original nickel radiator normally associated with an OHC engine had been replaced with a 1932 steel covered radiator, confirming the period when the overhead cam engine was changed to the side-valve. The hose connections to the engines are in different positions – hence the need for a matching radiator. The photo taken in 1960 (Fig.28) indicates that the car was vandalised after that date.

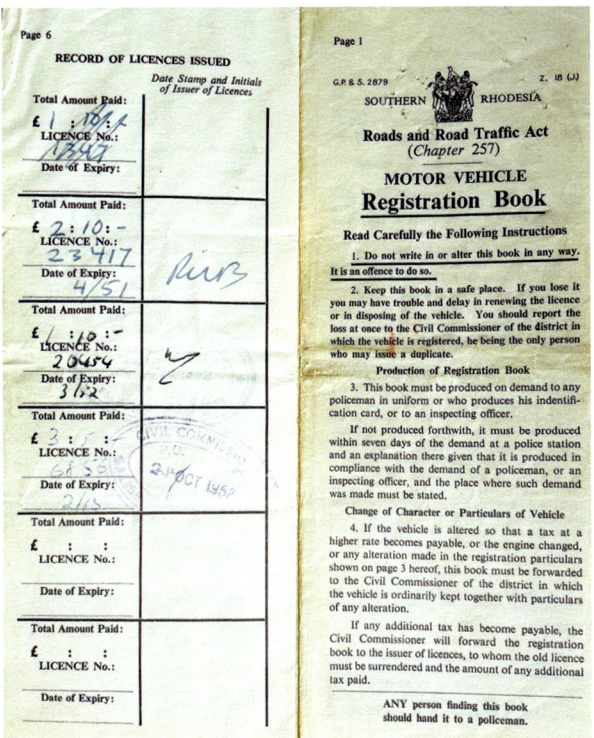

Fig.19: Southern Rhodesia Registration U750

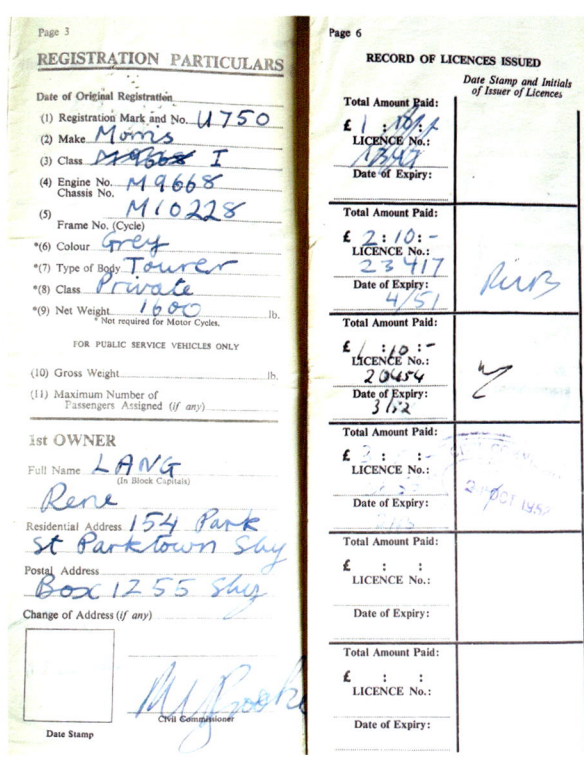

Fig.20: Mrs Lang taxed U750 1951–52

Fig.21: 1947 Salisbury – Donna Lang age 3, Morris behind the geese

Fig.23: *c.* 1950, Steel radiator when the OHC engine must have been replaced with a 1932 side-valve engine

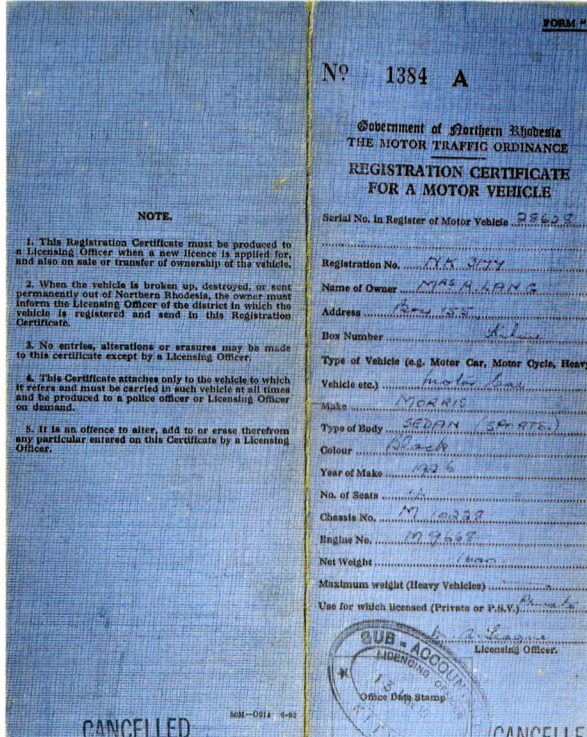

Fig.25 Northern Rhodesia "Blue" Log Book registered to Mrs Lang, NK3177

Fig.22: 1949 Salisbury – Donna and John Lang – original radiator, Ford T lamps, 1936 wheels

Fig.24 1952 – Mrs Rene Lang dressed for town, gloves and all. 154 Park St. Parkview Salisbury Southern Rhodesia

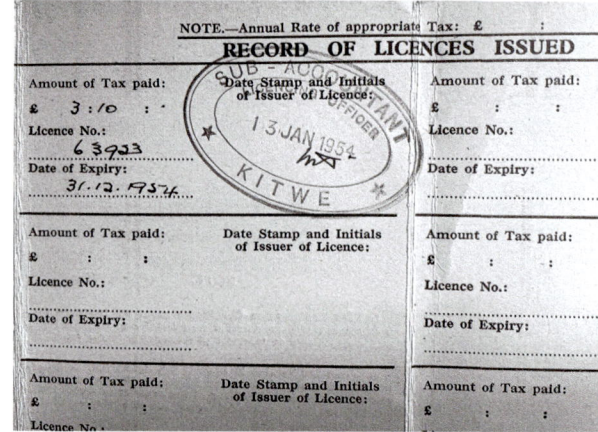

Fig.26: Tax paid ending 1954 – we assume the car was abandoned after that date

Fig.27: 1960 Donna with Morris at Itimpi before the Morris was vandalised

Fig.28: Donna Trott Putney London 2016 replicating the 1960 photo 56 years later!

We remain close friends with Ian and Donna who are regular visitors to London. The one person who deserves the BTA mug is without doubt Donna who was delighted to receive it (Fig.30) especially as she has fond memories of her *Tjorrie*.

Fig.29: Son, Jonathan Trott English Cricketer 2009 and coach for Afghanistan

Fig.30: Ian and Donna Trott London 2023 with BTA mug, highly treasured by them

I hope that with wider publicity relatives of other past owners may come forward to add to the history of this little car that like the phoenix has risen from the ashes.

Chapter 3

Restoration Zambia and England: Out and About

Inspiration

To condense a 22 year car restoration project covering three countries into a few sentences is quite a challenge. The story of the discovery of a wreck in 1970 to Concours condition in 1992 took many twists and turns. Success was not possible without dogged determination and the full support of my patient wife, Sandy, and my many friends both locally and abroad. In 1969 we toured Europe to collect a Fiat 124 Sports Coupé in Rome that was shipped to Cape Town in order to drive back to our home in Zambia (Fig.32). While in Cape Town a family friend, André du Toit, visited Sandy's parent's home in his recently restored 1909 Model-T Ford (Fig.31). He had started with a complete wreck and that inspired me to tackle something similar. See Sandy, her sister Sharon Quenelle (née Lowden), brother Graham Lowden admiring the vintage Ford in Kenilworth Cape Town.

Fig.31: 1909 Model-T Ford

Back in Kitwe I put out the message that I was seeking a vintage car. I located a 1928 Model-A Ford tourer that was in restorable condition, but the owner did not wish to part with it. Then I found a complete Derby Bentley at a remote farm outside Kitwe – again the owner refused to sell it to me as he felt I was too young (25) and did not have the funds.

In June 1970 my pal Roy Scott informed me that his aunt, who lived in Itimpi on a smallholding outside Kitwe, knew of some old cars at Plot 7, Azurite Road (Fig.33). We followed up this lead and found several wrecks of trucks and the Morris in a very sad state (Figs.34, 35) – or what could best be described as the remains of a car! Elephant grass and small trees had grown through the chassis; it was covered with rust. There were some remnants of the original ash frame (probably eaten by termites or burnt in bush fires) and a few body panels lying around. It had wire wheels, cable brakes, the hand-brake was on the transmission shaft, the petrol tank was under the dashboard, the accelerator pedal was between the brake and the clutch, and the engine and gearbox were in place. Wow! This car must be old, perhaps vintage, I must have it – surely love at first sight!

Since there were bits of scrap car parts spread all around, Roy and I searched the *bundu* (forest) for anything that might belong to the Morris. We located the two rear mudguards and the offside rear body panel. Wandering into a nearby village of thatched mud huts, I noticed, on an open fire, a wheel hub fixed to a sheet of metal with a large hole cut out to support a cooking pot; it was used as the villagers' hot plate. After some pleading and compensating them with several Kwacha, the villagers released the rear body panel to me as seen among the items that were used as templates and then scrapped (Fig.37).

Fig.32: Zambia (was Northern Rhodesia)

Fig.33: Plot 7, Azurite Rd Itimpi, Zambia

Fig.34: Wreck as first seen Roy and Peter 1970

Fig.35: Registration plate NK3177 – rear

Fig.36: Taking the Morris home

Fig.37: Rear body panel (note cut-out for a pot)

Fig.38: Chassis shot blasted and undercoat

Fig.39: VIN M10228 on front dumb iron

Fig.40: Restoration of chassis as of 1972, next, install the engine and wheels

Fig.41: Typical Rhodesian strip road that eroded the Morris's steering track rod

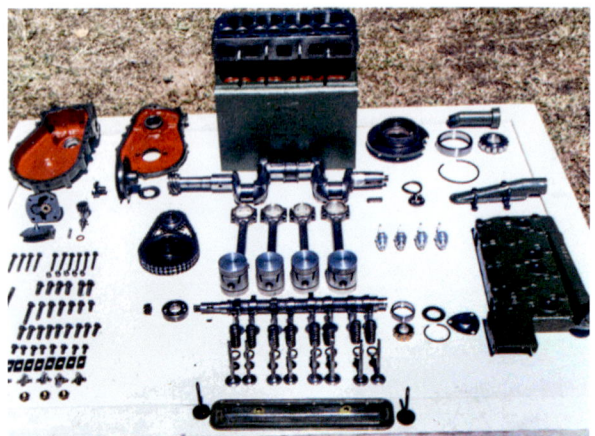

Fig.42: Model 1936 Side-Valve engine reconditioned and ready for assembly

Fig.43: Model 1936 Side-Valve engine started on 1 May 1973

Living rough in a nearby hut was an elderly gentleman, a Mr Heath. I asked him if I could have the Morris wreck and he agreed. At that time wars were raging around the borders of Zambia and all supply lines were disrupted or closed. Only the essentials were available – there were no luxuries like butter, make-up, perfume, clothes, camera film. I had to be thrifty in taking photos – selfies were not the norm. Even as a keen photographer, it did not occur to me to have a photo taken of me next to the wreck of the Morris – a pity!

Fig.44: My Dad, "Chilupala", my guru for engine assembly and fault finding

Fig.45: On the road with Peter Ashcroft and "Kwacha" our dog around Kalulushi

Fig.46: London – first view of an original Morris ash body – underneath view

Fig.47: Base made of Oregon pine from templates and guesswork – top view

Restoration in Zambia

I borrowed a truck to collect the wreck (Fig.36). When we arrived at our Kitwe home, I told my wife Sandy, "The man gave it to me." Shocked at the sight of a pile of scrap metal arriving in our garden, she said, "I'm surprised he did not pay you to take it away."

I soon stripped the car to its basic chassis and had it sandblasted to base metal (Fig.38). This revealed the chassis number (VIN) on the front dumb iron as M10228 (Fig.39), a key piece of information. I also noticed that the chassis front cross-member was severely corroded; so I arranged for a welder in the boiler shop at the Rhokana Mine to fabricate a copy. Working for an isolated mining company in Central Africa with very long delivery lines has its benefits. We had comprehensive workshops: pattern making, mould foundry, forge, boilers and welding, sheet metal fabrication, machine shop, tool room, electrical and instrumentation facilities. It was the friendly and helpful chaps in these workshops who wished to be associated with the Morris's restoration that spurred me forward. Later I had a stainless-steel plate engraved with all their names and other friends and family: it is now screwed to the Morris's firewall (Fig.48).

Fig.48: Helpers' names mounted on the Morris's firewall

I contacted the Morris Register and the club historian informed me that the car was a 1929 Morris Minor Four-Seat Tourer supplied with an overhead cam engine. The as-found fitted side-valve engine was from a later model (1934+). I purchased the basic *Morris Minor Handbook* that provided details of the various models and specifications. This guide was a godsend as, working in isolation in Zambia, it was my only reference for the restoration. It also ensured that I avoided restoring non-standard parts – and caused me to rework other parts completed before I had the document. While I was renovating the chassis, I outsourced the machining of the side-valve engine elements as it was the only engine I had at the time!

I undertook a detailed dimensional check of the chassis and found it to be accurate. After fitting the newly fabricated front cross-member I treated the whole chassis with zinc chromate followed by several layers of black enamel paint. Later in the UK all exposed chassis parts were powder-coated. The front and rear axles were fitted with sealed bearings.

The differential had remnants of 1953 oil that protected it from corrosion and seemed useable. After disassembling and cleaning I fitted new bearings with seals remaining on the outer sides to prevent seepage to the rear wheel brakes. All brake shoes were relined with a modern bonded material that later proved too hard for the Morris to get any sort of purchase and hence effective braking and were replaced. A local steel-wire rope company made up new brake cables with fittings – courtesy of Graham Brooklyn, a national sports star – we both played for Diggers Rugby Club.

The firewall was renewed with marine plywood sandwiched between thin galvanised steel sheets identical to the original, which was very tatty. I fabricated a battery box as per the original – which was only held in place by flakes of rust! The original steering column was bent and corroded; so after straightening the inner rod a new outer pipe was nickel plated. The car was now starting to take shape (Fig.40).

During this work I noticed that one of the steering track rods had a strange groove worn in the centre. Later it dawned on me that this was the result of driving on the old tar strip roads in Rhodesia (Fig.41) – an economic solution for the long distance between towns in the early days. When an approaching car was seen, each vehicle would pull over with one wheel in the dirt, the other on the strip of tarmac. Often there was a considerable drop and the track rod would scrape on the rough tar verge.

News of my Morris spread around Kitwe. In 1972 Bob Crisp asked to look at the car. When he was at university in England, he had a 1933 MG J2 that used the same engine block as the OHC Minor. He made a photocopy of his *J2 User's Manual* that proved very helpful several years later in the UK. We maintained contact over the years and, moving forward to January 2023, he visited me in Cape Town not only to see the Concours Morris but my latest project, a 1933 MG J2 that is painted British Racing Green and waiting for me to install the engine. Bob was similarly "green" with envy!

I used to photograph go-karts, bikes, saloon cars and Formula Fords at the Chingola Race Circuit north of Kitwe. At some point I mentioned my restoration project to Derek Dutton one of the course stewards. Out of the blue in 1972 Derek came to our home carrying a Morris Minor radiator: "Will this be of any use to you?" He had spotted it in a scrapyard but could not find any more associated parts. A fantastic gift as the one in the original wreck had been vandalised beyond repair – this would be a perfect replacement. Its honeycomb core was sound, although it was piped for the side-valve engine. Later I had the radiator re-cored and converted to the OHC configuration. In May 2023 I contacted Derek, now in his nineties and living in Australia. He was delighted to hear of the car's progress and planned tour around Zambia.

Side-Valve Engine Started

Rebuilding the single-valve engine became an international effort. I purchased pistons and rings from Johannesburg, the cam shaft was reground in Durban, the conrod journals that were originally white metal were converted to shell bearings by Ace Auto in Kitwe. The engine block was rebored, and the head was slightly skimmed to ensure that it was flat. Replacement cam followers were made and case-hardened by the Mine Tool Room. New valve springs were found locally but the head gasket was imported from the UK (Figure 42 shows the engine elements). I also stripped the dynamo and starter motor, cleaned and attended to as needed, and fitted new bearings. I wanted to ensure that the car would have its best start even though it had the later model engine.

Several ancillary parts of the engine were missing. To bring it back to life I found a distributor from a 1960s Mini and SU carburettor of a similar period that fitted perfectly. With a temporary fuel tank and a new battery, after a few splutters the engine burst into life and sounded rather smooth (Fig.43). From a rusty lump of metal where I had to chisel out the pistons seized in the engine block, it was such a thrill to see something inanimate returning to life. My father, an experienced automotive engineer, assisted me in the assembly of the engine (Fig.44). I now had a running chassis and even ventured out on the road (Fig.45).

Early in 1973 I was transferred on promotion to the Zambia Mines' Research and Development Laboratories based at a small village called Kalulushi, only 13 miles from Kitwe. This meant re-establishing a garage for the Morris. In the mining industry a promotion is often accompanied by a better and larger house. I must have been doing quite well as we moved home four times, but this interrupted the restoration progress. I was at the stage of creating the wooden body frame, but with few images or drawings to guide me I was stuck.

In 1974 a Morris Minor enthusiast in Sheffield (England), Dr Matt Vincent, then a PhD student, who had been sourcing his own Morris spares, offered to assist me. After receiving many "exciting" spares, he reported that a complete OHC engine was for sale but "very expensive at £80". I mailed a cheque to him at once and the engine was crated and sent to my sister's home in Hampshire. The plan was to have it shipped to Zambia once hostilities had ceased, but ultimately it remained in Ann's garage for the next 11 years, much to her chagrin.

During 1975 I was on a training course in the UK and took the opportunity to contact Roger Payne, another well-known Minor enthusiast. He had an original body of a 1929 Morris Minor Tourer off the chassis in a lock-up garage somewhere near London and was prepared to let me view it. This was the first time I was able to see the ash frame and body in detail. I took multiple photos that proved invaluable for the eventual body restoration (Fig.46).

Ash wood is not available in Zambia; so I used Oregon pine. In the mining industry in Zambia there were many British expatriates. One colleague in particular, Roger Holmes, returned from his annual UK leave with bits of Morris body frame that I was able to use as patterns – Roger, you are a star! These enabled me to make a start on the wooden base frame in Oregon pine (Fig.47). I managed to fashion the scuttle, base frame and a temporary seat. Progress was slow due to more house moves and life intervening, but occasionally we had fun driving the chassis around the neighbourhood with friends and their children (Figs.49, 50). In 2015 our goddaughter Susan repeated the drive in the Morris – but this time with her two children in London (Fig.51). Thirty-nine years later (2023) I placed the car in that very same spot in Kalulushi, (Fig.52). My nephew and namesake Peter Douglas Youngblood Hills was living with us in Zambia up to the time we departed for the UK; so he posed in the Morris before it was packed up (Fig.53). Later Peter starred in a movie, *Michel Vaillant*, about a French racing driver (Fig.54). So the wheels turn.

Restoration continued in England

In 1984 I was recruited to work in the UK and granted an allowance to transport our personal effects there. Apart from some books and ornaments, the Morris was just about the only possession worth bringing that came within the allowance. It was air freighted to the UK (Figs.55, 56) (John Hammond organised the crate) but it was a year before I was able to resume the restoration, after purchasing a home in the Chester area. Now in our new home the crate was opened (Fig.57) and after consulting with many users in the UK I was able to develop a project plan. Having searched for original parts I now had a better understanding of the various Minor models released from Cowley. I made an early policy decision that, while the car would be a true "bitsa" (bits of this and that), all parts fitted would be original to the marque. However, there was no point pretending that the body and upholstery were original: it would be the correct shape and build with ash frame and skinned with steel. Keep in mind that most vintage and pre-war cars were seldom garaged. They were exposed to the elements, wood rot and rust took their toll, and many cars are rebuilt. Most restorers ensure that their vehicles are constructed as close to the original specification as possible, using the traditional materials and to a finish that is realistic and economic.

Once settled in the UK my first priority was to replace the guesstimated Oregon pine base with a precision-made ash frame. This work took longer than expected because, apart from a new career and studying for my Master's degree, I spent many weeks travelling around Southeast Asia, India and the United States. At one stage I thought I had lost the Morris: it was outsourced for six months to a remote workshop and it took six years before I could recover it. When it was finally back in my hands, I completed the ash frame. On 12 August 1991 Sandy had a significant birthday: family and friends were present when my nephew and godson, Robert Macpherson and his fiancée Ailsa, suggested, "Uncle Peter, why don't you complete the car for our wedding in 342 days' time?" (Fig.58) It was this challenge that accelerated the restoration: I had a target date but could I manage the project while being out of the country so often? I needed to find and appoint someone to skin the wooden frame, paint it and then undertake the upholstery.

Before sending the car to be skinned, I needed to fabricate the frame of the hood so that the body could be aligned and completed. Conveniently, the nearby Moldsworth Museum had a 1930 Morris Minor Tourer that I was allowed to take measurements from. I fabricated the hood frame using steel conduit, the closest profile to the original. Forming the shape of the hood loops, cutting spars and levers (some riveted, some tapped and screwed together) was quite complicated. When I finally mounted the hood frame on the wooden body frame, I noticed that when it was lowered it was partially raised above the rear of the car – more like an F1 wing than flat like other tourers. (Figure 59 shows my Mum, Peggy Hills, admiring the hood.) I realised that I had taken measurements from a worn frame but failed to account for its wear and stretch. It only takes a few millimetres to affect the shape of the frame. After adjustment I sent the frame for powder-coating as I had observed the hood fabric of most other cars tended to be stained with rust. Later the frame was covered with double duck cloth; it was as tight as a drum and looked great. The body frame could now be sent for skinning and painting.

Although I can handle most mechanical work, I realised that I was not sufficiently skilled or equipped to form the metal body double curves calling for the "English wheel". If I wanted the car to be restored to Concours standard, a body specialist was required. A nearby upholsterer John Cartlidge suggested that I speak to Ken Hall based in Stafford. Ken was well equipped with a spacious fabrication and spray workshop based at his home. Fortunately, he had a slot to undertake the work and committed to meet my deadline. After several meetings and sharing of technical data Ken proceeded to skin the wood frame and make the doors (Fig.60, 61). He sent me progress photos and we visited him at each stage to discuss details and the way ahead. When Ken showed me a book of car colours, I selected the caramel as it worked well with the black wings – a very distinct combination (Fig.62).

An oft-asked question is: "Was that the original colour?" This is another story. Almost all "original" Minor tourers and saloons on the road are blue body, black mudguards and blue upholstery. At the time I was spending a lot of time in India on business and took the opportunity to buy in Chennai, famous for its quality leather, six blue-dyed super-soft leather skins for the car's upholstery. On returning to England, I decided to clarify the colour blue for the body with the venerable Harry Edwards, the historian of the Morris Register (Ref.3). He said the blue should be the same as that of the Brasso polish tin. But on checking the chassis number of my Morris, he stated, "Oh, but your M10228 was brown not blue." Few, if any, original brown Minors exist and the particular shade of brown is not known. I suspect that it was a chocolate brown. I now had a problem: the pile of blue leather upholstery had to be replaced! Fortunately, a fellow Morris member needed blue leather for his Minor and we did a deal.

The upholsterer, John Cartlidge, was trained at Rolls Royce in Crewe. He had set up his own business and was delighted to upholster the complete car as most jobs are small fixes. His work was to the highest standard and to the exact same dimensions as those that came out of Cowley. (Fig.62, 63). With the car body caramel, the upholstery had to be brown. I had to decide on the material: originally it was Rexine (painted linen) but as the upholstery labour cost would be similar irrespective of material used, I selected leather for the long term. John carried stocks of Connolly hide (Rolls Royce quality) and I decided the expense was worth it, having come so far with this restoration. Prior to this work my old friend Roy Hogg from Dorset, a retired upholsterer, who owned an identical 1929 Morris, made up the seat bases with proper springs as per original (rather than using foam). Roy provided detailed paper patterns for me. John also fabricated the hood covering and side screens to a very high standard.

While this outsourced work was progressing, I had time to attend to the assembly of the overhead cam engine (OHC) (Fig.64). The contents of the crate despatched from Zambia – after 11 years in a damp garage – revealed the engine to be in a pretty poor rusty condition. After stripping it down to every component I proceeded to source replacement new parts. The crankshaft oilways were almost blocked; so I went to great lengths to clear them and all other lubrication ducts. The piston bores showed little sign of wear and the pistons and rings were excellent, indicating that the engine had not done much work. So why was it sold? I took the conrods to the well-known Sports and Vintage in Shropshire to be white-metalled, but Mike Dowley advised that it was not necessary: if they were redone, in only 25 miles they would look just the same. Each conrod was checked and balanced to the equivalent weight. Not having experience of the overhead camshaft engine, where the valve ends are ground to set the clearance to the camshaft, I decided to outsource the rebuild as it needed many new components. The first fix was a special seal to solve the perennial oil leak from the cam drive to the dynamo. A further fix was a rear pedestal bearing to support the overhung cam followers to improve actuation and reduce the chance of pivot shaft fatigue. New valves, springs and cam followers were supplied and fitted by Mike – the complete cylinder head assembly was rebuilt to the optimum standard by a specialist.

On the Road – OHC Engine

In Zambia I knew a chap called Vic Ryan. He lived in a nearby mining town, Luanshya, and we had been in the same barrack room in the Rhodesia Regiment in Bulawayo. As an electrician, Vic had developed a skill and reputation for rotor dynamic balancing. Around 1976 I recruited him to head up our embryonic vibration diagnostic and balancing service at Mining Industry Technical Services at Kalulushi Zambia. Later he too moved to the UK to join the same company as me in Chester (IRD Mechanalysis), designing and manufacturing vibration measurement systems and rotor balancing machines. Vic had become a highly respected specialist in dynamic balancing, I could not ask for anyone better to balance the Morris crankshaft and flywheel, which he did at our company works.

As soon as the assembly was set in the balancing machine and commenced rotation, it wobbled violently: we discovered that the flywheel was "running out". The face plate to the crankshaft was plastically distorted with hammer marks and did not fit properly. Before I owned the engine, if it had been running, it must have created an unacceptable level of vibration. Was this the reason it was sold so soon after a major engine rebuild and being unaware of the basic cause?

Fig.49: Taking friend's kids for a spin in the Morris around Kalulushi Zambia 1982

Fig.50: Susan Shand and Clare Cummins, at No 2 Mwaiseni Kalulushi 1982

Fig.51: Susan McIntyre (Shand) with her James and Charlotte – London 2015

Fig.52: Chilupala returns to the same spot No 2 Mwaiseni Kalulushi, 26 April 2023

Fig.53: My nephew Peter D.Y. Hills prior to airfreighting the Morris to England1984

Fig.54: Peter D.Y. Hills as Steve Warson: movie *Michel Vaillant* Le Mans 2003

Fig.55: Morris and tools in crate 1984

Fig.56: Airfreight to Manchester UK

Fig.57: Unpacking the Morris in Chester, UK, Dad and young Peter assisting, 1985

Fig.58: "Uncle Peter, we would like the Morris for our wedding in 342 days"

Fig.59: Mum checking the hood frame!

Fig.60: Wood is skinned with steel sheet

After having the mating faces of both flywheel and crankshaft skimmed to a perfect fit Vic balanced and combined them to achieve better than F1 racing standard.

"The cobbler's children have no shoes." Among my varied skill sets, I am a Fellow of the British Institute of Non-Destructive Testing – or, as my wife calls me, a "crack finder". Why did I not undertake a magnetic particle crack inspection at the assembly stage of the crankshaft? Of course, hindsight is an exact science. Later I learned that these two-bearing crankshafts (called bent-wire) are known for their propensity to crack, which is why MG enthusiasts acquired Morris Minors for spares and why OHC Minors are so rare. Almost 40 years later I asked myself the very same question: why no NDT?

Fig.61: Ken Hall skinned the body

Fig.62: John Cartlidge – upholsterer

Fig.63: Seats in Connolly hide

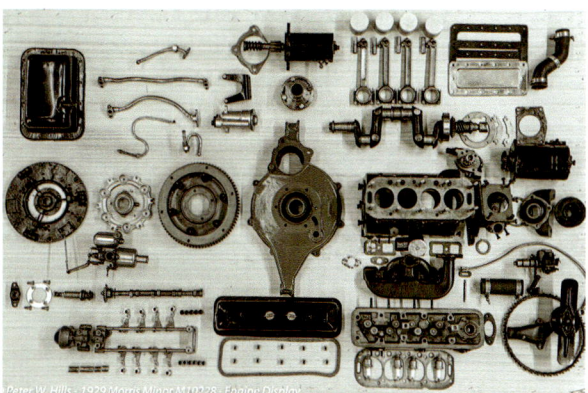
Fig.64: OHC engine ready for assembly

The completed Morris body (painted and upholstered), minus engine, was delivered to our home near Chester on 1 May 1992 and by my birthday on 31 May, with my brother Colin and his wife Margaret, we had fitted the engine into the chassis (Figs.66, 67). Given my long association with Vic and respect for his motor racing background, he joined me to check and start the Morris engine for the first time. On 6 June 1992, we broke out the champagne when the engine sputtered into life – it sounded as smooth as a sewing machine (Fig.68). All that remained was to connect the ancillaries: a few tweaks here and there, a quick drive around the block (Fig.69) and we had a car ready for its official road test (Fig.70). Some fast talking was required as the brakes had not yet bedded in, but Dave Baker appreciated my attention to detail and was confident that the brakes would improve over time. He issued the essential Ministry of Transport (MOT) Test Certificate.

Table 2: Summary of Restoration Costs to 1992

Description of Costs to 1992	Cost (£)	Description of Costs to 1992	Cost (£)
Chassis, new springs, bearings, brakes	500	Body	1,500
Engine, ring gear, OHC modifications	450	Painting	568
Differential (new 1/11/2003)	550	Upholstery and hood	1,300
Radiator re-cored	350	Electrical, lights, horn, et cetera	300
Wood framing	400	Tyres, wheels, stove enamelling	400
Total (excluding my labour)	**£6,368**		

Fig.65: OHC engine ready for installation

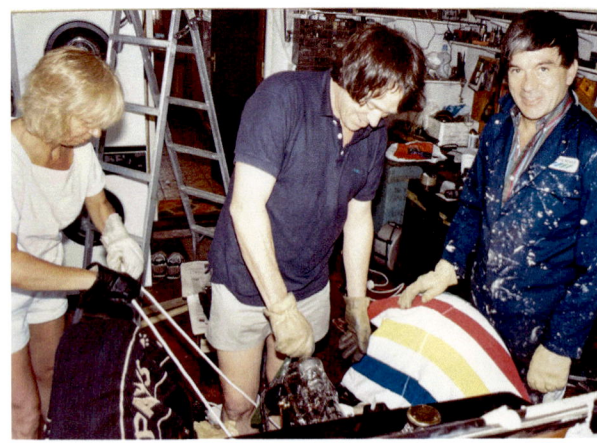

Fig.66: Colin and Margaret fitting engine

Fig.67: Engine started with Vic and family

Fig.68: On the road again after 40 years

Fig.69: MOT Certified roadworthy – "just!"

Fig.70: Wedding car on time 18 July 1992

Fig.71: First Prize Morris National Rally 1992

Fig.72: Lady Stamford presents the Cup

I needed to travel to Thailand for business and Robert and Ailsa's wedding was due to take place a few days after my return. The car had not yet been registered with the UK DVLA and did not have a registration number; Sandy, armed with documents and photos, went to the local DVLA office who recognised the car's provenance. Fortunately, rather than issuing a modern number plate, they awarded the car with an "age-related" registration number: DS9936 and issued its first UK Tax Disc (Fig.73). Several years later these were discarded when UK technology and registration plate recognition reveals a vehicle's details and owner.

Two days before the wedding I returned from Thailand and realised that the car did not have registration plates. A quick trip to the DIY shop to make a cardboard number plate and attach it to the car. The car was

Fig.73: DS9936 First Tax Disc in 40 years

delivered to Hampshire on a car transporter. On 18 July 1992, I drove the bride and her father to the church and then the happy couple to the reception (Fig.71). The Morris then returned by transporter to our home in Chester, 220 miles away.

Awards and out and about

A month later at the annual 1992 Morris Register National Rally, the Morris's first official outing, the car was awarded Best Vintage Minor – clearly, our hard work had paid off (Figs.71, 72). We then participated in the Morris Register's Manneken Pis Rally to Gerardsbergen in Belgium, and later the annual Club London to Brighton Run, the Prescott Hill Climb and many other club runs and natter meets.

Fig.74: Four walls rally winner, Wales

Fig.75: Five page article on Morris 1993

Fig.76: Peter's 50th birthday cake, Kariba Dam

Fig.77: Wirral Golden 100 Jubilee Rally

Fig.78: Cheshire Life "Out of Africa" theme

Fig.79: VMR – Peatling Magna Rally 2004

Fig.80: Mallory Park, Minors line up 2004

Fig.81: Prescott Hill Climb, 2014

In 1993 (Ref.4) *Classics & Sports Car* published a five page spread of the car's heroic restoration in their September edition (Figs.75, 82). This global magazine soon caught the attention of people associated with the car from Australia to Zimbabwe, adding to its past life and history.

Over the years the Morris has won many awards and attended many car club events and hill climbs (Figs.77–81). I celebrated my 50th birthday on Kariba Dam (between Zimbabwe and Zambia), Patti Bromfield had this Morris cake made for me (Fig.76). The car had done over 4,400 miles when, during a hill climb trial in a Chester meadow, the original differential made a clicking sound: the crown wheel and pinion had failed catastrophically. The car was off the road for a couple of years (I was busy and doing my Master's degree) before I could procure and fit new parts. I have since continuously fine-tuned and reworked many of the earlier jobs done less well in Zambia. I progressively powder-coated several parts fitted to the chassis since I wish to ensure that they are preserved with a reduced chance of corrosion. They are also easier to keep clean. In 2004 I undertook a major overhaul following a blown cylinder head gasket. I then reground the OHC valves,

1929 Morris Minor 4 Seat Tourer - MT0228

Fig.82: Classic & Sports Car Photo Shoot Cheshire

had the dynamo field windings renewed (an excellent charge rate now) and took the opportunity to tighten up the body frame and windscreen.

During 2004 I decided to accept an appointment in India to rebuild an ailing industrial electronics company that I knew quite well. Sandy thought it was for just a couple of years; in fact, we lived in Mumbai for nine fun years that decided our future lifestyle; so we hibernated the car (Fig.83). By 2011 we sold our country home in Cheshire, moved our effects and the Morris hibernated again this time in London, and then we returned to India until late 2013.

The attention to the Morris hibernation proved worthwhile as on our return to London and with little preparation the engine started first time (see technical guide TG01). The experience of living in a flat (after several large homes with gardens) convinced us to spend our retirement commuting between "lock up and go homes" in London and Cape Town: we will follow the sun while our health remains good.

One day in 2015 while walking down the Upper Richmond Road in London I noticed that the new Mini Cooper was advertised on a billboard. It had the identical colour scheme to my 1929 Morris that I had selected back in 1992. I subsequently parked the Morris in front of the advert to take a comparative photo – since my Morris is the Mini's great-great-grandfather (Fig.84) this shows the evolution of two great marques.

Going over the famous London Hammersmith Bridge (Fig.85) shortly before it was closed for major repairs was not only an excellent opportunity but I was accompanied by David Bromfield who has been a close friend since the age of seven. We continued to tour with the Morris attending the 2018 Morris Register National gathering in Thoresby, near Nottingham. The Morris again won best Minor in the show, a repeat of the same award in 1992 (Fig.86).

During the summer of 2019 in the UK, we continued to participate in club events. We took the opportunity to visit the home of the Morris Minor that is now the Mini in Cowley Oxford (Figs.87–89). We were invited to participate at the exclusive Chateau Impney gathering at Droitwich where hundreds of historic and amazing vintage racing cars performed around the track (Fig.90). I have never seen so many 1930s Bentleys in one place. I am building a collection of Morris photos at iconic sites. After some planning and persuasion, I was able to park the Morris in front of the Concorde preserved at Brooklands (Fig.91). This historic home of British Motor Racing, where the brilliant engineer Barnes Wallace designed many aircraft including Concorde, is better known for the WW2 "Bouncing Bomb". We returned to Prescott for the annual Vintage Minor jamboree and hill climb where we were caught at speed! (Fig.92)

The constant shortcoming of many vintage cars is their inability to retard or stop suddenly. On the open road we endeavour to leave a significant distance from the vehicle in front but inevitably someone – usually a youngster – overtakes, moves into the space created and then brakes, not appreciating the limitations of the older vehicle. We have had several near misses of not shunting the car ahead because the Morris brakes are just not good enough compared to modern cars.

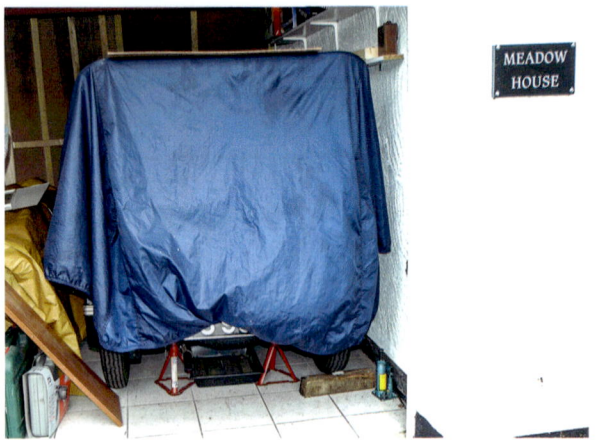

Fig.83: Left for India hibernated 2004–13

Fig.84: Great-grandfather and son 2015

Fig.85: Hammersmith Bridge London 2018

Fig.86: First prize Morris National. Rally 2018

Fig.87: William Morris's garage Oxford

Fig.88: Back to my birthplace 2019

Fig.89: Cowley Oxford the steel body shop

Fig.90: Chateau Impney Droitwich England

Fig.91: Concorde at Brooklands 2019

Fig.92: Speeding at Prescott track 2019

Fig.93: Brake shoe contact is <50 percent

Fig.94: New drums made with ribs

Fig.95: Home-made brake shoe profiler

Fig.96: Now skids on tarmac road

Fig.97: Blockley tyres fitted for Africa trip

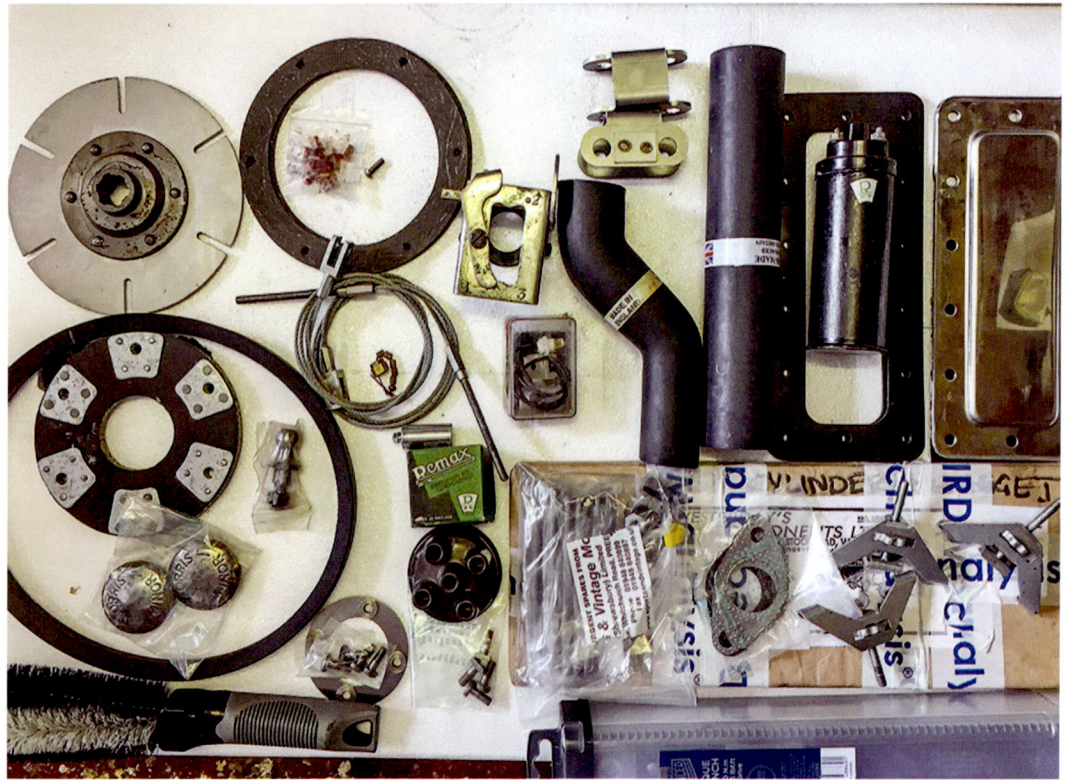

Fig.98: Spares for Back-to-Africa tour

Over the years I made many adjustments and modifications to improve the Morris brakes – unfortunately with little success. I realised that the real issue was that the car's brake drums had become oval and were hardly making effective contact with the brake shoes. (Fig.93). Due to overheating and stress, they had become distorted. Since there was insufficient metal to correct the ovality, I contacted a specialist company in Birmingham to make new drums. They created a detailed CAD drawing but instead of machining the outer rim like the original I asked them to create grooves that look like cooling fins but would add rigidity to the drums and prevent future distortion (Fig.94).

The drums were machined from a solid billet to the eight-inch standard internal diameter. To return the Morris's brakes to original specification I attended to the following: new steel slippers on the aluminium brake shoes, new soft linings, brake cams reshaped and new bushes.

However, the new drums appeared to be too small for the brake shoe linings. I later discovered that new brake linings are now supplied two millimetres thicker than the original because most vintage cars' drums are worn. To overcome the extra diameter of brake shoes, I converted an old brake drum as a jig to grind down the linings but also to ensure perfect roundness (Fig.95). This process gave the Morris superior stopping ability, even skidding on tar! (Fig.96) It proved to be one of the major improvements for driving the Morris in traffic, especially when in Zimbabwe and Zambia (see TG3).

Before the car's arrival in South Africa I took out a comprehensive insurance policy to cover the Morris for use in South Africa, Zimbabwe and Zambia. Despite this I still had to take out third-party insurance at the border posts. The value of this document is highly questionable and perhaps another money-making scam to "foreign" road users. To comply with Zimbabwean and Zambian regulations the car required the approved patterned white and red reflective tapes on the front and rear bumpers.

Never once was I stopped by police apart from them expressing great interest in this special little car. It did attract considerable smiles wherever it went. I think its distinctive colour helped as it is so noticeable.

Chapter 4

Travel, Planning, Logistics

The Dream is Realised

I had often dreamed of returning the restored Morris to Zambia where I had discovered it in 1970. Now retired and living between London and Cape Town following the sun, the dream started to seem possible. Stage one of the plan would be to get the car to Cape Town. As luck would have it, while in Cape Town I was invited to make a presentation to the Rotary Club ("India Through My Eyes"). I finished off mentioning the planned Morris trip. A fellow Crankhandle Club member, John Ryall, who ships cars back and forth to the UK, was present. We got talking and he offered to fit the Morris in his 40 foot container along with a 1911 Sunbeam and D-Type Jaguar from London to Cape Town. What luck! This shared cost certainly reduced my expenditure and with a known person experienced in transporting cars I felt more comfortable that the Morris was in good hands.

In 2019 before shipping the Morris to Cape Town I replaced all the tyres (27 years old) with new Blockley racing tyres because I was advised that the older tyres might not survive the heat on the Southern African roads (Fig.97). I also needed to assemble a range of spares that I hoped I would never need (Fig.98).

In order to drive a vehicle across national borders, without paying custom duties, a carnet is required. This statutory document requires a deposit of £3,000 in the case of the Morris. The administration charges and the printing of the carnet were extra. In reality the deposit is an insurance in case the vehicle is not returned or is damaged beyond recovery, which would then mean the £3,000 deposit would be forfeited. When the vehicle is returned to the UK the deposit would be returned. To comply with UK regulations, I had to submit, online, a SORN (Statutory Off Road Notification) indicating it would be off the UK roads until further notice.

The next stage was to get the car to John Ryall's container in Suffolk. During August 2019 the Morris was collected from London (Figs.99, 100) and was soon on the container ship *MSC Phoenix* (Fig.101). After about eight weeks at sea and then cleared by South African Customs, it was delivered to John's works in Cape Town on 4 November 2019. When removed from the container it was in perfect condition. Phew – back in Africa! (Fig.102)

When the Morris arrived in Cape Town, I was very excited to collect and get the engine started. After topping up with water and activating the battery isolation switch, the engine burst into life (as usual). Our first stop was to fill up with petrol (Fig.103), then drive the 28 kilometres to our home in the suburb of Kenilworth (Fig.104) being greeted by car horns all along the way.

Marketing

My first action in 2018 was to rough out a Marketing Plan in the hope of getting sponsorship but ultimately, I did not bother. However, the document did provide an outline of requirements, materials, budgets, travel logistics and planning. Furthermore, I had to develop new computer skills as well.

Fig.99: Loading in the transporter Aug. 2019

Fig.100: On its way to Felixstowe dock

Fig.101: MSC Phoenix on the high sea

Fig.102: Out of the container, Cape Town

Fig.103: Filled with petrol and driven home

Fig.104: Arrived at Oaktree, Wynberg

Fig.105: Crankhandle Clubhouse (CHC)

Fig.106: Houw Hoek Annual Rally 2019

I was aware that this "major event" would involve family, friends and new contacts who expressed a continued interested in the trip. In 2019 I created the BTA logo (Fig.107) and then the website (Back-to-Africa-in-a-1929MorrisMinor.com) to inform all of the plan but also hoping that it would open doors for us in Zimbabwe and Zambia – which actually proved to be the case. This site was updated due to changing events as the project kept being postponed.

I hoped that we would be assisted in various ways and that many people would be offering their services free or at highly discounted rates. To express my appreciation and as a token of the memorable event I had ceramic mugs printed with "before and after" images of the Morris. These mugs were highly appreciated by all who received them (Fig.108).

As part of the Team Building and presentation at various receptions, I purchased several polo shirts and had them embroidered with the BTA logo (Fig.109) that proved a hit with the Team. As I would be driving in an open tourer, I also needed long-sleeved khaki shirts to reduce the exposure to the fierce African sun; these were also embroidered with the BTA logo. To recreate the period when the Morris was used in Africa, I obtained a khaki pith helmet that raised a lot of laughs.

I felt we needed a large banner to display at group events and at the final destination to illustrate what this trip was all about, especially the Cecily's Fund (Fig.110). Fortunately, a long-time friend, Steve Martin in Johannesburg, had a banner printing company. He insisted that he print the banners and vehicle decals with all fixtures free of charge including delivery to Cape Town. This was his contribution to the tour (Figs.111, 112). The decals pasted on the box trailer created much interest making us look very professional: most police officers waived us through, recognising our mission. I also had business cards printed with the BTA logo that proved most convenient for providing contact details.

To keep family and friends aware of our daily progress I used social media through Instagram (peterw.hills) that linked the reports to a public audience on Facebook. The feedback received was most encouraging totalling some thousands of responses.

I wanted a video taken throughout the journey – that was David's duty. I also fitted the Morris with a dash-cam that recorded most of the travel and had to be downloaded daily. Perhaps once the BTA Book is published a TV documentary company may assemble the story. However, I will make a series of YouTube clips to create awareness for the book.

During the trip I maintained a PowerPoint presentation covering the preparation, the challenges and the trip itself. The before and after tour was presented to members of the Crankhandle Club as well as the Club in Mutare and elsewhere. It has proved to be a very useful reference for preparing this book.

Marketing Collateral

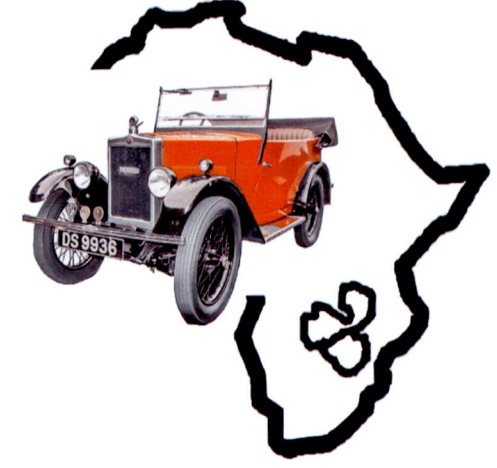

Fig.107: BTA logo showing Zimbabwe and Zambia

Fig.108: BTA mugs as gifts 1970, 2020, 2023

Fig.109: BTA polo shirts with BTA logo   Fig.110: Cecily's Fund – decals and brochures

The Morris History Board (Fig.111) displayed on both sides of the trailer created considerable interest along the way. It was a constant talking point wherever we stopped – particularly as the Morris was secured inside. Also mounted on a board at car shows, it creates considerable interest and saved retelling the story!

1929 MORRIS MINOR 4 SEAT TOURER – HISTORY SUMMARY TO DATE

Fig.111: Morris History Board Decal for the Trailer

OUT AND BACK TO AFRICA IN A 1929 MORRIS MINOR

Fig.112: BTA five-metre banner – a noticeable backdrop at all events

The *Vintage Minor Register* and the *Morris Register* published articles in their magazines creating greater awareness of the Back-to-Africa trip that startled many of its members. The *Morris Register* claims to be the largest pre-1940 car club in the world. (Refs.11, 12, 16)

Recall that in 1993 the *Classic & Sports Car* magazine in the UK that is published internationally, did a five page article on the Morris. Their June 2024 issue had a report on six pages about the Morris BTA tour 31 years later (Fig.113). I hope this article will awaken people's memories of their association with the car as happened with Bruce Beckley of Bulawayo (Fig.228).

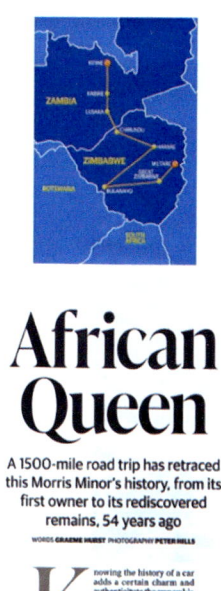

African Queen

A 1500-mile road trip has retraced this Morris Minor's history, from its first owner to its rediscovered remains, 54 years ago

WORDS GRAEME HURST PHOTOGRAPHY PETER HILLS

Knowing the history of a car adds a certain charm and authenticity to the ownership experience. While keys often change hands with a file of MoTs and receipts, details of past keepers can be more tricky to establish. Especially when the car is 94 years old and from another continent. Except in the case of Peter Hills' 1929 Morris Minor, which originally appeared in the September 1993 issue of C&SC.

Acquired as an abandoned wreck in rural Zambia in 1970, its ownership can be traced back through 10 previous keepers, all the way to when it was delivered new to neighbouring Zimbabwe (then Southern Rhodesia) as the first Morris in the land. And not just names, either: Peter has formed a list of all 11 addresses where the car was kept during its lifetime.

Peter W. Hills 1929 Morris Minor M10228

Fig.113: Classic & Sports Car Magazine June 2024 – Six Page Article on BTA trip (Ref.17)

Maintenance and Covid-19

After ensuring that all was well with the car, five days later we joined the Crankhandle Club (Fig.113), for its famous annual Houw Hoek Rally. Originally it was a Reliability Trial started in 1903 but in 1956 the Club started a commemoration rally and in 2003 the club repeated the original 1903 rally with veteran cars. The first task was to climb Sir Lowry's Pass, rising 453 metres above sea level, quite a challenge for the Morris – often in first gear. After that, despite the many subsequent hills that tested the car considerably, we just managed to keep up with larger vintage vehicles that had superior torque. Nevertheless, we often arrived a little later at the many destinations (Figs.106, 115). At the rally awards ceremony, while we came last, we were awarded a "Tea Strainer" for the car that took the most strain! The Club Members were amazed at its performance as they had never seen such a model and at subsequent club outings the little Morris gained a reputation for its grit and reliability.

Little did we know that our lives were about to change. The Back-to-Africa tour had been scheduled for April–May 2020 but the Covid-19 pandemic brought all plans and activities to a halt as South Africa was placed under lockdown.

During this period there was an attempted coup in Zimbabwe; the subsequent death of President Mugabe created an uncertain political climate; a hurricane and petrol shortages exacerbated the desperate situation in Zimbabwe.

The long-planned BTA trip had to be postponed (Fig.114), with no indication of when it would recommence. Naturally, I was devastated after all the planning and expense: we had trunks of provisions already packed: including the banners, polo shirts, ceramic gift mugs, camping equipment, oils and greases, and car spares. I had to cancel various accommodation bookings as well as a reception in Johannesburg. The box trailer also had to be cancelled and deposit returned. The original BTA Team was told to stand down, the air ticket for my brother in Germany cancelled and reimbursed – "The best-laid plans of mice and men…"

Since I had already attracted considerable interest in the trip on social media and folks were contributing to the Cecily's Fund Charity, I decided to create a virtual journey to justify these initial contributions and generate interest and fun during lockdown.

Using creative photography, I posted on the Instagram and Facebook sites photos of things we expected to encounter throughout the trip. This had attracted quite a following; some even believed it was the real thing!

Later the exercise proved to be a useful guide and formed the basis of the actual tour in 2023. During that trip I posted daily updates on Instagram that were automatically copied to Facebook. Based on the hundreds of Comments and Likes, I can only assume the reports were well appreciated – especially by those who had grown up in the former Rhodesias – seeing familiar sites and reviving their memories.

Fig.114: Covid postponed the 2020 trip

It was gratifying that at the Crankhandle Club end-of-year awards, the Morris was voted the "Best Vintage Car of 2021" – see the certificate (Fig.116). Considering that the 500+ membership has an amazing range of veteran, vintage and classic cars, it is quite an honour for the modest Morris Minor to be recognised so highly among world-class vehicles.

The original *Carnet du Passage* was valid for one year; but because of Covid I was able to justify an extension in the UK and South Africa; this involved the tax and customs authorities and the AA of SA. The original carnet document had to be couriered back to the UK and then to Cape Town. There was a renewal cost as well as additional surety deposits. This process was done twice and then the

SARS (South African Revenue Service) stated that the Morris must leave the country by July 2023. The clock was ticking; decisions had to be made.

By 15 December 2021 Covid lockdowns had eased. I was able to join an MMM group of MGs on a drive to Glencairn, towards Simonstown. After the gruelling climb up the Ou Kaapse Weg Mountain pass, mostly in first gear then a long downhill cruising at 50 mph I suddenly heard a different engine noise. At the bottom of the hill the dreaded "tuck-tuck-tuck" emanated from the engine. The car was transported home to avoid any consequential damage. On removing the oil sump, we found that number one cylinder's big-end bearing had failed. It now seemed an ideal opportunity to give the engine a complete overhaul so that it would be in perfect condition for the Back-to-Africa trip. After all, it was 27 years since it was last assembled and at that time I had zero experience of this particular engine.

Once the engine was removed, I noticed that one of the cylinder head's cast-iron stud water-jacket sealing pods was broken. Also, there was a new crack from the water jacket propagating down the engine block. The engine I purchased in 1974 also had a pre-existing weld along the block – perhaps a crack repair due to water freezing in the block. As luck would have it, I came across an identical engine block locally in excellent condition in the Cape. After acquiring the replacement block it was sent for re-boring to 58 millimetres. The existing pistons were good, but the worn rings needed replacing. I decided to convert the big-ends to shell bearings which would be better in the long run than white metal. Basticks Engine Reconditioners of Cape Town were contracted to do the work. Coinciding with this machining, we had an existing booking on a cruise ship to Marion Island along with some 1,500 bird watchers, a unique opportunity. The next morning the vessel was probably 180 kilometres out of Cape Town when to my surprise my mobile phone rang. It was Ronnie McFarland of Basticks: "Peter, Number One conrod is 2 millimetres shorter than the others, can you get a replacement, its cast number is 178240A?" Now here I am literally "all at sea" and needing to find a 1929 Morris Minor conrod! I phoned a fellow MG enthusiast in Knysna and bingo! One conrod was couriered to Basticks the next day. Phew, got out of jail again!

Back in Cape Town, having received the new piston rings via a friend visiting from the UK, the assembled engine was ready for installation. At the same time, I took the opportunity to further improve the noisy three-speed gearbox. I replaced the layshaft locking pins and replaced the thrust washers so that the various spur gears meshed better (TG8). I noticed that the rivets securing the clutch lining were loose; they were resecured.

Finally, the engine was installed in the car and all connections made. I filled the engine with Ravenol "breaking-in oil" to bed in the new rings and big-end bearings. The oil is recommended to be used for some 622 miles (1,000 kilometres). The first long drive (105 miles) was to Philadelphia with my pal Barry Pardey and then we made several local trips before it was time to replace the oil with the standard SAE40 non-detergent oil. The engine ran well but there was a mysterious sound, a slight "tick-tick" that increased when the Advance/Retard was adjusted. Some thought it was a type of pre-ignition or pinking but time would tell.

On 20 November 2022 we participated in the Cape Town Century Rally – 100 cars meet at Century City and travel 100 kilometres, the stipulation being that the age of the car and owner must exceed 100. With my co-driver, again Barry Pardey, we toured through the glorious Cape countryside and ended up at a wine estate in Stellenbosch.

The Morris gearbox continued to be very noisy; so after Christmas I removed it again – only to discover that the sealed spigot bearing had seized in the flywheel after only five years. I then decided to remove the flywheel to ensure that its taper was finely polished and fully lapped in. I also took the opportunity to replace the worn clutch, foot brake pivot shaft bushes and have the shaft built and polished to a perfect fit. Examining the gearbox meshing in considerable detail I replaced the spigot shaft with a spare that improved the gear meshing further. Since I also had spare gear selector arms, I fitted the least worn units. At the rear of the gearbox casing I found one securing bolt thread stripped that was fixed with a Helicoil system. After polishing the flywheel flange slipper-bearing, we tightened the flywheel bolts to a torque of 110 foot-pounds. The cylinder head was torqued down to 25 foot-pounds and the tappets were set to 0.006-inch inlet and 0.008 inch exhaust. Then we started the engine. It burst into life but did not seem as powerful as I expected because of a leak at the exhaust manifold. I was about to replace the fibre gasket with solid copper gasket but noticed that the exhaust manifold face was not flat – in fact one millimetre out. After correcting by milling, the sealed unit made the engine lively.

The gearbox: first gear had greatly improved although the second gear was still noisy. I rationalised that since I had installed a variety of used gears, they would need time and miles to bed in, especially going uphill! The car was now running better than ever – apart from the annoying and unidentified slight "tick-tick-tick". The lesson to learn is that no matter how much you wish away a strange noise, something is not right – as we would soon find out!

The final touch before the BTA trip was fitting leather gaiters to the main suspension springs that I had custom made in Cape Town. I first wrapped Denso tape (grease-impregnated linen) around the springs and then laced over the gaiters. Such fittings are a luxury for the Morris but quite common on high-end cars such as vintage Bentleys and Rolls Royces. I thought it would benefit the suspension during the forthcoming trip and in future. To ensure that the car was fully reliable I made several trips around mountainous Cape Town visiting many iconic sites and of course the monthly natters at the Crankhandle Club (Figs.117–122). Recording views of the Morris at well-known areas of the Western Cape including the Wine lands was memorable. I was even permitted to drive the Morris round the Killarney International Raceway, where many notable race cars and world-famous drivers have spun their wheels. (Fig.123). At a Crankhandle Club natter the E-Type and Ferrari put the modest Morris in perspective (Fig.124). The members reminded me of a "senior moment" for owning an English car (Fig.125)! The classic image of the Morris against the fabulous Table Mountain proved to be an iconic image (Fig.126) illustrated in several publications.

Wedding – a "Lucky Disaster"

On 5 March 2023, having delivered Sarah Millward (now Black) to her wedding the previous day (Fig.127), Sandy and I were making our way home from the West Coast back to Cape Town when on the motorway the "tick-tick-tick" heard previously increased and then "Bang!" I managed to coax the car to an off-ramp where it stopped altogether.

As usual, my brother-in-law Graham Lowden came to our rescue. We towed the Morris back to our workshop, but it was a Sunday afternoon and guests had arrived to stay the night: the next day would reveal the problem. A quick check indicated that the compression seemed okay. Was it the gearbox? Next morning, on removing the sump all was revealed: the crankshaft had snapped in two at Number One journal (Fig.128). Despite this, the broken unit rotated against the other part, giving the impression of compression.

My departure date to the North was 23 March – just 18 days to go and I had a broken engine. Clearly, I was devastated – was this the closure of years of planning? Where would I find a replacement crankshaft and conrods for a 1929 Morris Minor in Cape Town? Could the engine be restored by 23 March?

The Morris had to return to the UK according to the Carnet and South African customs by July 2023. A very stressful situation but not as stressful as that on that very day we learned that our dear friend's son, Iain Bromfield age 46, had passed away after a short illness. That loss put priorities into perspective.

The early MGs and 1929 OHC Morris Minor share the same engine block. One option was to use the crankshaft customised to fit in my newly assembled J2 engine block but it lacked the flexibility to fit the Morris without major modification. I immediately informed my local MMM group who thankfully responded immediately. Feliciano Martins offered his spare J2 crankshaft along with matching P-type conrods that, with minor alteration, would fit the Morris. Feliciano's only condition was that I replace the crankshaft, which I agreed to do.

The crankshaft (Fig.129) was made locally in 1993, one of two designed for a racing J2, but this spare unit was never used and had changed hands several times. Nevertheless, it appeared sound and this time I did an NDT; it was crack free. In the time available I had to do a lot of pleading to raise the engineering priority for the Morris engine to be fixed in my time frame.

Fig.115: Crossing a classic Bailey bridge

Fig.116: Morris best CHC vintage car 2021

Fig.117: St Patrick's charity – R100 a ride

Fig.118: Cape Town's iconic hotel

Fig.119: Wale Street Cape Town

Fig.120: Wine lands rally with CHC

Fig.121: Slanghoek Wine lands CHC Rally

Fig.122: Timour Hall, CHC monthly natter

Fig.123: A spin on the Killarney Race Track

Fig.124: Beauty and the "beasts" (Supercars)

Fig.125: Car nut friends, a senior moment?

Fig.126: Cape Town to Kitwe in 35 days' time

Since number one conrod was damaged beyond recovery and the replacement crankshaft journals were at least 10 millimetres larger in diameter, I had to use matching MG P-type conrods. My first contact was my dear friend and excellent toolmaker, Aubrey Springer of Glencairn (near Simonstown) who rose to the occasion and my priority. He machined the complex rear-tapered flange bearing and then shortened one end of the crankshaft to fit in the Morris's engine block. We took the opportunity to install front and rear lip seals on the crankshaft to reduce the perennial oil leaks so common to these vintage engines.

Fig.127: Sarah's wedding 4 March 2023

Fig.128: Crankshaft failed 5 March 2023

Fig.129: Replacement crankshaft 6 March

Fig.130: Morris Flywheel lightened by 2.5kg

The replacement crankshaft was a superior design to the original but was 3.5kg heavier. To compensate Aubrey lightened the flywheel by 2.5kg (Fig.130). It was appreciated that the heavier assembly would mean a lower top speed but have better torque.

Next, I delivered the conrods to Basticks Engine Reconditioners in central Cape Town to be converted to shell bearings by Ronnie McFarland. The two engineering facilities are 43km apart and our home is somewhere between. To get the work done, each needed different parts to measure and check at different stages of engineering – I spent a lot of time and distance driving back and forth. By 17 March I collected the engine block with new crankshaft, conrods and pistons fitted, it was an amazing achievement by all concerned

Engine rebuilt in 13 days

The next day Graham Lowden and I, assisted by Graham Pringle, assembled the engine and placed it in the Morris (Fig.131). Before fitting the flywheel, gearbox and radiator I said, "Let's fire up the engine first." All I wanted was to hear engine combustion so that I could fit the gearbox and other parts with confidence. The battery was not at its best as the engine was rather tight to turn but, after a couple of sluggish rotations, it burst into life. What joy! We then proceeded to fit the gearbox, the propshaft, radiator and ancillaries.

I drove home, collected Sandy and rushed off to the Foresters Arms in Newlands to make our lunch date with friends. From failed crankshaft to a working car in 13 days and no "tick-tick-tick" – an amazing (Fig.132) effort by all involved.

The support from Aubrey and Ronnie in expediting the work made it happen. Further, the encouragement and assistance by the two Grahams was invaluable – in fact Graham Pringle, the former

Fig.131: Installing engine, two Grahams 17 March

Fig.132: Back on the road,18 March – Yay!

banker, had an accelerated learning curve in overhauling and rebuilding engines that would come in useful for the pending BTA trip.

Why did the original crankshaft fail? The evidence is provided on its fracture face (Fig.133). A non-destructive test using the MPI (magnetic particle inspection) method on the remaining journals revealed that all were cracked to some degree.

My previous life involved forensic engineering (failure analysis): the crankshaft fracture face was free of obvious striations that would be typical of a rapid fatigue failure. In this case their absence is indicative of very slow crack propagation over many years. I concluded that this crankshaft had been cracked long before I purchased the engine in 1973.

It is amazing that it lasted some 11,300 miles (18,100 kilometres) and is a credit to the early balancing to F1 standard. Feliciano had an identical Morris Minor crankshaft that I also crack-detected: it too was cracked at most journals – so sadly is only of scrap value. The original Morris two-bearing crankshafts did not have counter-balancing lobes like the replacement and so would be subject to high-cyclic bending stresses that, despite radiused journals, have failed frequently at the changes in section.

Recall that in December 2021 the number one big-end bearing had failed. When the crankshaft broke in two, the car had done a further 1,241 miles since the complete overhaul in January 2022. Had a crack detection test been carried out on the crankshaft then, the situation might have been different. Keep in mind that the pre-1974 crankshaft journal crack had continued to propagate over the next 10,157 miles of my usage. The increased flexing at the increasing crack opening would have

Fig.133: Crankshaft fatigue fracture face

Fig.134: Golden "balls" (speed governor))

progressively eroded the bearing surface, thus lowering its local oil pressure. That would reduce the cushioning feature of the oil and finally lead to journal-bearing failure. Another lesson learned: when a failure happens, don't just fix – always find the cause, especially at an isolated fracture area.

In summary, how fortunate were we? Locating and replacing the crankshaft and conrods customised to the 1929 Morris engine in Cape Town and getting it running in 13 days is remarkable. The Back-to-Africa trip was back on schedule with a superior crankshaft and larger bearing journals making the engine much more robust. Thank goodness Sarah had asked me to drive her to the wedding because without doubt the engine would have failed in Mutare and that would have scuppered the whole project. Certainly, lady luck and the good old "golden balls" have followed us (Fig.134) and long may this continue.

Financing the Trip

Since this trip was about my Morris Minor and my dream, the cost for the enterprise was entirely mine. I invited the BTA Team to an all-expenses paid holiday and kept my word.

A major cost was shipping the car to Cape Town and back; here again the "golden balls" clanged. As mentioned earlier John Ryall, a Crankhandle Club member, offered me space in his personal 40 foot container in both directions (UK to RSA to UK). This probably saved me 70 percent of what I might have paid. It was comforting to have contacts in the UK who could collect and load the car securely and have the assurance of an experienced shipper.

Obtaining the *Carnet du Passage* enabled the Morris to cross international borders without paying duties. This was a cost, as was the annual renewal charge, but I managed to return the Morris to the UK unscathed and was refunded the £3,000 deposit (after 4 years).

Preparing the Morris mainly required replacing the tyres – they were 27 years old and although they looked almost unused, they would probably have broken up on the hot African roads. I also purchased a selection of spares that were never needed! I was advised to get a half-shaft and I did. If the half-shaft had failed, what would the consequential damage have been? Hindsight is great – I should have brought my spare Diff as well.

In Cape Town I upgraded several aspects of the Morris to ensure that it was robust and reliable for the planned journey along roads reported as terrible in both Zimbabwe and Zambia: the expense was anticipated. The car did not have a tonneau cover – an important consideration for when the car is parked and left alone – as a precaution against light-fingered onlookers.

The multiple reworking of the gearbox and improving the various gear mechanisms and worn bushes was done to bring the car back to original standard.

Later, the required replacement of the crankshaft to Feliciano Martins in Cape Town as promised was a major expense – but again I got lucky in obtaining an unused quality crankshaft in the UK at a very reasonable price that I was able to bring in my suitcase to Cape Town. The P-type conrods also had to be replaced. After the trip the BMW (our support car) needed a replacement tyre and the front shock absorbers that were found to be bent. Removing the defective towbar assembly and repairs to the rear body mudguard were added expenses but collateral damage was relatively minor.

Over time I had accumulated US dollars in cash as that is the currency of Zimbabwe. I also carried British pounds that I could convert into dollars as needed. Apart from accommodation, the biggest expense was fuel: it cost at least US$100 to fill the BMW each time in Zimbabwe. In Zambia I was able to use a credit card or draw cash from an ATM.

One expense I overlooked in my budget was convivial refreshments at the end of the day. Of course, I had committed to the team that the trip was on me and I kept us stocked with beers and cool drinks and paid bar bills, but extras such as exotic liquors were up to the individual. David does not drink alcohol, but Graham and I purchased our own nightly *dop* (brandy). Wayne was a Coca-Cola addict; so ice-cold Cokes and a cigarette kept him happy. Cold beers were essential to rehydrate and slake our thirst after a hot day's drive.

I have attempted to capture most expenses as summarised in Table 3 below. Keep in mind that a 7 week touring holiday for four adults works out at 86 GBP per person a day. However, excluding shipping, maintenance and repairs, and taking only the direct travel costs, it actually worked out to an economic 43 GBP per person per day – quite inexpensive for a dream and adventure. Only on a couple of occasions was accommodation poor but thankfully the BTA Team adjusted which is a credit to them.

We travelled a total of 9,607 kilometres (6,068 miles) – the distance between Cape Town and London as the crow flies!

Table 3: Summary of BTA Expenses

	Currency (£)	Share (percent)
Shipping and transport	3,396	19.4
Collateral: Mugs, polo shirts, banners, printing	766	4.4
Maintenance and repairs	3,305	18.9
Documentation: Visas, insurance, entrance fees	2,473	14.1
Accommodation	2,375	13.6
Carnet costs (excluding deposit returned)	1,600	9.2
Fuel: Petrol and diesel	936	5.4
Restaurants, self-catering, drinks, snacks	817	4.7
Morris spares (most unused)	450	2.6
Other: Camping, utensils, miscellaneous items	350	2.0
Road tolls	111	0.6
Garmin – dash-cam	102	0.6
Birding guide	50	0.3
Cecily's Fund (Accommodation compensation)	750	4.3
Total	**17,481**	**100.0**

The savings arising from complimentary or discounted accommodation as well as some benefit enjoyed by the shared shipping container £750 was paid to the Cecily's Fund. In reality accommodation would have been around GBP 3,000 a major proportion of the trip costs."

Team Appointment

The Back-to-Africa Team consisted of four chaps. Most of the time I would be driving the Morris along with a companion to assist with navigation and an extra pair of eyes on those busy roads. The support car with trailer would travel behind the Morris to warn of incoming traffic and protect the diminutive Morris from large vehicles behind.

The roles of the BTA Team were as follows:

1. Driver of Morris and mechanic
2. Diarist, navigator, companion
3. Photographer/Video recorder
4. Driver of back-up car and trailer

The difficulties of finally assembling a committed team are outlined in Chapter 10, covering all the challenges that were overcome (p.194). None of the team knew each other – except me and then not all that well (Fig.135). It soon became obvious that I did not have an intimate understanding of each person's character and so it was steady as we go, sometimes requiring extreme tact and calm at periods of tension and in a few crisis situations. It is creditable that all pulled together to meet the objective of the tour.

David Forgus   Graham Pringle   Wayne Taylor   Peter Hills

Fig.135: The BTA Team line-up

David Forgus   – Video and still photographer, former Mechanical Fitter – aged 70
Graham Pringle   – Diarist, Birder, Photographer, former Banker – aged 80
Wayne Taylor   – Driver, Vibration and Electronics Engineer – aged 73
Peter Hills   – Coordinator, Birder, Photographer, former Engineer, CEO – aged 79

Our collective ages totalled 302 years – a bunch of old men having the adventure of a lifetime! Sadly, the other three members are widowers. This was probably a benefit since there was less for them to worry about back home. My wife Sandy is used to me taking long business trips around the world and she has family and friends in Cape Town for support. She recognised that this was a boys' trip that might require "roughing it" and was happy to wave us goodbye and bon voyage.

Route Planning

The first task was to transport the Morris from Cape Town to Johannesburg, collect Wayne and then drive to Mutare in Zimbabwe where the Morris would start the "Official Tour".

Driving the Morris requires full concentration; so we planned to cover around 100 miles a day. The stretch from Gweru to Harare – some 173 miles on a good road – would be the longest single day stretch of the trip.

I had contacted the Secretary of the Hillside Golf Club of Mutare, who suggested that he could arrange club members to attend a brunch on Sunday 2 April. This would give us a few extra days in Mutare where Graham and I could do some birding – the Bvumba forest has several endemics in the area. The BTA Team could also relax, get to know each other and prepare for what was to come.

The Vintage Car Club of Zimbabwe in Harare had asked if we could arrive for an Easter Monday braai (barbeque) which required leaving Bulawayo a day earlier.

The planned route and overnight stops to our destination (Itimpi, Zambia) were as follows:

Mutare to Birchenough Bridge – 1 night
Birchenough Bridge to Zvishavane (via Great Zimbabwe Ruins) – 1 night
Zvishavane to Bulawayo – 3 nights

Then Bulawayo to Matopos

Bulawayo to Gweru – 1 night   Gweru to Harare – 3 nights
Harare to Chinhoyi – 1 night   Chinhoyi to Makuti – 1 night
Makuti to Siavonga, Kariba (Zambia) – 3 nights   Siavonga to Lusaka – 2 nights
Lusaka to Kabwe – 1 night   Kabwe to Ndola – 2 nights
Ndola to Kitwe/Itimpi – 3 nights.

Accommodation

Booking accommodation in Zimbabwe and Zambia was achieved by seeking advice of various friends and contacts. Some were aware of the "long-planned tour" and perhaps sceptical that it would ever come to fruition, but I maintained contacts in both Zimbabwe and Zambia.

Complimentary accommodation was offered by Dudley Searle in Harare, Maurice Diamond in Siavonga (Kariba), Ken and Mairi Cummins in Lusaka and Lynne Quarmby in Kitwe. Also, at Masuku, Choma, courtesy of Rory and Dori McDougall, another paradise in Africa. These fantastic offers certainly helped save expenses, but I had made a commitment that any money saved by people's generosity would result in a significant contribution to the Cecily's Fund Charity.

Finding the Paddocks in Bvumba, Mutare was a big win as it was self-catering, complete with swimming pool and a workshop – and at a discount. However, more especially, it was a unique birding area and not far from the internationally famous Leopard Rock Hotel where the Queen Mother, Princess Diana and other VIPs have stayed.

Our first night of the actual tour was at the Birchenough Bridge Hotel; it was offered as complimentary, but it has hardly been maintained since Graham last stayed there in 1978! The nearby *shebeen* (bar) and loud disco continued into the early hours – so none of us got a decent night's sleep. The food reminded us that we were back in rural Africa!

An online booking was achieved with Flame Tree Cottage in Masvingo and the Hotel Boutique in Zvishavane, both modern and within budget. In Bulawayo, Bruce Beckley arranged with the fantastic Granite Park Lodge who kindly gave us two cottages as their upstairs mezzanine bedrooms would not be safe for us older fellows at night! It was the Easter weekend with many people out of town and so they had several cottages empty. This self-catering accommodation was first class and among the best we would encounter. Next stop was Gweru; the Bradley Experience that I had booked online. On arrival we learned they only had one room with two double beds. Wayne used the floor, Graham was in his sleeping bag on the double bed with David. They insisted that I take the other double bed. Despite laying duvets down, poor Wayne had an uncomfortable night.

Staying at Dudley and Prue Searle's Pangoula Farm was like paradise. A large homestead, wonderful setting, trees and a lake – ideal for more birding. They were extremely generous and entertaining.

Dudley booked the Zebras Dazzle in Chinhoyi for us: it was just 73 miles from Harare. We had two double-bed rooms, costing US$70 per room including breakfast. It was clean and comfortable. Next stop was Makuti, 107 miles north where we stayed at the huge granite and thatched Makuti Lodge, also kindly arranged by Dudley. It was very well provisioned for self-catering at a reasonable US$30 per person. It had double rooms with single beds, a nice porch and swimming pool. We also managed to photograph some new birds there.

After crossing the Kariba Dam Wall into Zambia, we stayed at the Lake Safari Lodge hotel, courtesy of Maurice Diamond. What a super place! Large comfortable modern rooms with balcony views of the lake. Our 3 nights were a great experience: good food and the opportunity to cruise the lake and take a drive along the Zambezi River just below the dam wall.

Travelling 126 miles to Lusaka, Ken and Mairi Cummins hosted us and arranged a dinner party of old friends of mine who have remained in Zambia and are still doing well. Then 90 miles to Kabwe where we stayed at the Kabwe Safari Lodge. We had two rooms with single beds. The beer was cold and the dinner was excellent. Next day the terrible 110 mile road trip to Ndola was ameliorated by the luxury Protea Marriott Hotel at US$160 per person; we had to stay two nights – our most expensive accommodation. I had a business meeting in Ndola and it was the only suitable accommodation available.

Arriving in Kitwe and then on to Kamushi Farm on the Chingola Road: another paradise in the bush – much like Pangoula Farm in Harare. We were treated royally. For the third time we adjusted our schedule to meet other commitments. After three wonderful nights, the Morris was placed back in the trailer as we dashed 360 kilometres to Lusaka as we had been invited to attend the Cecily's Fund 25th Anniversary dinner. The hotel, Sandra's Creations, booked by the Cecily's Fund local organiser, was also the venue for the dinner. The chalet was quite basic regarding sleeping arrangements but we managed.

The next 2 nights were complimentary at Hans Sportel's establishment after the BMW's radiator burst. After repairs, we got to Masuku in Choma for a fantastic time birding and recovering from the trauma of the BMW and our rescue. Arriving in Livingstone we took a chance to find rooms and struck gold at Fawlty Towers, simple but clean, well-managed at US$55 per double room including breakfast and coffee/tea on tap.

Crossing back to Zimbabwe we booked a self-catering cottage at Hwange Main Camp game reserve. To our surprise the chalet was not self-catering, but if we wanted one the price doubled. We made do but after the second night we decided to cut our losses and headed for South Africa. This was the toughest day's drive, covering 720 kilometres and passing through Zimbabwean and South African borders. We arrived at 21:00 at the Northbridge Lodge in Louis Trichardt (Machado) where we had stayed on the way up. Fortunately, the gatekeeper was still there; so I paid R1,300 (US$71) for a chalet that slept four.

The next morning, we dropped Wayne off in Johannesburg before proceeding to the Winburg Hotel in Free State: 290 kilometres and arriving after sunset. We had not booked but found the hotel and managed to get rooms that appeared unchanged since it was built in 1857! By now winter was setting in – it was so cold that we slept with our clothes on! At R1070 (US$58) for two rooms it seemed a rip-off for one of the most basic hotels. Nevertheless, there was a reason for staying at this hotel, I wanted to replicate the photo of when Gilg and Kay stayed there in 1933 with their Morris Minor.

Not wanting to arrive in Cape Town in the dark I managed to book the superb Lemoenfontein Hotel outside Beaufort West. The evening dinner for three was voted the best of the trip (Karoo lamb), it cost R3,400 (US$186) – the comfort and stunning rooms were worth every cent.

Arriving home in Cape Town and back in our own beds: simply the best of all accommodation.

Chapter 5

Outbound – South Africa

Day 0: 22 March – Presentation to Crankhandle Club, Cape Town

The Crankhandle Club is perhaps one of the best car clubs in the world, boasting a fantastic range of cars from a 1901 Benz to the present. Their clubhouse is in the Little Chelsea area of Wynberg in the Southern Suburbs of Cape Town, and houses a huge collection of memorabilia and a comprehensive library. As a member of the club, I was invited to give a presentation on my long-planned tour "Back-to-Africa in a 1929 Morris Minor" at one of their regular Wednesday meetings. This was set for 22 March 2023 and thus fixed our date of departure – the next morning. Two of the members of the Back-to-Africa Team, Graham Pringle and David Forgus, accompanied me at the meeting.

The event was well attended by members and guests, despite the rain and cool weather. After thanking the chairman for hosting us I introduced Graham and David and explained that Wayne Taylor would join us in Johannesburg. My presentation covered details of the proposed trip in the Morris, an account of the car's restoration, research into its history and names and addresses of all previous owners. I outlined our plan to visit the addresses of the 10 owners, retracing the Morris's journey through Zimbabwe and Zambia to its "final" resting place in the Itimpi bush outside Kitwe where I found it in 1970.

When I explained that 21 days earlier that the crankshaft had sheared in two (Fig.136) there was a gasp from the audience. What now, was this the end of a crazy adventure? On telling them that I had been offered a replacement crankshaft the next day and we had got the car back on the road in only 13 days, many were in disbelief. "Where is the car, it's not on show in the clubhouse?" I convinced them that it was packed in the box trailer for an early morning departure.

Fig.136: Failed crankshaft

I expressed my grateful thanks to all the people who made the recovery possible: especially Aubrey Springer (the Beetle man) for lightening the flywheel, making the flange bearing and fitting the crankshaft into the engine block, Ronnie McFarland at Basticks Engine Reconditioning company, and my brother-in-law Graham Lowden.

Also present was Peter Price of Priclo Trailers and Caravans who had gone the extra mile in preparing the trailer, including emergency spares. The upholsterer Peter Crowley had worked on the tonneau cover and leather gaiters for the suspension. With Peter Truter also in attendance, I counted at least four Peters in the room! Then Peter Crowley took the floor to present me with a beautiful custom-made leather bag with Morris and MG logos to match my respective cars. The official business being over, I announced an open bar. "Is this a wake for this reckless small vintage car trip into the unknown?" some said. A lot of chat ensued – the broken crankshaft on display created much debate, especially as it only has two support bearings.

At 22:00 we headed home and hitched the trailer to the BMW – Graham and David slept at our residence overnight to ensure no delays to our departure early next morning and to avoid the Cape Town traffic.

Day 1: 23 March – Depart Cape Town to Gariep Dam (827km)

The box trailer was loaded with the Morris and strapped down. The food provisions, tools, engine oil, extra Morris wheel, spare BMW tyres, four jerry cans for fuel and a water container along with our personal baggage (Figs.137, 138) were loaded in the space around the car as well as in a front compartment. Documents, cameras and tog bags were stored in the BMW.

Fig.137: Morris and trailer with BTA decals affixed to its sides, the day before departure

Fig.138: Morris loaded in the trailer, spare tyres for the BMW and trailer

After so many weeks and months – in fact years of planning and preparing for the Back-to-Africa trip, the day had arrived. We were as prepared as we could be to set out from Cape Town on what we hoped would be an historic and epic adventure. After our wake-up call, we bade farewell to my ever-supportive Sandy and set off from Wynberg at 04:20, heading for the N1 out of Cape Town. This highway would take us the length of South Africa to the Beit Bridge border into Zimbabwe. Once there, we would travel across the country and into Zambia. We would go all the way to Kitwe on the Copperbelt where in 1970 I discovered the 1929 Morris Minor wreck that took me 22 years to restore.

The going was easy as there was not much traffic, but I had to get used to towing the high box trailer against the wind. We maintained a speed of between 90 and 100 kilometres per hour which was matched to our projected travelling speed. Within an hour we passed through the Huguenot Tunnel that many regard as the gateway between the Greater Cape Town area and the interior. This is where the holiday begins. The tunnel through the Du Toit's Kloof mountains was opened in 1988; it is 3.9 kilometres long and cuts 11 kilometres off the pass over the mountain. Apart from saving travelling time, it is a lot safer. After exiting the tunnel, we drove along the Molenaars River towards Worcester and then on towards the Hex River Valley, famous for its vineyards.

Passing along the Hex River Valley the scene was like a patchwork quilt with all the vineyards in various stages: autumn shades changing from green to yellow, orange and brown depending on their vintage. Several vineyards were covered with sheets of white plastic or netting, which detracted from the natural beauty. That is the cost of progress.

After climbing the Hex River Pass between De Doorns and Touws River we started seeing vast tracts of typical Karoo, surprisingly very lush and green after recent good rains. At 07:45 we stopped for breakfast at Laingsburg, halfway between Cape Town and the next big town Beaufort West (Fig.139). Laingsburg gained notoriety in 1981 when a flash flood from various parts of the Karoo caused the Buffels River to burst its banks and sweep through the lower-lying areas of the town causing major destruction: more than a hundred people were drowned – their bodies were swept downstream and never recovered.

We had decided to share the driving: after Laingsburg, Graham took over until Three Sisters and David then drove to Colesberg. I did the last 50 kilometres to the Gariep Dam, our overnight stop.

The reduction in rail transport means that these days there are thousands of trucks on the N1 daily; we needed to be constantly alert and ready to take evasive action as the truck drivers seem to believe might is right. We observed several near collisions; we even saw a police car overtaking a truck on a blind rise, ignoring the double white line and forcing the oncoming vehicle onto the shoulder of the road – a close call.

Just beyond Beaufort West we noticed that the large dam was full to the brim. This was pleasing since at the height of the recent drought drinking water had to be trucked in. After Beaufort West we passed several small towns until we reached Colesberg, a fairly large town where the main highway from the Eastern Cape joins the N1, and the truck traffic going north increased. After Colesberg we crossed the Orange River; it was very full with brown muddy water from the recent rains and lived up to its name – although it was actually named after the Dutch House of Orange. We had booked our overnight stay at the Hamerkop Cottage. It had a large secure parking area and the owners, Drikus and Liesl Smit, were on hand. Drikus offered to park our trailer in a position for an easy exit in the morning. A local restaurant delivered a simple hot meal for us; then it was early to bed in comfortable accommodation after a long and tiring day.

> About a hundred kilometres north of Bloemfontein lies the small historic town of Winburg, the oldest proclaimed town in Free State. It is also one of the two oldest settlements in South Africa north of the Orange River, the other being Griquastad. On their epic trip in a 1933 Morris Minor Tourer, Gilg and Kay stopped over at the Winburg Hotel. On our return journey to Cape Town we planned to visit Winburg to see if the hotel still exists and try to repeat a similar photograph.

Day 2: 24 March – Gariep to Johannesburg (588km)

We all seemed to have slept well; so after a shower and cup of coffee we set off from the Gariep Dam at 05:45. It was still dark and slightly overcast, which meant that the rising sun did not affect visibility. The traffic was light and we made good progress; we bypassed Bloemfontein and travelled for 80 kilometres on an excellent, mostly dual carriageway toll road. I drove the first stretch, then Graham took the wheel as far as Kroonstad where we stopped for breakfast at 11:45 after covering 469 kilometres.

The N1 crosses the Vaal River which forms the border between Free State and the provinces of Mpumalanga, Gauteng and Northwest. Travelling through the northern Free State and the provinces north of the Vaal, the countryside is generally agricultural, with many crops under irrigation, especially maize and sunflowers. This area is referred to as the "Maize Triangle" and is responsible for some 80 percent of South Africa's maize production.

The Gariep Dam (formerly the Hendrik Verwoerd Dam) is a proclaimed heritage site. It lies on the Orange River and forms the border between Northern Cape and Free State. The dam was constructed between 1966 and 1972 and its wall was subsequently raised in 1988. It has a height of 88 metres and the crest length is 914 metres. It is the largest water storage facility in South Africa for domestic and industrial irrigation. It supports a small hydroelectric scheme.

We had arranged to rendezvous with Wayne at the Kroonvaal Engen 1-Stop, just past the Grasmere Toll at 11:15. After introductions and loading Wayne's belongings in the trailer, we headed for coffee at the Wimpy. I had not seen Wayne since 2009 and it was good to catch up. His daughter was to be married the following day; so he would only join us on the Sunday morning in Johannesburg.

At around 12:00 we left Kroonvaal to go to Jack and Shirley Downsborough's lovely home in Bryanston, a suburb north-east of Johannesburg, arriving at 14:00. They had offered us accommodation for 2 nights. Our GPS assisted us in finding our way through the busy city and it was a relief to sit on their patio and enjoy a cold beer while we all got to know each other and catch up. Jack and I had worked closely together from 1973 to 1982 in Zambia.

There was insufficient space in their parking area to manoeuvre the trailer: our only option was to disconnect it from the BMW and position it manually. We wanted it to be in the right place so that we would have no problems leaving the property on Sunday. The first lesson we learned was that we needed to put the BMW into neutral with the handbrake off to facilitate disconnecting. Another problem was that, with the trailer having four wheels, it would not pivot but only move forwards or back. We left the trailer as it was for the time being.

Shirley had prepared a delicious dinner for us. The others learned that Jack and Shirley are seasoned travellers with a great interest in nature and especially birds. Graham was impressed that for all their extensive off-road trips around Southern Africa they use the diminutive Suzuki 1.5 Jimny that negotiates the most difficult of 4×4 terrains. Doing self-catering trips in this little vehicle over long distances is impressive – although luggage space is limited. After an enjoyable evening we retired at about 22:00.

Day 3: 25 March – Johannesburg

Graham and I had planned to visit the Walter Sisulu National Botanical Garden to do some birding but it was raining quite heavily and we called it off. David had arranged to meet a friend who was at university and living in Johannesburg; so Jack gave him a lift to a shopping mall nearby where they could connect.

With the rain continuing unabated we just relaxed and enjoyed a quiche for lunch. Jack and Shirley arranged for a family get-together that afternoon. Jack's daughter Linda and partner Sherri-Lee visited with her parents Brian and Lynn. Nine of us enjoyed a celebratory drink, followed by savoury snacks and cakes. Sherri-Lee's father, also interested in older vehicles, arrived in a 1949 Ford Prefect that was in Concours condition. Before they left, the whole gang combined forces and with some expletives managed to "bounce" the trailer into a suitable position from where we could set out the next morning.

In the early evening when the rain stopped, there was a sudden eruption of termites on the lawn next to the patio. Within minutes there were dozens of bats in a feeding frenzy in close proximity to us. This phenomenon was a rare live experience and I even managed to capture a few photos of the bats with a flashlight.

To thank the Downsboroughs for hosting us, I invited them to a restaurant at the Monte Casino complex. The place was a real eye-opener for us – especially Graham and David. It was incredible to look down from the balcony at the hive of gambling activity in the casino. Forget about the negative economic news, lack of money and jobs, and cost of living: the whole place was buzzing and almost every restaurant was full. Finally, we obtained a table at an Indian restaurant. The meal was enjoyable if not to everyone's taste – it was Graham's first "Indian"! After a cup of coffee at home we all retired; it had been a most enjoyable day.

Day 4: 26 March – Johannesburg – Louis Trichardt (433km)

Wayne arrived at Jack's home at 07:30 and after a photo shoot the official Back-to-Africa (BTA) Team of four left at 08:20 (Fig.140). We arrived at the Zebediela Engen 1-Stop at 11:00 for a "non-negotiable" cup of coffee. At this stage Wayne took over the driving from me and for the rest of the tour he had to be almost prised out of the driver's seat of the BMW! The toll road from Johannesburg, through Pretoria and for some distance beyond, was excellent and the driving was comfortable. The countryside became particularly picturesque as we approached Limpopo: granite *koppies* and traditional villages all along the way.

We crossed the Tropic of Capricorn at 13:00; it lies 23.4° south of the equator, in the region of Venda, a former homeland in Limpopo province. Before we reached our overnight accommodation near Makhado (Louis Trichardt), we filled the BMW and three jerry cans with diesel and another jerry can with petrol in case fuel in Zimbabwe was scarce (Fig.141). We arrived at the Northgate Lodge (7km south of Makhado) by 14:45. The place was impressive: a large lawn with many trees, a swimming pool and entertainment area. The cottages were spaced equally around the perimeter. Our cottage, Number 22 (of 23), was on the border near a herd of Brahman cattle being kraaled (Fig.142).

While unloading things from of the trailer we were concerned to notice that one of its wheels appeared to be slightly splayed out of line. We jacked up the trailer, removed the offending wheel and replaced it. It appeared that the Priclo fitter had fully tightened one nut after the other rather than in a criss-cross pattern. Once we had sorted this, the wheels were perfectly aligned. Priclo had advised us to check the trailer wheel bearings for overheating throughout the tour; fortunately, they were always at an acceptable temperature.

The weather was much warmer and perfect for enjoying a cold beer outdoors. I cooked dinner – a pasta and sauce dish that went down well. The sleeping arrangements were agreeable: Wayne, Graham and David shared a large room while I had a separate room.

Day 5: 27 March – Makhado to Beit Bridge, SA Border (398km)

We were up early and keen to make an early start. With two border posts to negotiate, we knew that this day might bring its challenges. Beit Bridge was still about 100 kilometres away and with Wayne at the wheel we left Makhado at 07:15. In just under an hour, after climbing the Soutpansberg mountains from Makhado, we drove through the Hendrik Verwoed Tunnels that were built in 1961 to bypass the old Wyllie's Poort Pass through the Soutpansberg, an extremely scenic route.

Prior to arriving at Musina (Messina) we made a final stop to top up the BMW with diesel. I bought some delicious pies that took care of breakfast. After driving the final 27km, we arrived at Beit Bridge at 09:00. All went well with the South African Immigration and the carnet for the Morris was processed with ease. One official wanted to see the Morris in the trailer but waved us through after a cursory glance.

The next check at Customs seemed to clear us until the final check at the exit gate. There they wanted to see the original BMW registration certificate that to my shock and surprise was missing from my portfolio of documents. The original had been left in Cape Town. We had to drive back to the Traffic Department in Musina where we obtained a stamped letter listing all the details of the vehicle from the NaTIS system. I realised that this simple document might not suffice. I remembered that I had a copy of the BMW registration certificate on my laptop; so I downloaded it to a flash drive and had a couple of colour copies printed at the shopping mall. We returned to the border post and presented the copy to the official; he accepted it and waved us through. This was a huge relief; it could have caused a major delay to have the original couriered from Cape Town. At other checkpoints along the way, I had to do some fast talking when the validity of the copy was questioned, but I did have an associated BMW document stamped by the SA Police in 2020.

Chapter 6.1

Zimbabwe – Manicaland

Day 5: 27 March – Beit Bridge to Masvingo, Zimbabwe (398km)

Welcome to Zimbabwe! Having crossed the Limpopo River to the Zimbabwean border post tension was high (Fig.143). We filled in the immigration forms, but the officials did not even glance at them. Everything went smoothly; then the other three wandered outside while I completed the carnet and other paperwork. I struggled to communicate with the official dealing with third-party car insurance in my name. She wanted to know how I could drive two vehicles at the same time. All attempts to explain that the Morris was in a trailer fell on deaf ears. I produced proof that we were all listed on the vehicles' insurance to drive either vehicle in both Zimbabwe and Zambia. This was not accepted. Her supervisor confirmed that I could not be insured for driving two cars at the same time. Finally, I went out to find the team. I insisted we should always stay together until everything was processed and they agreed. The solution was simple: Wayne was made the registered third-party insured driver of the one vehicle and I the other. We made the payment and moved on to the next processing stage.

At Customs there were more forms but no search or problems and we headed for the gate – only to be turned back to pay the ZINARA road tax. When instructed to manoeuvre the BMW and trailer back out of the queue Wayne inadvertently put one wheel on the pavement and a policewoman started threatening a fine for a driving offence. Fortunately, this matter was quickly defused. After paying the tax, we saw the BMW's registration number light up on the screen at the gate and the boom opened. We were through at last. Four and three-quarter hours after arriving at the South African border we were on our way north by 13:15.

It is worth noting that at no stage was Covid mentioned or the need for Covid vaccination certificates. Soon after leaving Beit Bridge and travelling towards Masvingo there was a detour onto a terrible dirt road that had been chewed up by the many heavy trucks using it. After some 17 kilometres the dirt road changed to tar but only for a few hundred metres to drive through the first of many tolls and then back onto dirt for a further 20 kilometres or so.

The road was fully tarred but we soon had to deal with severe potholes. Our full attention was required for the whole journey. At times this meant driving on the wrong side of the road and, as there were vehicles coming from the opposite direction, we had to be wide awake at all times. This type of driving eventually became the norm.

Between Beit Bridge and Masvingo (Fig.144) we crossed several large rivers in the Lowveld but sadly all the bridge signs had been removed. This was a general observation throughout Zimbabwe and we pondered the reasons behind this. Were they repurposed as building material or sold for scrap? Such is progress in independent Africa where priorities are clearly different.

After losing so much time at the border we hoped to arrive at Masvingo (formerly Fort Victoria) just before sunset; there was a light drizzle but the road improved. At around 18:00 and only 2 kilometres from Masvingo the traffic came to a standstill. A kilometre ahead we could see the flashing lights of a recovery vehicle. It appeared that there had been an accident. What transpired over the next hour could be the script for a horror movie. This was a normal two-lane road (one in each direction). Cars and taxis began passing on the right-hand side in the oncoming lane and just pushed into the left lane on meeting traffic. Then they all started passing on the left shoulder until one tried to squeeze in where space was limited and ended up with wheels in a ditch and nearly toppling over into the marsh. A stream of cars heading towards us on the left shoulder met the taxis and simply crossed through the lanes onto the opposite shoulder. It was just an incredible mess, with everyone doing as they wished.

We crawled along at a snail's pace and eventually arrived at the scene where a small car was half under a large truck on a narrow bridge. The truck was being hitched to a crane wrecker that took up the other half of the road. After crossing the bridge things got even worse: we had large trucks on either side of us and two lanes of oncoming traffic, making five lanes in all on a two-lane road. To add to the mayhem a large 26-wheeler was "parked" right across the main road with the police diverting the traffic to left and right. We took a side road and guessed that the grid would return us to the intended road to Flame Tree Cottage.

It was dark, with no streetlights or signs; I phoned our host for directions that we recorded on our cell phone. Directions were vague: look out for a mosque, at the cell phone tower keep to the right. We were relieved to arrive at the cottage at 19:10. But the pre-ordered cooked meal of peri-peri chicken and chips scheduled for 16:00 was soggy after being heated in a microwave. We washed it down with a couple of beers as we were famished. The accommodation was comfortable and after a long and frustrating day everyone was in bed by 21:30 – our first night in Zimbabwe.

Day 6: 28 March – Masvingo to Mutare (297km)

In the morning, we discovered that a long bolt in the trailer door that had not been shortened or covered had chewed a hole into the Morris's rear hood and hood cover. The cause was due to the new car securing straps that had stretched and allowed the car to move back and forwards. We used a hacksaw to cut off the protruding bolt, but the damage had been done. This served as a warning that we should regularly retighten the securing straps. We departed Flame Tree Cottage at 08:00 in a light drizzle with Wayne at the wheel.

We stopped at a filling station called Tanda Tavaruva. *Thanda* means "like" in Nguni languages but we were unsure of Tavaruva. We discovered later that Tanda Tavaruva was the owner of a bus service in Zimbabwe and a soccer team (Masvingo United Football Club and lower-tier football side, Gutu Leopards Football Club). The diesel was the first of many different brand names we encountered: this was Gamma Energies.

The A9 road towards Mutare looked good initially with green verges, but after half an hour it deteriorated and there were many large potholes (Fig.145). Of course, the toll booths still required US$2 per vehicle, sometimes accepting SA Rands. The countryside was a beautiful verdant green with traditional rural villages dotted among picturesque granite outcrops and *koppies* that became more frequent the closer we approached the Birchenough Bridge (Fig.146).

We took a rest stop near the Chivaka Primary School where many villagers appeared, fascinated at the poster of the Morris and the map stuck on the sides of the trailer: people took photos with their phones (yes, everyone seemed to have a Smartphone). Throughout the trip selfies became the norm and we let onlookers have their fun. After leaving Masvingo, the altitude steadily increased as we approached the Birchenough Bridge in the Save Valley. Soon we noticed a greater distribution of baobab trees – indicative that this region is hot and dry, typical of the Lowveld. About 20 kilometres from the bridge the countryside became even drier where the vegetation is sparse. Due to the low rainfall, the heat and large numbers of goats grazing on the remains of vegetation, the area is tending towards desert.

The population became steadily denser, with pockets of stores and stalls along the roadside, but at the bridge itself both sides of the road were covered in stalls. They sold everything from hardware to fruit and vegetables to handmade toys. There were barbers, hairdressers, mechanics, second-hand clothes, curio stalls and taverns. Along this section of road there were many donkeys as well as goats (Fig.147). We were aware that goats are considered prize possessions and were careful not to injure them as they crossed the road. At 11:30 we travelled over the imposing Birchenough Bridge; the Save River was very full and running strongly after good rains. For many reasons this crossing was a momentous occasion. We wondered how best to photograph the Morris when it would drive over the bridge in a few days' time, bearing in mind that the Morris would be travelling along the same road, having to negotiate the same potholes, goats, cattle and donkeys towards Bulawayo.

Fig.139: Fuel, Laingsburg 23 March 2023

Fig.140: BTA full team and hosts Joburg

Fig.141: Makhado, reserve diesel and petrol

Fig.142: Overnight at Northgate Lodge

Fig.143: Crossing Limpopo to Zimbabwe

Fig.144: Road to Masvingo Zimbabwe

Fig.145: Masvingo to Mutare – potholes

Fig.146: Amazing scenery, balancing rocks

Fig.147: Birchenough Bridge market

Fig.148: Arriving in Mutare, anything goes!

Fig.149: The Paddocks Bvumba Mutare

Fig.150: Self-catering, the cooks in action

Fig.151: Mutare Club built 1897 and the Morris

Fig.152: Mutare Club Kevin Woodward

Fig.153: Modern supermarket Zimbabwe

Fig.154: Supporting the local market

The bridge crosses the Save River, connecting Masvinga with Mutare and Chipinga. It was completed in 1935 and is 329 metres long. At that time, it was the third longest single-arch bridge in the world. It was designed by Ralph Freeman, who also designed the Sydney Harbour Bridge in Australia, and was constructed by Dorman Long. The bridge is named after Sir Henry Birchenough, the Chairman of the Beit Trust Foundation that funded and planned the construction of the bridge. His ashes are interred in one of the concrete pillars supporting the bridge.

We arrived at the outskirts of Mutare at about 13:00, where the traffic and potholes and general road deterioration were a nightmare (Fig.148). Our accommodation for the next 5 nights was a small farm named The Paddocks run by Nancy Morgan. The Paddocks is high up in the Bvumba Mountains, about 20 kilometres from Mutare (Fig.149). On arrival it was still drizzling, and the lawns were wet and soggy. Later we decided to unload the Morris from the trailer with the help of the local helper Jonathan. He and some others were astounded when they saw the Morris. Again, many photos and selfies were the order of the day. During the unloading we discovered that the welding on one of the hood support brackets had failed and needed repairing. Next to the Pool Cottage I noticed a lock-up workshop with a pit. So I asked if we could park the Morris under cover. This was very convenient since I was able to undertake lubrication of some awkward grease points and final checks for the start of the tour.

Our stay at The Paddocks was self-catering (Fig.150) but we had not had an opportunity to buy fresh food; so that night we went to the nearby White Horse Inn for a most pleasant meal. A side benefit was that they had a decent Wi-Fi system and we were able to inform our respective homes that we had arrived safely. Earlier I had set up an Instagram account to post daily updates that were automatically copied to Facebook so that people could follow our progress. After dinner we retired after a momentous day's travel.

Lying in bed I realised that what I had planned for so long had finally come to fruition. I was full of trepidation: had I prepared properly for the tour ahead? I was responsible for three others on this mad-cap adventure. I had to ensure that all were safe and satisfied with the arrangements for food, accommodation, transport and other conditions. I was financing the tour, but had I considered all the other essential details to cover every eventuality? Had I planned for each scenario to ensure that the tour was a success? Did I have a back-up plan? The next few weeks would tell if I had got it right or not!

Day 7: 29 March – Mutare, The Paddocks

Dawn broke on a beautiful morning with cloudless skies and no sign of rain. Graham was up early to do a bit of birding in the garden and surrounding forest. I soon joined him. As the sun rose and it got warmer so the population of birds increased, many sunning themselves after the cool night. They were predominantly sunbirds but of more than one species, presenting great photo opportunities (see www.WorldBirdPhotos.com). Once everyone was up, we enjoyed a cup of coffee, a light breakfast and then set off for the city of Mutare at 08:15.

Mutare, one of the four main cities in Zimbabwe, originated as Fort Umtali and was built by gold prospectors in 1890. The name is derived from a local word meaning metal, probably referring to nearby ancient gold-workings. It lies about 8 kilometres from the border with Mozambique and is 290 kilometres from the Mozambican port of Beira, earning the title of Zimbabwe's Gateway to the Sea. It has long been a key terminus en route to Beira and is a hub with railway and pipeline links with Harare, the capital of Zimbabwe. It is the access to the eastern highlands of Zimbabwe, a popular tourist destination. I first visited the area with my parents at age 13; but in 1971, when married to Sandy, we stayed at the fantastic Troutbeck Inn where I caught my first trout by fly fishing.

On the edge of town there was a Total service station where we refuelled the BMW. Quite fortuitously within sight were the headquarters of the Tanganda Tea Company. I managed to meet the company secretary who was very well spoken and accommodating. She handed me a copy of their corporate brochure and agreed to arrange for us to have access to the premises on Sunday so that the Morris could be photographed in front of the building.

The next stop was to locate the Hillside Golf Club, the address of the first owner of the Morris. We needed to do a recce in preparation for Sunday's departure from there. Unfortunately, Kevin Woodward, a former professional golfer and the secretary of the club, was not available and, after looking around and deciding where to take our photographs, we drove back to town.

We were photographing an old building in the Mutare main road when a motorcycle pulled up alongside – it was Kevin chasing after us! He offered to take us to the Mutare Club for a chat and tour (Figs.151, 152). The Mutare Club (Umtali Club) was founded in 1898. It was originally designed as a hotel, but Cecil John Rhodes recommended that it should become a Gentlemen's Club. We were treated royally with coffee and freshly baked scones, strawberry jam and cream – just like the old days.

Next was a complete tour of the club with Kevin pointing out all the fascinating historic photographs and items of furniture. One photo was of the tramline that existed in the 1900s and ran from the station to the club. The tram was pulled by horses and, as it could not turn, it was then pulled backwards. To allow the passengers to remain facing forwards, the bench seats had a backrest that could be flipped over, and thus serve as a backrest in both directions. One such bench was in the bar.

Prior to our arrival Kevin had researched the club's membership register and found Arthur Ward's name, dated 16 December 1926 (Fig.15). He was the first registered owner of the Morris and his address was given as the Hillside Golf Club. This confirming evidence is of invaluable historical importance to my research of the Morris owners. It was a very real honour and privilege to visit and explore the Mutare Club and take photos of some of the interior and items, all thanks to Kevin. There was a need to repair the two damaged hood support brackets and Kevin said, "Leave them with me, I have a welder friend who will fix them."

On leaving the Mutare Club we stopped to get provisions. With loadshedding under way, all the traffic lights were off and every intersection was chaotic. Drivers simply did their own thing, no one giving way. One has to adapt to this chaos and go with the flow. It really was every man for himself.

The local PicknPay supermarket was extremely well stocked, well laid out and clean (Fig.153). While most items were available they came at a price, much higher than in South Africa. Having purchased what was needed and paying in US dollars, we had to accept change in worthless Zimbabwe bond notes. Few people are prepared to accept this local money, not even in the nearby open-air vegetable market. Hence the need to carry small denominations of US dollars.

Next to the PicknPay was a large market square where dozens of stalls selling mostly fruit and vegetables packed every available space. We shopped here for some items at possibly a lower price and were able to select smaller quantities as opposed to the pre-packaged supermarket goods. I purchased some vegetables and bargained for fun with the stall owners (Fig.154), all of whom were extremely friendly and enjoyed the banter.

There was no Wi-Fi at The Paddocks but at the nearby White Horse Inn, where we had dinner the first evening, the manager had provided us with the access code. Each day whenever we passed the Inn we would stop in their parking lot and update our communications. Our landlady had previously said that the White Horse Inn was within easy walking distance, but this was not the case: if one took the footpath through the forest one probably had a good chance of meeting up with a leopard or getting lost. After an enjoyable day of driving through the spectacular country-side, we sat on the patio and had a couple of sundowners while Wayne cooked dinner. We were then ready for bed.

Day 8: 30 March – Birding at Bvumba, Mutare

Prior to leaving Cape Town, Graham had made enquiries about birding in the Bvumba (Vumba) mountains. Kevin Woodward connected him with Ken Worsley who owns and runs a resort called Seldom Seen. This is a renowned birding location and their in-house birding guide, Buluwezi, is reputed to be one of the best in Zimbabwe. After settling in at The Paddocks we organised an outing to the resort for the next day at 06:30. Seldom Seen is about 25 minutes up the road towards the Leopard Rock Hotel. After meeting Ken Worsley and Buluwezi we set off on foot into the forest. The canopy restricted the light from above and presented a photographic chal-lenge. The weather was perfect for birding and we spent a rewarding 4 hours in the forest. We identified most of the target birds and were able to take good pictures. I added eight lifers and Graham seven from some 20 different species we saw. The real prize was the highly sought-after rare Swynnerton's Robin that took some finding and proved even more difficult to photograph (Figs.155 and 156).

Buoyed up by our successful morning we headed back to The Paddocks, stopping for a few minutes at the White Horse Inn to update our messages. On our arrival at The Paddocks we found Wayne in the pit seeking the position of the many grease nipples of the Morris. After charging the grease gun I greased those areas that I had not had time for before leaving Cape Town. We put the Morris on jacks and adjusted the brakes: the car was as ready as it could be for the journey ahead.

At 15:00 we departed for the Leopard Rock Hotel to see what the famous hotel looks like today. It has been completely renovated and painted pink – quite different from what Graham and I remem-bered. The only real resemblance was the towers with their round turrets. We ordered tea and coffee but, while the hotel claims to have five stars, the service left a lot to be desired. The hotel grounds and bordering golf course are beautifully maintained and the neat gardens are extremely attractive. They take security very seriously: to enter the grounds there is a barrier with multiple checkpoints. To leave we were required to hand in an exit token at the gate.

An amusing incident at the barrier was when the Zimbabwean security official, who obviously had a military background, stood to attention on opening the boom and I commented on his decorum. After this whenever I saw him I shouted "Attenshun", to which he would respond very smartly and salute. This continued until we left, and resumed when we returned in the Morris. All good-natured banter.

On returning home, after making the usual Wi-Fi stop, it was time to relax with a welcome toot. Dinner that night was meat patties (from PnP) grilled on the small gas cooker I had packed but using Wayne's special braai plate. Since there were no bread rolls the substitute was lightly toasted bread with olive oil instead of butter! A patty on toast with an onion ring and potato crisps was perfect: the meal went down well, with a beer or two.

Day 9: 31 March – Leopard Rock Hotel, Bvumba, Mutare

The day was overcast and cooler, but in a few hours it warmed up. I wanted to drive the Morris to the Leopard Rock Hotel and get some photographs of the Morris in front of this iconic and historic building. This trip would also help to run-in the engine by putting a few miles on the clock since it had only done 51 miles since the new crankshaft was fitted in Cape Town: the engine was still tight. The others had doubts about this plan but I was adamant. I was confident that the Morris would cope; otherwise the whole tour would be in doubt. Wayne and David went ahead in the BMW while Graham and I followed in the Morris. Later we decided that they would see us on our way, always following behind, never going ahead.

Just outside the gate of The Paddocks there is a steep incline on a muddy rugged dirt road. The new engine did not have sufficient momentum to climb the steep slope. Jonathan and friends came to our rescue and pushed the car up to the tar road. Once on the level the Morris got going but still lacked power; it was as if the brakes were binding, which was not the case. When we reached the main tar road it was a long steady climb towards the hotel which is some 512 metres in altitude above The Paddocks. The Morris could hardly get out of first gear. Eventually we came across a road sign, "Steep Hill" – a bit of an understatement. It soon became apparent that the Morris was overheating, with steam exuding from the radiator. I stopped the car and after allowing it to cool then slowly topped up the water. I attempted to proceed but realised that the car needed momentum to tackle the steep slope. As this was not practical I decided that we should tow the car to more level ground. Joined to the BMW we climbed some 5 kilometres before there was a downhill run (Fig.157). By this time the engine had cooled down and thereafter the Morris coped with the smaller hills and dales. The rest of the team wondered about the little car's capability but I was quite confident that, once the new crankshaft had eased as it was "running-in", it would be up to the task.

We arrived at the Leopard Rock Hotel at 11:30 and, after negotiating the various security gates, we parked in front of the main entrance to the hotel. A civil engineering conference was taking place there and it happened to be their tea break. Dozens of onlookers started taking photos of the Morris, as well as the obligatory selfies. After David had captured a range of views of the Morris against the hotel (Fig.158), we enjoyed drinks and snacks in the main bar (Fig.159).

I then drove the Morris around the hotel gardens, with David recording a video. It was time to make our way back to The Paddocks. Would the Morris return unaided? We did take a precautionary stop to top up the radiator but as it was mostly downhill the car cruised home with ease. At one point, I put my foot flat to get momentum but on approaching the base of a hill with a hairpin bend the passenger door suddenly flew open! The car's wooden frame is rather flexible. This gave Graham quite a fright and from then on he always gripped the door handle. The followers in the BMW saw it all and found it hilarious.

It is worth repeating that the hotel is at an altitude of 1,745 metres while The Paddocks is at 1,233 metres. We arrived home at 14:30. The Morris was running so much better and I was confident it would improve further as the tour progressed. The BTA Team generally started to feel a lot happier with its performance, recognising there would obviously be more hills and gradients to tackle. Those hills in the Bvumba were very severe and had tested the Morris much more than we were likely to experience in the future (I hoped).

Day 10: 1 April – Birding Bvumba, Mutare

Graham and I organised a further birding outing with Buluwezi at Seldom Seen but this time to do some *Miombo* woodland birding. We made an early start in the BMW. There was heavy mist on the higher ground and, as we neared the rough access path to Seldom Seen, I turned the wheel sharply, to hear a sudden "whoosh" with dust exuding from one side of the car. I assumed the front tyre had impacted a rock breaking the seal between tyre and rim as it was now flat. We quickly fitted the spare wheel – so no serious delay to our birding (Fig.160).

We left with Buluwezi, back-tracking towards The Paddocks, stopping at a couple of spots to listen out for particular species and continuing until we reached the intersection to Burma Valley. We parked the car and began walking along the road to find the path that led into the woodland. Before we left the road a vehicle stopped next to us and the driver advised us not to walk too far from the car as there were *tsotsis* (bandits) in the area.

The birding hotspot was not very far away and we continued on our way, identifying a few new species as well as a couple of lifers. The morning was not as successful as the forest birding but the different habitat did produce new species. We returned to The Paddocks to find Wayne and David packing the trailer in readiness for the next day.

At 13:00 we set off for Mutare town to get the burst tyre pumped. After enquiring at a couple of garages, we found that none had functioning tyre pressure pumps. Eventually one attendant told us we should go to Leon's Tyre Services on the opposite side of a large parkland area (Fig.161). It turned out to be a piece of open ground with three compressors on one side and piles of old tyres on the other. There were also half drums of water to check for punctures and various locally made tools for changing the tyres (Fig.161).

A Zimbabwean lady arrived and I explained that the tyre needed inflating. When they attempted this, it transpired that there was a concealed side-wall puncture. Being prepared for a side-wall puncture (not repairable) we had two spare tyres in the trailer but these were at The Paddocks about 25 kilometres away. This would mean going back to collect the spare. At this stage Mr Leon looked at the wheel, noted the specifications, and said he had such a tyre! In disbelief I followed him to the mountain of used tyres and after digging around he produced the correct one. BMW X5s are not common in Zimbabwe and the front tyre is a different size to the rear one. It was a used tyre in good condition and the correct size. Leon quoted US$50 plus US$2 for fitting. I accepted the deal as this would mean that we had a spare tyre in hand.

Despite having no specialist equipment to remove the damaged tyre from the rim and fit the replacement, the whole process was all done manually in just a few minutes (Figs.162, 163). From the time of arrival at Leon's to leaving was no more than 25 minutes. I doubt that this could be achieved in a modern city anywhere, including South Africa with modern tyre machinery, and at that price. Although this front wheel tyre replacement was not perfectly balanced it served us all the way back to Cape Town.

We then headed again to PicknPay and the vegetable market to do some shopping in dollars and again getting change in worthless Zimbabwe bonds. Being a Saturday afternoon there was a festive atmosphere in the market and it was quite an education watching the people going about their daily lives. The general atmosphere could only be described as happy and friendly. We headed back to The Paddocks, taking our usual Wi-Fi stop at the White Horse Inn.

Fig.155: Birding – Bulawezi and Graham

Fig.156: The endemic Swynnerton's Robin

Fig.157: Steep road to Leopard Rock

Fig.158: The iconic Leopard Rock Hotel

Fig.159: BTA Team rehydrating

Fig.160: BMW X5 side-wall puncture

Fig.161: Used tyre US$50, fitting US$2

Fig.162: Removing the defective tyre

We loaded the Morris into the trailer and packed all the non-essential belongings, leaving a few personal items to be fitted in the following morning. We had planned for a braai and arranged with Jonathan to make the fire with real wood. We agreed to give Jonathan a good tip as he had really gone out of his way to see to our needs. I told him we appreciated his efforts and handed him a wad of the "useless" Zimbabwe bonds. His expression was priceless although he attempted to appear grateful (Fig.164). He then saw the joke when I handed him the real tip in US dollars! His grin was as wide as the Limpopo. He joined us for a beer.

The braai consisted of pork medallions and boerewors with a fresh salad prepared by Wayne. A couple of beers washed down this most enjoyable meal. We retired to bed around 21:00 as tomorrow was to be the big day: the start of the Back-to-Africa tour in the 1929 Morris Minor that started its life at the Mutare Hillside Golf Club.

Fig.163: Leak testing the "new" tyre

Fig.164: Jonathan, a gem, looked after us

Fig.165: Unloading at Hillside Golf Club

Fig.166: Presentation to club members

Fig.167: BTA mug to Kevin, me in his blazer

Fig.168: Staff Sergeant Harry Springer of 1963

Fig.169: Morris demo around the 18th green!

Fig.170: The BTA trip starts at Hillside Club

Day 11: 2 April – Mutare, Hillside Golf Club, the trip starts

We were all up bright and early as we knew that a full and exciting day lay ahead. After hitching up the trailer to the BMW we left The Paddocks, taking a last Wi-Fi stop at the White Horse Inn. Arriving at the Hillside Golf Club at 09:00 our first task was to remove the Morris from the trailer (Fig.165). It would not return for another 1,509 miles. We fitted the repaired hood brackets that Kevin handed us. I then drove into the grounds of the club and parked the Morris on the lawn near the 18th green in front of the clubhouse.

The chaps had mounted the 5 metre banner, "Back to Africa in a 1929 Morris Minor", on the pillars as a backdrop to the Morris for the welcoming party. Club members began to arrive, taking great interest in the Morris while I outlined its history. Later everyone assembled in the clubhouse hall where Kevin Woodward introduced me and the team to the 46 attendees and insisted that I

should wear the club blazer. Unfortunately, they were unable to arrange a projector and screen and the electricity supply at the time was doubtful. As a result, I faced my laptop towards the audience and commenced the show-and-tell (Fig.166). I thanked Kevin for all his assistance in arranging everything and presented him with one of the special BTA mugs (Fig.167), he was the first official recipient. We subsequently gave these mugs to all who assisted us; they proved quite a hit.

The club was supposed to lay on brunch before our official departure but, with time constraints, Kevin arranged sandwiches for us. We chatted

Fig.171: Ray Musto

Fig.172: Mutare Hillside Golf Club Members – "Bon Voyage!"

with many members who were delighted that an "old Umtali" car had returned to the club. One fellow Harry Springer reminded me that he was one of the Staff Sergeants at Llewellin barracks in Bulawayo when both Graham and I did our basic training in 1963 (Fig.168) and was a pal of Sergeant Ben Erasmus who was my platoon instructor. Surprisingly Ken asked me to drive the Morris around the hallowed 18th green (Fig.169) which certainly demonstrated the sprightly the little car's performance to the club members looking on in awe.

An elderly gentleman Ray Musto (born 3 years before the Morris) asked to sit in the Morris wearing my pith helmet and enjoyed the experience. Sadly, later I have learned that he passed away in December 2023, aged 97!

Before we departed on our momentous journey, all the club members gathered around the Morris for a group photograph (Fig.172).

At 12:45 we headed for the club's exit gate to the applause of the members (Fig.170). David recorded this significant event on video. The official start of the Morris on its long journey home to Kitwe Zambia was happening at last.

Graham joined me in the Morris, with Wayne and David following in the BMW and trailer. Earlier I had realised that by the time we departed Mutare we would have to spend our first night at Birchenough as we could not reach Masvingo in the daylight hours. I booked overnight accommodation at the Birchenough Bridge Hotel, explaining that the trip was also a fundraising event. The Chairman of the Authentic Group of Companies, that owns the hotel, Dr. Eng. Mutezo, was impressed with the noble purpose of this historic car trip. He stated, "It is thus befitting to donate accommodation and food at the Birchenough Bridge Hotel for the team." A very magnanimous gesture indeed.

Travelling along Mutare's main street we passed the Mutare Club and classic but abandoned Customs Building (Fig.173). As arranged we proceeded to the Tanganda Tea Company head office for a photo shoot (Fig.174). Departing Mutare at 13:50 we headed for Birchenough Bridge, knowing that the proper journey had begun. Once out of the city we steadily dropped in altitude towards the Save River Valley with the Morris coasting comfortably, mainly downhill (Fig.175).

Fig.173: Old Customs House Mutare

Fig.174: Tanganda Tea Factory

Day 11: 2 April – Mutare to Birchenough Bridge (140km)

There were several uphill stretches but nothing like the inclines of the Bvumba Mountains. Nevertheless, we planned to stop after 1½ hours to top up the radiator with water and give Wayne his essential smoke break (Fig.176). To the delight of all and my relief, the Morris was now running easily doing 40 mph (65km/h) or more and making good time.

Having already travelled on the A9 road to Mutare the countryside had little new to offer but was still enjoyable with the number and size of the baobab trees along the way. After 87 miles (140km) we arrived at the iconic Birchenough Bridge at 16:10, a remarkable average speed of 37 mph. As we neared the bridge Wayne and David went ahead and parked on the other side so that they could record a video of the Morris crossing the iconic bridge (Fig.177).

We turned in at the historic Birchenough Bridge Hotel that offers excellent views of the bridge (Fig.178). At Reception the hotel manager, Rachael Garawiro, made us feel very welcome. She wanted a photo taken in the Morris. This attracted a lot of attention and again staff and bystanders took several photos and selfies. While this was happening and before we had been allocated our rooms, a young German couple arrived on bicycles. They had ridden from Masvingo that day and, after inspecting the chalets, they opted to pitch their small tent in the garden area.

After seeing our rooms and recognising that the Germans had higher expectations, we understood their decision. Sadly, the main building was run down, with everything in dire need of renovation. The ceilings had collapsed, taps were broken and there was no hot water. Fortunately, it was a hot evening and the lack of hot water was not the end of the world. The beds were not too soft, but the linen and towels were clean. Graham remembered the hotel in much better condition from years gone by and found it difficult to hide his disappointment. Despite that, the staff and Rachael in particular, were very friendly and helpful.

Dinner had to be pre-ordered. Options were Chicken and Chips, Chicken and Rice, or Chicken and Sadza [*sic*], all with coleslaw optional. Before dinner, we had drinks in the bar where Graham and I were introduced to Zambezi beer – which became a firm favourite for the trip.

The first day of the tour had gone to plan and was a great success, made possible through the efforts of Ken Woodward of the Hillside Golf Club and its members. The Morris had done well and we could look ahead with confidence.

After dinner we retired to our two twin bedrooms: Wayne and David sharing, Graham and I sharing. This arrangement became the norm for the rest of the tour. Not long after our heads hit the pillow very loud music began pumping from a nearby shebeen. This music, accompanied by drums, singing and whistling went on long after midnight; so none of us slept soundly. Mosquitoes, not put off by the loud music and even though the hotel laid on mosquito burning coils, were buzzing around. It was really one of those nights best forgotten.

Day 12: 3 April – Birchenough to Masvingo to Great Zimbabwe (272km)

This was to be one of the longest days of the whole trip, in terms of distance for the Morris. I had always planned to visit the Great Zimbabwe Ruins, but this required reaching Masvingo, then a detour of 56km to the Ruins, and back to Masvingo for the road to Zvishavane.

Fig.175: Left Mutare towards Birchenough

Fig.176: Rest stops every 1.5 hours

Fig.177: Birchenough Bridge

Fig.178: Our complimentary hotel

Fig.179: Traditional roadside cattle kraal

Fig.180: Many baobab trees seen on the way

Fig.181: Amazing scenery to Masvingo

Fig.182: Balancing rocks common

Fig.183: Villagers waved as we passed

Fig.184 Dodging potholes was the norm

Fig.185: Admirers at Masvingo petrol stop

Fig.186: Great Zimbabwe Ruins

Fig.187: Note chevrons at top of wall

Fig.188: Great Zimbabwe Ruins Tower

Fig.189: Boutique Hotel, Zvishavane

Fig.190: The kitchen was unbelievable

Fig.191: Wayne – not pasta again!

Fig.192: Toll Zvishavane to Bulawayo

As breakfast at Birchenough Bridge was complimentary and we had no idea when the next meal would be available, we sat down at 06:30 for an early departure. The meal turned out to be an eye-opener. It was a fixed menu: two fried eggs (well flattened), chicken liver, a sausage, baked beans and some potato crisps accompanied by a large flask of weak tea. This was our first introduction to the real Africa and perhaps a sign of things to come. However, we were always appreciative of what was provided as it is probably a lot more than the general population enjoys.

The food was presented on a plate sealed with cling wrap. They explained that this protocol was developed during Covid and was being continued. Whatever the case, the food was protected from flies and insects and it made good sense. I informed the chaps that my brother Colin had worked for Union Carbide in the early 1960s and was personally responsible for launching "Glad Wrap" to the Federation of Rhodesia and Nyasaland, along with UCAR batteries.

The early morning greeted us with the sun filtering across the magnificent Birchenough Bridge: a sight to behold and an abiding memory. We departed Birchenough at 07:20, topping up the Morris at the first available petrol pump. Some of the fuel stations we came across were just a bare area of ground consisting only of two pumps, Petrol and Diesel. Throughout our tour we came across several unfamiliar brand names, including some stating "Blend" – so we never really knew what we were getting. We passed several African hamlets and small farms, some with traditional wooden cattle kraals (Fig.179). We came across a very large baobab tree at the side of the road, for a convenient photo with the Morris (Fig.180).

The drive was just as enjoyable as the incoming trip: great weather, little traffic and amazing scenery (Fig.181). The balancing rocks (Fig.182) and traditional villages, along with the locals who waved and whistled as we drove along, contributed to a most enjoyable drive (Fig.183). Despite this we had to negotiate multiple potholes every now and then (Fig.184). The original tar had just peeled away. The road looked like a patchwork quilt, requiring a lot of swerving around.

Day 12: 3 April – Great Zimbabwe, Zvishavane (plus 56km)

We arrived at Masvingo where we topped up both vehicles with fuel at a very busy filling station in the centre of town. Crowds descended on the Morris, with many selfies taken. It was quite surprising to see how interested the people were in our vintage car (Fig.185). Most could not believe its history. I was bombarded with many pertinent questions: "Is it automatic?" "Is it diesel?" "What is its top speed?" But the most frequent was, "What is its value?" Another was: "Please sell it to me." My standard response was, "Would you sell me your children?" "No!" "Nor will I, this is my baby!" Lots of laughter followed. Graham said I was in my element but the team soon realised that this level of interest would follow us at every stop.

The spirited crowd included a police officer with his arm on Graham's shoulder, insisting on a photo together with his son. One persistent youngster asked me how he could get an education in the UK. Clearly, most of the people had never ever seen such an old car before and were keen to have some sort of record to show their family. We managed to leave the petrol station at about 12:15 and headed for Great Zimbabwe. After a comfortable ride on a good and quiet road, we arrived at 13:15.

The task was then to try to position the Morris as close as possible to the World Heritage Site. Wayne had been to the Ruins before (as had Graham and I) – so he elected to guard the BMW and trailer near Reception. To avoid paying international rates especially for just half an hour (Graham refers to me as the Arch Negotiator), I managed to pay a modest non-receipted amount and arrange for the three of us to go to the site, along with their security guard. With four in the Morris we drove towards the Ruins some 750 metres away, proving that the Morris Minor is indeed a four-seat tourer (Fig.186). Near the entrance the security guard alighted and the official guide, Champion, joined us in driving right up to the Great Enclosure, positioning us close to the unique Chevron Wall (Fig.187). David was able to capture on film and video rare footage of the Morris driving around a section of the enclosure. We toured the enclosure on foot wondering what the purpose of the distinctive "solid" stone tower was (Fig.188). This visit was a major accomplishment and an important "tick in the box" for the tour. On the road from Great Zimbabwe we were surrounded by a troop of baboons; they soon scattered as we headed back to Masvingo en route to Zvishavane.

We took the A9 to Zvishavane, our next overnight stop. The general condition of the road was good, possibly because it did not carry much traffic. For the first 50 kilometres we encountered only three potholes. Further on there were patches where the road had deteriorated, and care was needed. Again, name signs of the rivers and bridges were absent or had rusted away.

We arrived at Zvishavane at 16:20 after an excellent run, the longest so far. The team was more than happy to move into the Hotel Boutique Runde (Fig.189). The lodgings were very comfortable with excellent showers, "plush" compared to the previous night. It was possible to order food but since we had perishables, I decided to cook a vegetable curry while Wayne prepared the rice. The hotel's kitchen was used only by the staff but could be likened to the black hole of Calcutta. All the pots were stored in a chest deep-freeze that was obviously not working. The state of cleanliness was more than questionable (Fig.190). However, we all survived Wayne's curry and rice that was washed down with a few Zambezis (Fig.191).

We agreed that this was a very successful day: we achieved a huge milestone, and the amount of travelling was a credit to the Morris that was improving mile by mile. On some downhills we achieved 40 to 45 mph and were able to mount the hills with ease. The disturbed sleep at Birchenough the night before ensured that we all slept well despite the mosquitoes.

Chapter 6.2

Zimbabwe – Matabeleland

Day 13: 4 April – Zvishavane to Bulawayo (184km)

Leaving Zvishavane the A9 road was quite good to start with. Thankfully there was very little traffic except for a few large trucks and buses – and the usual toll charges (Fig.192). The bus drivers were the worst drivers on the road: they drove at great speed irrespective of the potholed roads and oncoming traffic. The truck drivers were a bit more courteous. Wayne was driving shotgun behind us and would give a loud hoot or blast on the walkie-talkie when a large vehicle was approaching and wanting to overtake. The countryside became very dry and, although many trees were quite green, the ground remained parched. All the rivers and streams had evidence of water; so there must have been recent rainfall.

The road became somewhat undulating with some long uphills that caused the Morris to strain and overheat, requiring frequent stops to top up with water. Along this stretch of road there were very few settlements of any kind but at one place we came across a dead and very bloated *mombi* (cow) that must have lost the argument with a truck. We were surprised to see it lying there, considering the wasted food value of the dead beast.

Fig.193: Long climb over Esigodini Hills

Fig.194: Top of climb at 36° C, more water

Fig.195: Bulawayo 10km to go. Phew!

Fig.196: Graham's school, Milton

Fig.197: Lovely Granite Lodge, Bulawayo

Fig.198: Comfortable accommodation

Fig.199: Paying US$ change in Zim. paper

Fig.200: The Office – Tony Clark VCCZ

At 09:15, after travelling 80 kilometres, we took the regular smoke break for Wayne and for us to rest from the concentration of driving. This allowed the Morris to cool a bit before topping up the radiator. Although it was relatively early in the day, it had become very hot, at least 36° Celsius, and the Morris was struggling to keep cool in that environment. Furthermore, the long inclines were tackled mainly in second gear. I maintained a keen eye on the oil pressure. Dropping from 65 to 30 psi was indicative of an overheating engine more than the water boiling.

Shortly after Mbalabala (Ndebele name for kudu) the A9 road joined the A6, the main Bulawayo to Beit Bridge Road. The next town was Esigodini (Essexvale). Here was the turn-off to Falcon College where we stopped to photograph the sign to send to my godson Steven Bromfield who had attended the college. Once again, the Morris was crowded by onlookers. After leaving Esigodini we climbed the steep Esigodini Hills (Fig.193). This took a toll on the Morris; the radiator was nearing boiling point, requiring several short stops to add water (Fig.194). The day was now extremely hot and we noticed that the car would not start immediately due to petrol evaporation. We experienced this effect on several occasions throughout the trip. The engine started with a "pop-pop" sound but after a short while it went away once the petrol was flowing normally to the carburettor.

We arrived at the outskirts of Bulawayo at 12:30 (Fig.195), stopping outside Milton School, which Graham had attended for 6 years (Fig.196), leaving as a prefect. The essential photo shoot was for Graham to keep as a memory of happy school days. Bulawayo is where Graham was born and, while he knew it like the back of his hand, he found it quite difficult to recognise the suburbs as many of the roads had broken up, the verges were uncut and any visible road signs were generally illegible.

Bulawayo (place of slaughter) takes its name from *bulala* (to kill in Ndebele) but was initially called Gibixhegu. Graham penned the early history of Bulawayo:

In 1893 the Matabele were starting to become a threat despite the assurance of Chief Lobengula that no harm would come to the white settlers. However, the young Matabele warriors in Mashonaland were threatening to drive the white people into the sea. A French prospector was killed, and the settlers feared for the lives of their wives and families. The Matabele were raiding and stealing the cattle of the Mashona and taking their women into captivity and slavery. As a result, three columns were sent to Matabeleland, one from Tuli, one from Fort Victoria and one from Fort Charter to settle things. Prior to this Chief Lobengula had moved his first kraal, called Gwobuluwayo, on the fringes of the Matopos Hills, to the present site of Bulawayo. When the columns arrived Lobengula had fled but had burnt his kraal before leaving. The flying column was then despatched from Bulawayo in pursuit of the Matabele and to capture him. When they reached the Shangani River Major Allan Wilson and a small band of men, taking the freshest horses, crossed the Shangani. They were surrounded and trapped on the banks of the swollen river by more than 3,000 Matabele warriors. In the ensuing battle that lasted for more than 2 hours the band of 33 men were all killed, fighting to the end. The Matabele were reputed to have said, "These were men of men." In later years some world historians likened this battle (Wilson's Last Stand) to the Battle of Little Bighorn or the Battle of the Alamo. The imposing Shangani Memorial stands on the granite slopes at the Matopos not far from the grave of Cecil John Rhodes. It is a lasting memorial to the bravery of Major Allan Wilson and his men. Chief Lobengula died on 23 December 1893 when the Matabele acknowledged defeat. On 1 June 1894 Leander Starr Jameson declared that Bulawayo was now "open".

In 1894 a further pioneer column travelled to Bulawayo from Tuli on the same route as the two previous columns. Graham's grandfather, Donald Squair, who was born in Edinburgh in 1881, travelled with this column in the company of his parents, Hugh and Mary Squair (great-grandparents of Graham) and settled in Bulawayo. Like his father he became a builder and later a master-plasterer. He is credited with plastering the facade above the stage in the Palace Theatre in Bulawayo.

Our GPS took the Morris down Winnies Way, a bumpy road past the Bulawayo Golf Club and then on towards Hillside and into Burnside. Here the tarmac on the roads had totally crumbled basically to dirt and was mostly washed away. Before the 1980s Burnside was considered the most affluent and most sought-after suburb in Bulawayo. It is set among the granite *koppies* with houses attracting the highest prices.

After a few wrong turns we arrived at Granite Park and finally Granite Lodge where we had booked accommodation for the next 4 nights (Fig.197). This had been referred to us by Bruce Beckley. The lodge comprised five individual, beautifully appointed thatched cottages, each able to sleep four but with two being upstairs on a mezzanine floor. The owner, Gale Moore, kindly agreed for us to have two cottages so that everyone could sleep on the ground floor. The steps to the mezzanine for an older person presented a hazard especially for those wanting to go to the toilet during the night. After some negotiation Gail agreed to a discounted price in view of our charity drive. Another factor was that it was the Easter weekend with most folk out of town; so bookings were very quiet. This was an extremely generous gesture on Gail's part as the accommodation was first rate; the cottages were well constructed from granite, with high thatched roofs, well-appointed and with a fully equipped kitchen (Fig.198).

Graham and I managed to do some birding in the gardens. For all of us it was a privilege to enjoy this fantastic accommodation and setting. At about 15:00 Tony Carter, the chairman of the Vintage Car Club of Matabeleland (MVCC), came by to introduce himself and chat about our visit. He had been resident in Bulawayo since the 1970s and knew what went on and whom to contact.

As we needed to stock up with groceries and beers (not necessarily in that order) we followed Tony to the Hillside Shopping Centre where we obtained all the necessary items (Fig.199). The amounts quoted on the individual items made no sense at all and we had to convert everything to dollars before we could have any understanding of value. After shopping Tony took us around the corner to a small pub called The Office (Fig.200). This was the watering hole and meeting place of the Hillside Lions Club. There is a plaque in the pub referring to Gerry Muirhead, who was the owner of Greys Inn Hotel in Bulawayo, a great friend of Graham's father. The plaque reads: "Lions Club of Bulawayo, The Gerry Muirhead Den". After a couple of drinks, it was time to head home where dinner back at the self-catering Granite Lodge was a Thai green curry that I was confident in cooking but David was not impressed – I thought he would be familiar with the cuisine as the Cape offers a wide range of Malay and Indian dishes (Fig.201) but he said "I won't eat that again!"

Day 14: 5 April – Bulawayo and Matopos, Hartsfield Rugby Club

We awoke to a much cooler overcast day. After breakfast we planned to travel 50 kilometres to the Matobo National Park to visit Rhodes's grave, which was on our list of iconic sites. The cooler weather would also suit the Morris's engine. We left the lodge at 09:20, topped up the Morris with petrol near the pump at the bottom of the Old Gwanda Road – close to Graham's old home before he left Zimbabwe in 1981. He was unable to take a photo of his house as it is now surrounded by a high wall. High-walled houses seem to be the new norm everywhere we went – perhaps a security issue?

We arrived at the Matopos Road (Fig.202) and headed for the main gate of the park. (Fig.203). Naturally, there was an entrance fee (never in the past for a national monument)! We decided to take the Circular Drive to reach the grave of Cecil John Rhodes. After a short distance we arrived at the columbarium, a MOTH shrine (Memorable Order of Tin Hats). This is in a beautiful setting and has been extremely well cared for by the Bulawayo MOTH Club. There is a facility where soldiers can have their ashes interred and there is also a comprehensive Military Roll of Honour (Fig.24). It was a real privilege to stand at this famous spot and soak up the atmosphere. Wayne played a version of The Last Post on his phone; for some of us ex-army blokes it made the hairs stand up on end and brought a tear to our eyes.

Travelling further around the circular drive (Fig.205) took us past Shumba Shaba, a very large granite feature and then the gates to Gordon Park, which is the scout camp site where Graham spent so many of his younger days (Fig.206.) The Morris was doing extremely well and coping with the undulating terrain. We arrived at the parking area below the site of Rhodes's grave, surrounded by huge boulders at World's View. Again, there was an entrance fee, but after I negotiated by mentioning the charity trip, we paid the Zimbabwean citizens' rate of US$2 per person. We hiked up the mountain to the grave site where we took photographs of the graves of Cecil John Rhodes (Fig.207) and Leander Starr Jameson, and the Shangani Memorial. From there we stopped at World's View (so named by CJR); the vista is unequalled and not easily forgotten (Fig.208). I reflected on what we had achieved thus far and what thrills lay ahead.

Visiting this Heritage Site was a major honour and event that all appreciated. It is worth noting that there were very few visitors in the park that day and very little game to be seen. There used to be a resident herd of sable antelope in the vicinity of the MOTH Shrine and the Gordon Park. Upon completing the Circular Drive (Fig.209) we spotted several baboons along the way and the Morris just avoided running over two warthogs dashing across the road in front of us. Later I had to dodge a donkey who decided to own the road (Fig.210). We departed Rhodes's grave site at noon, making our way to Bulawayo city centre to seek the Hartsfield Rugby Grounds.

Arriving in the city, down Matopos Road, we passed Number 79, home of Graham's late wife Barbara before they were married in 1970. Further along on Matopos Road was Number 17, 19th Avenue where Graham had lived from 1947 until 1964 with his parents (their first home). Seeing this established home of his youth was both nostalgic and fulfilling for Graham.

Next on the agenda was finding the Hartsfield Rugby Grounds, where in 1963 I had represented the Rhodesia Regiment Under-19 rugby team to play a curtain raiser for Ronnie Hill's Rhodesian team against a South African invitation team (Figs.212–215). As with many other locations, things had not been properly maintained and were nowhere near their former glory. One of the grandstands had been opened by Sir Roy Welensky, Prime Minister of the Federation of Rhodesia and Nyasaland (Fig.216) in 1961. We learned that all the club's artefacts had been moved for preservation to the Bulawayo Club.

The second owner of the Morris is listed as Mary O'Gorman, Matron of the Isolation Hospital in 1940. This hospital was subsequently closed; she was then based at the Ingutsheni Psychiatric Hospital. The hospital is situated near an industrial area called Belmont which borders on the southern suburbs of Bulawayo (Figs.217, 218). I managed to speak to a senior nurse who agreed to fetch the matron,

but she never arrived. At this stage David was able to take group photos of us with some of the staff at the main entrance. Later the Human Resources matron aggressively wanted to know if we had permission to take photos; so we departed having ticked another box of a Morris owner's address.

Bulawayo city centre was extremely busy and, although the traffic lights were working, the inter-sections were a real challenge. The road surface was breaking up in places: there were many potholes in the city centre but they were much worse on the outskirts. There are still many of the early original buildings but also a lot of new ones. It was sad to see the deterioration due to lack of maintenance of what was once an organised city.

We got the impression that the people in the city were less friendly than those in the countryside; they showed little interest in the vintage Morris. However, there was a group with several American tourists who were fascinated at the history of the vehicle. After a busy day and having covered a total of 125 kilometres, we arrived back at Granite Lodge at about 15:30. We were ready to relax and enjoy a couple of Zambezis beers. Dinner was stir-fry vegetables with pasta that Wayne and I cooked – voted delicious.

Fig.201: Home cooking – exotic Thai green curry

Fig.202: Road Bulawayo to Matopos

Fig.203: Motopos National Park, Matobo

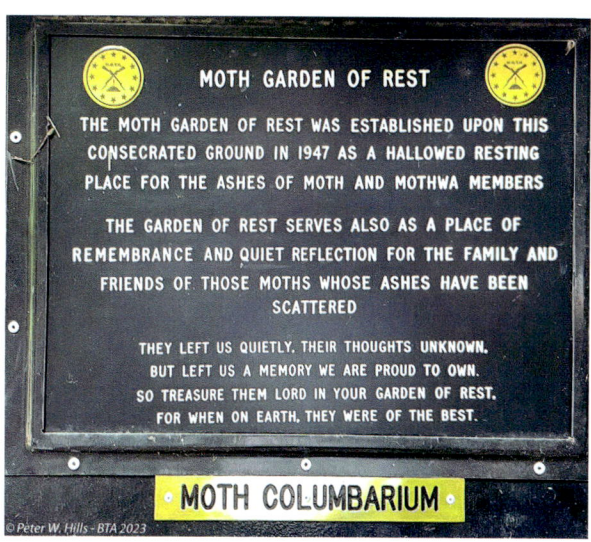

Fig.204: MOTH "Old Soldiers Never Die"

Fig.205: Motopos Circular Drive

Fig.206: Boy Scout Camp Park, Motopos

Fig.207: Here lies Cecil John Rhodes, Motopos

Fig.208: World's View: "Is this trip a crazy idea?"

Fig.209: Departing Motobo National Park

Fig.210: Donkey on the road back to Bulawayo

Fig.211: Hartsfield Rugby Ground Bulawayo

Fig.212: I played a curtain raiser here in1963

Fig.213: Royal Rhodesia Regiment U19s

Fig.214: Peter in the main stand 60 years later

Fig.215: Hartsfield Rugby Club, new player

Fig.216: The Federation Prime Minister

Day 15: 6 April – Bulawayo – Diff Failure, VCCZ Mashonaland

The plan for the day was to take the Morris to the home of Bryan Christie, who has a workshop and pit that would make the needed engine oil change so much easier. Bryan lives in a suburb called Matsheumhlope some way out of the city, east of Bulawayo and generally comprising smallholdings. First, I wanted to visit an old family friend from Kitwe days. We found Diane (née Wood) in Paisley Crescent, Famona on the way to Bryan's. She was at home – although our visit was a surprise to Diane, she invited us in for a chat and tea. She had five yapping dogs of various breeds and sizes that were quite a nuisance. We caught up on her family history and our times in Kitwe as her mother, Muriel, was a good friend of my Mum's. I reminded her that 65 years ago her father Ernie often took me fishing at Mindola Dam outside Kitwe – I picked up my fishing skills from him. After a short visit we bade farewell and set off for Bryan's smallholding.

Suddenly I noticed a constant clicking noise emanating from the rear of the car that became increasingly louder, especially when changing gear. This was very worrying as it seemed to come from the differential and clearly needed urgent attention. Arriving at Bryan's place required driving up a narrow tree-lined tunnel 50 metres to his workshop area. Our initial impression was one of surprise: the entire place appeared to a scrapyard. It was littered with classic car chassis, trucks and wrecks, apparently all beyond repair rusting in the bush (Fig.219). The large workshop looked just as disorganised but seemed to have all the necessary tools and equipment. Typical engineer: "I know where everything is in my garage, don't move stuff or try to tidy up my place," said Bryan. First appearances can be misleading and this proved to be the case. Bryan is just a regular guy working hard to make a living, an accomplished motor mechanic and well known in the vintage/classic car circles.

We placed the Morris over the inspection pit, where the planned oil change was no longer the priority. We immediately removed and checked the half-shafts, finding them in good order. I had carried a spare half-shaft that fortunately was not needed. My biggest fear was that the crown wheel and pinion may have failed. On removing the cover plate to my relief both looked perfect, almost as new. With Wayne "supervising" from a distance (Fig.220), we then removed the complete differential and as soon it was opened the problem was evident (Fig.221). Each spider gear had two teeth missing – fortunately the bits had adhered to the diff's magnet debris collector (Fig.222) avoiding further damage. Bryan diagnosed the cause of the problem: with potholed roads, if a rear wheel leaves the ground spinning, returning to the ground places severe stress on the spider gears and can ultimately fracture them. Clearly, we had experienced this several times especially "gunning" downhill and crossing the expansion gaps between bridge and road. The Morris would go airborne for an instant and return to earth with a jolt.

Having established the cause of the noise, the priority was to obtain replacement spider gears. Bear in mind that the next day was Good Friday and during the Easter weekend all services would be slow or nonexistent. For the next couple of hours Bryan and his friend Colin phoned all their local car contacts around Bulawayo without success. Many people were already away for the holiday weekend and others were unable to assist. I topped up Bryan's phone for the number of calls he made. Eventually, I decided to phone Rodney Wayland-Green, an MMM (MG) pal in White River near the Kruger Park in South Africa who has piles of MG spares, many compatible with the Morris. He confirmed that he had a set of spider gears but delivery by courier would only be possible for the following Wednesday (after Easter). To maintain our travel plans and accommodation arrangements delivery would have to be to an address in Harare. This meant that the Morris would have to be transported from Bulawayo to Harare in the trailer, which was quite a disappointment. Wayne, Graham and David returned to Granite Lodge to collect the trailer. During their absence good fortune struck again (those "golden balls" clanged). Bryan located two 1936 Morris 8 differentials owned by Tim McAlastair who lived almost around the corner.

I went with Bryan to view the units in Bryan's "done-up" Ford Fairlane – it went like a rocket! I was aware that the internals of the Morris 8 differential would be compatible if intact. Although the exterior of Tim's Diff was rusted, I anticipated that the gears would be protected by retained internal oil (Fig.223). I offered to pay Tim for the differential, but he only wanted the unused parts to be returned to him. Thanks Tim, you saved us. I then informed Rodney to cancel the DHL delivery for his set of spider gears – with grateful thanks. We removed the spider gears from the rusty unit: they were dirty but as expected in remarkably good condition. After a good rotating wire brushing, we fitted them back in the Morris differential (Fig.224). As it was getting dark and since we had arranged a get-together with the Vintage Car Club Matabeleland branch (VCC-M) at Granite Lodge, Bryan told us to go ahead – assembly of a Diff is not to be rushed – he and Colin would continue with the job and join us later.

We returned to Granite Lodge where the Vintage Car Club of Zimbabwe (VCCZ) – Tony Carter and 12 members – were waiting for us with snacks and drinks. Unfortunately, the Morris was not available for the guests to view, but I gave a summary of the car's history and the trip so far. When Bryan and Colin arrived, having brushed up well since we last saw them in the garage pit there was much banter. The atmosphere was very relaxed, and it was good to meet some of the older former Rhodesians. Graham chatted with Cliff and Vicky Gillies – Cliff had also been a member of the 9th Battalion Rhodesia Regiment in Bulawayo in the seventies, a few intakes after Graham and me. Vicky had been a professional golfer for a while and knew a lot about the Old Bulawayo. After a few drinks and a photo session with all the VCCZ (Fig.225), I presented Bryan Christie and Colin Bail (Fig.226), Tony Carter (Fig.227) and Bruce Beckley (Fig.228) with the BTA commemorative mugs and that was greatly appreciated. Bruce then gave a video interview – the transcript is recorded alongside his photo. The links he revealed to this Morris Minor are remarkable. The fact that Bruce's grandmother knew Mrs Rene Lang, the 10th owner, was a revelation.

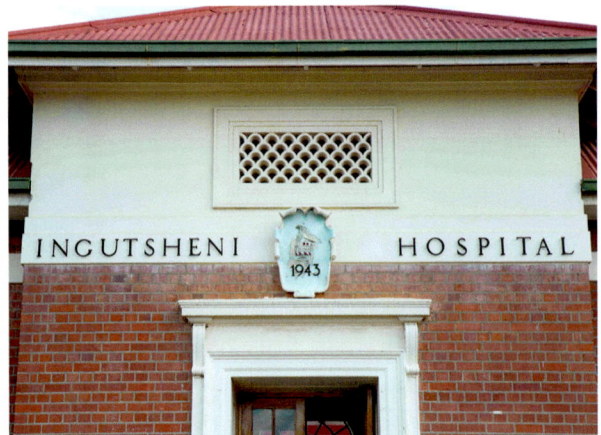
Fig.217: The Ingutsheni Psychiatric Hospital

Later we had a dinner of boerewors and fresh salad that went down very well. The day had been stressful but ended with a bright light at the end of the tunnel and high hopes for the next morning as the old "golden balls" had done the trick once again.

The plan was to return to Bryan's workshop the next day to complete the fitting of the differential, make the oil change, then freshen up for a visit to the venerable Bulawayo Club that seemed to have a strict dress code.

Fig.218: Mary O'Gorman 2nd owner matron here

Fig.219: Bryan's farm and scrapyard

Fig.220 "Houston, we have a problem!"

Fig.221: Spider gears – catastrophic failure

Fig.222: Diff oil drained, magnetic plug debris

Fig.223: Jewel in the Crown – M8 Diff in Bulawayo

Fig.224: Bryan and Colin replacing spider gears

Fig.225: Vintage Car Club Zimbabwe at Granite Lodge 6 April 2023

Fig.226: Colin Bail and Bryan Christie

Fig.227: Tony Clark Chairman VCCZ

Fig.228: Bruce Beckley (with transcript of interview recorded by video).

Bruce Beckley's video interview 6 April 2023 in Bulawayo: "I first heard of the 1929 Morris Minor in the 1993 Classic & Sports Car magazine. My father then contacted my grandfather, Alderson James Lewis Beckley who was with RAF 237 Squadron from 1939 to 1945, serving in North Africa and the Middle East during WW2. Before he went to England, he left the car for his wife to use but fitted the Model-T Ford headlights and the Morris 8 wheels and tyres as new Morris Minor tyres were not available in the 1940s."

I found the car in 1970 with these non-standard fittings, Bruce is convinced that it is the same Morris Minor. His grandfather also changed the engine and fitted Wolseley Hornet pistons to the engine. Along with the RAF chaps his grandfather drove the car. Also his grandmother was a close friend of Mrs Rene Lang (the 10th owner).

Fig.229: Installing Diff half- and propshafts

Fig.230: Bryan tightening up, now add oil to Diff

Fig.231: We fixed the Diff – a good Friday

Fig.232: Downtown Bulawayo, Rhodes Ave

Day 16: 7 April – Bulawayo Club Tour

It was Good Friday, and it was indeed good for us. After a leisurely start to the morning, we made our way back to Bryan's workshop. Bryan, Colin and I immediately began installing the repaired differential into the axle banjo housing (Figs.229, 230).

We used a silicon gasket sealant instead of the traditional paper type to reduce any chance of oil seepage. The work progressed steadily: connecting the propshaft, half-shafts and then wheels back on. Finally, we added fresh SAE 140 oil into the Diff housing. The original purpose of using Bryan's pit was to replace the engine running-in oil with a standard non-detergent SAE 40 oil designed for vintage and classic cars. The Ravenol running-in oil (thinner) has two objectives: to flush any debris in the overhauled engine and to bed in the working elements. Since the piston rings were already seated, the stiffness of the new big-end shell bearings needed to be eased. Many years ago I placed a rare earth magnet in the oil filter basket, which does its job very well. This time I found it covered with all sorts of debris, not only wear particles but minute metal swarf, fibre (from cleaning cloths) and jointing adhesive that is always difficult to remove completely at the engine assembly stage. At the subsequent 500 mile oil change there was hardly any debris evident on the magnet, which was very encouraging. With better access in the workshop pit, I also took the opportunity to grease the spring shackles, steering and other moving links and levers.

When all was ready, we started the engine and reversed the Morris off the pit. To the great relief of everyone, the job was completed by 11:45 – good going by the three mechanics. Bryan asked us to deliver a parcel of car spares for a friend in Harare as well as a tray of two dozen fresh free-range eggs.

We obviously agreed to this but we were also given a further two dozen eggs for the team to consume. After farewells all round we left for the lodge after 12:00.

Bryan's wife had indicated that times were not always easy: a fair bit of mutual bartering takes place among the neighbours where she swaps eggs and the occasional chicken for vegetables and fruit from the opposite neighbour. Hens and a few turkeys range freely between the workshop and the house. The municipal rates are high and are constantly escalated on smallholdings; the council believes that if the properties are subdivided to develop individual plots, this will bring in more revenue for the council. Whatever the situation and despite the long weekend, Bryan and Colin came to our rescue and saved a potential disaster to the trip and the schedule. I was happy to give them US$150 for their trouble and this was greatly appreciated (Fig.231). We arrived back at Granite Lodge at 12:30 with the Morris running smoothly. That afternoon we had the engagement at the exclusive Bulawayo Club.

Tony Carter had arranged for us to visit the historic Bulawayo Club and we were advised to dress smartly in long trousers. This time we went downtown in the BMW along the former Rhodes Avenue (Fig.232). What had been the Barclays Bank DCO building on the corner of Main Street and 8th Avenue, where Graham had started his banking career in 1963, has now been renamed. Next door, on 8th Avenue, is the Bulawayo Club. In the centre of the intersection there used to be a statue of Cecil John Rhodes but this has now been replaced by a statue of Joshua Nkomo, leader of the opposition party to Mugabe (Fig.233).

Along many residential roads were numerous topiary gardens that were well cared for with many depictions of animals and birds (Fig.234) – a surprising and pleasing sight. The Bulawayo city roads were originally designed so that a wagon train could undertake a complete turn. There were many street vendors (Fig.235), the traffic was heavy (Fig.236) and every now and then there was evidence of Bulawayo's magnificent early days (Fig.237). We finally arrived at the Bulawayo Club where the original hitching post (Fig.238) was still present inside the security railings.

Tony Carter met us at the main entrance where there was a broken parking meter (a past relic of an organised city) and the odd street vendor. Entering the large wooden doors of the club was like walking into a different world. At this hallowed place Tony signed us in at the magnificent entrance hall, with its gleaming polished parquet flooring and woodwork: it took some time to take in the historic opulence on display (Fig.239). The walls are adorned with historic photos, paintings and relics. One corner is devoted to Cecil John Rhodes and his adversary Chief Lobengula (Fig.240). Soaking up the atmosphere and picturing the many famous personalities from the past who had stood in this very room and had dined there was very moving (Fig.241). One wonders what strategies and plots were hatched over a bottle of fine port. They must have concluded historic business deals, some affecting the history of Central Africa and the lives of many, including us, for many years to come. After viewing the numerous framed photographs and artefacts we adjourned to the bar where a welcome cold beer hit the spot (Fig.242). From the club's inception only gentlemen were permitted in this bar, and this is still the case today. As planned, Bruce Beckley, a chartered accountant and committee member joined the party; we exchanged details of our various activities and association with the two Rhodesias. Bruce is a very amiable fellow who sadly lost his wife due to illness a few years ago; he is now raising their 12-year-old daughter, which no doubt has its challenges.

Graham discussed with Bruce his earlier years in Bulawayo; Bruce knew some of Graham's school friends and folk from Gwanda where he had been posted with Barclays Bank. After a few more beers Barry Knight took us on a complete tour of the club, including the kitchens and residential section. One large room houses the regalia from the Hartsfield Rugby Club which particularly attracted my interest. There are some amazing records: signed rugby jerseys, trophies, medals, rugby balls and photographs in glass-fronted cabinets – all irreplaceable (Fig.243).

Before we departed Bruce proudly introduced his daughter to us, still dressed in her horse-riding attire, a very quiet and well-mannered young lady. After a wonderful and privileged tour of the club, a reminder of times gone by, we said our farewells with the obligatory photo outside the club (Fig.244) and with Barry Knight posing with his 1960s Morris Minor in excellent condition (Fig.245). We then returned to Granite Lodge after collecting provisions at the Hillside Spar supermarket.

I cooked a Thai green curry for dinner, with salad prepared by Wayne, to our surprise David found it too spicy for his taste! After ensuring that our personal packing was sorted and ready for an early start, it was time to retire. Dudley Searle in Harare had arranged a braai (barbeque) for the Easter Monday. Since we had achieved all our targets in Bulawayo, we decided to leave for the North a day earlier than planned.

Fig.233: Joshua Nkomo replaced Rhodes

Fig.234: Topiary gardens seen everywhere

Fig.235: "Oh yes, we have bananas today"

Fig.236: Heavy traffic was evident everywhere

Fig.237: Bulawayo old and new

Fig.238: Club hitching post

Fig.239: The Bulawayo Club entrance

Fig.240: Cecil J. Rhodes and Chief Lobengula

Fig.241 The Bulawayo Club dining room

Fig.242: After the tour by Barry Knight

Fig.243: Hartsfield Rugby Club mementos

Fig.244: Bulawayo Club entrance and VCCM

Fig.245: Barry Knight and his Morris Minor

Fig.246: Leaving Bulawayo for the north

Fig.247 Mzilikazi (Ex-Brady) Barracks Bulawayo

Fig.248: Ex-Llewellin Barracks

Fig.249: 1963 "61932 Rifleman Hills, Sir!"

Fig.250: "It's a long way to Gweru" (Gwelo)

Day 17: 8 April – Bulawayo to Gweru (162km)

We arose early to find that there was no electricity – loadshedding! We decided against taking a cold shower in the dark – so a quick splash and wipe down. A light breakfast and coffee, packing and loading the trailer, and settling the account (I left a BTA mug for Mrs Moore), we departed Granite Lodge at 07:15 in convoy. Once again negotiating the very potholed road towards the city then along the now well-travelled route via Beryl Drive, Old Gwanda Road and Matopos Road. Stopping for fuel in Hillside, then making our way along Grey Street to Selbourne Avenue, we turned onto the Harare Road, At the corner was a building with "cape town < 1,150 miles" on one side and "cairo > 3,500 miles" on the other (Fig.246). For fun I took a photo. At the same time Graham took pictures of the Greys Inn Hotel, previously owned by Gerry Muirhead, whose plaque was in the pub we had visited with Tony Carter on arrival.

On the outskirts of the city we drove past Brady Barracks (now called Mzilikazi Barracks) where, in the past, the territorial battalions in Bulawayo were based, as well as the Corps of Signals. As we passed the entrance we took a couple of quick photos, but moved on as the guards came rushing out gesticulating. Both vehicles sped off very quickly (Fig.247). About 12 kilometres out of Bulawayo there is a large cement works known as Cement Siding. In the distant past, when passenger trains operated daily between Bulawayo and Salisbury (Harare) and beyond, if you missed the train in Bulawayo there was still time to drive to Cement Siding to board the train. Just beyond Cement Siding is Heany Junction and the turn-off to Imbizo Barracks where Llewellin Barracks (now Lookout Masuku Barracks) are situated. This is where both Graham and I did our National Service Training in the 1960s when there was conscription (Fig.248). The father of my pal, Frank Jenkins, took a rare colour slide photo of me in 1963 when most photos were monochrome. I obtained this picture in 2003 from Eileen Robertson (née Jenkins) among others taken when I was in the army at Bulawayo. Many years later I contributed to two books on the history of the Rhodesia Regiment and one book created a draft cover jacket for the book using my original photo because it was in colour (Fig.249). The second coffee table book included the photo and many more I took with my ever ready but simple Halina 35mm camera.

The road out of Bulawayo was better than most, and the going was easy, but we still needed to make regular stops to top up the evaporating radiator water. Like many roads in southern Africa, they are straight for as far as one can see (Fig.250). After an excellent run, we arrived at Gweru (formerly Gwelo) around 11:30. As seemed to be the norm whenever we approached city precincts, the roads deteriorated with crumbling tarmac and potholes; this state extended to the general cleanliness of the streets and buildings. Finding our overnight accommodation started to become a mystery tour leading us out of town and into an area of smallholdings along narrow tracks surrounded by bush (Fig.251). We began to wonder where we were heading when the Bradley Gardens Experience came into view – a new venture, with modern fittings but still a "work in progress" (Fig.252). The lush extensive lawns and gardens were well manicured. We were greeted with loud music – a children's birthday party with a bouncy castle in the garden. A wedding was also under way with many guests staying overnight.

Despite having booked ahead, we were dismayed to be allocated only one room with two double beds: not the ideal situation for four men. I pleaded with the manager, who intimated that another room might become available. However, that was not the case and our only option was to manage with our allocation. Graham agreed to sleep in his sleeping bag on top of one of the double beds while David was under the sheet alongside. Wayne elected to sleep on the floor on a double duvet, a decision he later regretted. I took the other double bed. It was a "cosy" arrangement with the potential for noisy group snoring. The shared modern toilet and shower facilities were quite acceptable.

Fig.251: Bradley Gardens Experience Gweru

For dinner we had pizzas and beers at the restaurant. Their piped music seemed to become louder and louder as the other guests enjoyed themselves. We were amazed at the size of some of the food portions. Six huge sausages with almost half a kilogramme of chips seemed the norm for a single person, especially the women! We asked what time the music would stop. "Maybe nine o'clock." This proved to be far from the truth; it was well after midnight before we managed to get some sleep despite our room being over 100 metres away from the restaurant.

Fig.252: Our accommodation – 4 to a room!

Fig.253: Impressive Gweru Council Office

Fig.254 Presbyterian Church, Gweru

Fig.255: Stone laid 10 days after Morris was made

Fig.256: Mosque, leaving Gweru

Fig.257: Easter Sunday – Morris astonishes

Fig.258: Tomatoes were the order of the day

Fig.259: Maize ready for harvest

Fig.260: Dual carriageway entering Harare

Fig.261: Housing estate under construction

Fig.262: Green at the end of the rainy season

Fig.263: The Chinese are here and expanding

Fig.264: Arrived downtown Harare

Fig.265: Central Business District Harare

Fig.266: Ex-colonial offices, CBD Harare

Chapter 6.3

Zimbabwe – Mashonaland

Day 18: 9 April – Gweru to Harare (278km)

Leaving the Bradley Gardens Experience at about 07:30 we agreed it was an experience we did not wish to repeat. We drove into town along a dirt road track and came out near the impressive City Council Offices with neat gardens (Fig.253). I spotted the Anglican Church with a square Norman style tower in brick and decided to investigate further. The foundation stone was laid by the Hon. H.U. Moffat CMG, Premier of Southern Rhodesia on 27.07.1929. How strange. Just 10 days before, on 17 July of the same year, my Morris was exported from the Oxford factory in England to Southern Rhodesia (Figs.254, 255). What are the chances?

It was Easter Sunday. Gweru to Harare would be a 182 mile drive, but the road was in good condition and we made good time. At the next rest and radiator top-up stop I suggested that David should accompany me instead of Graham who had been my passenger to date. This would give David personal experience in the Morris. We chatted about the importance of his photo-journalistic role in recording the BTA journey. It was up to him to be proactive and creative in recognising photographic opportunities. Having spent some 680 miles in the Morris, Graham remarked at the difference in comfort when he joined Wayne in the BMW!

We approached Kwekwe (Que Que) at 10:00; this stretch was by far the smoothest and cleanest we had encountered. I made a sudden stop to photograph the Morris near the local mosque (Fig.256), with Wayne stopping ahead just past the roundabout. Before he realised it, two police officers wanted to charge him for parking illegally – that carried a US$50 fine or face arrest. At the same time a local drunk was bothering Wayne for money. So, while the police were busy getting rid of the drunk, Wayne sped off. I was unaware of all this; somehow they ignored the Morris that was parked virtually on the roundabout itself. At the next rest and smoke stop I heard Wayne's story. We chuckled at his dilemma and evasive action.

At 11:00, on the outskirts of Kadoma (formerly Gatooma), we made another fuel stop, this time at a fancy new service station complete with a food market (Fig.257). Again, the Morris attracted many admirers and we were faced with multiple questions and disbelief that such a vehicle was still on the road. At this new service station there were several convenience outlets awaiting occupants. I returned from the only store selling snacks, hopping like the Easter Bunny with a slab of chocolate each for Graham, Wayne and David – it was Easter Sunday after all!

Continuing through Chegutu (formerly Hartley) at midday and a bit further on before Norton, we made a stop at a roadside stall selling all sorts of fruit and vegetables. All the roadside stalls seemed to have the same produce for sale: oranges, bananas, watermelons and other vegetables (tomatoes were in abundance on every main road) (Fig.258). We wondered how the stall owners survived: much of the produce would go to waste in the hot sun. Since we were attending the VCCZ braai in Harare I decided to buy some sweet potatoes, but the pile marked US$2 contained far more than I required. The lady vendor agreed to accept US$1 for half her pile but when I handed her a well-used US$1 note she refused to accept it. I said, "Okay if I can add one more sweet potato to my pile here is a fresh crisp new note." She agreed and we both laughed at the amusing exchange. Continuing along the road it was encouraging to see evidence of extensive fields of maize ready for harvesting (Fig.259).

As we approached Harare, Graham re-joined me in the Morris to help with navigating through the city and finding the road to Dudley Searle's farm where we were to spend the next 4 nights.

For a while the single road ran alongside what seemed to be an abandoned dual carriageway with weeds growing through extensive roadworks. Had they had run out of funds to complete the job? Eventually we came to a completed section of dual carriageway as we got nearer the City (Fig.260) from the south. We passed what looked like a new and extensive housing estate still under construction – clearly, new developments indicate improvements in infrastructure (Fig.261).

We passed Lake Chivero, a potential birding spot but awkward for us to get to as it was on the opposite side of the City from where we were staying. The area was now becoming green and lush (Fig.262). The traffic became more and more dense, not helped by the road rapidly deteriorating. We became engulfed in the general traffic mayhem. We reached the suburbs of Harare at 14:00 and it was not surprising to observe the presence of the Chinese who tend to construct their own enclosures and create a little bit of China in Africa; this became common as we progressed north (Fig.263). We motored through the CBD with its familiar skyscrapers, much as Graham and I remembered it (Figs.264–266). Unlike in the rural areas, the locals took little notice of the Morris; all seemed too busy with their own affairs. The heavy traffic, modern cars and general activity everywhere gave the lie to the reports of the economy being a disaster. We did not see any beggars or any informal settlements such as are widely established in South Africa. This was a pleasant surprise.

Harare was called Salisbury until 1980 when Zimbabwe became independent. The first Pioneer Column travelled from Tuli to Fort Victoria, then Fort Charter (Enkeldoorn) and then Fort Salisbury. The Column reached Fort Salisbury on 12 September 1890 and they raised the British flag the next day in what was then known as Cecil Square. This was part of Cecil John Rhodes's dream of colonising the area north of South Africa. Development was rapid as the colonists set about transforming a land of hunter gatherers into a rich agricultural behemoth able to be the bread basket of Africa. The rest, they say, is history

I had obtained the grid coordinates for Pangoula Farm, our next accommodation; so we followed my iPad through the centre of Harare and on to the Enterprise Road but we made little sense of the directions and could not find where to turn off towards the farm. Further down the road we passed a most outlandish entrance to a property (Fig.267) that we later discovered was some guru/preacher who sold bricks to his worshippers for entry to heaven. Clearly, it was a profitable activity.

After driving up and down without success, I phoned Dudley Searle who drove out to meet us. We had passed the turn-off to his farm by 2 kilometres and this meant turning back against the heavy traffic. While we were attempting to do this, a bunch of unruly youngsters suddenly mobbed the Morris. They put their shoes on the mudguards, jumped on the running boards and stood in front of the Morris, bending the bumper badges for photos. This could have been an ugly situation; so I put my foot on the accelerator and forced them out of the way. This kind of behaviour was not the norm. We guessed that the guys were drunk – not an experience to be repeated! The event was recorded on our dash-cam.

Dudley was waiting at the turn-off. We then followed him on a road that was very poor and lined with many half-built domestic houses on either side; the last 3 or 4 kilometres were really challenging. The convoy arrived at Pangoula Farm, the home of Dudley and Prue Searle. Their farm is situated on a slope with rolling lawns, surrounded by fabulous flower gardens, leading down to a lake. The large house is very spacious, constructed from several prefabricated units assembled without any evidence of a joint. We each had our own room – mine was in an annex with a full-size snooker table nearby. Considering all the days on the road thus far, this was the most idyllic and peaceful setting: no people or traffic noise – just the sound of the birds (Fig.268).

Dudley has an interesting bar decorated with all sorts of artefacts, and the drinks were very welcome after our long drive (Fig.269). Bear in mind that I met Dudley at the Beaulieu International Autojumble in the UK in 2017; it was not long before we made multiple mutual connections and shared experiences of living in the former Rhodesias.

Dinner was laid on by Prue: spaghetti bolognese with all the trimmings, washed down with excellent red wine in their formal dining room. As an initial thank you for their hospitality I gave them two bottles of Stettyn wine that I had brought from the Cape for such an occasion – and the two dozen free-range eggs from Bulawayo (Fig.270). We then adjourned to the recreational lounge where Dudley had set up an overhead projector, large screen and fantastic music system. He was proud to entertain us with a couple of music DVDs of live shows from some of the stars of our era. His powerful speakers blasted out music so loud that it felt as if we were present at a live event. After a few toots in Dudley's bar (Fig.271) it was off to bed at around midnight for the BTA survivors but not before a final shot of Dudley's fine single malt whisky that he insisted we imbibe. This certainly put me to sleep very quickly after the longest drive covering some 278 kilometres (172 miles).

Day 19: 10 April – Pangoula Farm, VCCZ Harare

It was a beautiful Easter Monday morning; so Graham and I got up early to take advantage of our time at Pangoula as there were birds at the house and lake. We were quite successful in spotting several new species including a pair of Cardinal Woodpeckers, Variable Sunbird and African Jacana. The prize, however, was the pair of Bat Hawks roosting in a tree just above the braai area. Even Dudley and Prue were very surprised at this sighting – a lifer for me.

After breakfast it was "all stations go" to prepare for the visit by the members of the Vintage Car Club of Zimbabwe with their cars. Wayne and David mounted our BTA banners on the veranda while Graham helped me to clean and polish the Morris (Fig.272) and Dudley organised his workers to set out the braai area with chairs and tables. The braai drums were loaded with real wood, not charcoal. Prue prepared large bowls of salad.

The VCCZ members parked their impressive cars in a row on the lawn (Fig.273). As is normal practice, everyone brought their own drinks and meat. The host lays on the braais (barbeques) and Graham managed the fires. By 12:15 there were 16 members with their cars: Ford Mustang Mach 1, 1973 E-type V12, 1972 Alpha Spider, 1968 MGB, 1951 Mercedes 170, 1960 Morris Minor, 1985 Toyota Corolla, Sunbeam, 1990 MGF. How they managed to negotiate the horrible road to the farm (especially the E-Type Jaguar) was a wonder.

Dudley formally introduced the BTA Team and I then summarised the Morris's history, the trip thus far and our future plans. I thanked Dudley and Prue for their generosity in hosting us for so many days and then I presented Dudley with one of the special BTA mugs and Prue with a WPB mug (www.WorldBirdPhotos.com) (Prue is a bird enthusiast) (Figs.274–276). We then positioned the Morris in front of the BTA banners with everyone grouped together for a historic photo (Fig.277).

Then it was time to start the braai: steak, chicken, chops, boerewors – and the sweet potatoes! Everything was cooked to perfection; some serious feasting was washed down with a few beers and wine (Fig.278). The weather could not have been better and everyone chatted well into the afternoon. Graham spoke with Ginty Melville (ex-Lusaka), who had also worked for Barclays Bank DCO and in some of the same branches as Graham including Gwanda; they knew some mutual ex-colleagues. Another chap, Allan, recalled much about his early days in Rhodesia and the RAF.

Dudley and Prue's two daughters and grandchildren popped in to say hello. One of the daughters is in a joint venture with Prue involving organic market gardening; the vegetables are sold at local markets. She also has a range of herbal teas, with the leaves being packaged and sold locally. It is her aim to go commercial in due course. Having eaten and drunk their fill, the visiting folk started leaving for home and by 17:15 all had departed. The entire event was most enjoyable and a great success: our thanks to our hosts having made these special arrangements for the BTA Team. Satiated and satisfied, we all relaxed before heading for an early bed. Later when we arrived in Choma in Zambia I sent Dudley an update of our progress – his reply was so heart-warming (Fig.279). Clearly, we will maintain contact as firm friends.

Day 20: 11 April – Pangoula Farm, Harare

Graham and I were up early to go out birding again. On this occasion we walked along a track adjoining the nearby wetland that produced several birds enjoying the early morning sun, including a breeding family of Black Crakes. On returning to the house, I photographed a pair of African Black Ducks on the lake – a plus for the collection. At around 08:30 everyone sat down to a real breakfast: muesli, fruit salad, fried eggs, bacon, fried tomato, fried banana, coffee, toast – we were spoiled rotten!

After breakfast I drove the Morris over the pit in Dudley's workshop. There was a constant oil leak at the pipe leading to the sump and I knew it was reducing the oil capacity. The flange-securing nuts did not have sufficient purchase: the presence of a very thick gasket meant that there was not enough thread. I removed the old gasket and replaced it with a thinner version with sealant and was able to tighten the flange fully. We hoped that the oil leak would be a thing of the past (it proved to be a permanent fix).

Travelling towards the city off the Enterprise Road we came across a modern-looking shopping complex where I purchased mobile data at the PicknPay. An upmarket café nearby, Café Nosh, served excellent cappuccino and chocolate cake. Wayne decided to go outside for a smoke, David declined the cake and it was left to me and Graham to devour a large but delicious slice each. They had fast Wi-Fi and we were able to catch up on international news.

We drove to Halstead's Hardware to purchase engine oil for the Morris as I was worried that our stocks might run out. Later I realised that after fixing the sump pipe the subsequent consumption of engine oil was minimal. The store was comparable to any found in South Africa; they carried a range of engine oil and we purchased two 5 litre cans of SAE 40. The cashier suggested that I get a loyalty card at the information desk. This resulted in a discount of US$20. Well worth the effort of filling in a form! Coincidentally, Halstead's was on the road leading to the main Harare–Chinhoyi road and the route would be familiar for the way out in a couple of days. Then the heavens opened and it began to pour very hard – time to return to Pangoula. Close to the farm, at a dip, the rain had converted the clay road into a greasy slide and, despite being four-wheel drive, even the BMW slid down the hill. This may not have had a happy ending had the trailer been attached. As for the Morris: it would not have coped at all.

Back at the farm Prue served tea, coffee and home-made biscuits. It was still drizzling outside; so we attended to our travel records. Graham was writing up the daily diary with much dedication. Later we joined Dudley in his bar to enjoy a drink. The conversation turned to past events in Rhodesia during the Bush War. After some prompting by Prue, Dudley regaled us with the story of how he and a friend were captured by Renamo "freedom fighters" in Mozambique. He and a friend were held for 8 months before managing to escape. What they endured shows the mettle of the man, having survived such a terrifying experience. Dinner was a relaxed affair, with us sitting around the kitchen table. We chatted until 22:00 and were offered a cup of Horlicks, a happy reminder of bygone days. However, Dudley insisted that we have a tot of port before bed to ensure a good night's sleep.

Day 21: 12 April – Harare City, Owners RAF Stations

Once again Graham and I went on an early morning birding walk, this time around the garden and up the road behind the dam. Prue alerted us to a very accommodating Hamerkop sitting on the surfboard floating in the swimming pool. We spotted several species and were back in time for an excellent fruit salad breakfast.

While we waited for the weather to clear, I needed to download records from the Morris's dash-cam, a time-consuming job. We then drove into Harare to seek out the listed Morris past owners who had lived in the then Salisbury.

Fig.267: Guru sells holy bricks, does well!

Fig.268: Stunning Pangoula Farm Harare

Fig.269: Relaxation after 263km trip (163 miles)

Fig.270: Thanks Dudley and Prue, our hosts

Fig.271: Dudley's "office" – a late night for all!

Fig.272: Polishing for Easter Monday braai

Fig.273: VCCZ members' cars of many models

Fig.274: Dudley our host, thanks, a BTA mug

Fig.275: Dudley was so appreciative.

Fig.276: Prue our hostess, a bird enthusiast

Fig.277: Vintage Car Club Zimbabwe – Harare honoured us by bringing their cars and friendship

Fig.278: The braai was enjoyed by all

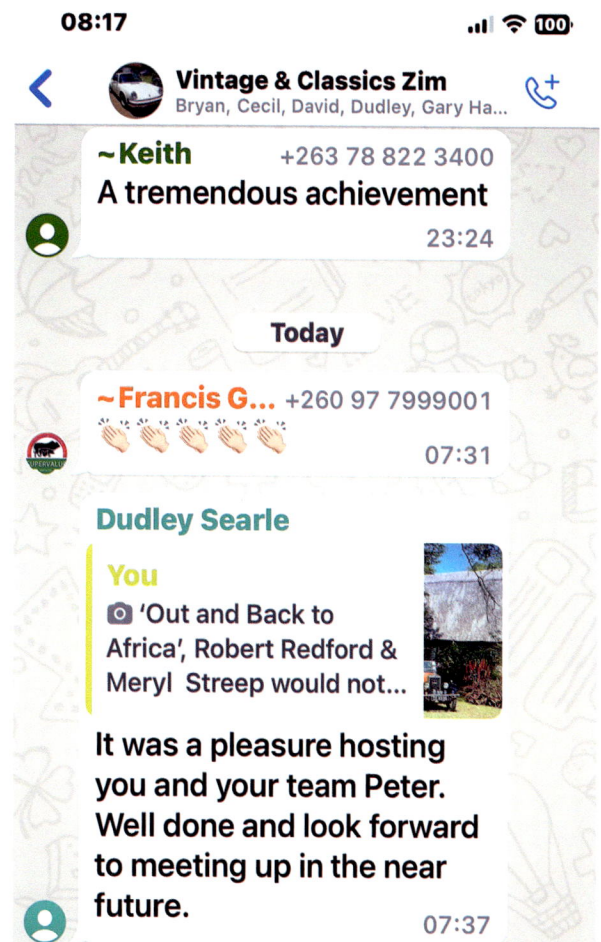

Fig.279: We had a wonderful stay there

The first stop was in the city centre, to locate the 9th/10th owner's address. Mrs Rene Lang's address was given as Parkview, P.O. Grand Hotel, Salisbury (Fig.280). That was at the junction of First Street and Speke Avenue. Our information was that the hotel had been knocked down many years before and replaced with a new building. The area has been pedestrianised – so we had to park some distance away. David and I set off on foot to locate the site of the hotel. It proved to be quite easy with road signs, but I noticed a plaque set into the pavement engraved "First St and Speke Ave" (Fig.281). Deciding which of the four corners the hotel would have been on was based on the age and look of the replaced building compared to others (Fig.282). Street sellers had their wares laid out on the pavement in impressive order (Fig.283).

We headed for the suburb of Belvedere having obtained an old street map of the area (Fig.284) where there had been an RAF Airport during World War Two and where the 5th and 6th owners were based (Corporal Charles Edward Haines and Flight Lieutenant Graham Willy Bates, respectively). We noticed that most of the streets were named after aircraft (Lancaster, Wellington, Cessna, Boeing, Skymaster, Concorde). We came across one particularly wide, straight road called Ganges Road that was around 800 metres long (Fig.285). Surely this was the original runway? Further along the road, we spotted the Meteorological Station that is still functioning; its proximity to the Belvedere RAF base makes a lot of sense (Fig.286).

RAF pilots undertook flight training with the Rhodesia Air Training Group (RATG), part of the Empire Air Training Scheme. The RATG trained over 7,600 pilots and 2,300 navigators during the war.

Leaving the city centre we drove out to Parktown to find the 8th owner's address, (Donald Lewis Mayor) in the suburb of Waterfalls, Plot 1, Fraser Road (Fig.287). This suburb is adjacent to an industrial area with many large plots and smallholdings. In 1964 Graham had attended a Barclays Bank course in Harare (then Salisbury) and was accommodated at a smallholding in the Waterfalls area.

The roads were almost nonexistent and street names were few and far between. After a lot of driving around and asking residents, we located Fraser Road but could only assume that the original plot has been subdivided into residential stands. Number 1 is a very large stand and is now a Children's School (Fig.288). Another tick in the box.

Fig.280: Mrs Lang, 10th owner at Salisbury 1951

Fig.281: Grand Hotel First St and Speke Ave

Fig.282: The hotel has been replaced

Fig.283: Harare street sellers everywhere

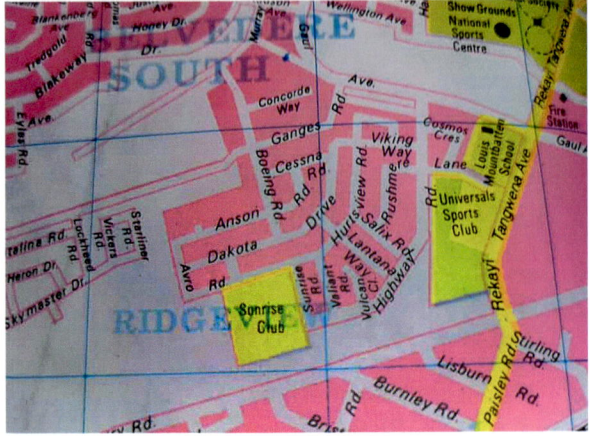

Fig.284: RAF owners; area of the airport

Fig.285: Urbanised; the original runway

Fig.286: Nearby the Meteorological Station

Fig.287: 8th owner Donald Lewis Mayor

Fig.288: Plot 1 Fraser Road 8th owner's home

Fig.289: RAF Pilots 3 and 4 Kaguvi Barracks

Fig.290: Kaguvi ex-RAF Cranborne Harare

Fig.291: Departing Pangoula Farm, Harare

As it was 15:00 we headed back to the farm via Cranborne Barracks (now Kaguvi Barracks) where during World War Two the RAF pilots Corporal Sydney John Hammond and Flight Sergeant William Owens were stationed with the Morris U750. Although the entrance is some way from the road, when we stopped to take a photo at some distance, the guard ran out waving angrily and we sped off (Figs.289, 290).

On the way back to Pangoula we stocked up with groceries and beers for the next stage of our tour. Since Dudley and Prue had gone out to a family braai, we rustled up a quick meal. When Dudley returned, we enjoyed chatting late into the night.

Day 22: 13 April – Harare to Chinhoyi (116km)

After a hearty breakfast of fruit salad and muesli followed by real ham on toast, we said our farewells and left the farm at 08:30. Dudley offered to trailer the Morris across the farm road but since it had not rained over the past two days the clay road had dried; we did not take up his offer. Instead he instructed one of his workers to lead us out on his motorcycle along a much better route to the main road (Fig.291).

We made good time, taking a rest break at 11:00 to top up the radiator. Soon we arrived at Banket, where the 7th owner of the Morris, Mary Sims, had her farm on the Glen Atholl Estate. We made numerous enquiries as to where it was located and it was difficult to know where Banket began or ended (Fig.292). Next stop was Chinhoyi (formerly Sinoia). Driving through the busy town we were greeted by loud whistling and clapping from the locals seeing the Morris (Fig.293). Our overnight accommodation was at Zebras Dazzle. The owner was friendly but a bit alternative, in tatty jeans and barefoot; she was from the Netherlands and married to a Zimbabwean. Two rooms were available: one with a double bed, the other with twin beds. But she provided an extra mattress for David. Graham and I had the two single beds in the other room where one wall was covered with wallpaper of Van Gogh's Starry Night (Fig.294).

Fig.292: Banket, 7th owner Mary Sims

Fig.293: Arriving in Chinhoyi (formerly Sinoia)

Fig.294: Zebras Dazzle B&B Chinhoyi

Fig.295: Dirk Kriel, knew the Sims family

Fig.296: Theo Pieterse's Formula Ford, right

Fig.297: Mary Sims's Glen Atholl Farm was seized

Fig.298: Glen Atholl Farm now a gold mine

Fig.299: Glen Atholl Farm, artisanal gold mine

We could easily have travelled on to Karoi, but I had been unable to find accommodation there. This stop turned out to be fortuitous as "golden balls" had clanged again. We settled down to a relaxing afternoon ahead of the more challenging trip the next day to Makuti known for potholes and numerous trucks. At 15:15 I received a phone call from Theo Pieterse in Siavonga (Zambia) that altered our plans for the afternoon.

Theo provided me with the name and address of his pal, Dirk Kriel, who apparently had known Mary Sims, the 7th owner. It was a remarkable connection via Facebook, Theo had started to follow the BTA tour on social media and something in the back of my mind rang a bell. I managed to check his profile on Facebook and to my surprise there was a photo of him with his Formula Ford racing car that I had taken during 1972 at Chingola race circuit in Zambia (Fig.296). This connection triggered a renewed friendship that developed further when we reached Siavonga.

We set out for town where Dirk owns a flour mill and bakery at the Chinhoyi industrial area, Graham and I in the Morris followed by Wayne and David in the BMW. After a bit of a run-around we located Dirk's factory. He was delighted to meet us and the Morris (Fig.295). Over a cup of tea, I informed him of the purpose of our trip and then Dirk told us his story. Back in 2002 his farm and that of Mary Sims had been taken over by Mugabe's "War Veterans", a gang of thugs. Dirk was forced out of his property but has subsequently managed to set up his business in the town. However, Mary's descendants, Gulam and Janet Sims, had had enough. They packed up and left Zimbabwe to settle in the UK. When the War Veterans attempted to farm the Glen Atholl area, to everyone's surprise, they found rich deposits of gold. The area is now an open mine – just like the Klondike gold rush with folk digging open pits and panning for gold all over (Figs.297–299)! How ironic it is that the

Sims family was unaware that they were living on a gold mine! There is still the possibility that I may locate Gulam and Janet in the UK. To date I have drawn a blank as I cannot find their names on the UK electoral role.

We headed back to Zebras Dazzle after topping up the Morris with petrol. Once again this attracted a large crowd of excited and admiring locals. The proprietor offered us a complimentary dinner: a stodgy pasta dish that filled a hole as we had, as usual, missed lunch. The ice-cream accompanied by a Fanta orange cleared our throats.

Day 23: 14 April – Chinhoyi to Makuti (175km)

We set out for Makuti at 08:00 after breakfast, knowing that the day was going to be challenging and mentally prepared for the bad road ahead. Not far from town are the Chinhoyi Caves (Fig.300) where in 1980 I had sub-aqua dived in the crystal clear water of the amazing sinkhole. All except David had visited the caves before and as he had never ventured north of the Limpopo, we were surprised that he was not interested in seeing this fantastic geological occurrence – so we moved on.

Back on the road a "ting-ting" noise emanated from the bonnet. I discovered that a loose segment of the fibre fanbelt was impacting the radiator housing. After securing it, we pressed on towards Karoi but a little later the noise returned but louder. The fan support bracket was now loose causing the fan blade to rub against the honeycomb radiator fins. This fan bracket had been repaired and remodelled twice before we left Cape Town; so it was quite a surprise that it failed again. I could not risk it coming away and damaging the radiator; so I removed the fanbelt completely. This meant losing the cooling effect of the fan; now we had to monitor the temperature and oil pressure gauges even more closely.

Lower oil pressure is a sensitive indicator of an overheating engine. I was also aware that my 1933 MG J2 with basically the same engine has no radiator fan. Surely if the ambient temperature is sufficiently low, we should be okay? A calculated risk I was forced to take.

On the rather poor and remote road to Makuti we were surprised to find a toll booth where they are demanding a toll of US$2 for each vehicle. It was quite amusing when the operator asked if the Morris was a motor bike. Perhaps we could have avoided the toll fee. After coming across the second toll of the morning, and given the road conditions, we could only wonder what we were paying for – certainly not maintenance. Along the way there were large fields of maize, it was no surprise to see a huge bank of grain silos, showing that some farming is taking place in Zimbabwe these days (Fig.301). On the way to Kariba, we saw many adverts for "marvellous fishing worms" – obviously for fishermen (Fig.302)! A road sign said Lion's Den – a name that both Graham and I were familiar with, yet had not thought about for many years.

Between Chinhoyi and Makuti there were three police roadblocks that we approached with trepidation. Contrary to reports of the police demanding dollars for the slightest reason, they were all smiles and adulation and requested to take photos of the Morris; our little car certainly opened doors for us.

For at least 50 kilometres between Karoi and Makuti the road was the worst we had experienced – with potholes, sinkholes and troughs stretching right across the road. The road edges had crumbled away so that in places there was a 10 inch drop-off from the jagged edge of the tar. This made the road very narrow in places and meeting one of the many heavy trucks could result in us being squeezed into a pothole. Dodging potholes required driving on the wrong side of the road at times. Later Graham said he thought I enjoyed the challenge of successfully overcoming the road conditions but he always kept a firm hold on his door. We had been warned about this section even before leaving Cape Town and, when any local was asked, they confirmed that it was one of the very worst roads – it certainly lived up to its reputation. However, we were amazed to see some sort of road maintenance taking place. For about 100 metres workers were repairing the road, carrying a mix of tar and aggregate in buckets and then manually compacting the potholes. No mechanisation, not even a wheelbarrow was used; it was all very primitive and the repair was likely to be short-lived but they were doing something! This was the only occasion over the whole trip in both countries that we came across roadworks.

We arrived at Makuti at 12:30 and while I was unable to avoid hitting a couple of bad potholes we arrived in Makuti with all four wheels and springs intact and pointing in the same direction (Fig.303)! To locate our overnight accommodation required some searching over rough dirt roads – the Makuti Lodge was in a remote area. It is a picturesque building in a peaceful bush setting, constructed in

Fig.300: Chinhoyi Caves – I was there in 1980

Fig.301: Grain silos on the road to Makuti

Fig.302: Worms for fishing sold on the road

Fig.303: The road to Makuti was awful

Fig.304: Makuti Lodge B&B, lots of bird life

Fig.305: Makuti to Kariba and Siavonga

rock and with a thatched roof – a classic "Out of Africa" homestead (Fig.304). It was well appointed with a comprehensive kitchen and comfortable rooms and, as the only occupants, we had the run of the place. There was a swimming pool and a large natural garden area. The Zimbabwean caretaker showed us around to our assigned twin bedrooms with adjoing bathroom, we did the usual split.

There was a lovely stoep where we could sit in comfort and survey the African countryside and enjoy a cold beer. What a pleasure! We realised that there were several birds in the bush garden and environs; so Graham and I went out with our cameras, clicking away and adding to my Zimbabwe collection. Wayne prepared a simple pasta dinner and we all retired early.

Day 24: 15 April – Makuti to Siavonga via Kariba, Zambia (88km)

The beds were comfortable, there were no mosquitoes and the showers were hot. Arising early for a bit of bird photography and a quick breakfast, we set out from this very convenient overnight accommodation (Fig.305). This stage of our journey would be exciting and crossing the great Kariba Dam wall into Zambia would get us closer to our goal. It was 07:15 but still fresh, the best time of the day. After refuelling, the Morris was hard to hold back: the road was in good condition, we met very little traffic and there were no large trucks. The drive through familiar scenic bush country was most enjoyable and the large baobabs became more frequent (Fig.306). We spotted a large raptor flying out of a nearby tree circling above us but as our cameras were packed no decent photos were possible. We quickly unpacked the cameras, as we should have done earlier!

We made our usual radiator top-up stop as the ambient heat built up. The altitude dropped steadily as the road wound down into the Zambezi Valley. The Morris enjoyed some long steep descents that allowed the radiator to cool. We reached the outskirts of Kariba at 09:30, stopping to photograph the lake as soon as it became visible and reminding ourselves that it is the longest man-made lake in the world, going back some 114 miles towards the Victoria Falls (Fig.307). After some twists and turns, we arrived at the Kariba Dam wall for Customs and Immigration. By 10:00 it had become blisteringly hot.

As I had always wanted to have a video recording of the Morris crossing the wall of the Kariba Dam, I needed to work out the logistics. Based on past border crossings, I calculated that, once we had been processed by Zimbabwe's Immigration and Customs and obtained the essential stamps on a piece of paper, there was no time constraint to exit. David and I visited the observation point in the BMW to see if it was practical and if the video would capture the Morris in motion (Fig.308).

In 1959 I was returning from the Central African Jamboree from Salisbury to Kitwe with fellow scouts in Scout Master John Cheverton's Chevrolet. He decided to swing past Kariba Dam that was still in construction. This was a rare opportunity: my trusty Kodak Brownie camera recorded the image (Fig.309). The top of the wall was yet to be cast.

First, we had to be processed. Immigration went smoothly, and all was going to plan until the police (Interpol), who were housed in a tent away from the main building, wanted to see the original Vehicle Registration Certificate of the BMW and the South African Police Clearance certificate (neither of which I had – apart from a 2021 police-stamped car document). They seemed to accept the older stamped document but were not happy with the colour copy as it had not been certified and things were not looking good. After some pleading, I explained the purpose of the trip and that it was a charity drive. We apologised very humbly for not having the appropriate documents. The two officers got together and after some discussion eventually said, "As you guys are all old, we will let you through." For once age was on our side!

Chapter 7.1

Zambia – Central Province

Day 24: 15 April – Kariba Dam crossing to Siavonga, Zambia

Welcome to Zambia! At last we had the stamped papers for two persons in each vehicle. It was time to put our cunning plan into action: Wayne and David would go to the observation point while Graham and I crossed the Zimbabwe border barrier. The whole plan was nearly derailed when, apart from the stamped paper, we had to show passports. Damn! Graham had left his passport in the BMW that was now somewhere up the mountain beyond the range of our walkie-talkie. The official would not permit him to proceed. The only option was for Graham to wait at the barrier until Wayne and David collected him. However, their stamped paper was for two persons not three. Would that be a problem? The security chap said he would remember and allowed me to drive through alone. Poor Graham had to sit in the hot sun at the boom feeling rather frustrated at this silly omission.

I waited for David to get into position at the observation point. Luckily the radios worked and I commenced driving the Morris along the wall. Due to all the civil works being done only one vehicle is permitted at a time as it is a single-lane road. I proceeded slowly to the midpoint of the dam wall, then waited until the BMW and trailer arrived.

The Kariba Dam is currently undergoing repair and is a massive construction site. Extensive work is being done in the area below the dam wall: the spillway water has impacted and undermined the wall's foundations, causing erosion (Fig.310). They have built a coffer dam at the base of the wall to retain the Zambezi River and there is a huge hole in it. At some stage they will pump the water out of the hole and presumably fill it. The plan is to redirect the spillway water over a sort of slide or chute so as not to impact the foundations of the dam in future.

I recall that in 1978 I undertook a consultancy assignment to investigate the cause of metal debris in the oil filter on one of the 150MW Francis turbines. This involved going inside the dam wall. At one point we came to a huge oval steel plate with water dribbling from its base. Our chaperon told me that behind that gate is 114 miles of water! It was a memorable experience but, due to tight security and the fact that we were in a war situation with the then Rhodesia UDI (having dropped the Southern from its name), I was not permitted to take photos. All we could do was sketch our findings. We concluded that there was not a serious problem as cosmetic weld debris had lifted from the bearing surface ending up in the oil filter basket.

Fig.306: Brilliant early morning drive downhill

Fig.307: First sighting of Kariba Lake

Fig.308: Nyami Nayami Serpent God – Kariba Hydroelectric Dam from Zimbabwe, 2023

Fig.309: I was here in June 1959, the dam was still under construction, it opened in1960

Fig.310: Repairs to fix spillway hole, April 2023

Fig.311: Crossing the dam wall 15 April

Fig.312: Arriving in Zambia, my old home!

Fig.313: Customs official amazed at the car

Fig.314: Lake Safari Lodge, Zambia, superb

Fig.315: Relaxing after an exciting days drive

Fig.316: Crystal Diamond, Sid's granddaughter

Back to today's venture: the top of the wall roadway along the west lane was covered with masses of equipment and cranes, reducing the width of the single lane. This could be a problem: I parked the Morris close to a chained-off area at the centre section of the wall but leaving sufficient passing space. A Health and Safety Officer asked me to move on, but after some discussion and the usual selfie with the Morris she permitted me to wait until the team arrived. The charming little Morris had done the trick again (Fig.311). Graham then joined me in the Morris while David positioned himself at the Zambian end of the wall to record us driving along the remainder of the dam wall and up around the mountain into Zambia. I was back in the country where I grew up. Home at last!

We arrived at Zambia's Customs and Immigration at 11:45 (Fig.312). It was a relatively modern, air-conditioned building and clean. The officials were in uniform – a pleasant change compared to the Zimbabwe post where it was difficult to know who was who in civilian clobber. Processing through immigration was straightforward except when an official asked me, "Where are you going?" I replied, "Kitwe." "How long?" Thinking she was just interested in my Kitwe visit I replied, "Five days." She then stamped my passport with an entry visa for 5 days instead of the required 25 days – shock and horror! Graham and Wayne pointed this out to me and, when I informed her of the misunderstanding, she said it was in the system and could only be changed by the office in Lusaka. No amount of pleading would alter her decision. Meanwhile I moved on to process the vehicles at Customs. Thankfully, Graham and Wayne did some smooth-talking: the lady wandered off and returned with my passport extended to a 25 day stay. Phew! We later realised that the computers being down had worked in my favour: the network had not been updated and the entry could easily be changed (golden balls went "clang clang" again).

Our next problem was that all payments for third-party vehicle insurance and toll and carbon tax had to be made in Kwacha. They did not accept US dollars or British pounds. Fortunately, Wayne had some Kwacha, which saved me having to go to the money dealer in the car park to exchange forex to Kwacha at a questionable rate. With the computer systems offline, they had to photocopy all legal documents for their records. During this delay Graham, Wayne and David stayed near the Morris chatting to an off-duty customs official who was very interested in the history of the car (Fig.313).

I emerged from the building at 13:00 only to be called back to make another payment: for the Zambian Road Maintenance Certificate. Surely was this yet another scam? Later it proved to be an essential document as it was demanded at every toll gate where the most recent receipt was stapled to it. As in Zimbabwe, these money-making exercises had never been there in the days before independence – we used to pay income tax and car tax for the very purpose of having well-maintained roads. Granted, that was another time and culture, but neglecting the maintenance of the transport infrastructure inhibits a country's trade and growth.

At long last we made our way along rough roads to Siavonga and the Kariba Safari Lodge (Fig.314). We thought we had landed in heaven. The lodge is like a five-star hotel: each of us had a spacious en-suite room, with a double bed and a large glass door across the front, leading to a personal balcony overlooking the lake. Wow! This was luxury compared to some of the places we had stayed at over the previous 3 weeks. We met the owner, Maurice Diamond, the grandson of Sid Diamond who had owned most of the stores in Kitwe when I lived there and where my mother had worked. I knew Maurice's late father (of the same name) as well as his aunt, Maxine Sifis (née Diamond), with whom I am in regular contact and who had kindly arranged our stay. After a "meet and greet" we enjoyed welcome beers in the hotel's impressive modern bar (Fig.315).

Graham, Wayne and David retired to their rooms while I joined Maurice's family and friends and his sister Crystal (Fig.316). We chatted all afternoon; the kids enjoyed the pool while we were plied with drinks and delicious snacks, especially Kariba langoustine. Later, being fully satiated, I decided to skip dinner and suggested that the team should enjoy a meal on their own. They had fresh Kariba bream fillets that were apparently delicious.

From our balconies at sunset we watched the kapenta fishing boats heading out from several harbours for the night's fishing. The beat of the single-piston diesel engines transmits over the water and can be rather disturbing. The boats operate through the night until sunrise, but the noise did not bother us. Each boat has a power plant to supply the bright neon lights that attract the miniscule kapenta fish (Fig.317). Once on land the fish are laid out to dry on a large rack in the early morning and due to the high level of sunlight and low humidity, they are ready for bagging by midday (Fig.318). Later we learned that Theo Pieterse makes the kapenta fishing boats.

The kapenta is a small high protein fish that was introduced to Lake Kariba in 1967 from Lake Tanganyika where it is exploited in huge quantities and marketed fresh or dried. It enhances the staple diet of maize for the local population. Many people have made a fortune investing in the industry. Some resort owners on the lakeshore rent out their own small fleets of kapenta boats that the locals operate.

The clear sky and blue water, the warm evening, the stunning sunset – it was really "heaven on earth". While Graham was sitting on his balcony writing up our daily diary, he counted at least 46 boats with their twinkling lights. It had been a momentous day: successfully recording the crossing of the Kariba Dam wall, overcoming the entry documentation for Zambia, and now relaxing in a wonderful part of Africa. We had checked off all the past Morris owners' addresses and were now on the last leg of our trip to take Chilupala home near Kitwe, some 545 kilometres away! Staying at such a spectacular place for a few days was a real treat that would allow us to take a breather. But as we would learn in the morning, more adventures were awaiting us.

Day 25: 16 April – Siavonga, Kariba Lake

After an excellent night's sleep, most of the team were up early. At sunrise I popped my head around the wall of my balcony to find Graham in his pyjamas watching the sun rising over the lake. We made our way to the dining hall for an excellent breakfast that would keep us charged for the rest of the day. Then Theo Pieterse phoned to tell us to get ready: he was taking us on a cruise and would collect us in his Toyota Prado. We stocked up with drinks in an icebox and then headed to Theo's home where there were several boats bobbing about in his private harbour (Fig.319). A JCB digger and D9 bulldozer were parked next to his large boat-building workshop. We boarded his 40 foot motorboat powered by twin Perkins diesel engines and made our way to open water (Fig.320). I had not met Theo since 1972 at the Chingola Race Track where he had built a Formula Ford racing car that I had photographed. I thanked him for all his subsequent assistance in finding Dirk Kriel (Fig.321). Theo then offered the wheel to Graham – much to his delight (Fig.322). After crossing the bay near the shoreline Theo took back control so that Graham and I could photograph "coastal" birds. We passed numerous bream farms where tilapia fish fingerlings are enclosed in floating circular nets, then fed and grown to table size for local restaurants. Travelling slowly along the edge of the shoreline and islands, we saw locals whose subsistence depends on their numerous gill nets. I also spotted a beautifully crafted bamboo basket being lowered into the water (Fig.323) by a Tonga fisherman. They use gill nets suspended from plastic bottles as floats. Unfortunately, the mesh size is not controlled and the nets capture all fish sizes, sadly reducing the fish population.

Along the lakeshore wherever there is a sheltered inlet, kapenta boats are moored alongside small villages. Theo informed us that there had been a licensing procedure but, with the new government, this has fallen away and overfishing of the kapenta is reducing the stock.

We had excellent sightings of the African Fish Eagle – I managed to photograph one carrying a fish (Fig.324). After 4 hours we returned to the harbour where Theo invited us to his home and his wife Gladys offered us welcome cold beers.

Theo has a photo collection of his many oil paintings, some of which have been sold in the United States for as much US$60,000 (Fig.325). His animal paintings are excellent, but sadly his eyesight is failing and he can no longer achieve the same standard. In addition to his remarkable artistic talent, he has built racing cars, boats, farms, engines and is a qualified pilot to boot. He offered me a small painting of a leopard and after exchanging some cash I have brought my precious acquisition home. Later I learned that Theo worked with the famous Norman Carr in the Luangwa Valley, and he was a friend of the famous wildlife artist, David Shepherd. David gave Theo painting lessons, which explains how his artistic skill developed. I included a bit extra to cover the cost of the fuel for the boat and the car since he had given us such a special experience. Gladys drove us back to the lodge just before sunset.

The road between the lodge and Theo's house is rather rough with many ups and downs, twists and turns. We passed through two small settlements where shops and market stalls have encroached onto the main road. Between the houses along most roads we saw many small racks and mats of kapenta drying. Most of the community are in some way involved in the kapenta trade; their livelihoods depend on it.

There is a huge divide between the locals living some 500 metres away from the lake and the walled-off tourist hotels on the lakeshore – the hotels are luxurious, but they do provide employment. Gladys told us that these primitive settlements were originally squatter camps, but the government has permitted them to become permanent – a function of their economic situation.

Fig.317: Kapenta fishing Kariba lake, Zambia

Fig.318: Kapenta drying, locals' staple diet

Fig 319: Theo Pieterse's private dock – Wayne & Graham delivering the beers!

Fig.320: Cruising Lake Kariba, Zambia

Fig.321: Theo's motor launch on the lake

Fig.322: Captain Graham at the wheel

Fig.323: Tonga fisherman, handmade basket

Fig.324: African Fish Eagle with fish

We needed to return to the lodge before sunset as I had planned to have the Morris photographed on the edge of the lake. I positioned the Morris at the base of the slipway with its rear wheel in the water. There is a saying that once you have drunk the water of the Zambezi or Kafue you will never get Africa out of your system. David took several photos at various stages as the sun went down including some with Maurice Diamond sitting in the driver's seat. It was "Maurice in Morris" – very appropriate (Fig.326)! Later Maurice joined us for a couple of drinks before dinner. The end of another enjoyable day, especially our time on the lake.

Fig.325: Theo Pieterse is also an artist

Fig.326: Maurice Diamond, our host

Day 26: 17 April – Siavonga, lower Zambezi

We had to have an early breakfast, because Theo had insisted on taking us on a drive along the lower Zambezi on a stretch of river below the dam wall but upstream from Chirundu. Arriving at the Tamarind bush camp we had the rare opportunity to get photos of a Southern Banded Snake Eagle sitting in a tree overhanging the Zambezi. We then followed the river downstream close to several villages where the land was parched and devoid of any grass – the Tonga villagers still sweep the ground clean around their huts. There were several thatched grain storage huts and even kilns, perhaps for making charcoal (Figs.327–329). Away from the Zambezi, the countryside around the villages is totally barren due to the hot dry climate and the foraging goats who eat anything and everything. We explored many roads and forest areas, seeing several species of birds. Theo informed us that he and his son Reynard built a 30 foot steel boat for the local chief. For payment he was given the land; it has been officially registered and he holds the title deed. This seems to be the way things are done in rural Africa.

It was getting late in the afternoon and I asked Theo if we could return before sunset. Driving rally style in his Prado Theo put his foot flat, applying his skills as a former racing driver to give us a ride to remember and arriving in good time. Again, we drove the Morris down the slipway but this time we waited for the sun to set, giving a wonderful red glow across the lake. This produced some stunning photos of the Morris (Fig.330) against the background of sky illuminated in red, almost matching the colour of the car. To create this stunning photo, we used "fill-in" flash.

I then presented Theo with a BTA mug (Fig.331) thanking him for making our stay in the "real" Africa so memorable. Pleased to receive the mug, Theo became quite emotional as we bade him a fond farewell.

We met Maurice Diamond for a drink in the bar where I also presented him with a BTA mug and one for his wife, Cilla, and his sister, Crystal (Fig.332). Unfortunately, it was bedtime for the kids; so the two ladies were unable to attend. I also handed Maurice a bottle of Stettyn Pinotage wine, that I had carried from the Cape, as a token of our appreciation for his generosity in hosting us. After dinner with Maurice, we said farewell as we planned to leave early the next morning while it was still cool.

Fig.327: Tonga village, lower Zambezi

Fig.328: Tonga village grain storage

Fig.329: Tonga Kilns, lower Zambezi

Fig.330: Farewell Kariba, my toe in the Zambezi

Fig.331: Thanks, Theo, for your hospitality

Fig.332: Thanks, Maurice Diamond, our host

Day 27: 18 April – Siavonga to Lusaka (190km)

We had packed most of our equipment in the trailer the previous day and we were up early; we settled our bar account and then departed from Kariba Safari Lodge at 06:15. The morning was cool and conditions were perfect for the hills that the Morris would have to tackle (Fig.333). I had decided that if it became too hot when climbing out of the Zambezi Valley escarpment, we would remove the bonnet of the Morris to aid cooling. Not far from Siavonga we passed a heavily potholed stretch of road, but after that the going was pretty good with hardly any traffic. The cool fresh morning air made us feel very much at home – especially as the scenic countryside was so lush at that time of the year. With the familiar bush and the many baobabs all along the way, Graham and I were both reminded that this is the Africa that we love and miss!

After an hour of making good progress, we came to a straight stretch of road leading to a makeshift road barrier made up of rusty dented oil drums, poles and tyres. There was a derelict building nearby, supposedly an office. The chaps in plain clothes demanded 50 Kwacha per vehicle for road tax. This was highly questionable, but we had no option but to pay what they claimed was a District Council tax. Eventually, we arrived at the main junction between Siavonga and the Chirundu–Lusaka Road where we topped up with fuel (Figs.334, 335) at a rather new modern petrol station. We noticed an increase in the roadside sale of charcoal; this practice is decimating the forests and there seems to be no control of this impending environmental disaster (Fig.336). The next few kilometres of road were shocking – the potholes and trenches proved to be among the most treacherous we had to negotiate – yet, the scenery was stunning and we noticed the mix of traditional and modern housing at the same site (Fig.337, 338).

There were several steep, almost continuous, inclines to climb out of the Zambezi River escarpment with several large 26-wheeler trucks coming down the hills in the opposite direction. These trucks are subject to brake failure due to long downhills and overheated brakes; if they fail to lower their gearbox ratio before starting the descent, they can lose control and become a danger to themselves and oncoming traffic. We had been warned that the road was treacherous and within a few kilometres we passed several sites of road carnage (Fig.339). At one spot a very large truck was parked across half of the road – the truck's cab had jack-knifed, and the remains of a small pick-up were crushed and mangled beneath it (Fig.340). We found out that six people had died there about 3 weeks earlier; yet there had been no attempt to remove the vehicles or clean up the road to make it safer again. Perhaps this was left as a warning sign to other drivers.

As we came over the brow of a hill the police waved down the Morris and the BMW. They claimed that the BMW was speeding at 60.1 on a 60km/h stretch of road! They showed us on their camera that the amount exceeded was just 0.1km/h. Wayne and I explained that as electronics engineers we understand the technology: 0.1 is not excessive speeding or even a valid number! Furthermore, our vehicles could not have been speeding as we were heavily loaded and going uphill. I think they saw us as soft targets but realised that we had "local knowledge" and were not an easy source of Kwacha. We went on our way, leaving them empty handed.

Fig.333: Sunrise drive Siavonga to Chirundu

Fig.334: Next stop Lusaka via Kafue

Fig.335: Zambia had many new fuel stations

Fig.336: Sadly, charcoal is sold everywhere

Fig.337: Stunning scenery in Chirundu valley

Fig.338: Traditional and modern Chirundu

Fig.339: Warning: the road is treacherous

Fig.340: Shocking highway accident, 6 dead

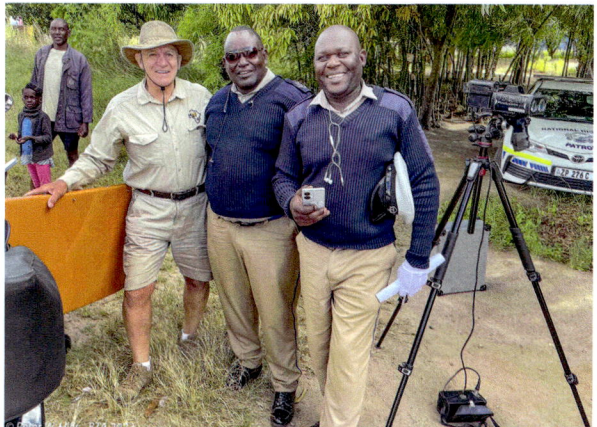

Fig.341: Morris stopped for speeding!

Fig.342: Zambia police "photo shoot"

Fig.343: Approaching Kafue Bridge

Fig.344: Lower Kafue feeds the Zambezi

Fig.345 Yet another vehicle checkpoint

Fig.346: Lusaka Car Club escorted us

Fig.347: Arriving to the chaos of Lusaka

Fig.348: Our escort's Mercedes was shunted

An hour later we were hailed down at another speed check; this time they called the Morris over to the opposite side of the road where their vehicle and camera were set up. This was just a ruse for them to admire the Morris. The overweight senior officer asked to be photographed sitting in the driver's seat of the Morris. Because of his size I needed to lever him in (Figs.341, 342). We then had a group photo with the police officers, who were all good natured, and we were soon on our way.

Shortly afterwards we arrived at Kafue, a town that hardly existed in the 1960s when Graham lived in Lusaka in 1965. He used to fish below the bridge where there are now quite fancy houses, even a houseboat. I paused on the bridge for Graham take a couple of photos of the river and he got out to get a better shot (Figs.343, 344). But as he returned two fellows in military fatigues apprehended him and frog-marched him to a tented army camp nearby to explain to a senior officer why he was taking photos. He said that he had lived in Lusaka in the 1960s and just wanted a couple of shots of the river as a reminder of where he used to fish. The officer smiled and said, "Thank you for your cooperation, you may go." Rather stressed, Graham hurried back to the Morris and we headed rapidly towards Lusaka. We remembered this sort of security in pre-Zimbabwe days with terrorist incursions and curfews in Zambia. Such practice seems outdated and unnecessary today, especially when we had free rein at Kariba and at Victoria Falls Bridge later.

As we approached Chilanga there were more vehicle checkpoints with traffic stretching back over a kilometre – the stopping and starting caused the Morris to overheat. Eventually we got to the front and were waved though (Fig.345). What the checking was all about was a mystery.

I had been in contact with the Lusaka Car Club who wished to escort the Morris into the city to our accommodation. I advised them of our progress by phone and just outside the Chilanga Cement Company we stopped off the road at the planned meeting spot. While we were there, a lady travelling in the opposite direction saw the Morris and came rushing back to have a look as she had been following us on my Instagram posts. Betty arrived in a cloud of dust in her 4×4 – very aptly named "Volcano". Soon afterwards René, Bruce and Andy of the LCC arrived and the obligatory group photo was taken (including Betty) (Fig.346).

Approaching the "chaos" of Lusaka, the capital of Zambia (Fig.347), we were very grateful for their assistance as the road system was new to us. Gary kindly led the convoy in his fine red MGB to the home of Ken and Mairi Cummins, our hosts for the next 2 nights. The route to avoid the city was rather circuitous and littered with speed bumps every 100 metres or so. Progress was very slow and the many gear changes caused the Morris to overheat. Suddenly, we heard a bang: René in his classic Mercedes had slowed for a speed bump and been shunted by a modern minibus, causing significant damage (Fig.348). They needed to wait for the police but as it was quite hot they said we should proceed to the Cummins home. Entering their property was through the blanked off large security gate with a local guard, which was now common. Wherever we travelled we saw many roadside businesses welding large steel security gates.

I had not seen Ken and Mairi since 2008 and there was much catching up to do (Fig.349). We had been friends since the early 1980s. After a couple of most welcome beers at Ken's pub, Wayne and David set off to get the Morris's hood support brackets welded as they had broken once again. Wayne's description of "engineering Zambia-style" was highly amusing:

"Repairing the two brackets was an experience of note. David and I were taken to the back streets of Lusaka to an area I would never have gone to on my own. I met a welder called Zebbie and, after showing him the bracket, he agreed that I could use his equipment to repair it. This is where the fun began. We were expected to work on a 2×3 metre concrete slab on the ground. They had only a large angle grinder to remove the existing weld. So I asked if he had a vice to clamp the bracket. Zebbie brought the vice, which was also placed on the ground. After setting the bracket up in the vice, I asked for the welding machine and a welding helmet. He gave me the spectacles that he was using but when the electrode took the first strike, I thought my head was going to burst. I then realised that I had been given a pair of ordinary sunglasses, not the automatic darkening type. As such I could not use his equipment; so I supervised while he did the welding. I looked into Zebbie's eyes and thought he was going to bleed to death. In what was an open-air storage-cum-storeroom another welder was building a braai, with no goggles or welding helmet, and we thought he too was going to bleed to death through his eyes. All that was left for me to do was to tidy up the weld to attempt to make the bracket respectable, pay the man 100 Kwacha and get the hell out of there."

The reason the brackets had failed again was the constant bouncing of the hood on each bracket due to the bumpy roads. To solve this, we secured both sides of the canopy struts to the brackets with cable ties. Later I discovered that on the early Morris tourers leather straps were fitted as standard to the brackets for this very purpose.

Fig.349: Mairi and Ken Cummins, Lusaka hosts

Fig.350: Bobby v d Merwe's Motor Museum

Fig.351: Lusaka experts inspect Chilupala

Fig.352: Dinner party with old friends, Lusaka

Fig.353: Thanks, Bobby v d Merwe

Fig.354: A scuba-diving friend, Gerard Fagan

Fig.355: Mairi Cummins, ex-Kitwe friend

Fig.356: Ken Cummins gets Cape Wine

Day 28: 19 April – Lusaka, car museum

After breakfast Andy Legg collected us to go to Bobby van der Merwe's home where he had a car museum. I accompanied Andy in his MGB and the others went in the BMW. The car museum was some way down the old Leopard Hill Road housed in a former dairy that has been renovated and looked quite modern (Fig.350). It contained an amazing collection of cars, perhaps more than 50 vehicles including tractors, trucks and a range of vintage motorcycles and outboard motors. There were classic cars in good running condition – a 1936 Stepside Chevrolet, a Pontiac Firebird and a Corvette.

There was also a Honda Accord with a bullet hole in the windscreen and into the seat – luckily the Somali diplomat who owned it survived the assassination attempt. There was a London taxi that still had its charge meter intact. The open-top Cadillac in need of love had been owned by President Kaunda, Zambia's first president. Apart from being a mechanic and car builder, Bobby has made all sorts of novelty items from scrap, such as tables with glass tops mounted on an engine block and a hand basin mounted on a gearbox.

On our way to our lodging we stopped at the Zambian Coffee Company for coffee and a bite to eat. They use only Zambian coffee beans and the coffee was excellent. Ken and Mairi Cummins had arranged a dinner party for us that evening. Guests included Bobby van der Merwe and his fiancée Corinne Thornicroft, the artist Quentin Allen, an older German lady named Brigetta, Gerard Fagan and his partner, Julie Sammons. After inspecting the Morris (Fig.351) we adjourned for dinner; thanks to Mairi and Ken.

I had not seen Gerard or Quentin since the early eighties; so there was much to catch up on. A most enjoyable evening with lots of chatting and reminiscing about the old Kitwe days and the Copperbelt.

In conversation with Gerard, Graham discovered that when he worked in Lusaka in 1965 he had known a Derek Gordon from Barclays Bank. They subsequently made contact via WhatsApp. With the BTA Team wearing our shirts the obligatory group photo was taken to record a special gathering (Fig.352). After dinner I presented Bobby, Ken and Mairi, and Gerard with BTA mugs (Figs.353–356) and a bottle of Stettyn wine to our hosts. They insisted that I sign each mug with a permanent marker pen.

Day 29: 20 April – Lusaka to Kabwe (139km)

In order to miss the early morning traffic we left after a light breakfast – only to encounter traffic that became progressively heavier as we approached the main Cairo Road. At a large, complicated traffic circle I was unsure of the exit and ended up going in the wrong direction on Cairo Road! We had to travel at least 1km before being able to do an about-turn. Wayne radioed that he needed to get fuel and we assumed that he would follow us to a petrol station. Graham and I were concentrating so hard on avoiding the heavy traffic that we did not notice Wayne and David passing the Morris. We were amazed to see this on our dash-cam later.

The situation turned into a complete farce (Fig.357). Realising that the BMW was no longer following, I pulled into a petrol station on the main road to the Copperbelt. I kept trying to make contact on the walkie-talkie but there was no response. Worried that they had broken down we back-tracked to the last communication point, stopping at three service stations along the way to check whether the BMW had been there. Eventually, having waited for 1½ hours, we decided to continue to Kabwe as they knew it was our next destination for petrol.

This drive was quite risky with so much traffic and the BMW no longer protecting our rear – also rather worrying and frustrating! Fortunately, we made good time despite stopping now and then in the hope that they would come along. Still silence on the walkie-talkie (Fig.358): where had they got to?

People had advised us that the road between Lusaka and Ndola was poor but the Kabwe section was quite good with only the occasional pothole. We had been conditioned to what was a bad road or worse – so "good" is open to interpretation. We reached Kabwe at 14:00 (formerly Broken Hill). While we were topping up with petrol the walkie-talkie suddenly crackled into life. What a relief! Wayne and David had made their own way to Kabwe and were parked about a block away. At the time I was quite annoyed that they had not followed our motoring protocol, especially as they were supposed to protect the Morris. They thought we had seen them passing us and assumed we would follow them. Had Wayne been more patient, I would have stopped at the next convenient petrol station for them as we usually did; they need not have passed us on such a busy road. When Wayne had filled up the BMW, his GPS took him on a short cut that we had missed; he had assumed that we were ahead. Hot, bothered, annoyed and relieved, we made our way to the Kabwe Safari Lodge (Fig.59). The solution was simple: a couple of ice-cold beers in the bar – always good for cooling down emotions. Thankfully we were back on plan and all together again.

Later in the afternoon, when it was cooler, Graham and I took the Morris into town to look for the location of the Boon Hotel near the railway line next to the main road into Broken Hill. This was where Gilg and Kay had stayed on their epic trip in 1933 (Figs.360, 361) from Liverpool, England to Cape Town, South Africa. No sign – the whole area has been given over to shops.

I wanted to accomplish a curiosity of the past. We drove around Kabwe and its parks seeking the ex-Mulungushi Steam Traction Engine. In 1928 this had transported the Prince of Wales to officially inaugurate the Mulungushi hydroelectric power station to supply electricity to the Broken Hill Mine. The mine was under development at that time. It was named after the Australian mine with similar lead and zinc deposits. I first saw this massive traction engine and trailer abandoned in the bush when

I visited the Mulungushi Power Station in 1969 in order to test their inclined hoist ropes (Fig.362). In 1970 when I next visited only the trailer remained in the bush (Fig.363). I was told that the steam engine had been rescued. In 1980 I photographed the painted machine that had been placed in the Kabwe City Park (Fig.364). I had hoped to see it again but despite asking many locals we could not locate it. I worry that this historic machine may have been melted down to make railway brake shoes at the failed Chinese plant set up for the TanZam or Tazara Railway, 1,870 kilometres from Kapiri Mposhi to Dar es Salaam. No one could tell us its fate or whether it was still in the country. By chance in August 2024 I learned from Tony Bowler living in Wimbledon (an ex Kabwe schoolteacher) that it had been taken to South Africa for restoration. I will attempt to establish its status.

We then visited the Zambia Railway Headquarters that had a 1940s steam locomotive positioned just beyond the entrance. Security would not permit us to enter and as the sun was in our eyes, photography was a challenge. Our next target was to locate the Mine Club Sports Grounds where I represented the Copperbelt's Under-19 football team playing against Midlands on 7 May 1961. Despite several enquiries again we abandoned the search and returned to our lodge for another beer. It seemed we had been looking in the completely opposite direction and we would try again the next day. The lodge was comfortable with a well-maintained garden and swimming pool at its centre. We had two twin-bed rooms that were clean, had fresh linen and showers that worked. For dinner we all had T-bone steaks – a change from our usual chicken and pasta sauce.

Zambia – Copperbelt Province – Mission Accomplished

Day 30: 21 April – Kabwe to Ndola – car overheating (183km)

At breakfast, we were surprised to meet Stephen Barlow and Cheryl Hooper, the organisers of the Cecily's Fund that I was supporting. They had also spent the night at the lodge having inspected one of their charity's remote bush schools. It was quite a coincidence to bump into them. We agreed to meet again in Lusaka as we had been invited to attend the 25th anniversary celebrations of the Cecily's Fund on 27 April. Stephen kindly agreed to arrange accommodation for us.

With clearer directions we located the Mine Hospital, but still no evidence of the Mine Club and sports fields in the same area. After more enquiries we made our way to the Broken Hill Mine plant area that is on the opposite side of the Lusaka Road from our accommodation along a road that ran parallel with the railway line. No longer a tarred road, it was a potholed dirt track populated with food and vegetable stalls that had encroached along either side. It was not easy to negotiate the narrow track with people everywhere. Finally, the mine shaft headgear came into view and we made our way through broken security gates to the plant area of Kabwe (Broken Hill) Mine. The whole place is derelict – totally neglected, with all sorts of heavy machinery and piles of scrap metal rusting away. It was so disappointing to see the deterioration of what used to be an immaculately maintained yet historic power station. In 1971 I had carried out sophisticated harmonic wave analysis of their electrical system and now it was a scrap heap. We positioned the Morris in front of the mine winder building and headgear, taking what may in future be a historic photo (Figs.365, 366). Once again, we were surrounded by admirers who expressed their amazement that such a car existed, that it had travelled so far and was still going to Kitwe – "Eish!" We were running out of time to search further for the elusive Mine Club and sports ground. We returned to the main Lusaka–Copperbelt road, just managing to squeeze through the heavy traffic – predominantly trucks.

After settling our bill at the Kabwe Safari Lodge and taking a group photo (Fig.367), we refuelled the BMW and headed for Ndola. From Kabwe onwards the road lived up to all the negative reports we had been given – even exceeding what we had already experienced and expected.

We passed through the crowded Kapiri Mposhi that was famous for being a bit of a one-horse town, but no more (Figs.368, 369). In my day it had only a corrugated shack with a petrol pump and store that sold ice-cream. I remember going to Lochinvar for a scout camp in about 1956: when we stopped to fill up, the manual petrol pump had two single gallon bottles that emptied in turns. In the early days, when leaving the Copperbelt and travelling south, once you passed Kapiri Mposhi you were on the way for your holiday south.

As we approached Kapiri, there was a hold-up with lots of traffic all around. We assumed it was an accident but it was yet another police road check. Before we realised this, we had seen an old District Affairs building that I asked Graham to try get a photo of "that classic old building". He did so but a police officer appeared at the Morris immediately, grabbed Graham's camera and walked away. I was directed to park on one side while two policewomen escorted Graham to the "classic" building. Graham was in the shit again but this time it was not his fault. The detectives explained to Graham that he was being charged for taking a photo of a public building without permission. Graham pleaded ignorance and offered to delete the photo, but they would not budge or return the camera. Graham's options were to pay a fine or be officially charged. How much was he able to pay? Graham offered US$10 but they said it would be difficult to give change as they required only Kwacha. Clearly, this was a scam. After some time, I was worried and went into the office "breathing fire and brimstone" (according to Graham) and demanded to know what the issue was and why the delay. Just then another police officer with pips on his shoulders arrived.

Fig.357: Leaving Lusaka, we lost Wayne!

Fig.358: Near Kabwe, Wayne where are you?

Fig.359: Kabwe Safari Lodge (ex-Broken Hill)

Fig.360: Gilg and Kay at Boon Hotel 1933

Fig.361: Site of Boon Hotel Kabwe, Zambia

Fig.362: Search for the 1912 Steam Engine – 1969

Fig.363: Mulungushi – Engine's trailer, 1970

Fig.364: Engine moved to Kabwe Park, 1980?

Fig.365: Kabwe's lead mine now abandoned

Fig.366: Mine winder hoist mothballed

Fig.367: Leaving Kabwe for Ndola

Fig.368: The metropolis of Kapiri Mposhi

Fig.369 Kapiri Mposhi bus station

Fig.370: Zambia–Tanzania Railway Terminal

Fig.371: The plastic tar and deformation   Fig.372: Challenging driving to Ndola

I greeted him in the local Bemba tongue, which delighted him and turned a tense situation jovial. However, he said the matter was in the hands of his good lady detectives! Graham informed me that they wanted 250 Kwacha (£10). I then tossed the cash on the desk and left saying, "Enjoy the party". This seemed to upset one of the ladies but Graham retrieved his camera, deleted the photo and returned to the Morris. No receipt was issued as this would have made the whole matter official. This unpleasant experience was simply extortion, which annoyed and disappointed me as I expected Zambia to have matured after almost 60 years of independence.

Later, as we passed through the now sprawling town of Kapiri Mposhi, with shops and street traders encroaching the main highway, we were stuck in traffic and I got out of the car to take a photo of the Tanzania to Zambia Railway Terminal (Chinese-built in the late seventies) from a bridge (Fig.370). It was unchanged in comparison to a photo I took from the same position in 1980. Just my luck, it was now my turn to be in trouble – a police car going in the opposite direction pulled up; the officer wanted to charge me for obstructing the traffic. Again, I offered the traditional Bemba greeting and explained our charity tour, but he wanted me to turn around on the narrow highway that was now nose-to-tail vehicles going back as far as one could see. I said that this was impossible with the Morris's large turning circle but if they could turn around and follow us up the road we could settle things. I knew this was virtually impossible for them. Eventually I simply climbed into the Morris and drove off. They did not follow! Sadly, it appears that Zambia has not shaken off its post-independence "police state" mentality: believing that the former Rhodesia was to blame for all their problems. They also appear to view the whites as soft targets for a few extra Kwacha.

Added to the driving conditions was the volume of huge trucks. These were really frightening as they thundered by – especially when our miniscule car hardly reached the height of some truck tyres. Apart from potholes, the heavy trucks had squeezed the hot tar into ruts that at times were 4 inches (100mm) deep; it was like driving on tram rails (Figs.371, 372). Keeping the Morris stable was very tricky and dangerous; its narrow wheelbase was totally unsuited to the deformed road, especially having to cross from one lane to the next when a vehicle overtook us. It was very easy to lose control if a wheel dropped off the edge of the jagged tar that could be anything up to a 10 inch drop. This could easily destroy the tyres and or make it very difficult to return to the road. Such conditions would continue for kilometres, making that stretch of driving very stressful.

Notwithstanding the state of the road, when we arrived at a clear downhill, I needed to pick up as much speed as possible to get up the steep hill ahead. Often there would be a bridge at the base of the hills, usually with a bump on entry and exit. Once when we were barrelling down, Graham was monitoring the speedometer needle flicking over 70km/h. He recalls being shocked when I casually remarked, "Graham, at this speed we are basically out of control."

Some of the trucks were 26-wheelers with two long trailers, others were left-hand drive; on more than one occasion they almost squeezed the Morris off the road. Once I had to brake heavily to allow a truck to overtake with an oncoming truck – the swinging trailer only just missed the front of the Morris (Fig.373, 374) recorded by our dash-cam. It was a close call for a head on collision and unnecessary as the road was subsequently clear. My language at this stupidity and near miss is not printable.

Fig.373: Double trailer truck cutting-in the Morris   Fig.374: Truck avoids head on collision – JIT

After a fuel stop and our nerves had subsided, we finally arrived at the outskirts of Ndola near the Indeni Refinery, where a brother freemason, Dilip Desai, had arranged to escort us to the hotel via the least difficult route. A large crowd gathered around the Morris and again there were questions and more photos (Fig.375). Dilip kindly led us through Ndola centre, but the going was so slow that it caused the Morris to overheat, severely. Apart from the state of the road, the markets along the sides were filthy, with piles of black charcoal dust adding to the mess. We entered Ndola via an uphill underpass to a junction where the traffic light was on "Stop". The Morris stalled – usually a sign of fuel evaporation but the engine was particularly hot – it re-started momentarily but stalled again in the middle of the crossroad, holding up traffic from all sides. Suddenly, several youngsters appeared to give us a push start but when we got going one of them hung onto the rear hood and would not let go. After a few hundred metres he finally jumped away. We then chugged along but the car was not happy. In the centre of Ndola, I pulled into a service station to allow the engine to cool and top up the radiator. Back on the highway, negotiating probably the largest speed hump we had ever seen, the Morris petered out once more with no power and then refused to start again. This was very worrying. Dilip informed us that it is illegal to use a tow rope or chain in Zambia; we had to load the Morris into the trailer for the remaining 4 kilometres to our booked hotel.

Anywhere in the African bush one can come across a small, old, heavily loaded bus that has broken down and parked off the road. The frustrated passengers are all standing around or sitting on their belongings and goods on the ground next to the bus awaiting transport. Graham said that is just what we looked like! The only items missing from our scene were a bicycle, a couple of sacks of mealies, a wire cage with chickens, and a bundle of sugar cane (Fig.376).

With the Morris loaded in the trailer, we passed Ndola's new international sports stadium, an impressive sight (Fig.377). I recalled that in the late 1950s Ndola built a dual sports stadium with a concrete cycle track inside it. My pal, Roy Scott, was a sprint cyclist and I assisted him at the start of each race on the inclined track.

Fig.375: Indeni, outside Ndola many admirers

Fig.376: Chilupala stopped, heat exhaustion

Fig.377: Ndola new sports stadium

Fig.378: Protea Hotel, our most expensive!

In the 1970s the Ndola Council decided to build a more modern and larger sports stadium: they brought in the wrecking ball and flattened the existing structure. Only then did they realise there was no money to replace it and so Ndola had to wait many years before this new stadium was built to comply with the latest safety regulations for World Cup matches.

We followed Dilip's Toyota Fortuner to the Protea Marriott Hotel; it is very plush but quite a lot more expensive than I had expected (Fig.378). We were to spend 2 nights there and had no other option but to accept the expense as I planned to attend a Masonic meeting in Ndola. After settling in we had dinner at a nearby Indian restaurant, expecting it to be cheaper than our fancy hotel. Unfortunately, our experience was not positive – the quality of food and service was below expectation. Feeling tired and a bit depressed as we did not understand the Morris's condition, we headed to bed. We had come so far – yet just 42 miles to our destination and the Morris had said, "Enough is enough." But was this the end? I hoped not; I know my Morris!

Day 31: 22 April – Ndola, lodge meeting

After a comfortable good night's sleep we headed for breakfast – an excellent spread of fruit and cereals, eggs, bacon, sausage and more – certainly sufficient to last the day! We then tried to start the Morris in the trailer but to no avail: it would not fire up. I removed the spark plugs to check the compression, only to discover that there was almost none. I imagined all sorts of issues: pistons burnt through, dropped valves, leaking head gasket – what else? Because it was very awkward to investigate further in the enclosed trailer and my time was limited I decided to wait until we had a decent working area.

I needed to prepare for my Lodge meetings. After a shower I changed into my tux – the full regalia as Provincial Assistant Grand Master – one minute a bush mechanic, the next looking like the city mayor wearing a gold-plated chain. I think the chaps were impressed with the transformation. Dilip collected me for the meeting and, to my surprise, I found that the members had created a new Masonic Lodge building – so much bigger than the facility I remembered from the early eighties. It now has several meeting rooms and a large banquet hall with a kitchen attached. I had long planned to attend the Zambia Provincial Grand Lodge quarterly meeting to represent the Southern Cape Province of South Africa and many of the travel plans had been worked around their meeting date. The Provincial meeting was followed by the annual installation of Shannondale Lodge (Fig.379). It was a great honour to attend and be welcomed so warmly: in addition, I was lucky enough to win the raffle for a bottle of vintage Jameson Whiskey. There were many brethren of Indian heritage present and the banquet was Indian cuisine. The Asian brethren were amazed at my knowledge of India, the food and some basic Hindi. My dear friend David McCabe had come from Lusaka with a contingent of Provincial Lodge Officers in support. Dave was my candidate in Kitwe in about 1974 and had risen to be the Provincial Grand Master of Zambia Irish Constitution (now retired), which made me feel very proud of his achievement.

After I left for Lodge, Wayne and Graham relaxed by the hotel's swimming pool. They had planned to visit the Copperbelt Museum in Ndola but discovered that it closed at 12:00 on Saturday. While sitting outside they noticed a pair of birds visiting a hole quite high up in a dead tree – feeding chicks. Graham identified the Northern Grey-headed Sparrow, a lifer for him. With time on their hands, they counted the trucks on the Kitwe–Ndola Road passing outside the hotel at a rate of two to three trucks every minute. Dilip informed us that Ndola's new revenue stream was their truck distribution and consolidation hub, especially from the Democratic Republic of the Congo. We now understood why we had seen so many huge left-hand drive trucks along the way.

Wayne, Graham and David discovered that the hotel's menu was surprisingly reasonable and in fact cheaper than the outside Indian restaurant of the previous evening. I returned at 21:15 with my bottle of whiskey that was soon imbibed by all. It did not take long before we were sound asleep.

Fig.379: Irish Prov. Grand Lodge, Zambia

Fig.380: Upper Kafue River near Kitwe

Fig.381: Welcome to Kitwe, my old home

Fig.382: Road accidents are a common sight

Fig.383: Mine slag dump (black mountain)

Fig.384: Slag pouring at night

Fig.385: Roadside markets common

Fig.386: Kitwe town centre on a Sunday

Fig.387: Kaunda Square, was "Coronation"

Fig.388: Hotel Edinburgh was "The Place"

Fig.389: Peter's 18th at that Scout Hall stage

Fig.390: Ex-Scout Hall Kitwe, now YMCA

Day 32: 23 April – Ndola to Kitwe (62km)

Awake at 06:00 and after an early shower we had a hearty breakfast before setting out from Ndola for Kitwe. Wayne wanted to swing by Luanshya to take a couple of photos. The road was terrible and it took some time negotiating the potholes. Soon we were back on the dual carriageway to Kitwe, first crossing the Kafue River (Fig.380), then past Wusikili compound where I ran a Cub Pack in 1961. The welcome to Kitwe was nostalgic for me as I was returning to the town of my formative years: school, employment, marriage. (Fig.381). Again, we came across crashed and abandoned vehicles along the roadside (Fig.382). We passed the mine slag dump that is so memorable to many who have lived in Kitwe. The molten waste slag from processing copper has been poured there since the 1920s and is a sight to be seen at night (Figs.383, 384).

Along the roadside were the many vegetable sellers (Fig.385), which was a common sight wherever we travelled, even around the towns. It was a Sunday morning and the centre of Kitwe near Kaunda Square was quiet – lacking the hustle and bustle of a normal city centre (Figs.386, 387). Wayne and Graham decided to stay with the trailer while David and I went on a photo tour to places on my wish list that held special memories for me, and to share with ex-Kitwe friends. I located the former First Nkana–Kitwe Scout Hall, now a YMCA facility hidden behind a shop front (Fig.390). I was surprised and delighted that in the large hall the parquet floor was still intact and polished. As boy scouts, we used to play "duster hockey" with our staves and a rubber puck on this floor. The stage where I had my 18th birthday photo taken was still there (Fig.389) – now a pulpit for preachers.

Other familiar locations we visited were the Hotel Edinburgh (our first honeymoon night, now a hostel) (Fig.388) and then St Michael's and All Angels Church, where Sandy and I were married in 1967 (Fig.391). Next door is the Anglican Church Hall (Fig.392), where we spent many a Friday or Saturday evening dancing. As mentioned in the Morris Owners Section, this is one of the halls where Mrs Rene Lang organised dance sessions for us teenagers.

As you see in most parts of Africa, street vendors set up vegetable stands outside large supermarket chain stores in competition (Fig.393). One wonders how this is permitted.

I stopped the car to show the chaps the colonial BOMA (British Overseas Military Administration) (Fig.394) that was common in all towns built around the 1940s. Many folk in South Africa and elsewhere think of a BOMA as a cosy enclosure around a central camp fire, usually in upmarket game camps or boutique hotels. Not so in Northern Rhodesia: they are still referred to in Zambia as the BOMA. This houses the magistrate's court and the office to license your car, dog and bicycle among other taxes.

We made our way along the former Cornwall Avenue to find the home of Maurice Diamond's grandparents, Sid and Molly Diamond: Sid was the local millionaire who in the early 1930s established the Standard Trading Company and eventually bought up and merged the main shops in the Kitwe town centre. Their large double-storey house (unusual for Kitwe) was greatly admired but today it is unrecognisable as it is Chinese-owned and has been converted into a block of flats and offices with a high surrounding wall and security gate.

Nearby is St John's Convent that looks in excellent condition, as does the Kitwe Primary next door where I attended school. In the past the properties had a low wire fence but now a concrete wall surrounds them. We then passed the Copperbelt Battalion Headquarters where I was a member of the 7th Battalion Rhodesia Regiment and, after independence, the Zambia Rifles. There was no sign of the former squadron of armoured cars that used to be there.

We located my first home (in 1950), Number 17 Border Motors Flats, Galway Avenue (Fig.395). At the time this was at the perimeter of Kitwe, with open bush across the road. I decided to replicate a photo: me sitting in front of Number 17 wearing a similar pith helmet at the same spot as in 1950 when I was 5 years old (Fig.396). Our third home, Number 32 Moss's Flats, was almost next door but again behind a high wall. Security walls around properties seem to be the norm both in Zimbabwe and Zambia.

It was so hot after driving about that we made our way to what I knew as the Kent Park extension – now it is a huge shopping mall that sadly has been built over a wetland. We went to the Spur where we had huge milkshakes and coke floats – four elderly gentlemen having a fun time like kids! A pity we did not record this event.

After quenching our thirst, we made our way to Nkana East. Very bumpy or nonexistent urban roads brought the realisation that this was the new normal. We headed for Number 12 Stanley Street (now Lilongwe Street), our first home after we married in 1967 and where restoration of the Morris began in 1970 (Fig.397). I hardly recognised the place: the old garage is now a house and the main house has been extended towards where we sunk a portable swimming pool. When I was transferred to Kalulushi, I had to return the property to its original state and we filled in the pool. Local builders were only too pleased to dump their rubble in this 15 metre diameter hole, to which I added the remains of the Model-T Ford headlamp brackets and other scrap items that were on the Morris in 1970. Later I regretted doing this as some of the items would have been of great interest to other car enthusiasts.

It gets dark by around 18:00 – so it was time to head for our accommodation at Lynne Quarmby's home on the Kamushi Farm, some way out of Kitwe on the Chingola Road (Fig.398). Another horrible surface to negotiate but Lynne kindly met us and guided us to the farm. We settled into our respective accommodations over three properties. I stayed in Lynne's cottage to spend some quality time with her – she had lost her husband a week or so before and the wake was to take place on the day we were due to leave (Fig.399). She had some health issues due to swollen legs and it was rather a stressful time for her. Later I was sad to hear that Lynne had passed away on 19 February 2024 from lymphoma.

Wayne and David stayed with Dimitri and Charlotte Klironomos (Lynne's stepdaughter) and Graham with George Klironomos and his wife Tonia; they are all related. The Kamushi farm is like a family commune but with separate homes; it also has stables and a butchery and grows its own vegetables (Figs.400, 401).

Day 33: 24 April – Kitwe to Itimpi – Morris home after 53 years

Graham and I did some early birding in the forest area: we did not see many species but noted the large anthill that is common in this region of Zambia (Fig.402). Breakfast was simple: fruit and cereals, proper coffee and toast. Graham was offered home-made lemon curd, the first he had tasted in years and was hooked. After breakfast we made our way to Plot 7, Azurite Road at Itimpi (Garneton) that was nearby – a few miles along the Chingola Road (Fig.403).

The Morris was in the trailer as the condition of the roads continued to be poor. To locate the spot where I had discovered the wreck in 1970 I walked through the bush searching several plots – only to find that some had been divided. Signs were nonexistent but I came across a remarkable residence with laid paths, fountains, artworks – in fact rather out of place for the area (Fig.404). I walked to a nearby house to make enquiries: this was Plot Number 5 Azurite, so Number 7 would be next to it, about 200 metres away.

While I was searching in the bush, a 4×4 truck drove up to where our BMW was parked. It was Kerry Macfarlane who had been following our trip on Instagram and recognised the BTA trailer. The previous evening, she had enquired on Facebook where and when we would be; I did not know her and was a bit sceptical about her questions. She took a chance and came over from Chingola (32 miles north of Kitwe) with her husband and mother to meet us. Kerry's assistance was invaluable: she drove me around the bush paths in her more suitable 4×4 until we finally located the very spot where the Morris was found in 1970 on Plot 7. So much had changed – even from the photos that Mairi Cummins took in 2008. The rock columns along the original road had been removed and the original hut had been modernised and extended. The trees and bushes were so overgrown that the area was almost unrecognisable.

We unloaded the Morris from the trailer (Fig.405) and Kerry asked to sit in the car, which she surely deserved. She described it as a fun experience (Fig.406).

With the Morris correctly positioned with our Back-to-Africa banner – kindly supported by two local Africans – and the BTA Team assembled at the place where I had rescued it 53 years before (Fig.407), it was Mission accomplished! (Figs.408–410). We made a celebratory jump in the air, having achieved our objective after covering 1,506 miles over 32 days on the road in the Morris to finally arrive at Itimpi (Fig.411).

When I reflect on all the events leading to 24 April 2023: airfreighting the Morris from Zambia to the UK in 1984, completing its restoration by 1992, shipping the car to Cape Town in 2019, the global pandemic, a coup, politics, a hurricane, petrol shortages, seeing the tour becoming a reality after assembling a committed BTA Team ready to go. Then the broken crankshaft only 20 days before our departure seemed to be the final straw but we overcame that. Despite having to make a complicated repair to the Morris during the journey, we had achieved a long-held dream. My team members were an essential element in this crazy enterprise and I will be forever grateful for their dedicated commitment and assistance. *Zikmo Bemba* and *Tatenda*, as they say in Shona, "Thank you."

We then loaded the Morris back into the trailer and set off back to the farm. Along the way we spotted a pub in the "middle of nowhere" where we celebrated with some well-earned beers at midday! On our return to Kamushi Farm, I could now focus on establishing the cause of the engine's loss of compression. George, an experienced engine mechanic, was happy to assist me, particularly as he had never seen anything like the Morris engine before and was fascinated with the overhead cam system.

Once the cylinder head was off, I was surprised at the amount of carbon on the pistons and valves after 1,500 miles. This was probably due to the blend petrol (based on alcohol from sugar cane) so common in Zimbabwe (Fig.412). We did a leak test and found that the valves were leaking; this would certainly have contributed to the loss of compression, but I doubted that it would have made such a difference. George said that his company had all the skills and equipment to regrind the valves and that they could do the job by noon the next day. I was welcome to supervise the work but I had other jobs to do on the car and trusted George to get the work done.

George and his brother Dimitri own a number of companies in diverse fields, including a fleet of some 100 trucks and workshops and engineering facilities in Kitwe. Luke the driver took the cylinder head into town at 15:00 and George would collect it the following day. With the cylinder head off I could clean the piston heads and check everything else in readiness for assembly. I discovered the cause of the defective fan: the weld supporting the main shaft had failed. We fixed this so that it would be able to cool the engine again.

To celebrate our exciting and successful day, Charlotte and Dimitri hosted a dinner at their stunning home (Fig.413). The meal, mainly Greek cuisine, was delicious and accompanied by fine wines. We chatted at length, telling of our exploits and getting to know one another. We had quite an early night because the next day would involve visiting numerous landmarks in and around Kitwe and then returning to Kamushi to assemble and commission the Morris engine.

Fig.391: St Michaels – married here in 1967

Fig.392: Church Hall, pop sessions that Mrs Lang ran to raise money for girls' softball

Fig.393: Kitwe street vendors compete with the corporates without compunction

Fig.394: Kitwe BOMA where your car, dog or cycle is licensed, also Magistrates Court

Fig.395: 17 Galway Ave – first home 1950

Fig.396: Me 1950 and 2023 at 17 Galway Ave

Fig.397: 12 Lilongwe St, Morris's 1970 home

Fig.398: Edinburgh Ave, Kitwe to Chingola

Fig.399: Lynne Quarmby (Casson) our host

Fig.400: The stunning Kamushi Farm, Kitwe

Fig.401: They stable horses and have events

Fig.402: Huge anthills are common in Zambia

Fig.403: The search for the 1970 Morris site

Fig.404: Jungle and then this smart development

Fig.405: Unloading the Morris in the forest

Fig.406: Kerry Macfarlane "followed" us

Fig.407: Morris as discovered in 1970, Itimpi

Fig.408: Back in the same spot 2023, Itimpi

Fig.409: The BTA Team made this possible

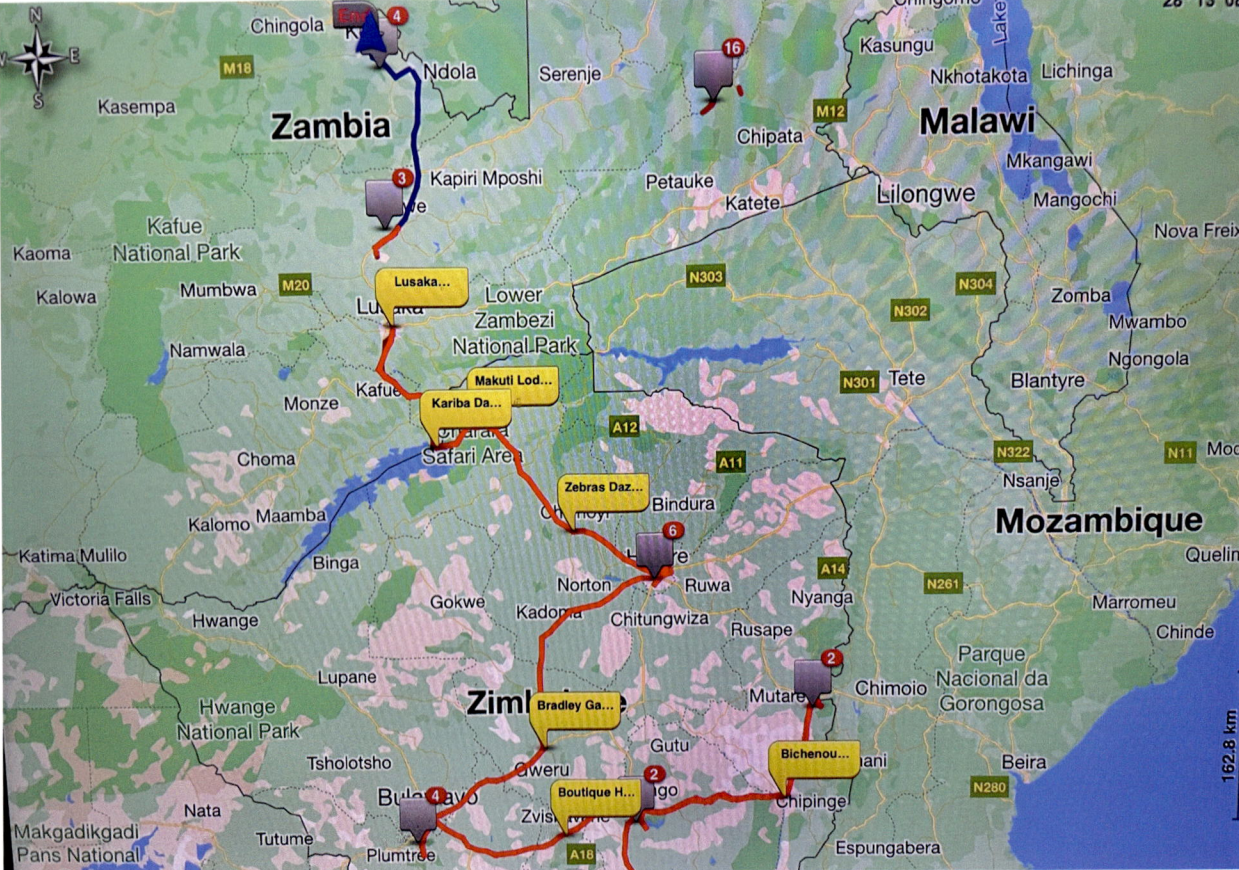

Fig.410: Mission accomplished, "Yay"

Fig.411: Tracking map 24 April 2023, Morris returns after 53 years, Mutare to Kitwe – 1,509 miles in 22 days

Fig.412: Morris valves encrusted with soot

Fig.413: Charlotte and Dimitri hosted a dinner

Fig.414: Scout Hall now a supermarket, very sad!

Fig.415: Former Rhokana Mine Head Office

Fig.416: Former Nkana Mine Hospital

Fig.417: Mine Club from Diggers Rugby field

Fig.418: Nkana Cinema, enjoyed flicks here

Fig.419: Olympic Swimming Pool 2023

Day 34: 25 April – Kitwe Around Town

We drove the BMW into Kitwe to visit as many of my old haunts as possible in the time available before lunch. In 2008 when I visited Kitwe, it was a bit ragged round the edges, and not much had changed since 1984 when we left for the UK. Now in 2023 there had been an explosion of new buildings, some occupied, many still works-in-progress. We raced around Kitwe reviving memories of my past home and places of significant events but the poor state of the urban roads slowed us down at times. It was certainly a whistle-stop tour: it was a matter of click pictures, move on.

One disappointing sight was the "new" 1st Nkana–Kitwe Scout hall located on the Kuomboka Drive (ex-Salisbury Drive). The old hall in the Kitwe town centre was sold and is now a church but the new hall (*c.* 1960) is now a supermarket (Fig.414). How can this happen when the site was created by public subscription and dedicated to developing all youngsters?

Passing the former Rhokana Corporation Central Offices on Central Avenue (Fig.415) now named Mopani Mines and opposite the Nkana Hospital now called the Sinozam Friendship Hospital (Chinese) (Fig.416) where Sandy was in charge of the Maternity Ward.

At the top of Central Street is what remains of 1st Avenue, now just a rocky stretch – like driving over a quarry! I had last seen the abandoned Nkana Baths in 2008 but felt the need to report on its latest condition – a sign of the times and an example of poor planning and the decline of a significant place of recreation. In my day, the swimming pool was the centre of most folks' lives – especially the kids who would ride bikes a considerable distance (over 5 miles) with towels wrapped under the bike's saddle. Entrance was 3 pence and Pop, the pool superintendent, was ever-present – to control the wilder ones, give swimming lessons and be the lifesaver in attendance. In the late 1970s I learned to scuba dive in the pool that has a 5 metre deep end. We had a room dedicated to our comprehensive diving equipment and compressor. The pool had a sweet and pie shop that was always popular: especially for having a picnic on the manicured lawns.

When one considers that in the 1930s the mining company built an Olympic-size swimming pool, vast sports grounds, cinema and a recreation club right next to the copper mine and plant, it seems misguided (Figs.417, 418). We accepted contaminants such as dust from the concentrator crushing plant, a smelter that spewed out sulphur dioxide, smoke and soot. I visited the Nkana Baths in 2014 and by then the pool had been abandoned due to the encroachment of the cobalt process plant that spewed out red calcine. Visiting in 2023 was like seeing a movie set of a broken-down deserted cowboy town. This was once the community centre where Olympic swimming and diving trials took place and where most kids learned to swim (Fig.419). The memorable fountain was smashed and the roofs of the change rooms had collapsed (Fig.422).

In January 1952 the company photographer took a photo of my sister Ann, her friend Anne, and me splashing in the baby pool. It was published in the mining company's monthly glossy magazine *The Rhokana Review* (Fig.420). I decided to position myself in the abandoned pool in 2023 (Fig.421). Such a sad sight with so much history of another era.

We made our way to the old Mine Pilot Plant where Alfred H. Knight, a UK company, that purchased the Mining Industry Technical Services (MITS) in the late 1980s, continues to operate (Fig.423). Originally MITS was based in Kalulushi where I helped to establish a range of specialist services after 1973 when I was transferred from the Rhokana Corporation in Kitwe.

In the past mine-hoisting equipment had to be exported to the UK and South Africa for testing and certification according to the Ministry of Mines regulations. Zambia had sanctions against South Africa and we could no longer use their services – also the railway lines to the coast had been blown up. The mines were under threat of closure if their safety equipment was not certified fit for use. Appreciating these issues, I wrote the first code of practice that established our organisation as the national testing and certification authority to undertake the inspection locally. This avoided the need to invest capital in duplicate hoisting equipment while other items were sent overseas. This service saved Zambia huge amounts of foreign exchange, giving recognition for our organisation to expand multiple specialist testing services where Zambian technologists were trained to undertake the work. I was welcomed by the Alfred H. Knight staff who gave me a tour of the facilities. It was a great thrill to see the production magnetic particle crack detection test rig that I designed and commissioned in 1974 still in daily use (Fig.424). The staff were very friendly and realised that I was the originator of their two codes of practice (Fig.425). Sadly, the place appears rather disorganised, with no evidence of ultrasonic, radiographic and vibration analysis equipment. I did visit the laboratories undertaking destructive winding rope tests and some oil analysis as part of a machinery health monitoring programme. What did make me proud was that over the past 40 years there has been no major failure reported of hoisting equipment in the Zambia mining industry.

We returned to Kamushi Farm at 11:30 and shortly afterwards George arrived with the cylinder head cleaned and valves ground-in. We started to assemble the engine (Fig.426) but when it came to fitting the dynamo we realised there was excessive play on the drive yoke on the camshaft. Investigating more closely, we found that the steel locking key had sheared and the yoke was no longer operating the camshaft and valves. The engine timing was thus nonexistent and the root cause for the loss of compression. Without a secured yoke, the valves had opened in the wrong sequence and the cylinders were not sealed by the valves.

The engine, with imperfect sealing valves would probably have run, with reduced power, for quite a while but since the dynamo shaft was badly worn the engine's timing would have been compromised (Fig.427). It would require a major repair but we needed a temporary fix as I had to have the Morris operating to complete the long-desired drive over Victoria Falls in Livingstone. George fashioned a replacement key from an Allen key of high-quality tool steel. We then made a shim from a Red Bull drinks can (giving the Morris wings!) to take up the excessive clearance of the drive yoke to the dynamo shaft (Fig.428) that worked very well and would probably function for years to come!

We installed the assembly in the engine and soon we had the engine running smoothly – a joy and relief. Since I had to depart for a long-planned Masonic Lodge Meeting in Kitwe, we would complete the assembly the next morning. While I was away, Graham, Wayne and David had dinner with Tonia and George – a big family event with everyone else from the farm. Tonia cooked two huge bowls of spaghetti bolognese with all the trimmings; George produced beers and wine – delicious fare and lots of light banter.

By the time I drove into Kitwe it was dark and navigating the potholes was pure guesswork. There were no streetlights and people would just cross the road anywhere; so I was extra-cautious. I had long ago asked to attend the Failte Masonic Lodge Number 805, Irish Constitution in Kitwe. It was my Mother Lodge that I joined in 1970 (coincidentally the same year as finding the Morris). The Lodge's regular meeting should have been a week later, but as I was making a rare return visit (being a life

Fig.420: Ann and I, Nkana baby pool 1952

Fig.421: Back in Nkana baby pool 2023

member since 1984), they kindly brought forward the meeting by special dispensation. Attending was a real honour – especially as brethren came from Ndola (40 miles away) for the occasion. It was good to see Bro. Dilip Desai again. The reigning Worshipful Master invited me to chair the Lodge Meeting; that was a great honour and pleasure for me. After the meeting they served a fine curry and rice and the usual drinks. I needed to ensure that my alcohol consumption was moderate, as I was quite nervous about the unfamiliar drive back on the bush track to the farm that would require my full concentration. Nevertheless, this was a memorable evening, especially being so well received by the brethren (Fig.429).

Fig.422: The Fountain at Nkana Pool 2023

Fig.423: My ex-forensic engineering services acquired, *c.* 1986, continues to function

Fig.424: Magnetic particle crack finding rig that I had made in 1974, now in Kitwe

Fig.425: Staff running the materials testing services for Zambia's mines, my legacy

Fig.426: Wayne and Graham: "Morris Consultants"

Fig.427: Morris's dynamo shaft worn

Day 35: 26 April – Kalulushi – Former Home

After breakfast, we completed the outstanding work on the Morris, then loaded it into the trailer and set off, leaving Kitwe for Kalulushi about 17 kilometres away. The Kitwe top road past the fuel storage tanks and light industrial area was problematic, almost impassable. We managed to take a diversion and finally got to the main road to the village of Kalulushi. Passing the Mindola Dam turn-off, we noticed several new houses, some under construction, others were like a modern housing estate – quite a pleasant surprise. As we neared the Chibuluma Mine (Fig.430) it was apparent that all the engineering workshops were deserted. Further along, the former Chibuluma Mine Hospital (for employees) had been renamed the Kalulushi General Hospital. My wife Sandra was Matron here in the late 1970s (Fig.431). Opposite is the former Chibuluma Mine Central Office, now the Kalulushi Municipal Civic Centre.

Around the previously model village it was overgrown: the very rough roads were almost impassable – I had difficulty in finding the Chibuluma Golf Club. The course looked well maintained but not a soul was there – no players or caddies standing by. Nearby was our third home (14 Lukasu Street). The friendly owner told us that the anthill at the rear with a brick Wendy house built on top had been removed for more space to grow vegetables. After negotiating the non-roads, we arrived at Number 2, Mwaiseni Crescent, our last home in 1984. Nuns are now living in this once-prestigious home with a large garden, but I noticed that the swimming pool was empty. There is a wooded area across the road where a resident Red-chested Cuckoo would often call its distinctive "Piet my vrou, Piet my vrou" (Fig.432). We unloaded the Morris from the trailer after gaining permission to drive it partially on and off the property's driveway. I wanted to recreate a photo taken in 1980 by my late pal Mike Shand of the Morris positioned next to our old home. The photo is of his daughter Susan Shand and Claire Cummins (Ken and Mairi, Lusaka) who were in the Morris as a running chassis for a fun ride along the tarred Mwaiseni road (Figs.50–52) mentioned earlier – then in excellent condition 1980 but sadly not the case today (Fig.433).

David had his video camera positioned through the open rooftop of the BMW; he recorded me driving down the driveway, out of the gate and then he followed me along the potholed road past the ZCCM Technical Library. It looked as though I was drunk, weaving along Maina Soko (excuse for a road), then splashing through a large puddle and mud patch. We arrived outside my former office at Mining Industry Technical Services that is now the Copperbelt University (Fig.434). I would have liked to have driven the Morris to the Kitwe city centre, but after experiencing such poor roads, getting there would have stressed the Morris to an unacceptable level. Even the BMW with the trailer was struggling due to the condition of the roads.

I decided that we should put the Morris back in the trailer and return to the farm. I found a convenient parking place in front of a couple of shops to do the loading. A couple of Zambians were showing considerable interest in the activity (Fig.435). It turned out that Mr Phiri had been following our tour on the Internet; he seemed well informed and was keen to relate the Morris's story to his young son. Then, disaster struck (again!): I was driving the Morris up the ramp into the trailer not knowing that the exhaust pipe bracket had broken. This lowered the silencer and impacted the lip of the trailer, shearing the cast-iron exhaust manifold flange. The Morris roared like a motor bike with no silencer.

To get the Morris into the trailer we had to remove the whole exhaust pipe that was dangling below. While I was under the car I asked Graham to pass me the *sandu* (hammer). Mr Phiri chuckled, putting his hand on Graham's shoulder and pointing to his son, saying, "This generation of Zambian will never know the meaning of *sandu*." Later Mr Phiri reminded me that we had similar names, both meaning "hill". He pointed out that my spelling of the Morris's name was incorrect and that it should be Chilupala. This was the nickname the locals gave to my father which means "one with no hair".

We arrived back at the farm at 15:15 where I informed George that the exhaust manifold flange had sheared. Once again, George came to our rescue: he immediately organised a car and driver to take me to one of his workshops in Kitwe. The welder, Gordon, seemed to know what he was doing: after preparing the joint and preheating it he laid down a substantial weld bead and after post-heat treatment let it cool slowly (Figs.436, 437). As Wayne had experienced in Lusaka, the work was done on the floor, no work bench or vice but at least the welder had a proper protective helmet with visor. Back at the farm I installed the repaired manifold and did a short test drive where some of the horses were exercising slowly (Fig.438). I purchased a replacement exhaust pipe support bracket that I planned to fit later. In retrospect this was a mistake as it was no longer supported at the centre of the silencer!

A farewell braai was organised by the three Kamushi families in their amazing entertainment area: the pool, braai facilities, drinks fridges, seating facilities combine to create a spot of paradise in the middle of the bush. They had invited some friends, including Bill Osborne who was married to Rose (who nursed with Sandy) who sadly died of malaria about a year ago. As the farm has its own butchery, there was plenty of delicious meat, along with piles of fresh salads and Greek specialities – a real feast.

After dinner Dimitri introduced me and the team to his friends and asked me to give a short talk about our trip, its purpose and what had been achieved. I thanked everyone for coming to the braai and expressed the team's appreciation to the three families for their friendliness and generosity: the accommodation, making us feel so welcome in their homes, and the assistance from George and his team in getting the Morris back on the road. I presented Lynne with a BTA mug and a bottle of the Cape Stettyn wine, and mugs to Dimitri and George. (Figs.439–443). They said they would cherish them. It had been a long and interesting day with a happy ending. We said our goodbyes as we needed to leave early the next morning.

Fig.428: Red Bull shim for the dynamo

Fig.429: Failte Lodge Kitwe, 25 April 2023

Fig.430: Rusting Chibuluma Mine

Fig.431: Ex-Kalulushi Mine Hospital

Fig.432: Red-chested Cuckoo in Kalulushi

Fig.433: Leaving our ex-luxury home down Mwaiseni Road, ex-paved road in Kalulushi

Fig.434: At my 1984 office R&D Kalulushi, now the Copperbelt University

Fig.435: Loading the Morris with Mr Phiri

Fig.436: Prepping the exhaust manifold

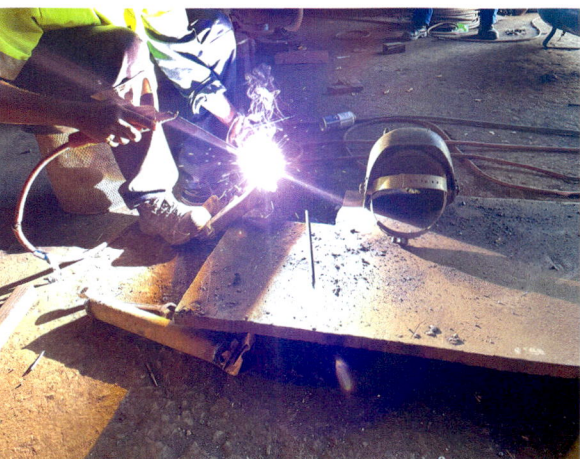

Fig.437: Welding the exhaust manifold

Fig.438: One horse vs eight horse power!

Fig.439: Kamushi farewell braai

Fig.440: BTA mug for Charlotte – thanks

Fig.441: BTA mug to George – thanks

Fig.442: BTA mug for Lynne – thanks

Fig.443: BTA with George and Dimitri

Chapter 7.3

Zambia – Southern Province

Day 36: 27 April – Kitwe to Lusaka (384km) – Cecily's Fund Dinner

Our destination was Lusaka; a 358 kilometre trip to attend the Cecily's Fund 25th Anniversary Dinner. We had experienced the road's condition and expected the journey to take about 8 hours instead of the expected 4 hours based on the distance. After coffee and a light breakfast, we left Kamushi Farm at 06:45 with snacks that Lynne had kindly prepared for us. Leaving Kitwe, we passed the famous O.B. Bennet Hall, a place where pop dances and boxing tournaments were held and where I had judo training (Fig.444). Mr O.B. Bennet OBE was the famous General Manager of Nkana Mine, a very tall and imposing Oxford man with an attractive wife: they were the royal couple of Kitwe and supported many sporting activities. Around 1962 Mr Bennet was appointed the Rhodesian Minister in Washington, USA.

There were more police checks with long lines of trucks causing congestion (Fig.445) as well as the ubiquitous mobile phone booths (Fig.446) whose main business is money transfer. We saw rows of these in Zimbabwean and South African towns and villages; this is an efficient means of transferring money, especially for migrant workers. This is how technology is helping enterprises to develop and grow – making huge improvements in rural areas particularly.

Nearing Ndola, between the two lanes of the "new" dual carriageway, there is a small, fenced area with a memorial. This is for Dag Hammarskjöld who was the Secretary General of the United Nations from April 1953 until September 1961 when he was killed in a plane crash near this spot. Sadly, the area appears neglected and overgrown.

It took us half an hour to get through Ndola and then once again we were exposed to the plastically distorted tarmac road towards Kapiri Mposhi. Seeing the road and traffic conditions from the comfort of the BMW, Graham and I were incredulous: "Did we actually drive the Morris on this?" It reminded us of the accomplishment of the Morris and the risks we had taken.

Approaching Kapiri Mposhi the fuel warning light came on for quite some time and, while we had fuel supplies in the trailer, we worried that we would run out and have to stop on the side of the road. Fortunately, we came across a new petrol station on the outskirts of town where we took 90 litres of fuel – the rated capacity of the X5 is 93 litres! Closer to Kapiri Mposhi Wayne overtook a very slow vehicle, only to be pulled over by the police. They wanted to charge him with negligent driving for overtaking on a white line. But, after telling them of our fundraising exercise and showing them the trailer, they let us go without a penalty.

At Kabwe we decided to get off the road and find somewhere to enjoy the packed lunch that Lynne had prepared. We spotted a flock of Marabou Storks circling overhead: some had settled in a field across the road and I decided to take photos. I thought the fence would be ideal to steady my large lens but then got a jolt as it was electrified – the rest of the team had a laugh! From the outskirts of Lusaka, it took a full hour to get across the city. Traffic was heavier than expected ahead of the public holiday and long weekend.

We passed through Lusaka on the main road south, arriving at Sandy's Creations at 16:00 (Fig.447). Since we were to attend the Cecily's Fund 25th Anniversary Dinner that evening, this was the most convenient option. Our accommodation was booked but the room charge was not the same as had been confirmed earlier. Finally, the manager agreed to the earlier discounted price. But it meant that three had to sleep in the lounge area of the cottage which was otherwise well appointed.

On to the dinner: we were almost the first to arrive at the venue, wearing the bright orange Cecily's Fund T-shirts that had been supplied back in 2019 (Fig.448) – we had our BTA Team shirts underneath! Stephen and Cheryl welcomed us and took a group photo before seating us. The other guests trickled in slowly and by 19:00 only 12 of an expected 30 had arrived. There was a lively opening and welcome by traditional drummers and dancers (Fig.449). The organisers had obviously gone to great lengths and expense to arrange the decor, entertainment and complimentary dinner. It was such a shame that those who had confirmed attendance had not shown up.

We were seated with two impressive young recipients of the Cecily's Fund Trust as well as a successful Zambian businessman who was both a sponsor and mentor. He was quite outgoing and generously kept the table in drinks! Wayne and David were at another table with sponsors. Stephen and Cheryl introduced everyone, then gave a slide show explaining the aims of the trust and its many successes (Fig.450). It was then my turn to give a short talk. After introducing the BTA Team I explained the aims of the trip, the history of the Morris and funds raised to date in support of the Cecily's Fund (Fig.451). I said we were like *bilimungwe* (the *Bemba* word for chameleon). At my signal, we all removed our orange shirts to reveal the black BTA polo shirts underneath. This resulted in a lot of applause and hilarity. I ended with the customary *hamba gashle* that in Zambia means go slowly – or a chameleon – but in South Africa go well, as announced on SAA flights!

Dinner was a first-class buffet with wine continuously served at the tables. Between dinner and dessert, three young Zambians who had been sponsored by the Trust to complete tertiary education had the opportunity to talk about their circumstances and how they had benefited from the trust. Each of them, Nora, Jackson and Evans, spoke very well and confidently, a good advert for the Trust's work.

Walking back to our chalet we had to duck under a metal boom. Wayne raised it but did not realise Graham had not passed through and released the boom on Graham's head. This was not well received, but no blood was drawn. After a whiskey in our room we were soon sound asleep.

Day 37: 28 April – Lusaka to Choma (aborted) – BMW Breakdown

Graham, our diarist, aptly named this Friday as "The Longest Day". It was a public holiday to celebrate Kenneth Kaunda's birthday (first President of Zambia). We had learned to expect the unexpected. After our usual early breakfast, we set off from Sandy's Creations and Wayne decided to take a "short cut" to join the awkward dual highway. Big mistake! The road deteriorated progressively into a track, making it very heavy going on the BMW and trailer. Eventually, we found the main road to Chilanga and, as soon as we were out of civilisation and on the open road, with Masuku, Victoria Falls and Hwange Game Park to look forward to, I said, "Chaps, we are now on holiday."

Successfully negotiating the permanent police checkpoint at Kafue, we were on the road to Mazabuka that had recently been rebuilt and was probably the best we had encountered (Fig.452). The BMW was cruising along when, near the crest of hill, the car's temperature warning light and alarm buzzer came on. Wayne immediately pulled onto the shoulder of the road and stopped. Steam was rising from the bonnet and water was trickling onto the road. We opened the bonnet expecting to find a burst hose but what we discovered was far worse. The plastic radiator expansion reservoir had split down the whole of one side. This was a very serious problem: we could not use our car, we were on a remote road 70 kilometres from Lusaka, it was a holiday weekend, there is no AA or national road recovery service. What now?

We put on our high-viz safety vests and then placed breakdown safety triangles some distance back from the trailer and in front of the BMW. We were on the crest of a hill and a dangerous bend and would come into view quite suddenly on this national highway (Fig.453).

Wayne and I did the usual *Boer maak 'n plan* (Farmer makes a plan), attempting to seal the cracked reservoir (Fig.454). We covered the crack with duct tape as far as we could reach – it was in a very confined space – then reinforced the repair with the corners of a plastic bottle bound with cable ties. David collected some water from a nearby dwelling. As soon as we added the water, it ran out of the base of the reservoir; obviously it was cracked well below where we had made the temporary repair. Since the water was no longer required, David returned what was left to the village – in this parched area water is precious and is often carried considerable distances. The villagers were paid a few Kwacha for their kindness.

I started checking on the Internet to find a car transporter that would take the BMW and trailer back to Lusaka for repair on a public holiday. The transporter is essential as towing the BMW would damage its 4×4 drive and gearbox. I assumed we would have a better chance of finding a BMW agent in Lusaka. To add to my stress, my phone was low on data and call time. Eventually, I contacted Tip Top Motors, a 24-hour towing service, who agreed to collect our vehicle but needed its VIN number and a copy of the licence disc. They would come in a few hours and all we could do was wait. By now my phone was on its last Kwacha.

As Graham has observed, I have the ability to take catnaps at will and so I reclined the car seat to take a rest while waiting for the progress call. Wayne and Graham sat on the cooler box, watching a grasshopper trying to climb out of the culvert: each time it almost reached the top it slipped and fell back. They were considering taking bets on whether it would succeed. A sorry sight: two old men watching a grasshopper. David was spotted sitting on an ammo box watching another beetle climbing up the side of the culvert; when it reached the top he dislodged it with a stick and it had to start climbing again. Close encounters with the real Africa!

After some time of boredom, on a lighter note Wayne played a song from The Animals, "We gotta get out of this place" – most appropriate considering the helpless situation we were in. There was nothing else to do but watch the trucks passing by in both directions. Lunch was lemon biscuits and water. I made a cappuccino with cold water but it tasted vile; so I unpacked the kettle which we had not yet used on the trip to make a cup of tea. The others stuck to water.

After 4 hours of patiently waiting and no missed calls I again tried to contact Tip Top Motors but their phone was turned off. I then texted them and a chap responded, claiming he had tried to call me but now they were all going on holiday (so much for a 24-hour service). What could we do? Were we going to have to spend the night without food or water on this barren highway with heavy traffic passing? I also had to think about accommodation when we managed to get to Lusaka. The BMW agents would only open in 4 days' time (Tuesday); so the most convenient option would be Sandy's Creations.

Our predicament seemed to be dire. Finally, I contacted Bobby van der Merwe who was fishing at Siavonga. He said, "Leave it with me." Then I called Gerard Fagan: he was en route to Kitwe but could remotely load 50 Kwacha onto my phone – another problem solved.

I then managed to contact René Lourens who was still in in Lusaka. Thankfully, he arranged for Richard Baldy's Transport to collect us. It was now 17:00. René had also spoken to a Hans Sportel who has a workshop near Sandra's Creations. I did not know Hans but he contacted me and said that he was aware of our predicament and kindly offered us accommodation at his smallholding outside Lusaka. What a relief! Meanwhile Bobby van der Merwe had contacted his mechanic to obtain the radiator expansion reservoir and arrange to fit it at Hans Sportel's place the next day. All this on the start of a holiday weekend; it seemed that "Lady Luck" was smiling at us once again. That local folk would assist us unknowns in a foreign country confirms one's faith in humanity.

Hans phoned to say the transporter was on the way – hooray, we are saved! When the sun goes down in the tropics, it gets dark very quickly; by 18:00 it was almost black. We put on the side lights of the BMW, activating the fantastic rear large upper and lower bright LED lights of the trailer. We were now very visible to oncoming traffic and the awaited transporter.

On the opposite side of the road there was a clearing where several bags of charcoal were stacked ready for sale. The whole operation appeared to be run by women, who carried the bags to the site and even loaded the customer's vehicles. We noticed that they sold only three bags for K100 (£4) each bag the whole day and we could not help wondering how these folks managed on such a modest income. We chatted to one fellow who mentioned that a large tree would produce five to six bags of charcoal. We then asked what would happen when there are no more trees: he simply shrugged. In many places along the roadsides, close to settlements or villages, there are very few large trees to be seen and mostly just scrub.

Fig.444: O.B. Bennet Hall outside Kitwe

Fig.445: Police checks and congestion

Fig.446: Mobile money traders everywhere

Fig.447: Arriving at Sandra's Creations

Fig.448: Cecily's Fund 25th Anniversary Dinner

Fig.449: Traditional Zambian welcome

Fig.450: Steven Barlow, Director Cecily's Fund

Fig.451: BTA Cecily's Fund exceeds £2,000

Fig.452: Road, Lusaka to Choma 09:00

Fig.453: BMW overheats on the highway

Fig.454: Bust radiator expansion tank cracked

Fig.455: Transported back to Lusaka 19:15

Fig.456: Two nights at Hans Sportel's farm

Fig.457: Thanks Gea and Hans – BTA mug

Fig.458: BMW fixed, depart for Choma

Fig.459: Masuku, our quaint chalets

One bonus of being in a remote area with zero ambient light contamination and a dark night sky is that the stars are very bright. Orion with his sword and the Southern Cross were particularly brilliant. There is always a silver lining somewhere! As boy scouts Graham and I were in our element pointing out the stars to the other two "townies".

At long last we saw a vehicle coming over the crest of the hill with a bank of flashing orange lights on the cab. It was 18:45 and the transporter had arrived. Our salvation. The feeling of relief was palpable. The driver's name was Brave; he knew exactly what to do and had everything loaded and ready in just 20 minutes (Fig.455). There was no space for him to turn around and he decided to drive further up the road until he could find a suitable turning spot. When the tow truck and trailer disappeared out of sight Graham remarked, "There go all our worldly goods – we only have what we are standing in."

When he returned in a few minutes, Graham and I sat in the cab with Brave. Wayne and David had to sit in the BMW – this is not allowed but we had no option. At the Kafue police check (which we thought we had seen the last of) Brave was pulled over and was called to the police desk. Wayne and David kept a very low profile in the BMW. Brave said they wanted to charge him for having a black-and-white number plate and not a red one and demanded that he pay 450 Kwacha. He said that he only had 200 Kwacha which they accepted with no receipt – corruption at its best! Just before reaching the police check Brave had been telling us how rife the corruption is at these roadblocks.

With all the phone calls that had taken place to set up the recovery – Bobby, Gerard, Hans – directions had become complicated. Brave drove towards an area near the home of Hans and Gea Sportel but fortunately Hans met us at a nearby flour mill. We followed him home, arriving somewhere on the outskirts of Lusaka at 21:30.

We uncoupled the trailer and unloaded the BMW. I slipped Brave some Kwacha to cover his corruption losses and a little extra to show our appreciation for his efficient service. He was very grateful.

It had been an extremely long, tiring and frustrating day for everyone. After a cup of most welcome coffee, we were shown our accommodation: Wayne and David had a fully equipped cottage, Graham had a single-room cottage, and I had a basic room in the main house. Everyone had collapsed into bed by 22:30. It had indeed been the longest day, but we were safe, the cars were safe and there was a way forward.

The next morning Hans remarked that he had not in a long time seen a bunch of chaps who were so totally exhausted. Quite right. Hans came across as a quiet, self-assured and no-nonsense man but also very friendly and helpful. At some stage, sitting on the veranda, he casually mentioned that he had also completed an "epic" trip, driving his Citroën 2CV (*Deux Chevaux*) from Lusaka to the Netherlands on his own. It had taken him 6 weeks but in two 3 week stints. At the halfway stage, somewhere in North Africa he had garaged the vehicle and collected it later. He admitted that he had been very lucky in avoiding all the political issues along the way and had suffered no major mechanical problems. He said that the biggest problem was folding his 6'6" frame into the small car for such long periods of time!

Day 38: 29 April – Lusaka, BMW Repairs

Everyone enjoyed a late breakfast with Hans and Gea, who laid on fried eggs and bacon, and delicious bread made that morning. We then discussed how to proceed with repairing the BMW: Bobby van der Merwe's mechanic was to bring the replacement expansion tank to Hans's place. I had already sent a photo of the item together with the BMW's VIN number.

Hans lives on a 5 acre property that has three houses (Fig.456), a large workshop and a row of 40 foot containers that house his collection of classic cars. Most are Citroëns but there is also a Bentley. At the rear is a long, sheltered carport where Hans has six or eight 4×4 vehicles fully kitted out for camping. His business is hiring them to tourists who wish to undertake self-drive game reserve tours. He maintains the vehicles at his fully equipped workshop. Because of the high-value vehicles on the property he is extremely careful about who visits and only admits people that he knows or who are recommended.

Meanwhile, we took the opportunity to use Hans's garage pit to refit the Morris's exhaust system. I installed the new exhaust pipe support bracket and connected it to the repaired manifold. We fired up the engine and all was well: Chilupala was back in action.

Soon the BMW mechanic, Kennedy, arrived with the plastic tank and began to remove the damaged unit. This proved to be awkward to extract but with some brute force from Wayne it was finally removed. On inspection we found that the crack was bigger than we thought, it had propagated into the base. Then we realised that the replacement unit was for a BMW X3 not the X5. Kennedy made a phone call and, surprisingly, on a Saturday in Lusaka on a holiday weekend, the correct part was delivered by motorcycle. Owing to Hans's security concerns the delivery was accepted at the main gate.

When I enquired of Kennedy where he was trained, I was surprised when he said at BMW in the USA; he lived there for 9 years but did not like it and returned to Zambia. Kennedy soon had the correct part fitted, and the system was running by early afternoon. The replacement tank cost 1,500 Kwacha and 1,000 Kwacha for Kennedy's labour. We had both vehicles in running order; so we loaded the Morris into the trailer and hitched it to the BMW for an early getaway on Sunday morning. Once again, we had "got out of jail".

Hans organised a braai for the evening and invited René to join us. The team had been out of beers for some time; Hans disappeared for a while returning with a couple of life-saving six-packs of Castle Lite! We provided the sausages that Wayne had obtained from the Kamushi Farm butchery as well as chicken kebabs. Hans and Gea contributed beef fillet and a spread of salads. All the meat was delicious, especially the beef fillet washed down with ice-cold Castles! Another happy ending to our saga, resolved by the help and generosity of old and new friends. We were so appreciative of those who did not know us and yet were happy to assist. I presented each with a BTA mug which they were happy to accept (Fig.457).

Day 39, 30 April – Lusaka to Masuku, Choma (292km)

After a 06:30 breakfast that included Gea's fabulous fresh bread, ham and Dutch cheese, we bade farewell with grateful thanks. Before leaving Lusaka, I had to visit an ATM to pay for the towing service that cost 5,300 Kwacha (£225) and draw a further 100 Kwacha for telephone top-up. We were back on an excellent road to Choma (Fig.458), our next destination. We cruised past the spot where we had spent 9 hours waiting to be rescued and recalled the dreadful feeling of helplessness.

Our first stop would be Mazabuka where Graham had been posted to Barclays Bank and lived in 1966. Along the way we noticed that for long stretches before Mazabuka the land on the left side was green with maize under modern irrigation, yet on the right was mainly sugar cane. The Nakambala Sugar Estate had been established by Tate & Lyle of the UK who installed a large pipeline from the Kafue River to irrigate their sugar cane fields. This investment created much employment for the local population and the town of Mazabuka prospered. Many of the skilled workers building the pipeline came over from England, employed by John Sisk & Co. After hours these chaps supported the pubs of the Golf Club and Mazabuka Club.

We arrived at Mazabuka at around 09:30, making a bee line for the local PicknPay for supplies, especially ice; Wayne had to have his constant supply of ice-cold Coca-Cola. At the till we were told that they could only sell beer after 10:00; so we processed the other items and then at 10:00 loaded the beer and ice into the cooler box. Graham was quite disappointed with the appearance of the town where he had had so many happy memories. Buildings and roads were run down, street cleanliness and maintenance nonexistent, and shanties spread everywhere with no apparent urban planning. Next stop Monze.

The road started to deteriorate, with tar crumbling and potholes galore; the going was much slower. We had a rest stop to eat the pies I had bought and went on again towards Monze where we topped up with fuel. It is no longer a small one-horse town but a sprawling conurbation.

The turn-off to Masuku Lodge was at the precise GPS numbers I had recorded in 2015 when I first visited. At the control gate I had to register the BMW, then drive through a trough for prevention of foot and mouth disease, a necessary cattle control in this area. The dirt track towards Masuku was in fairly good condition and apart from occasional corrugations it took us steadily downhill through ever-denser indigenous forest. Graham remarked how much he loved this sort of countryside and type of bush.

At 12:45 we arrived at Masuku Lodge owned by Rory and Dori McDougall. They had recently returned from the Lower Zambezi Valley where they are setting up a tented tourist camp and it was clear they were quite exhausted. We were allocated two chalets (Graham and I in Number 3, Wayne and David in Number 4 (Fig.459). We unloaded all our personal gear and settled in. Graham and I did some birding in the expansive well-wooded gardens up from a nearby lake. As the day cooled the birds became more active and numerous and at first we could not easily identify them. At sundown we were invited to the main lodge for drinks at Rory's bar with Dori and four other guests who were spending the night. Everyone sat down together at a long table for dinner – an excellent spread that included roast beef, Yorkshire pudding and vegetables (Fig.460). Happy to be back in the bush, we retired to our chalets and Graham and I enjoyed our usual nightcap – a *dop* of brandy on ice. Tomorrow would be an early start to seek Zambia's only endemic bird, Chaplin's Barbet. Back in Cape Town I had promised Graham we would see one and he was eagerly awaiting this treat.

Day 40: 1 May – Masuku Lodge – "Out of Africa" House

We had arranged for Martin, the gardener, to meet us at 06:00. We unhitched the trailer from the BMW and set off under Martin's directions (Fig.461). We travelled about 12 kilometres through a neighbour's property following a little used road. We parked and walked along a track to a wooded area but did not see the Barbet. We drove a short distance further but drew another blank. Martin said he knew of another possible spot about 2 kilometres away. This time, after walking a very short distance, there was the Chaplin's Barbet perched on the top of a tree sunning itself (Fig.462). Hooray! Graham and I began clicking away. The Barbet then flew to a nearby tree where it was joined by another two. Seeing so many together was a rare opportunity. The light was perfect; and we both obtained several excellent photos. Mission accomplished! Along the drive back to Masuku we spotted Lizard Buzzard, Senegal Coucal, a Rufous-bellied Heron and an excellent sighting of Long-crested Eagle, Yellow-fronted Tinkerbird and Black-collared Barbets. A most successful morning and Martin was suitably rewarded.

We joined Wayne and David for a full-on English breakfast. We then unloaded the Morris from the trailer. It sounded like a Harley Davidson – the cast-iron exhaust manifold weld repair had failed. This may have been caused by the excessive vibration on the rough road after Mazabuka; welding cast iron is seldom successful, especially as the thin casting may have been too brittle. We needed to support and seal the exhaust manifold. Wayne bound it up with steel fencing wire and then used the Gun Gum sealant that Bryan Christie had given us in Bulawayo (Fig.463). If I wanted to drive the Morris across the Victoria Falls Bridge without disturbing the peace, this work was essential.

I then drove the slightly noisy Morris across the lawn to the front of the thatched manor house with a stunning lake in front (Fig.464). I wanted to record a classic image of the Morris in period with an "Out of Africa" backdrop of the homestead built in the 1950s. We also made a video clip with me attempting to take off David Attenborough (Fig.465). As the sun was setting, we took a further series of photos at the same spot. I then did a retake video with the narrative created by my London friend John Greenwood who sent the text on WhatsApp:

The 1929 species had been thought to be extinct in Zambia, but careful nurturing by a dedicated keeper has enabled this particular member of the species to make a rare return to the habitat where it once flourished.

Crazy, this ability to be in a remote part of Africa and yet talk to a friend 6,000 miles away! Graham added the sound of the African Fish Eagle in the background to create the atmosphere. We had a lot of fun. I posted the video clip on Instagram.

We returned to our chalets for sundowners, then to Rory's pub for a farewell chat as he and Dori were leaving for Lusaka early the next morning. Rory compiled and published a series of educational books for training nature guides for the ecotourism industry. The documents are highly professional, comprehensive and provided to each student in their appropriate field. Rory gave us a signed copy of his *Pocket Guide: Birds of Zambia* that he and Derek Solomon had produced. Some years ago, I had donated several photos of Zambia's birds for this publication but later learned that they required images in portrait orientation to fit the size of their small book – whereas my bird pictures are in landscape.

Before dinner we presented Rory and Dori with a WBP mug (my bird website) and BTA car mug. We also handed over a pack of 18 toilet rolls that Wayne had brought along but never needed – they were surplus to requirement. They had a good chuckle at that, wondering who was full of shit. After another scrumptious dinner, Rory and Dori retired early. Rory suffers from back problems; he wears a back support and was not looking forward to the long drive to Lusaka over rough roads the next day.

Graham and I then set out on a night drive to see if we could spot some Nightjars. We followed the road that Martin had taken us on and before long we flushed one. I expected to spot the birds' eyes in the headlights but found that we needed to drive slowly, keeping our eyes peeled for small, unusual lumps like rocks on the edge of the road – these were sitting Nightjars taking in the warmth of the road. In all we spotted eight nightjars and managed to get detailed photos of two species with the aid of my 4,000 lumen torch – using a camera flashlight not only disturbs the bird but also makes the birds' eyes appear blue. We spotted Square-tail and Fiery-necked Nightjars (Figs.466, 467). By the time we returned Wayne and David had retired; Graham and I celebrated our successful day and night with a *dop* of brandy and slept well.

Day 41: 2 May – Masuku Lodge, birding

Graham and I were up early and set out on foot for the nearby dam. The sun was just rising and many birds were perched on the tops of the trees preening and warming in the morning sun. Close to the dam Graham spotted an African Golden Oriole. We walked about 4 kilometres then headed back to the Lodge for breakfast.

In the afternoon we all did our own thing: washing clothes, catching up on WhatsApp messages. Later, we loaded the Morris into the trailer and prepared the rest of the kit ready for our departure the next day. We had a drink on Wayne and David's stoep, discussing the highs and lows of the trip. We laughed at what we had endured and agreed that the highs far outstripped the lows. Eugene, the cook, had prepared dinner for the four of us and really did us proud: Yorkshire pudding again, beef fillet, mixed vegetables, gem squash – prepared perfectly and just delicious. A wonderful end to our stay at this magical place. Off to bed after the usual *dop* of brandy but without ice or water!

Day 42: 3 May – Choma to Livingstone (212km)

After breakfast we assembled the staff. I thanked the five of them for their help and friendliness and then handed them each 100 Kwacha to show our appreciation (Fig.468). Martin had been the gardener for 28 years, the other gardener had been at the Lodge for 10 years, Eugene had been the cook for 7 years. Anna took care of housekeeping, assisted by another lady whose main job was to take care of Granny in her cottage.

We left Masuku at 08:00 (Fig.469), making our way along the 18 kilometres to the main road. Along the way we spotted a couple of small buck in the thick bush. Arriving at central Choma we got the impression that there was a lot of new development taking place; the town was one of the cleanest and best organised that we had come across in Zambia. We could not help being amused at the road-side sale of gravestones (Fig.470).

The road to Kalomo and on towards Livingstone was excellent: a real highway compared to what we had previously encountered. There were very few charcoal dealers along this stretch, which was good news. Unfortunately, closer to Livingstone we were back to poor road surfaces. I was unable to secure accommodation in Livingstone at Olga's Place where Sandy and I stayed in 2015, but they suggested an alternative which was just up the road. I came back smiling, having found suitable accommodation at a great price per room and secure parking. The team laughed when I told them it was called Fawlty Towers, after the British sitcom made famous by John Cleese (Fig.471).

The hotel's large back yard, locked from the street, was where the BMW and trailer were safely parked. The double rooms cost US$55 per room with breakfast included. A simple but smart feature of the Fawlty Towers hotel was that you could help yourself to tea and coffee in their restaurant area all day. We thought this quite innovative. At most other places each room had its own kettle, crockery, tea, coffee and milk sachets that would need constant refreshing.

After settling in, connecting with Wi-Fi and having coffee, we set off for the Zambezi Waterfront where they offer helicopter rides. I had thought that David might photograph the Morris from the air while we crossed the Victoria Falls Bridge. The cost would be US$150 per 15 minutes, but they could not fly lower than 1,500 feet. From that height the Morris would look like a dot and, if the weather was misty, it would not be seen at all; so we scrubbed that idea (Fig.472).

We planned to do the filming the following day. I would obtain a pass to drive the Morris across the bridge and back while David would film from the vantage point. Graham would position himself on the bridge and take photos with his camera. Wayne would stay with David and have the second radio to keep in touch with me.

The Zambezi River was quite full, with a huge amount of water thundering over the Falls and creating dense clouds of mist; depending on the wind direction it was at times almost like light drizzle. *Mosi-oa-Tunya* (the smoke that thunders) lived up to its name.

Fig.460: Dori and Rory McDougall, our hosts

Fig.461: Martin seeking Chaplin's Barbet

Fig.462: Chaplin's Barbet (Lybius Chaplini)

Fig.463: Morris's fractured exhaust temporary fix

Fig.464: Masuku, an idyllic setting in Zambia

Fig.465: The real "Out of Africa" homestead

Fig.466: Graham hunting Nightjars, Masuku

Fig.467: Fiery-necked Nightjar, Masuku

Fig.468: Thanks and appreciation to the staff

Fig.469: Departing Masuku for Livingstone

Fig.470: Roadside gravestones for sale

Fig.471: Our excellent Livingstone B&B

Fig.472: Vic. Falls Bridge from the air

Fig.473: Welcome to Victoria Falls

Fig.474: The magnificent Falls 1904 Bridge

Fig.475: Frank Jenkins and me, Bulawayo 1963

Fig.476: White-water rafting Zambezi, 1984

Fig.477: Zambia Customs and Immigration

Fig.478: Morris crossing the bridge

Fig.479: One vehicle is permitted at a time

Fig.480: This 1908 car visited Livingstone

Fig.481: Lt Graetz en route to Namibia, 1909

Fig.482: Gilg and Kay – Morris Minor 1933

Fig.483: Peter Hills – Morris Minor 2023

We drove to the Falls Bridge (Fig.473), obtained a temporary pass to walk across it and do a reconnoitre for recording the Morris on the bridge. Just before the crossing, on the Zambian side, is an official observation point, a covered deck and sales area but with a limited view of the whole bridge. Further along in open ground we found the perfect spot and at mid-afternoon the sun's angle would illuminate the bridge completely (Fig.474). We agreed that we would get full camera and video coverage from that position.

Graham was delighted to see the Zambezi and Victoria Falls again. The place holds many happy memories for him. He never imagined that he would have the opportunity to see these sights again. I too had visited the Falls several times: first in 1950 from the train but in 1963 over an Easter Weekend, with a pass from Llewellin Barracks in Bulawayo, Frank Jenkins and I hitch-hiked (in uniform) (Fig.475) to Livingstone. My parents had motored down from Kitwe in Dad's immaculate 1956 Chevrolet and picked my brother up from the School of Infantry in Gwelo (Gweru); we all stayed at the Livingstone Hotel. This was memorable because while Dad was playing dice at the hotel bar he threw five sixes and the hotel sent him a letter confirming this very rare "throw". In 1984, just before we left Zambia for the UK, a group of us from Kalulushi went white-water rafting down the Zambezi, starting from below the Falls (Fig.476). I have so many happy memories of this special place.

Feeling pleased with what we had seen and having agreed on a plan for the next afternoon we crossed the road to Olga's Place where they serve 30 centimetre diameter pizzas with generous toppings. Two were quite sufficient; there was even some left over to take away in a doggy bag. Feeling relaxed at how well the day had played out, we all retired to be full of energy for the busy day ahead.

Fig.484: The welcome guard with AK47

Fig.485: Livingstone Museum

Fig.486: David Livingstone – Zambia's first tourist!   Fig.487: Fawlty Towers – tea and Wi-Fi

Day 43: 4 May – Livingstone, crossing the Victoria Falls

When we visited the Livingstone Museum, they demanded 90 Kwacha per person for non-residents. I convinced them in Bemba that as a Kitwe resident we should only pay 10 Kwacha per head and they agreed! The museum has considerable historical records but unfortunately the displays are hardly readable. They were probably prepared before independence – over 60 years old and faded, as well as not being in tune with the modern museum format. There was quite a lot of political background about the colonial era, the "Struggle", and Kenneth Kaunda "Saving the Nation" but rather one-sided. You need to make up your own mind according to your personal beliefs or undertake a broader study. There was reference to Alice Lenshina's part in the Lumpa Uprising that was more balanced than I have read elsewhere but the deaths reported were less by a factor of 10 than my knowledge of the numbers when in Military Intelligence with the Zambia Rifles – I was in Chinsali during the conflict in 1964.

Outside the museum is a Provost Trainer Aeroplane. I wanted to have a photo with the Morris in front of the museum and would return later. Back at the hotel, we decided to grease the trailer's hydraulics and check the oil and water in the BMW to prepare for the return journey to South Africa.

At about 14:00 we made our way to the Falls Bridge for the photo shoot of the Morris with the sunlight in our favour. After being processed through Customs and Immigration we unloaded the Morris and drove to the entrance of the Customs Building (Fig.477). A very obliging young lady officer arranged the pass for me to drive the Morris over the bridge and return to Zambia. When she came to check the Morris's registration, she was amazed at what she saw. She asked to have her photo taken in the driving seat and departed with a huge smile on her face.

Wayne carried the heavy video tripod for David's video and had his first ride in the Morris as far as the steps to the viewpoint deck on the Zambian side. David and Graham, armed with all their cameras and video equipment walked to the bridge. I carried one walkie-talkie and Wayne the other to inform David when I was about to start driving across – David was further away from the deck to have an unobstructed view and a steady surface for the tripod. When I was in the best position, he started recording a video of the Morris driving across the bridge (Figs.478–479). Meanwhile, Graham was on the bridge itself near the railway track to take close-up photos. I made a couple of runs between Zambia and Zimbabwe without any hindrance by the bridge officials on either side: in fact, they seemed bemused at the sight of this old car. It was such a thrill driving the Morris with the light mist from the Falls cooling my face; I was exhilarated as this was a long-held dream being fulfilled.

Since the early 1900s many thousands of cars have driven over the famous Victoria Falls Bridge (Fig.480). The first car was an Argyll, driven by Captain R.N. Kelsey and his team on an unsuccessful attempt to drive from the Cape to Cairo in 1914. (Ref.8). Oberleutnant Paul Graetz and his Gaggenau tour across Africa from east to west in 1908 (Fig.481) passed through Livingstone en route to Namibia (Ref.9). Then Gilg and Kay on their 1933 African adventure (Fig.482) crossing the Victoria Falls bridge – note that the bridge framework is the same as that taken in 2023 (Fig.483). This excellent composition of the diminutive 1929 Morris with the gigantic Zambezi in the background is memorable.

On the Zambian side there was a checkpoint with a guard armed with an AK47 rifle (Fig.484). This soldier was so interested in the Morris that he seemed oblivious to the security of the 1905 bridge. How different was this from the attitude of the guards at the Kafue Bridge – where Graham took one snap – and other minor "infringements". The guard did not prevent Graham from taking a photo of him standing next to the Morris with his AK47 resting on the running board. Exhilarated at having ticked the final box of our tour, I wanted to get back to Livingstone town before we lost the light, but in my haste I forgot to collect my driver's licence from Immigration: they had retained it to prove that I had returned to Zambia; I planned to collect it the next day.

Since we had achieved everything, I drove the Morris back into Livingstone, taking David to the Museum for the photo shoot there (Figs.485, 486). We loaded the Morris into the trailer for the final time and relaxed at the hotel, enjoying tea, beers and Wi-Fi updates (Fig.487). To celebrate the successful day, crossing the bridge in the Morris, David recording a video and Graham taking photos at the bridge entrance, we had dinner at a fish restaurant called Sea Spice across the road from our hotel. It had been some time since we had had fish and the menu looked tempting. Graham, who always ate small portions, opted for the Kiddies Menu of battered fish fingers and chips including three prawns. After seeing a huge serving being delivered to another table, the rest of us decided to have same. It was more than sufficient and an enjoyable celebration dinner.

Day 44: 5 May – Livingstone Zambia to Zimbabwe Border

We cleared the Zambian Customs and Immigration at 07:15, I retrieved my driver's licence and we made our way (Fig.488) passing the Zambezi River in full flood to the Zimbabwe border. As we left Zambia, we reflected on the experience of traversing the country, meeting great people and enjoying their generous assistance in a country that has so much potential.

Fig.488: Leaving Livingstone and Zambia

Fig.489: The Big Tree, Zimbabwe side

Zambia was my home for the first half of my life. When we left in 1984 it was with mixed feelings but both Sandy and I knew that the decision was right for our future. If we make any trips to Zambia in future, they will be organised by others and only to the wonderful game reserves. Dealing with over-sensitive police and corruption is not a pleasant experience. I did hope that official attitudes had changed, but after almost 60 years of independence, there remains immature hostility towards foreigners. This is a pity because individual Zambians we met were generally polite, well-spoken and fun.

The many friends old and new who have made Zambia their permanent home appear to have sufficient finance to enjoy a high standard of life. Many seem to exist in their own isolated paradise while others are trapped with insufficient funds to settle and retire elsewhere. As long as their health is good they remain happy there. I was informed that there are super-rich Zambians who enjoy the high life but for the majority, post-independence has not brought the expectations they deserve. Sadly, for most, it is a daily struggle and life expectancy is low.

Chapter 8

Zimbabwe Southbound

Day 44: 5 May – Victoria Falls to Hwange Game Reserve (213km)

Back in Zimbabwe! However, at the Zimbabwean Customs and Immigration post, things did not go as smoothly as before; there appeared to be one obstacle after another to overcome. First, they claimed that the vehicle's third-party insurance had expired on 26 April as it only ran for 30 days – a fact that was not explained when it was taken out. I had to pay US$60 to renew the policy for only 2 days!

The next problem was that the trailer was now considered to be a commercial vehicle, which was not the case on entering Zimbabwe. It needed to be cleared by an official clearing agent who "happened" to be the well-dressed gentleman standing next to me. He had his documentation at the ready and after some form-filling at the same desk as the Customs officer and paying a further US$50, we were cleared to leave. Armed with the necessary pass, we had a further hold-up at the gate as the police wanted to inspect inside the trailer. After I opened it they took a cursory glance and allowed us to continue on our way. The whole procedure took an hour and it was now 09:45 and I had been fleeced of a total of US$110.

A short way from the border is the entrance to the National Park and the Rain Forest. David had never visited the Falls before and it would be a lifetime opportunity for him to see David Livingstone's statue, the Devil's Cataract and the rainforest. A couple of coaches were parked at the entrance and at least 50 tourists were waiting to get in. I went to the front of the queue to establish the cost. This turned out be US$50 per person. All except David had visited before but he was not that interested and since our time was limited, we decided to move on. We deviated along Zambezi Drive to see the Big Tree, a huge baobab that is reputed to be over 1,200 years old (Fig.489).

Departing Victoria Falls town at 10:15 we headed for Hwange following Wayne's GPS – not always reliable – but after travelling 51 kilometres the road seemed too good and very quiet. I felt we were going west and not south; so I checked my iPad's tracker programme that confirmed that we were heading for Kazangula: Wayne's GPS was looking for the huge Hwange Game Reserve and not Main Camp! We headed back towards Victoria Falls town and found the correct road south at 11:30. This lost us both time and diesel that we could ill afford.

The road between Victoria Falls and Hwange was not great, but about 30 kilometres before reaching Hwange it deteriorated so much that we rated it as one of the worst stretches we had encountered (Fig.490). There were some small coal mines nearby and the road was black and filthy from coal spillage; the heavy trucks transporting the coal had destroyed what was left of a paved road.

We finally arrived at Hwange at 13.30 to stock up with food and drinks at a PicknPay for the game reserve camp. There we noticed that the trailer hitch had dropped significantly. On further inspection we discovered that the hitch had torn away from the BMW's rear body panel. (Fig.491). This was extremely serious and needed urgent attention. At the entrance to Hwange was a Tiger Wheel and Tyre outlet where we stopped to seek advice. It was a Friday afternoon and most places were closing.

Fig.490: Victoria Falls to Hwange – poor road?

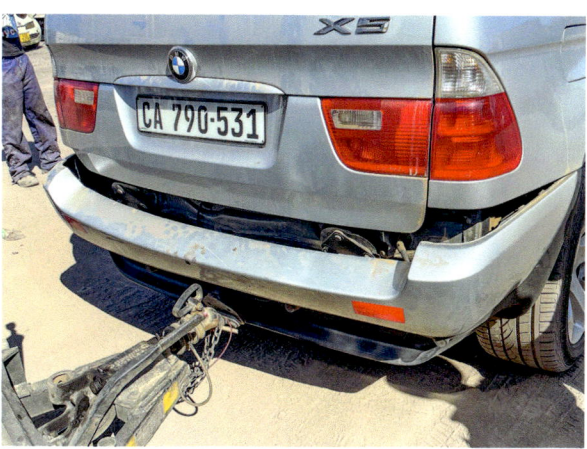

Fig.491: The trailer hitch was collapsing

Fig.492: The Zimbabwean mechanics and Supervisor

Fig.493: Found a welder, made good repairs

Fig.494: Oh dear, what can we do now?

Fig.495: Back in action but for how long?

Fig.496: The long drive to the Game Park

Fig.497: Late night check-in, exhausted

Fig.498: Morning relief, game and bird viewing

Fig.499: At the water hole, great views

Fig.500: U-bolts strengthened the trailer frame

Fig.501: Ground Hornbills at the exit

A mechanic said the problem was out of their league but suggested that we try a welding and panel-beating shop called Amora about 2 kilometres on the road out of town.

Amora was basically a container on the far edge of a very large open piece of barren dusty ground and we were very doubtful that anything positive could come out of this. It was too risky to attempt to reach the Main Camp game reserve as the trailer hitch was close to collapse. A couple of fellows were hanging around and the one in charge, a Tonga with a long name, introduced himself and asked me to reverse the BMW up to the container so that he could have a look. We later referred to him as Mr Welder.

After the trailer had been unhitched, Mr Welder lay underneath the BMW to assess the situation. He said that he could do the welding and fix the problem. "When?" "Now!" With the help of a couple of his chaps, they placed a large piece of cardboard on the ground and started to remove the rear bumper (Fig.492). This was a bit of a struggle but, once it and the metal plate behind it were removed, the problem was evident. The tow-hitch was clearly not designed for the BMW or the load it was pulling. It was a cheap after-market unit with thick metal plates bolted to the thin sheet metal of the car's body and these were in the process of being ripped off the vehicle.

The whole towbar was fastened to the vehicle with two angle-iron struts that were badly bent some 35° downward. Despite the angle, the struts remained bolted to the car's chassis channel with a couple of bolts. Surely after a few more kilometres of bad roads this would undoubtedly have led to disaster, releasing the trailer and its precious contents. Once everything had been stripped into component parts, we could understand the problem and the emergency solution. Mr Welder suggested that he weld another piece of angle-iron onto the existing ones to form a box section which would be much stronger. We agreed that this was an excellent solution (Fig.493).

On a lighter note, while all the work was being carried out, we had to sit around and wait, our future was in the hands of a bunch of bush mechanics. It was also very hot, dry and a dusty area; clearly, we were all worried and tired (Fig.494). Then a strange fellow approached Wayne and Graham. He said that he was a pastor presently out of work but would be prepared to say a few prayers for us (no doubt for money). Wayne and Graham declined and suggested that he go and speak to David – who was not impressed with either the pastor or his teammates for the referral!

First, Mr Welder had to beat the existing angle-iron struts with a 4 pound hammer until they were reasonably straight – as they say in South Africa, "he bent it straight". Bear in mind that these fellows function with no workbench, no vice, no safe electricity supply. Extension cables were connected without the use of electrical tape: they had simply bound plastic bags around the cables to insulate the connections! They attempted to work with limited or crude tools so I provided them all that was needed to get the job done quickly.

At one point there were five fellows lying under the rear of the BMW, all involved in bolting and assembling the tow-hitch. Amazingly the whole job was completed in 2½ hours (Fig.495) and for US$150 that I was happy to pay – anyway it was our only option.

The BMW's rear plastic bumper and bracket (about 1.5 metres long) could not be secured as its fittings were damaged. Despite limited space in the trailer we placed it alongside the Morris covered with sleeping bags to prevent it rubbing against the body of the car. We were on our way again by 17:00, hopefully with a secure towbar and a safe connection to the trailer.

After departing south of Hwange the road to the airport turn-off was excellent and not too bad after that – the moon was rising but it was difficult to see and avoid some of the potholes (Fig.496). At one stage Graham, who was seated in the rear of the BMW, remarked on a new noise that he could hear every now and then but it didn't seem to get any worse. It was dark and we were not in a position to investigate it.

From the turn-off to Hwange National Park, the road to Main Camp was excellent – which was comforting as it was now completely dark (Fig.497). Driving slowly, we did not spot any animals or birds along this stretch of road. We arrived at the camp at 19:00. The booked accommodation was a twin-bedroomed cottage but not self-catering as we had expected. This made food preparation difficult, but the beers were still ice-cold. Our portable gas cooker came in handy for boiling water and making a basic braai. Then it was off to bed after another tension-filled and tiring day.

Day 45: 6 May – Hwange Game Reserve (Main Camp)

The plan was that we would all go on an early birding/game drive but when the time came Wayne and David chose not to go. Wayne had visited many game reserves before, but David had not; so this came as quite a surprise. Graham could not believe that they would forego such an opportunity in a renowned game reserve, preferring to sit around the camp without even access to Wi-Fi. However, we could not persuade them – perhaps the previous few days had exhausted them. I was disappointed as the main reason for visiting the game park was to give the team a treat after the tour, when the focus had been primarily on the Morris.

When we unhitched the trailer we noticed that the towbar was again very loose; on inspection we found that all three of four bolts had sheared. Wow! We had driven 90km from Hwange to Main Camp towing the Morris in the trailer and wondered for what distance was the single remining bolt securing it? Surely the gods had been smiling on us again! Perhaps this was the noise Graham had heard the previous evening? I shudder to think of the consequences had the trailer come adrift. Certainly, it and the Morris, would have been smashed. I concluded that the Amora chaps had used the "cosmetic" low tensile bolts rather than the originals.

We set out on our drive around the reserve knowing that the hitch would have to be fixed before the trailer could travel any further. We put it out of our minds and focused – literally – on the birds and game to come (Fig.498). We saw several species of birds and were able to photograph most of them, but also saw a good variety of game. We came across three families of elephant, one of which was at a small dam being filled by a solar-powered pump (Fig.499). This family had two new-born youngsters who were covered in mud; baby elephants are always such fun to watch. There were also a couple of large lone bull elephants along the road that we kept at a distance.

Other game spotted included impala, steenbok, giraffe, zebra, kudu, warthog, hippo and a single crocodile. We had hoped to do a particular loop, but by 12:00 we had not even reached the halfway stage and decided to return by the same route arriving at the camp by 14:00.

We established that there was a workshop in the camp, but as it was a Saturday afternoon there was no one around and the workshop was locked. We spoke to a Ranger who was about to leave for Binga; he was unable to help personally but referred us to a chap called Gary who lived close by and had the key to the workshop. Gary was having his afternoon siesta, but eventually we met him. I explained our predicament and how I planned to fix the problem, but he was not overly concerned; his only comment on our getting the trailer back to Cape Town was, "Good luck".

I did, however, persuade him to allow us to use the pedestal drill – this was not attached to the floor as per normal practice. Once we had all helped to secure the drilling machine, we managed to drill two large holes through the box section of the hitch to house the high-tensile U-bolts on either side as the bolts available were not long enough. This done, we reassembled the hitch; the U-bolts were emergency spares for the Priclo trailer springs and appeared to be very secure and strong. Perhaps another Houdini escape (Fig.500).

One of the park employees came to help us and knew where to find things, but most of the equipment in the workshop, including their pedestal drill, was not in working order. Once again, electrical plugs were scarce and connections were crudely wired together and covered with a bit of insulation tape. Gary told us that the workshop and all the machine tools were a recent gift (from China) but in no time everything was "buggered".

The original plan was to move to a more organised bush camp the next day where food and accommodation would be provided at a reduced cost. This would involve travelling back an additional 60 kilometres on rough park roads. Together we discussed our options: the reserve was not that well populated with game or birds and since Wayne and David had little interest in game viewing there was no point spending more time there. We all agreed it was time to head home and calculated that if we left early next morning, we could cross the South Africa border late that afternoon. Graham and I enjoyed a last *dop* of my good whiskey before bed.

Day 46: 7 May – Hwange Reserve to Beit Bridge Border (720km)

We were up early, packed all our personal belongings, this time distributing most of the weight from the front storage section of the trailer into the rear section. We placed as many items as possible over the double wheel section of the trailer to reduce the load on the tow-hitch and perhaps help reduce the stress on the repair.

As we were departing the perimeter fence of the park, we spotted three Ground Hornbills right next to the road (Fig.501). These are highly endangered birds – so it was wonderful to see them up so close as they flew into the forest.

From the Hwange Game Park turn-off, the main road, as far as Lupani, was terrible and it was impossible to avoid hitting the odd pothole. This increased our concerns over the strength of the tow-hitch and we checked it regularly. We reached Bulawayo at about 13:00 making a short stop on the outskirts for refreshments. Graham managed to buy a six-pack of beers for the evening. The road from Bulawayo to Gwanda – where Graham had worked for 2 years before his marriage – was quite good and we arrived there at about 14:30. We stopped to fill up with fuel. The chaps were pleasantly surprised when I came back loaded with ice-cream cones and Colcom pork pies for lunch. Yes, we lived in style!

The next town was West Nicholson, home of the famous Liebigs and Colcom meat products. The sun was setting as we passed West Nicholson but just before crossing the Mzingwane River (a major tributary of the Limpopo) we were flagged down by a police officer in full uniform. He asked if we were heading for Beit Bridge and said he needed a lift. When he cheekily attempted to open the rear door to get in, I told him that there was no room as by law we were limited to four passengers. Wayne said "bugger him" and immediately put his foot down.

After West Nicholson the road was terrible; there was a 90 kilometre stretch that was undriveable (Fig.502). Bruce Beckley from Bulawayo had messaged me to warn us to take a dirt road deviation when we reached that section. This proved to be a lot better but had been in use for some time and the big trucks had done it no good. The dust permeated everything in the trailer, the colour of the Chilupala caramel.

Fig.502: The road to Bulawayo, the worst yet

Fig.503: Zimbabwe's hi-tech customs hall

At one stage we came to a toll where only one fellow was attending to the traffic in both directions and there was a bit of queue. A couple of vehicles drove up the left-hand side and pushed in at the last minute. One local tried to cut in front of our BMW but after a few choice words from me he was left to try his luck with the next car.

Day 46: 7 May – Zimbabwe, Beit Bridge Border to South Africa

Arriving at Beit Bridge at 17:30 it was now dusk; we cleared Customs and Immigration by 18:00 but not before I had to pay yet another road tax fee – a real joke as we were leaving the country (Fig.503). Zimbabwe had fleeced us at every opportunity! We returned to the BMW and trailer in the car park with all the necessary exit stamps when a very large electronic sign in the car park stated that CA750591 was free to leave. Wow – very hi-tech, Zimbabwe (Fig.504) – we were relieved to depart for South Africa!

Fig.504: Our vehicle passed to enter South Africa

When we arrived to cross the Limpopo River Bridge, we were at the end of a solid line of huge trucks parked the length of the 457 metre bridge. We wondered if it was designed to carry such a static load. The security guard at the entrance indicated that this was the queue to join.

While sitting in the queue on the bridge, a truck in the opposite lane came along heading for Zimbabwe: the whole bridge vibrated and our BMW bounced. In the long term this cannot be good for the structure of the bridge; it was no doubt designed for moving traffic but surely not a whole line-up of stationary trucks. Time will tell!

After about 20 minutes several trucks passed us heading north for Zimbabwe. Then on our side a few cars passed us going south and driving along the oncoming lane! Finally, we decided, "If they can go, let us try it or we will be here all night." We must have passed 50 trucks and, to our surprise, arrived at the South African border unscathed. Who dares wins!

Chapter 9

Return to Cape Town

Day 46: 7 May – Beit Bridge to Makhado, South Africa Border (120km)

Back in South Africa! We cleared South African Customs and Immigration by 18:45 with no hassles. In fact, there was a relaxed atmosphere as one of the young officials was celebrating her birthday and, when the staff sang Happy Birthday, we also joined in! It was dark and beginning to rain, and Makhado was some distance away over a mountain range. Leaving Musina, we commented on the world-class quality of the road, with good markings and cats-eyes. How different it was from what we experienced in the two countries to the North.

The dash from Hwange to South Africa was unplanned – there was no internet access on the way and I had been unable to book accommodation for the night. We headed for Northgate Lodge where we had stayed on the way up in the hope that rooms were available. Fortunately, there was a chap at the gate who checked us in. The electricity was off due to loadshedding but it came on within half an hour at 21:00. We used our gas braai to cook the pork chops we had purchased in Bulawayo; they went down very well with a couple of beers. Another long and tiring day, we covered a distance of 614 kilometres from Hwange to Beit Bridge, then 120km to Makhado (Louis Trichardt) – a total of 734km in one day. The stress and uncertainty of customs and immigration on both sides of the border, the terrible roads after Hwange, the rain before arriving at the Lodge had all taken its toll. A comfortable bed and sleep was needed.

Day 47: 8 May – Makhado to Winburg (718km)

From Northgate Lodge we headed for Johannesburg; the N1 highway was in excellent condition, and we made good time. We rested at the Kranskop Engen 1-Stop at 11:45 where we had breakfast and took a last group photo (Fig.505). Near Pretoria we ran into a severe thunderstorm that lasted all the way to Johannesburg. Fortunately, the rain cleared just as we dropped Wayne off at a shopping complex to wait for his son. We felt quite guilty leaving him standing under a tree in the parking lot when it started to drizzle. As we departed there was a flash of lightning and crash of thunder, and Wayne made a dash for cover in the mall.

Fig.505: Farewell to Wayne at Johannesburg

I took over the driving to head for Winburg in Free State; it was still some distance away and the weather was overcast. The plan had always been to locate the old hotel in Winburg where the two intrepid travellers, Gilg and Kay in their 1933 Morris had stayed. My intention was to replicate their photo taken outside the hotel's entrance.

Not having booked accommodation, we hoped to find a B&B in the Winburg area for the night. The town is 2 kilometres beyond the exit from the N1 to the N5, towards Bethlehem and Kwazulu-Natal. Winburg is one of the oldest settlements in South Africa. It used to be a popular stopover but the highway has cut it off. Graham had passed Winburg many times but never entered the town. It was 18:00 and dark, but we spotted a sign to a guesthouse. I asked for directions to the guesthouse and the old hotel and found that they are both owned by a chap called Deon. We decided to try our luck at the hotel (Fig.506).

Finding the Winburg Hotel was a challenge, the whole town was in darkness due to loadshedding and there was hardly a person on the streets. Eventually we came across a very large building that was the hotel. There were no vehicles in the huge car park and it appeared desolate; we wondered if it was actually open. Entering the Reception area with a stuffed caracal and an ostrich on display was rather creepy – like the set of a Hitchcock movie. A fellow emerged from the nearby bar and confirmed that they had rooms available and that our vehicle would be quite safe parked in front of the hotel. On inspection the rooms had antique furniture and appeared to be unchanged since the hotel was established in 1857. The price reflected the condition but, since we had few options in this "one-horse town", it was a bed and we were cold and exhausted.

The original entrance was almost the same as when Alan Gilg and Walter Kay stayed there in 1933. Inside the building there is a mahogany flight of stairs leading to the first-floor bedrooms that all access to a balcony that runs along the length of the hotel. In its day it must have seen grand times. The bath in the room that Graham and David shared was at least 2 metres long and proportionately deep!

Loadshedding lasted until 22:00 which meant that there was no power for their pumped water system. The toilets did not flush, which was unpleasant. There was no food served at the "hotel", but we had a pack of four sausages in Graham's cool bag and decided to use the hotel's portable gas braai. Fortunately, the gas lasted just long enough to cook our meagre "dinner". We then headed to the candlelit bar where Deon and his friends were having a drink. Graham and I decided to have a double brandy on the rocks while David had fruit juice. Brandy and Coke is the drink of choice in many parts of the country. Taking ours neat amazed the barman, who probably thought he was dealing with a couple of hardened drinkers – not far wrong (they were our sleeping pills)! The walls in the bar were similarly festooned with stuffed trophies: giraffe, springbok, kudu, eland, gemsbok, buffalo, warthog, impala and zebra.

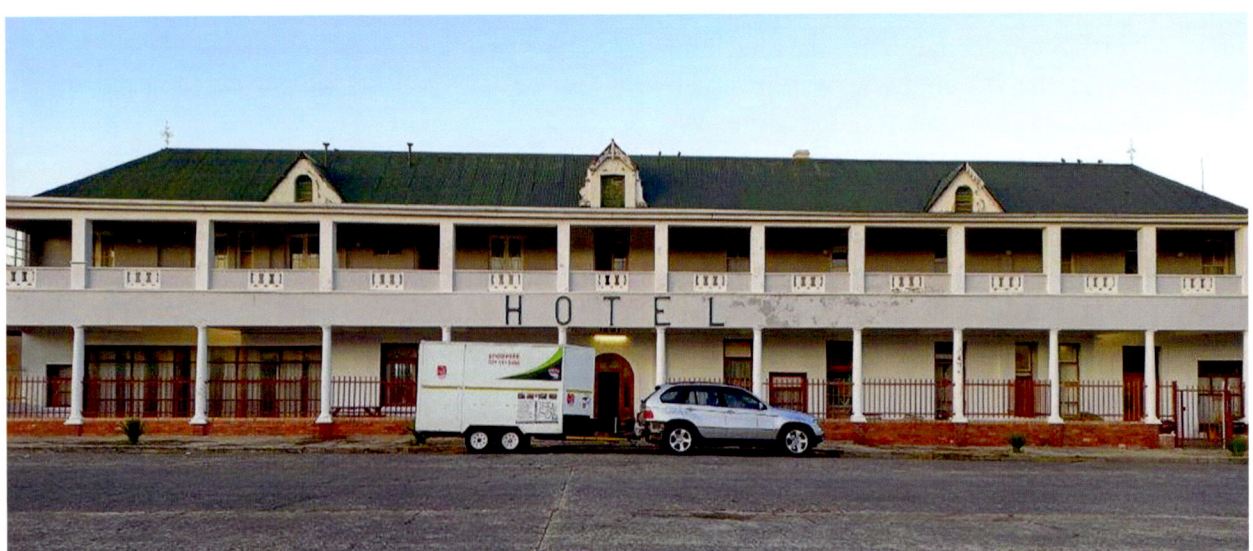

Fig.506: Overnighted at Winburg Hotel repeating the 1933 Gilg Liverpool to Cape Town stay

The night was by far the coldest we had experienced on the trip and, not being used to it, none of us slept well. I was disturbed at 22:00 when the power came on and the noisy toilet cistern started to fill with water before leaking onto the ceramic tiled bathroom floor and making it very slippery, in fact treacherous. My "bathroom" – a flattering description – was larger than my double bedroom and nothing worked properly. We needed to sleep in our fleeces and jackets; it was a cold long night waiting for the morning.

Day 48: 9 May – Winburg to Beaufort West (650km)

It was a relief to get out of a cold bed in the morning and put on some extra-warm clothes. There was no water and we had to use some of our bottled water to wash and clean our teeth. After loading our belongings into the BMW, we took our photos. The street was least 30 metres wide and it was easy to turn around with the trailer.

We replicated the 1933 photo of Gilg at the entrance of the hotel with me at the very same spot. (Figs.507, 508) with the 1929 Morris.

Across the road is an impressive Anglican Church and next to the hotel is the Post Office Building, dated 1938. Winburg once prosperous is now virtually a ghost town.

Fig.507: Gilg's 1933 Morris Minor – Winburg Hotel

Fig.508: Hills's 1929 Morris Minor – Winburg Hotel

Our plan was to overnight somewhere closer to Cape Town so that the following day we would arrive home at lunch time rather than in the late afternoon traffic when it was getting dark. We set off for Lemoenfontein Game Lodge outside Beaufort West where Sandy and I had enjoyed a stay before. I booked two rooms for us. After Bloemfontein we passed the Gariep Dam, then crossed the Orange River towards Colesberg where we had a hearty breakfast at 11:00.

Graham took over the driving; the road was good, with only a few trucks, and we made good time. The turn-off to Lemoenfontein is about 7 kilometres from Beaufort West – it's a dusty dirt road leading towards the distant hills. On the way we had a wonderful surprise when we saw a small herd of sable antelope feeding close to the road; these endangered animals are well protected by the lodge.

Lemoenfontein Game Lodge boosted our morale. We arrived at 16:00. The standard of accommodation is in a different league (Fig.509). I had my own room, while Graham and David shared. After a wonderful hot shower and changed into clean clothes, we relaxed before dinner. The view from my window was of typical Karoo *koppies*. The lights of Beaufort West in the distance twinkled in the evening sky. A very peaceful and relaxing setting: a few birds flitted about as the sun set. Dinner was

Fig.509: Lemoenfontein Game Lodge

Fig.510: Excellent Karoo lamb served

a buffet with succulent Karoo lamb and vegetables – out of this world – followed by a delicious dessert (Fig.510). After dinner, Graham treated us to a final drink and then we settled down for a warm comfortable night's sleep.

Day 49: 10 May – Beaufort West to Cape Town and Home (462km)

It was a beautiful morning with stunning warm light illuminating the whole area (Fig.511). As usual we were all up for an early shower and ready to hit the road. The car park was on two levels and rather tight with the large trailer, but Graham called on his trailer-reversing skills and positioned the rig for the exit. I took over the driving to Laingsburg. On the way out of Lemoenfontein we had fabulous sightings of the sable in perfect morning light (Fig.512).

The road from Beaufort West to Laingsburg was quiet: not too many trucks and the going was easy. The weather was a lot cooler than we had experienced in the previous few weeks and seemed to get colder as we neared Cape Town. At Laingsburg (10:30) we had a tasty breakfast of chicken-mayo toasted sandwiches and cappuccino. The petrol attendants remembered us stopping there 7 weeks before and were thrilled to see us and hear about our adventures. Graham was not feeling very well, having picked up a head cold just before leaving Hwange, and he decided not to drive. Having had a break, I was happy to continue.

We passed through the Huguenot Tunnel at 13:00 and arrived in Wynberg an hour later. As I drove into Oaktree hooting, Sandy rushed out with a huge smile on her face, giving me the biggest hug and so relieved that we had returned home safe and sound. Seven weeks away was a long time (Fig.513). We unpacked the BMW and trailer and sorted out our belongings. After I disconnected the trickle charger, Graham removed his car from my garage. I could then reverse the Morris out of the trailer and park it in my garage (Fig.514).

With the trailer now empty, we positioned the BMW and trailer so that I could drive straight out in the morning to return the trailer to Priclo. Graham set off for his home; after spending so much time together it felt strange to be saying farewell. Later David's lift arrived and Sandy and I went inside and had the best cup of tea.

For the BTA Team it was the end of a memorable, enjoyable, sometimes scary, yet successful adventure over 49 days. It was exciting and challenging but, thanks to years of detailed planning and support by many known and unknown folk, the trip was undoubtedly a once in a lifetime experience that will be cemented in our memory banks and fondly remembered for a long time to come. On 28 May I presented the car at the Crankhandle Club Natter in pristine condition after "Tracing its African Routes" (Fig.514) to the amazement of the club members..

Fig.511: Sunrise at Beaufort West

Fig.512: Sable at Lemoenfontein Lodge

Fig.513: "I will be back" – love Sandy's hugs

Fig.514: Chilupala made it with good fortune

Fig.515: Crankhandle Club Members

Fig.516: BTA 2023 mug to Graham Pringle

Fig.517: BTA 2023 mug to David Forgus

Fig.518: BTA 2023 mug sent to Wayne Taylor

31 May 2023 – Follow-up Presentation to Crankhandle Club

The Crankhandle Club requested me to give a follow-up presentation of the trip on a Wednesday that coincided with my 79th birthday! This time the Morris was placed inside the clubhouse and admired by all members who could not believe that this little car had travelled so far and endured so much – yet here it was looking splendid. The presentation covered the challenges and successes of the BTA trip. Most people were amazed that four elderly blokes had overcome so many issues (Fig.515). Many members were in attendance but especially Sandy and her cousin, Rose Malinaric, who has made a huge contribution editing and guiding me on preparing this book.

Since I had used up my stock of BTA mugs I had a fresh batch made but this time with 2023 – the initial batch in 2020 celebrated 50 years of the Morris since 1970. I took the opportunity to present my team members, Graham and David, with the new mugs – as well as one to Megan Greyvensteyn, the Club Chairperson. One mug was also despatched to Johannesburg for Wayne (Figs.516–518).

The Club's editor also requested that I provide a summary report for the *Crankhandle Chronicle*, that was subsequently published in two parts in the *Chronicle*'s issues (Ref.10). Similar articles were published in the UK's *Vintage Minor Register* Magazine, Summer (M186 and Autumn M187) (Refs.11, 12) and the *Morris Register*'s December 2023 issue (Ref.16).

Graeme Hurst, a freelance writer for the international UK based *Classic & Sports Car* magazine, attended the presentation and was keen to do a write-up of the BTA tour. When he heard that in September 1993 his magazine had done a 5-page spread of the Morris's restoration, he was even more excited to follow up this car progress and unique tour 31 years later. Together we prepared a fresh article that was eventually published in the June 2024 issue in the UK and then internationally (Ref.17).

Chapter 10

Trip challenges

Zambia, England, India

If you worry about all the things that could go wrong, you will never do anything.

Anon

In 1984 while working in Zambia I was headhunted to the UK. Many of my work colleagues were astounded! How could a local boy, trained as an apprentice in the copper mining industry, land a plum job in the UK? Since I had made a significant contribution to the safety of mine hoist-winding equipment, the engineers at Chililabombwe Mine presented me with a Lilly winder speed governor (Fig.134). The mechanism consists of two shiny brass balls and throughout my life it has seemed that these "golden balls" have clanged several times to do their magic when problems arise. Certainly, we appear to have had a charmed life – and no more so than during the Back-to-Africa trip.

A very dear lifelong friend kept telling me that this idea of driving the Morris around Zimbabwe and Zambia was "an exercise in futility". I wondered if he was envious. Had he been in better health he might have joined me. Was he worried about my well-being? (He often was!) Certainly, he was not alone in recognising the danger of this adventure but, as Del Boy of the successful UK sitcom *Only Fools and Horses* would say, "Who dares wins".

During our 9 years in Mumbai (India) leading up to my seventieth birthday, Sandy and I realised that we no longer wished to return to our beautiful home in Cheshire (England) which required regular maintenance of house and garden and certainly could not be left empty for six or more months. We no longer wanted to rent out the property: so, instead, we would be swallows spending summers in London and Cape Town with "lock up and go" homes in both locations. This decision was helped as Sandy had family in Cape Town and I had many school friends there. By 2014 we changed our lifestyle and hope to continue this pattern as long as our health permits.

A friend in the Crankhandle Club (Peter Truter) persuaded me to think about bringing my special Morris, Chilupala, to the Cape and this brought the Back-to-Africa dream one step closer. We began to formulate a plan to undertake the mad-cap adventure of driving our rather flimsy small 94-year-old car around Central Africa. Apart from the distances involved and the condition of the roads, the independent African countries had become wilder than when the colonists cleared the jungle to set up roads, rail, industry and agriculture. Huge trucks from the Congo, Tanzania, Zambia and Zimbabwe now make their way to South Africa transporting raw materials, usually destined for China. They return with imported items as few goods are manufactured locally. The roads, or what is left of them, are known to be very busy and the truckers would have little time for a little Morris puttering along at 50km/h!

Shipping the Morris to Cape Town in 2019 was straightforward. But there were political issues in Zimbabwe: President Mugabe was displaced and died soon afterwards. A destructive hurricane in Zimbabwe caused huge damage, affecting many rural people and then petrol became scarce. My contacts in Zimbabwe assured me that we would be okay as fuel was being smuggled into the country from Botswana. The last straw was when Covid-19 struck and the borders were closed.

Each year I had to apply for a renewal of the vehicle's carnet (at a cost) but in 2023 I was informed that it would not be extended beyond 27 July 2023. We were booked to return to the UK in June. A further worry was that my sister Ann was severely ill – sadly, she passed away a few days before our return. My window to make the trip was very narrow. It had to be at the tail end of the annual rains and the cooler autumn weather would be better for the Morris's engine. In fact, we did not have a drop of rain but the early part of the trip was very hot.

BTA Team Changes

Selection of the Back-to-Africa Team started in 2018. David Forgus had agreed to be the photographer and video operator. I had upgraded my cameras and passed on my Nikon D800 to him at a modest price; so he had a more powerful unit. Several members of the Crankhandle Club expressed interest in joining me but probably got cold feet or domestic pressure to decline. My brother Colin, a retired opera singer living in Germany, was keen to join me and become my diarist: his flight was booked to join us in Johannesburg. However, by 2021 Colin had debilitating medical issues that ruled him out. Next, my brother-in-law Graham Lowden, newly retired and winding down his consultancy in Cape Town, was very enthusiastic at the prospect of travelling around Zimbabwe and Zambia. Unfortunately, he too developed serious illness and could not be away from Cape Town for an extended period while undergoing treatment.

As luck would have it, a relatively new friend, Graham Pringle, with a mutual interest in birding lent me a book he had written during Covid lockdown on his life in Rhodesia up to 1980. Sadly, his wife had passed away a few years before and he had created a "family" book of their history for their grandchildren. I was fascinated by his background: both of us had grown up in the Rhodesias (North and South) and our respective early lives were almost in parallel – we both loved the bush, fishing and birding. Also, we were Queen's Scouts and attended the Central African Jamboree in 1959 (see Appendix IV: The Boy Scouts of Rhodesia). We were conscripted to the Rhodesia Regiment only a couple of intakes apart. Graham's professional writing and attention to detail rang a bell; I invited him to join me on the trip and asked him to be my diarist. He immediately accepted and proved to be a "golden" asset to the team and me. His career as a banker did not prevent him from assisting me in the preparation of the Morris especially when the engine needed serious repairs.

I needed a third person in the BTA Team as there would be two in the Morris and with David photographing from the BMW, we needed a driver. A close friend (Tony) had kept asking to join and all was set and ready. Since the three did not know each other, on 3 February, 7 weeks before our departure date, we held a braai (barbeque) at our home for members of the team to introduce themselves. This seemed to go down well but on 6 February Tony was forced to withdraw for business reasons – a huge shock.

Where would I find a fourth team member? We had only 45 days before departure. I contacted a school friend in Durban, but Rod Groenewald did not have a passport or time to get one. Sandy suggested Wayne Taylor in Johannesburg; our paths had crossed in business and socially in the 1970s and he too was recently widowed. Wayne agreed on the spot but had to attend his daughter's wedding; this meant staying an extra night in Johannesburg. What a relief! Now it was just a matter of packing and collecting Wayne. I thought I could relax as everything had come together – but read on. As Harold Macmillan said, "Events, events, my dear boy." My challenges had only just started!

Broken Crankshaft – Cape Town

When I was working for Rhokana Corporation in Kitwe (at a copper and cobalt mine), the many engineering facilities had assisted in the early restoration of the Morris. A colleague, Peter Millward, fabricated the complex bottom rail of the Morris's windscreen. He had married a nurse (Lynn) at the Mine Hospital where Sandy also worked. Sandy had been their bridesmaid. His daughter, Sarah, who lives in Cape Town asked if I would drive her to her wedding in the Morris, which I happily agreed to do. On 4 March 2023 we drove out to Big Bay, delivered Sarah to her Norman and were driving home the next day. For several months, when advancing the distributor control, there had been a slow "tick-tick" that some assumed was pre-ignition. Within 2 miles of our home on the motorway the sound increased, then "Bang!". Surprisingly, I was able to coax the Morris to the next off-ramp, where the car stopped altogether. After a tow to my brother-in-law's workshop, I confirmed that the crankshaft had sheared. Fortunately, there was no consequential damage as often a conrod breaks through the engine casing. (Full technical details are given in the Wreck to Restoration section.)

With so many issues, was I being told something? Should I simply cancel this crazy adventure? The fact that I obtained a replacement crankshaft and conrods the next day seemed to indicate that the gods were smiling on me and telling me not to give up – the "golden balls" had clanged. In 13 days the engine was up and running and ready for the tour only 3 days before our planned departure date. This was perhaps my biggest challenge but there would be more!

When we arrived in Mutare and attempted to visit the famous Leopard Rock Hotel, I realised that the engine was very stiff; it was like driving with the brakes on. We started off having to face a steep uphill and, since the engine had only done 51 miles since restoration, it needed momentum before it could attempt to climb a continuous incline. From the start the engine overheated and the radiator boiled over. I had never experienced that before. We then towed the car for the first 8 kilometres but after that it ran quite well and got better and better, handling the inclines all the way to Bulawayo.

Defective Diff – Bulawayo

The next issue was in Bulawayo on 6 April. The engine oil in the Morris was a low viscosity lubricant to aid running-in (to bed in the new elements). The engine had done 552 miles and was ready for an oil change – with the standard SAE40-70 non-detergent oil. Bryan Christie has a smallholding with garages and an open pit and he made these facilities available to us. On the way I noticed a "tick-tick" emanating from the rear and occasional jerking of the transmission. On arrival, greatly assisted by Bryan, we removed the differential and, on stripping it, found that the internal spider gears had failed catastrophically. The "golden balls" clanged again; later that afternoon we located a rusty Morris 8 differential in Bulawayo. Despite its appearance, the internal spider gears simply needed a wire brushing and they fitted perfectly. The next day, after replacing the engine oil, greasing the suspension and fitting the overhauled differential, the Morris was back on the road.

Engine Fan Failed – Chinhoyi

Not far from Chinhoyi we heard a "ting-ting-ting" emanating from the front – not to be confused with the familiar "tick-tick". On inspection, we found that a weld securing the fan support bracket had failed, causing the blade to touch the radiator. Rather than risk it coming adrift and impacting the radiator I removed the fan belt. Certainly, the fan aided cooling but was not very effective. Besides, my 1933 MG J2 has a similar engine without a fan; so I felt we could take the risk without the fan. If the engine was constantly hot, then one solution would be to remove the bonnet. As long as we maintained a decent speed, say over 30 mph, the air flow would be sufficient to keep the engine reasonably cool.

Engine said "Enough!" – Ndola

Chilupala did very well all the way to Ndola, but on entering the city the traffic was nose to tail and the road condition was so poor that we were moving at only 10 mph. The Morris was overheating and it eventually spluttered and refused to start again. I could not understand the reason. After checking into our hotel, I did a compression check. Shock and horror – there was hardly any compression. Had a hole burnt through the piston? Had valves dropped or stuck open? Or something else.

We spent the next 4 days at Kamushi Farm outside Kitwe where they had an excellent workshop. One of our hosts, George Klironomos, who was a skilled mechanic and fascinated by the "unusual" Morris overhead cam engine, assisted me in investigating the fault. We removed the cylinder head. Apart from thick black deposits, all looked quite normal. We did a valve leak test that confirmed that the valves were not sealing. I attributed this contamination to the "blend fuel" in Zimbabwe – a mixture of alcohol extracted from sugar cane and petrol. Later, we were advised that normal practice is to add a cup or so of diesel to the petrol to act as a lubricant.

Luck was with us again as George offered to have his off-site workshop regrind the valves by the next day, which would enable me to attend to other issues. We also had the fan support bracket welded – another small fix and improvement. I noticed that the dynamo drive yoke was loose and on investigation found that its locking key had shattered: the drive to the overhead camshaft was out of sync and had affected the engine timing. This explained why there was no compression: the valves were stuck open irrespective of the piston position! The yoke and shaft had worn as well; so we made a shim from a Red Bull can that took up the clearance – now my Morris has wings! We then shaped a replacement key from a scrap Allen key (tool steel) and with the addition of Loctite the yoke was again firm and in its correct position. Once all was assembled, Chilapula started immediately; we were back in business.

Exhaust Manifold fractured – Kalulushi

We decided to take the Morris to Kalulushi in the trailer as the roads leading out of Kitwe were abysmal. In Kalulushi I drove Chilupala around the roads near my last home in Zambia and where I used to work. Then we decided to load the car into the trailer. As we were going up the ramp there was a "Bang!" – the engine sounded like a Harley Davidson motor bike. Unbeknown to us, the exhaust pipe bonded rubber bracket had failed causing the silencer to drop a bit and it caught the edge of the trailer, shearing the cast-iron exhaust manifold flange. Back at Kamushi, George sent me to one of his workshops where a specialist welder fused the cast flange together.

We left Kitwe for the Cecily's Fund anniversary dinner, stayed on the outskirts of Lusaka for the night and the next morning made our way to Choma. Mission accomplished; we were now on holiday – but the challenges continued. Twelve miles past the Kafue bridge, it was the BMW's turn to complain. The water temperature suddenly went full-scale: the alarm sounded and we immediately pulled off the highway. The plastic radiator expansion tank had split down one side and was not repairable. At around 21:00 we returned to a farm outside Lusaka for 2 days. It was a public holiday weekend but help arrived: a mechanic brought the correct part and fitted a new expansion tank. We then left for Masuku farm outside Choma.

At Masuku, Graham and I had some fabulous birding, but discovered that the welded manifold had failed, probably due to the many bumps experienced by the trailer, especially along the bush road to the farm. Wayne then secured the exhaust pipe with binding wire and sealed it with Gun Gum that muffled the sound.

BMW Trailer hitch Defective – Twice – Hwange

After driving Chilupala across the Victoria Falls bridge and around town we packed it in the trailer for our visit to the Hwange Game Reserve. Refuelling at Hwange town, we noticed that the trailer hitch had lowered 30 degrees from its original position and found that its securing plates had torn metal away from the rear body of the BMW. It was a Friday afternoon, but we located a bush workshop with welding equipment. The trailer bar assembly was poorly designed and clearly not fit for purpose, especially for the potholed roads we had covered and perhaps the load of the trailer. After straightening and strengthening the two support brackets, we were on our way to Hwange Main Camp and arrived in the dark.

The next morning, Graham and I set out to go game watching and birding, but while unhitching the trailer from the BMW we noticed that one of the two hitch-securing bolts had sheared. Wow! Lucky once again, how long had we travelled with only one bolt securing the trailer?

That afternoon we stripped the whole assembly, drilled larger holes in the hitch box channel and used the back-up spare U-bolts supplied by Priclo and intended for the trailer's springs. These high-tensile robust U-bolts doubled the purchase area and did the job perfectly, getting us all the way back to Cape Town. This penultimate sector of the trip in Zimbabwe and the potholed road was the last of our challenges. If that final bolt had failed, the trailer would certainly have crashed and severely damaged the Morris. It does not bear thinking about: Lady Luck or those "golden balls" were with us all the way.

Back in Cape Town, I replaced the used front tyre on the BMW – the one we obtained in Mutare at the start of our tour. During fitting they were unable to get the wheels to align as both front shock absorbers were bent; they were subsequently replaced. The road conditions had taken their toll on the BMW too; so really the Morris did pretty well.

I also reworked the Morris's dynamo and had its shaft rebuilt – new bearing, keyway and yoke – it is like new again. With the many bumps on the roads the hood impacted on the side support brackets; they had to be repaired twice on the trip. However, their distortion caused dents of the rear body and there were several dings from stones in the wings, and other body parts. The car was last painted in 1992; so I decided to have all the dents repaired and the car completely resprayed in the same colour before returning the car to the UK. Mr Chin of Cape Town completed the brilliant job in just 6 days. In the meantime, Aubrey Springer fabricated a new set of more robust hood brackets to my design.

The car was ready for shipping in a container from Cape Town. It arrived at our home in Putney, London in an impressive transporter (Fig.244) looking in perfect condition. But when I attempted to start it, the oil pressure was low and the gauge was fluctuating. I discovered that the oil was now a white emulsion – as my friend Robin stated, "it got sea-sick". On investigation, the rear NS cylinder head stud sleeve in the water jacket, after 94 years, had corroded through, allowing water to mix with the oil. Perhaps the container ship's vibrations had exacerbated the leak. After replacing the stud sleeve and reassembling the cylinder head, the engine now runs like a sewing machine.

In Cape Town I had swapped the Blockley tyres from the Morris to my 1933 MG J2 under restoration with older traditional tread tyres. I ordered a new set of Blockleys in London and had them fitted on the Morris; it is back to standard. Chilupala subsequently made a trip to Surrey and then did a photo tour of London's iconic sites. It is going as well as it has ever run, having covered 160 miles since its arrival back in the UK. I anticipate that its reliability will be maintained for many years to come.

Without my lucky charm – those "golden balls" – this adventure might never have been completed. Long may they "clang"!

Chapter 11

Return to England

Wrapping Up and Return to the UK

The temporary fix to the dynamo yoke drive done in Zambia needed to be addressed. We removed the dynamo and found the yoke shaft severely worn and the top bearing very loose. I had the shaft built up with low temperature metal-spray, followed by precision grinding. We fitted a new sealed bearing and shaped a keyway to fit. My friend Ted Borcherds lent me a new yoke that fitted perfectly. We replaced the dynamo, set the timing and recommissioned the car. This was essential to deliver the car for the next exercise of giving the Morris a thorough makeover before returning to the UK: some damage to the rear body had to be fixed and it needed a new hood bracket to be designed and manufactured.

The car was delivered to Mr Chin in Lansdowne Road (Imam Haron Road) to repair the rear body dents and other dings in the mudguards and respray the whole body. Mr Chin worked his magic and completed the job in only 6 days; it looked brilliant. On return to our workshop in Diep River I fitted the more robust replacement hood support brackets that should prevent body damage in the future.

The Morris had to return to the UK because its carnet was due to expire. I had embarked on restoring a 1933 MG J2 as a vehicle to use at the Crankhandle Club's events in the future. This car needed tyres that coincidentally were the same size as those fitted on the Morris. A simple solution: exchange tyres – the MG would have excellent Blockleys and the Morris would get a new set in the UK.

On 1 June, after changing the engine oil, I drove the Morris to John Ryall's workshops in Montague Gardens to be packed in his 40 foot container along with other cars to be shipped to London. Soon the container was loaded on the vessel, *The Kalahari Express*, that was scheduled to arrive in Felixstowe on 16 July (Fig.519). The actual arrival date was later because the ship developed a fuel pump problem and had to call in at Morocco for repairs. This meant losing its slot at Felixstowe and having to be re-routed to Rotterdam. The container was transferred to another vessel for London taking a further two weeks.

Morris Back in London after Four Years

On 28 July the container with the Morris was finally delivered to Bridge Cars in Suffolk, UK (Fig.520). They then transported the car to Putney at a cost of £396 (Fig.521). I calculated that travelling to Suffolk, spending the night and then driving the Morris back would not have made much of a saving. However, a subsequent discovery revealed that it could have damaged the car's engine.

After offloading the Morris, I started the engine and noticed that the oil pressure was surprisingly low with the needle fluctuating. The priority was to have the old tyres removed and the new set of Blockley tyres fitted by Waddams Garage of Putney – once again.

Fig.519: The Kalahari Express to London

Fig.520: Arrived in England, out of container

Fig.521: Delivered to Putney, our home

Fig.522: Touring London – Westminster

Fig.523: Doing the London Ritz

Fig.524: Two icons, Buckingham Palace is one

When I investigated the low oil pressure, I found that the oil had turned to a white emulsion. This was caused by water contamination – perhaps indicative of Chilupala being sea-sick after 6 weeks of vibrations in the shipping container.

There could be many reasons for water to leak into the engine sump: an overhead cylinder gasket, a welch plug or – worse – a cracked cylinder head due to severe overheating during the African expedition. I raised the question on the Vintage Minor Forum. The collective view was that the rear NS cylinder head stud is fitted inside a sleeve in the water jacket. Probably after 94 years that sleeve has corroded through causing water to leak in the oil system. Sure enough, I found this to be the case and subsequently removed the cylinder head and drilled out the remains of the corroded sleeve. I replaced this with a new sleeve suitably sealed into the cylinder head. On commissioning the engine sounds as sweet as ever.

Future of the Morris

I will continue to maintain and drive the Morris for as long as I am able; now aged 80 and thankfully blessed with excellent health I look forward to many years of driving pleasure. One ongoing objective is to record the car at as many iconic sites as possible (Figs.522–524). London is pretty well done – so perhaps a visit around the Continent of Europe could be on the cards. Who knows? The *Vintage Minor Register* had tentative plans for a United States tour or even an Australian tour; anything is possible. What I am confident of is that the Morris engine is as good and robust as it could ever be and I expect many maintenance-free miles for years to come. No relatives have expressed interest in the 1929 Morris: I only hope that a future custodian will treasure it as much as Sandy and I have.

Was it worth it?

- Yes, the whole programme of events proved that with determination, focus, detailed planning and the availability of known and local assistance, all challenges were overcome.
- We achieved all of our objectives: the Morris toured the two countries and, despite some mechanical issues, performed very well – I was especially proud of the suspension.
- Visiting iconic places was special: Leopard Rock Hotel, Birchenough Bridge, Great Zimbabwe, Matopos, Kariba and Victoria Falls.
- The BTA Team worked well together and, despite occasional frustrations and concerns, we managed to solve issues along the way.
- The freely given support and assistance we received wherever we went was outstanding: without that the trip would have been aborted.
- The hospitality was fantastic: we made many new friends and connected with old.
- For Graham and me, returning to our old homes and stamping grounds was nostalgic, yet we were sad to see so much deterioration and disrepair.
- We managed to do bird photography, at every opportunity adding new species. All birds seen in Zimbabwe and Zambia can be viewed on my web site www.WorldBirdPhotos.com (Ref.14), some of which are published in the latest *Bradt's Zambia Safari Guide* (Ref.15)
- The BTA Team all agreed it was the adventure of a lifetime: full of history and discovery, but above all enjoyable. We had a lot of laughs!

Chapter 12

Charity Fund and Footnote

The Cecily's Fund – Educating Zambia's orphans

According to their website the Cecily's Fund is an international development NGO, established in 1998 after Cecily Eastwood died in a road accident while volunteering in Zambia.

Over the past 25 years the fund has raised over 6 million pounds to help more than 50,000 children in an effort to break the cycle of poverty in Zambia. The country was crippled by the HIV/Aids epidemic, leaving a stark reminder: 54 percent of the population is under 18, over 60 percent of the population live in extreme poverty, and the cost of schooling is far beyond their means. Many households are headed by children. The programme supports children and young people and helps them to succeed and to prepare for a better future.

My formative life in Zambia certainly helped my personal development and future growth. I have always wanted to give something back and associating the Back-to-Africa trip in my 1929 Morris Minor with the Cecily's Fund seemed the perfect opportunity to make a contribution and widen the awareness of the needs of Aids orphans in Zambia.

Later in the year, back in the UK, we attended the Cecily's Fund 25th Anniversary black tie dinner at Bristol on 16 September. The event was held on Brunel's *SS Great Britain* ship (Fig.525). Built in 1843, at the time the world's largest, and first all-iron, propeller-driven ship. It was recovered from the Falklands and returned to its original dry dock in Bristol during 1970 for restoration. We had a most enjoyable evening of fundraising, especially among several ex-Zambia folk (Fig.526).

Fig.525: SS Great Britain, Bristol UK

Fig.526: Cecily's Fund 25th anniversary dinner

See page 10 to make a donation to the Cecily's fund.

Footnote – Crankshaft repaid – Cape Town

I returned to Cape Town in October 2023 armed with the replacement crankshaft and conrods as committed to Feliciano Martins. At an MMM gathering at his restaurant I presented him with a high-quality unused Phoenix crankshaft machined from a solid billet. It is considered to be the best in the market (Fig.527). Understandably, Feliciano was delighted. In addition, I also replaced the set of MG P-Type conrods (Fig.528). Obligation completed: a win–win.

Fig.527: My obligation to Feliciano fulfilled

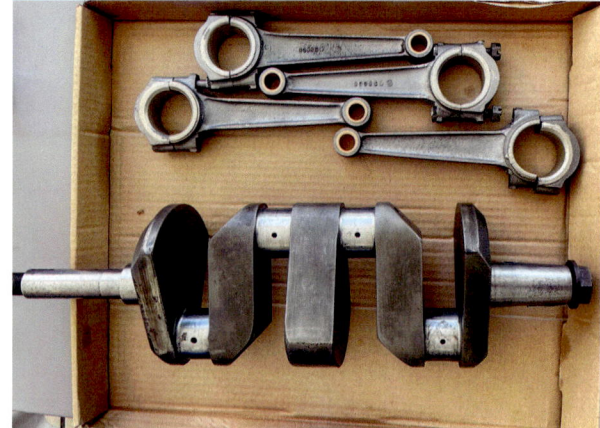

Fig.528: Phoenix crankshaft and conrods

Car Clubs are Essential for all Aspects of Support

Without car clubs our veteran, vintage and classic vehicles would not be sustainable. They provide an essential service: passing on expertise, buying and selling of spares, and even funding the manufacture of consumable spares such as hoses. Our cars need to be used and not left to rot in museums or owners' garages. One massive benefit from a common interest is that you one acquires a global network of friends on which you cannot put a value.

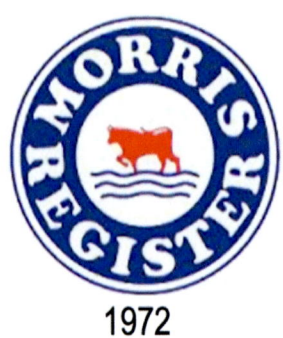

1972

2000

2013

Fig.529: Car Club Badges and recognition of my association

Chapter 13

Technical Guides for the 1929 Morris Minor

I initially published these technical guides for the *Vintage Minor Register* and made them available to the *Morris Register* of the UK. With hindsight, and having gained knowledge and experience from my recent exploits, I have brought them up-to-date.

While these documents are specific to the vintage Minor, the basics apply to many vintage cars on the road of the same era. It is hoped that they will be a useful reference to future custodians who venture into the unknown annals of vintage car mechanics.

TG01: Hibernating Vintage and Classic Cars

Introduction and Background

This article describes my practice and experience in hibernating and re-starting my 1929 Morris Minor 4 Seat Tourer.

Prior to my retirement I lived in India for 9 years and have had to hibernate my car for extended periods. We then decided to live like swallows commuting between London and Cape Town. This requires me to lay up my vehicle for up to six months (UK winter) while enjoying Cape Town's summer.

Depending on climatic conditions, especially in the Northern hemisphere, it is essential to protect against freezing temperatures. However, in hot climates and those with high humidity, different solutions are required to prevent degradation of rubber tyres and drying of upholstery, especially leather. Mould is a particular problem in both hot and humid conditions.

A poorly stored car can be an ideal home for bugs, rats and other creatures that breed, leave droppings and even eat car materials. Consider using mouse traps and other deterrents for protection against rodents and insects.

The ideal storage facility should be dry and dust free, have good airflow, low humidity and be at a temperature above freezing.

Hibernating and Storage

Read this checklist for hibernating and storing your car along with your particular vehicle's operating and maintenance manual:

- Body and chassis
- Petrol
- Engine oil
- Engine lubrication
- Cooling water system
- Tyres
- Battery
- Exhaust and carburettor
- Upholstery and hood.

Body and Chassis

It is advisable to wash and polish the car before putting it into storage. With careful application I use a pressure washer to remove any debris and mud from the chassis, springs, wheel arches, running boards and engine area. If the car has been used on salted roads, washing under the chassis will prevent corrosion.

A good wax and polish of the body will improve protection against rust and damp and will look nice. Depending on how long the car is to be stored, you can spray a light engine oil over the chassis, springs and steering gear for added protection. Some spray wax polishes would be equally suitable and easy to apply.

Petrol

It is an established fact that petrol goes off. Anyone who tries to start a lawn mower that has had petrol left in it during winter will know that it seldom starts. If left for extended periods, petrol creates a gel that messes up carburation and combustion. You should drain as much petrol as possible and then run the engine until the supply runs dry. The car is made safer without volatile liquid left in it.

One view against emptying the fuel tank is that condensation could cause rust, that would in turn affect combustion. The solution to this is to fill the tank full of petrol but I have not done this because my Morris's petrol tap is internal and seeps a bit. There are fuel preservatives that promise to ward off corrosion, oxidation and keep the fuel in good condition, but I have no experience of these.

Engine Oil

Depending on the age of the oil and the period the car is to be stored, I always drain the old oil and store the car with new oil. Diesel contains 50ppm of sulphur and higher for industrial grade. When combined with water this can create sulphuric acid that will cause severe corrosion if left in an engine. Although petrol is different, I apply the same logic to replace the standing engine oil. Remember, relative to the value of the engine, oil is cheap. It is far better to change the oil every 500 to 1000 miles.

In my cars I fit rare earth magnets in all oil compartments: the wisdom of this protection is shown by agglomerating metal debris (Fig.1). Removing any grinding media reduces wear of all moving elements and extends machinery life.

Fig.1: Magnet in oil filter before and after 1000 miles, showing metal wear debris

Run the engine until it is hot and then drain the oil, removing any residual in the oil filter housing. Then re-fill with new oil. It is good practice to check and clean the oil restrictor as is recommended in the *Morris Minor Handbook*.

Engine Lubrication

Once filled with new engine oil, remove the spark plugs and rotate the engine until the pressure gauge indicates normal. This will ensure that the new oil has reached all parts and diluted or replaced any residual old oil. Then squirt some new engine oil into each cylinder and manually crank the engine so that oil is spread around each cylinder. Refit the plugs (not too tight as engine may be still warm).

Cooling Water System

By now the engine should have cooled and you can drain the radiator and engine of water. My Morris has a radiator drain tap that evacuates both the radiator and engine but some vehicles also have taps in the engine block. Ensure that there is no residual water left that could freeze and expand, resulting in major engine damage during severe winter weather. This was my practice in the past, but I now add a coolant and inhibitor to the radiator and find that I no longer see brown water due to corrosion: it comes out crystal clear.

If I fill my Morris's radiator to the top, it soon drains via the overflow pipe – at least half a litre of water due to expansion. The guide is to fill the radiator so that you can just touch the water by inserting your index finger or see if it is two inches below the rim.

If my Morris had a pressurised cooling system, I would fit an overflow expansion tank like that fitted to the early Minis. The excess water would collect in the expansion tank and then syphon back into the radiator when the water cools down.

Tyres

Pump up the tyres to greater than specification (say by 20 percent) and then jack up the car and place it on metal stands or wooden blocks (Fig.2) to take any load off the tyres. Otherwise, they will distort and crack when deflated for long periods. The new Blockley tyres on my car (not shown) hold their pressure very well. They have valves with rubber sealed caps.

Fig.2: Car on stands, tyres pumped

The various tyre polishes look nice for Concours events but I am not convinced that they afford any long-term protection. Perhaps the contrary.

Battery

The battery is an expensive item to replace if not cared for. I have left mine on a trickle charger for over a year and found it to be in excellent condition. There are two competing chargers/battery conditioning units on the market. I have had good experience with both brands in the UK and South Africa: Optimate (www.optimate.co.uk) and CTEK (www.ctek.com).

These "smart" chargers re-condition the battery by cycling charge and discharge, thus keeping the battery healthy. They come with permanent charger connections (Fig.3) that are superior to crocodile clips as they optimise connectivity. They have an insulated quick-fit socket that conveniently and efficiently connects to the charger unit.

Fig.3: Battery with permanent charger connections fitted

My 6 V battery is the lead acid type that needs to be topped up with distilled water from time to time due to evaporation. However, when stored for extended periods with the smart chargers, it has not lost an appreciable amount of electrolyte as there is no excessive load or heat generated for evaporation. Remember to apply petroleum jelly to the terminals and to loosen the battery filling caps to allow any gas (hydrogen) to escape during the charging process.

Exhaust and Carburettor

To prevent rodents living in the exhaust, stuff an old oily sock or cloth up the pipe but remember to remove it when starting the engine. Also stuff an oily rag in the carburettor intake to reduce any condensation and corrosion on the inlet valves.

Upholstery and Hood

After cleaning the upholstery (especially leather) feed it with a proprietary product to retain its original suppleness. In high humidity conditions, mould grows when the temperature is below 35°C and humidity exceeds 60 percent. But in colder climates it will not grow below 4°C or grow when temperature exceeds 40°C. In Mumbai (India) we used low wattage light bulbs in our wardrobes to expel mould on clothing and leather.

I always place the hood in the raised position so that it remains tight and smooth. Over this I fit a "breathable" dust cover so that the car is almost ready for the road (Fig.4).

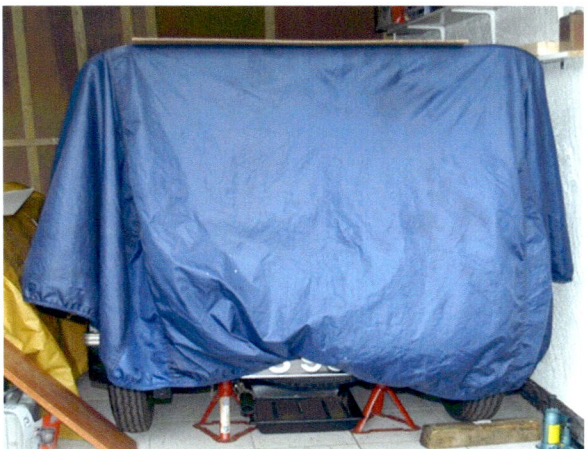

Fig.4: Breathable dust cover and stands

Commissioning after Hibernation

If the following steps are observed, the car's life will be extended and the engine should start easily after hibernation. Make a checklist of what needs to be done for your particular vehicle. The following is my practice:

- Tyres and car stands
- Battery condition
- Water in radiator
- Engine and camshaft pre-lubrication
- Petrol
- Starting the engine.

Tyres and Car Stands

Check the tyre pressure and if needed, pump up the tyres before removing the stands. Remember to check the spare wheel's pressure.

Battery Condition

Disconnect the smart battery charger and, if water based, check the levels in each cell. For good measure use a battery hydrometer tester (Fig.5) to assess whether each cell is of a similarly charged condition based on the density of the electrolyte.

Fig.5: Battery hydrometer: Electrolyte density tester

Water in Radiator

If you used a coolant and rust inhibitor, check if the radiator is filled to the desired level. If you drained the radiator; then check that the drain tap is closed and fill the radiator with rain water – preferably. It is good practice to remove the lower return hose from the engine and flush through with water to remove any deposits. Often some yellowish rust-like fluid comes out. I then fill the system and check hoses and water jackets for any leaks. After long storage gaskets can dry out, causing some initial seepage that soon stops.

Engine and Camshaft Pre-Lubrication

This section is the most important when a car has been stored for an extended period. Most moving components will have dried out and, if started "dry" without lubrication, then you are simply reducing the life of these moving parts, especially the camshaft and rockers. Remove the rocker box to expose the camshafts, drives and followers. Lubricate these and all moving parts liberally (Figs.6, 7). This is the most important action when re-starting an engine that has been out of use for an extended period.

Fig.6: Lubricate camshaft and drives

Fig.7: Lubricating overhead camshaft

Next, remove the spark plugs and again squirt some light oil into each cylinder and hand-crank the engine a few turns. After this press the starter and allow the engine to rotate while watching the oil pressure gauge until it indicates almost normal operating pressure. This will confirm that oil has reached all moving elements.

Petrol

Fill the tank with fresh petrol. Ensure that it has filled the carburettor float chamber. If you use an in-line petrol filter, make sure this does not have any old petrol gel in it. Vehicles with cork- sealed petrol taps may have some seepage at the tap as the cork may have dried out and shrunk a bit. This should self-correct soon.

Starting the Engine

Remember to remove the sock or cloth plug from the exhaust pipe and carburettor. If your battery is good and the distributor points are clean and there is sufficient petrol, then apply the choke and a gentle pressure on the accelerator and the engine should start easily. Initially there will be a smoky exhaust as the oil in the system clears.

Closing Comments

Many vintage and classic cars are stored for extended periods and yet we expect them to function at the press of a button. This seldom happens unless the practices outlined here are followed. Consult your vehicle's operating manual for any specific actions. The main hibernating issues are attention to lubrication and fuel. Tyre life will be extended if the tyres are not allowed to deflate under load during extensive periods of storage.

Over the past 40 years my 1929 Morris Minor has started first time, every time despite a long hibernation. This can only be attributed to the care and attention outlined.

TG02: Steering Overhaul

Introduction and Background

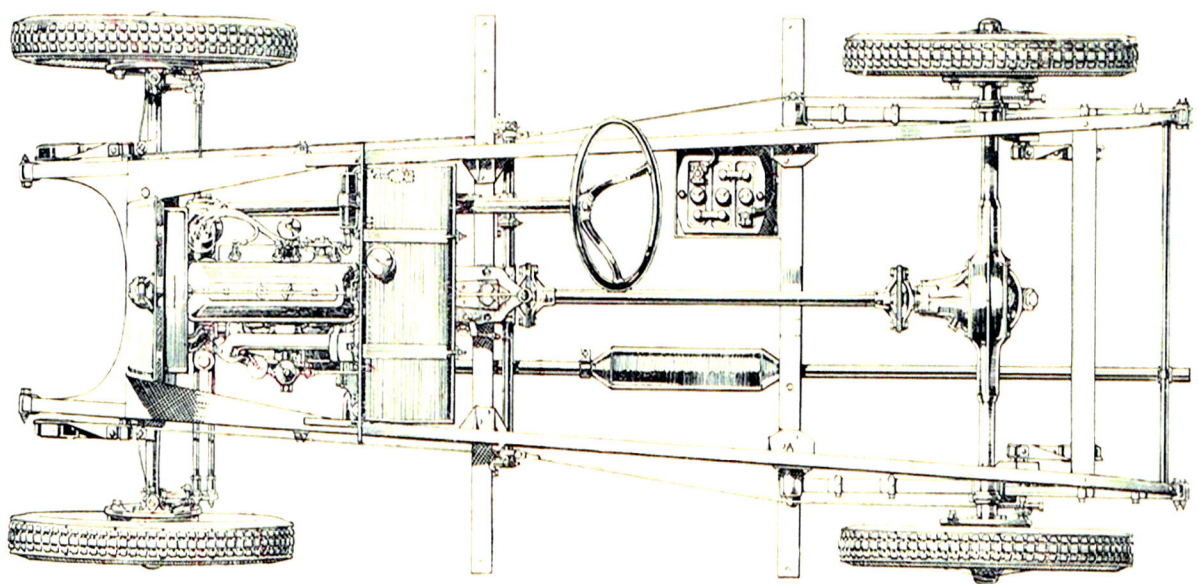

Fig.1: 1929 Morris Minor Chassis

A car's handling, steering and braking are fundamental to safe motoring, let alone the joy of driving a vintage car. The restoration of my 1929 Morris Minor 4 Seat Tourer started in 1970 using local engineering facilities in Zambia to manufacture worn components. By 1984 the car was brought to the UK where I was able to source "original" new parts to a more exact specification. Over the years I have upgraded or replaced components to bring the car as close as possible to the original specification when it left the factory.

The restored car was on the road by 1992 when it commenced building up mileage but it was less than perfect. New components began to bed in, but I found driving needed absolute concentration, especially as the car tended to wander.

The first step towards my dream trip (returning the car to the place in Zambia where I found it in 1970) was shipping the car to Cape Town, South Africa. There I commenced a range of upgrades to ensure that the car would be as reliable as possible for the journey around Zimbabwe and Zambia. A priority was addressing the complete steering system, having obtained a range of replacement parts as part of the preparation.

This article covers replacement of the kingpins, the key elements in the steering drag and track rod assembly, as well as setting up the wheel alignment.

Kingpins

In the late 1980s I replaced the Zambian-made kingpins with ones that had the correct extension for the brake cable pulley, supplied by the *Morris Register*. The car was on the road in 1992 but by 2020 it had only done 8,000 miles – so one assumed little wear.

When the vehicle was jacked up, I discovered considerable vertical movement back and forth on both front wheels. It seemed incredible that there was so much wear but for good measure I had fitted a new set of kingpins and bushes from Ian Harris Morris Spares Ltd. Ian suggested that perhaps only the pins needed replacing as the bushes were unlikely to have worn much. However, I could not take any chances and decided to replace the complete system, including bushes.

Referencing the *Morris Handbook,* originally by Harry Edwards then updated by John Nagle (Ref.13), this article refers to part numbers illustrated below (Figs.2, 3).

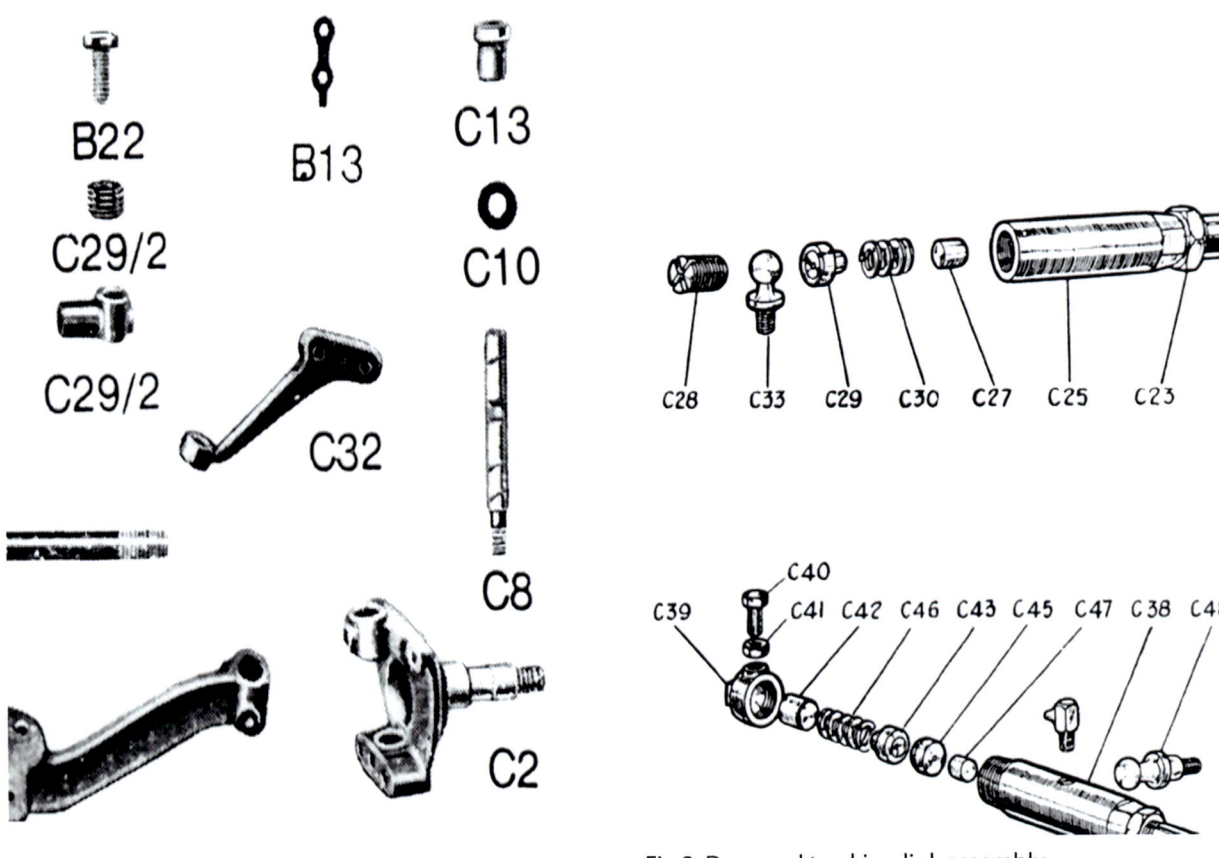

Fig.2: Kingpin assembly schematic

Fig.3: Drag and tracking link assembly

Once the kingpins have been removed, you need to secure the steering knuckles with the wheel back plate in a vice (Fig.4) to extract the two bushes. Use a brass drift and/or a long punch to remove them carefully as they may be recoverable or could be recycled for another use. On inspection, the kingpins showed very little wear. So why the vertical wheel movement?

Notice that the older cotter pin (Fig.5) is smaller than the new one (Fig.6). The cotter pin I had used before was typical of that fitted to a bicycle pedal crank. The larger pin was not standard supply 30 years ago. The cycle cotter pin had been inserted to its maximum depth and was just not tight enough. This, as well as the material being relatively soft, was the cause of the loose wheel movement (another lesson learned). The larger more robust cotter pin supplied with the new kingpins subsequently proved to be fit for purpose.

Fig.4: Steering knuckle – kingpin bushes

After comparing the older kingpins (Fig.5) with the new ones (Fig.6) they were found to be quite a different configuration. The old pins have lubrication grooves and smooth bushes while the new pins are quite the opposite: they are smooth and the bushes are grooved. Why this is so I cannot say – or decide if one system is better than the other.

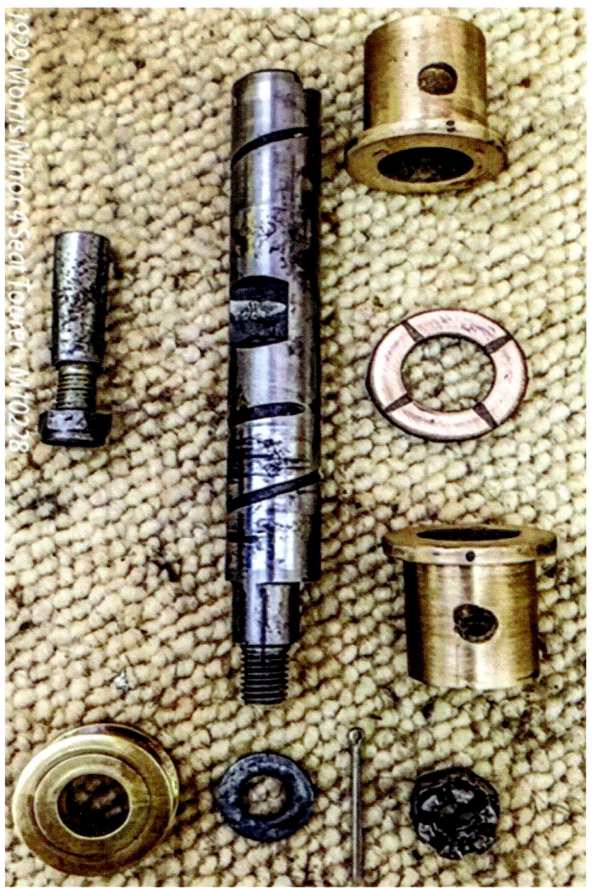

Fig.5: Kingpins removed – grooved pin, plain bored bushes and brake pulley stub (at base of pin)

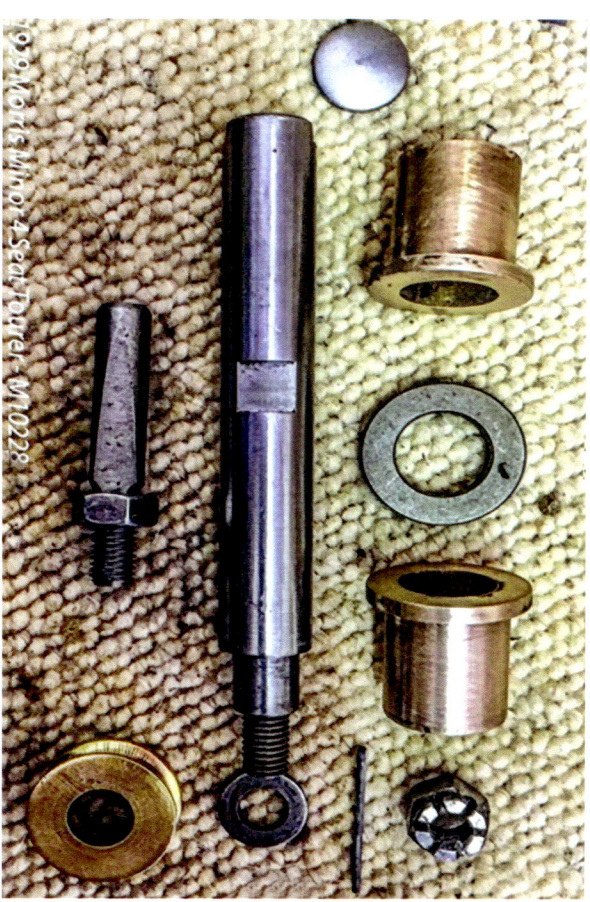

Fig.6: Replacement kingpins – smooth pin, grooved bushes and brake pulley stub (at base of pin)

Perhaps with the grooved kingpin it may be hit or miss when greasing, unless the grease nipple mates with the pin's groove? In the case of the grooved bush it will always distribute the grease along its length and onto the plain pin. It is probably better but has marginally less contact area than the grooved pin. Hobson's choice?

The original bronze thrust washer (Fig.5) is similar in shape to the steel type used in the gearbox. The new type was sintered iron (absorbs grease) but on tapping it in for an interference fit it shattered. Ian Harris now supplies steel thrust washers with the kingpins (he replaced mine). The steel thrust washer contact to the brass bush shoulder is probably a superior arrangement.

Fitting the new bushes in the wheel hub was straightforward. Make sure the lubrication hole aligns with the casting's grease nipple hole. The bush's interference fit in the steering knuckles appears to compress and the new kingpin would not fit the bush without excessive force. I was fortunate to have a friend with engineering facilities. They used a line-boring machine to ream the bushes accurately so that the kingpins were perfectly aligned in the steering knuckle and were a firm fit.

When inserting the kingpin, it is important to position it so that the flat face is towards the inside to accept the cotter pin. The top slot (Fig.7) of the kingpin enables it to be rotated into position as required. The eccentric pulley stud located at the bottom of the kingpin will then be in the right position.

Fig.7: Kingpin below recess in top bush

Fig.8: Welch plug protects kingpin

In fitting the cotter pin ensure that the kingpin is about 2mm below the top bush (Figs.7, 8) so that the welch plug can be fitted. This welch plug seals the top of the kingpin and prevents ingress of dirt and water.

Fig.9: Brake pulley at base of kingpin

Fig.10: Brake cable fitted

Before fitting the wheel hub to the axle, check that the brake cable pulley runs free (Figs.9, 10) (specific location to my model M10228). On later models the cable routing is different. This early cable routing can cause the front brakes to bind when the steering is in full lock but I have never found this to be a problem.

Fitting the kingpin can only be done from the top. Use a copper hammer to move the kingpin carefully into partial position and then insert the thrust washer below the axle (Fig.10). Continue to position the kingpin, making sure that the top is sufficiently below the recess for the welch plug. Then insert the cotter pin: give it a good knock so that it secures the kingpin firmly. Tighten up its associated nut with a locking spring washer.

Next, position the brake cable with a generous amount of grease on the pulley and adjust the brakes. With a grease gun apply grease to the upper and lower nipples so that the grease exudes from between the thrust washers. Note that it is always better to grease points "off load" when the car is jacked up to ensure that the grease distributes fully. Twisting the wheels should feel firm and secure – a job well done.

Steering Box

The first action is to remove the steering lever off the splined spigot shaft at the base of the steering box. Then unbolt the cover plate. To inspect the worm wheel, remove the steering wheel and top bearing assembly (Fig.11).

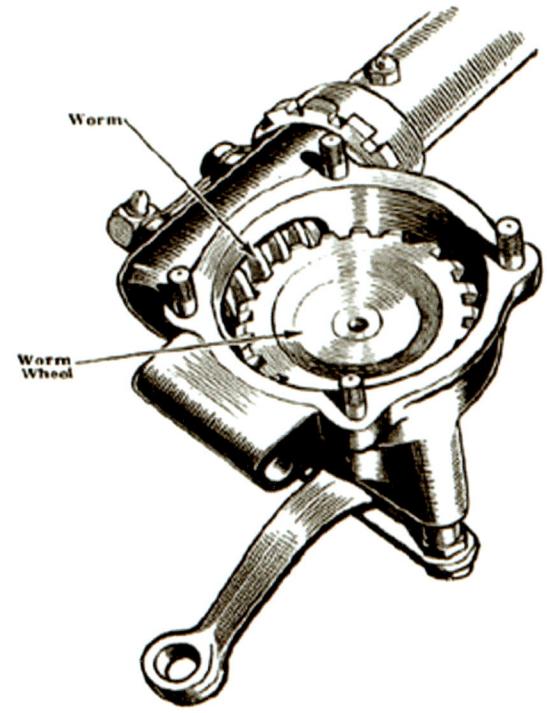

Fig.11: Steering box schematic

Also loosen the lower slotted nut at the steering box that secures the steering column. By gradually rotating and moving the steering mast (column internal rod) upwards it is possible to disengage the worm drive from the worm wheel gradually so that it can be removed and inspected. On my car, the worm wheel teeth showed no discernible wear: the teeth flanks were partially polished.

First pack grease in the steering box, then fit the worm gear and set the cover thrust screw. The ball race at the steering wheel end needs greasing and adjusting so that it is firm. To present a new gear contact area to the worm gear rotate the steering wheel (say 180o) to then fit the drag link ball and position the extremity locking plate. The change in gear contact can also be done by removing the arm to the drag link, rotating the steering and re-securing the link in the splined shaft.

Track and Drag Links

The track and drag link has adjustable ends (C25) (Fig.3) (left- and right-hand threads) that should have shaped openings so that the knuckle ball can be inserted and moved to the narrower end where it is secured by the spring and pushed up to prevent it from popping out. In my car the openings were badly worn (Fig.12). If the spring is not secure enough, a severe jerk to the front wheels (by a pothole) could cause the ball to jump out and result in a loss of steering.

The parts schematic assembly (Fig.3) shows the spring and ball cup on the rod side of the adjustable ends; mine is the other way around. The knuckle spring (Fig.12) is visible and reversed to what is shown on the schematic. It seems odd to locate the pivot ball at the larger opening. In the 1970s I had fitted end caps on either side of the ball for added pivot ball security.

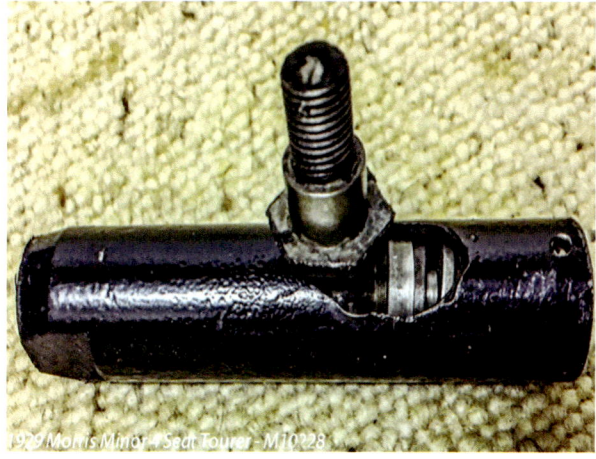

Fig.12: Drag link adjustable end

Fig.13: Fractured springs

I removed the track and drag links and stripped all assemblies of ball cups, springs and pivot balls and inspected them. This was quite a revelation. My initial restoration was done about 48 years ago. Some ball cups were distorted, springs were different lengths and some were broken (Fig.13).

The parts schematic (Fig.3) shows a plug (C27) that is fitted inside each adjustable end. Its only purpose seems to be to prevent grease from filling the unit's cavity. This plug was missing in my arrangement and seems superfluous.

For comparison, based on sound engineering, Figure 14 shows the better assembly of the spring, ball cup, pivot ball and end cap.

The lever, track and drag adjustable ends (Fig.14) were stripped and found to be in a similar condition with enlarged holes (Fig.12).

Fig.14: Spring, ball cup, end cap

Fig.15: Adjustable drag and track

All the adjustable ends (Fig.16) were stripped and also had enlarged holes that needed attention. The pivot balls were in surprisingly good condition. Most of the ball cups were plastically deformed and needed replacing – some of them did not have a central lubrication duct. This was done for all replacements (Fig.18).

The internals of the adjustable ends have a shoulder that secures the spring and cup; in some fittings the shoulders were chamfered due to wear or distorted due to uneven load. This was corrected by slight machining and using a heavy-duty washer to take up the lost space. The spring and ball cup abuts against this washer or internal shoulder.

The openings of the four adjustable ends were built up with TIG welding and reshaped prior to painting (Fig.16).

I created a sufficiently round area so that the pivot ball could be inserted. When assembled the pivot ball then moves closer towards the elongated area that safely retains it and provides full movement.

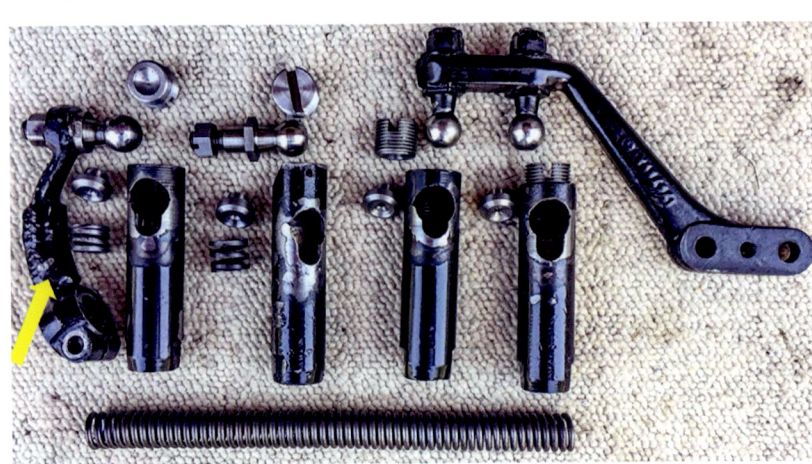

Fig.16: Track and drag link steering assembly ready for installation

Notice that the steering lever attached to the steering box (arrow) has been reinforced by welding on an extra plate. This must have been repaired in Southern Rhodesia in the late 1940s. I decided to retain it as part of the car's patina!

Below the adjustable ends is a long spring (Fig.16). This was just one piece made by a specialist spring company in Cape Town from which the replacement springs were cut.

Fig.17: Adjustable ends – springs ⅝"

Fig.18: Ball cup lubrication duct

After the springs (measuring ⅝" in length) were cut the ends were ground flat to the original size (Fig.17). The new springs proved to be suitable for the application. After assembly of all elements and positioning the steering wheel so that its centre spoke was vertical, all links were connected. On the road the steering felt so much firmer than before. In fact, the car no longer wandered on the road and when the steering wheel was hands-free the car maintained a straight line.

Wheel Alignment

The *Morris Minor Handbook* recommends a simple yet practical method of setting the wheel alignment and the ⅛ inch toe-in. This calls for fitting two equal wood planks with a cut-out around the axle stub and holes for wheel nuts to secure it.

Fig.19: Wheel alignment tool

Fig.20: Wheel toe-in set

The top edge of the plank must be the centre line of the stub axle. The plank on each wheel is set level; then the wheel is clamped to the back plate. Ensure that the car is level, then with a tape measure modify the adjustable ends of the track rods accordingly. This tends to be a two-person job for holding and viewing the tape measure. First, you need to achieve an equal distance between wheels front and rear of the plank (Fig.19). Then set the ⅛ inch toe-in; using a tape measure is a bit fiddly for accuracy (Fig.20) but it seems quite effective.

Back on the road the car handled rather well but a local specialist garage (Drive & Align of Wynberg) offered a free laser alignment check. I was curious see how effective the basic alignment was.

Once the computer was calibrated, to the amazement of the operator, the laser alignment of all four wheels was found to be a perfect alignment in a rectangle (Fig.21). They could not believe this accuracy; so the boss re-checked and was extremely impressed. This confirmed that the suspension is aligned correctly and is a tribute to the accuracy of the set of springs I had made in the UK around 1990.

Fig.21: Wheel alignment

Fig.22: Laser wheel alignment

They did find some play on the recently set steering lever pivot ball to the drag link adjustable end. I had not tightened the end cup sufficiently; it required a half more turn against the stiff spring before replacing the locking split pin. The ⅛ inch toe-in that I had set was just a ¹⁄₁₆ inch out but good in all other respects.

The computerised laser alignment test (Fig.22) was perhaps a bit over the top for a 90-year-old vintage car. Nevertheless, it was satisfying to know that the car set up was precise as confirmed by the technician (Fig.23) who had no experience with such an ancient vehicle yet recognised all the basic elements that have evolved to modern cars. On the road the car is fairly precise without constant adjustment to remain in line and handles comfortably.

Fig.23: The Drive & Align engineer, impressed with 1929 technology

Closing Comments

Ensuring the integrity of the complete steering system – kingpins, steering box, track and drag links – is fundamental to safe motoring; but a matched set of suspension springs suitably set to specification is fundamental to a balanced system.

Reviewing past work is always worth the effort because, over time, the Morris owner will incrementally improve the car's reliability, performance and enjoyment.

The investment in my Morris's suspension, steering, brakes and tyres was fundamental to the success of my Back-to-Africa tour covering 1,509 miles over everything from rough to diabolical roads and potholes. The suspension did its job perfectly.

TG 03: Brakes – Making the Morris Stop

Introduction and Background

I rescued the wreck of my 1929 Morris Minor 4 Seat Tourer from the Zambian jungle in 1970 and brought it to England in 1984. It was restored and roadworthy in 1992 but, despite countless adjustments and modifications over the years, I could never get the car to stop effectively or safely. In 2015 I decided to address the situation.

I was aware that the original 1929 brake drums were very worn and had severe pitting from corrosion. After detailed measurement I found that the drums were oval and only braking on 50 percent of the surface area. I sent them to a specialist engineering company in the UK to be ground. They reported that there was insufficient metal to make the drums effective. The solution was to manufacture new drums and I had a new set made by BG Developments Ltd of Bromsgrove.

This article discusses the issues and the actions taken in trying to return a vintage Morris Minor's brakes to 1929 standard.

The 1929 Morris Minor Braking System – Cable Routes in Green

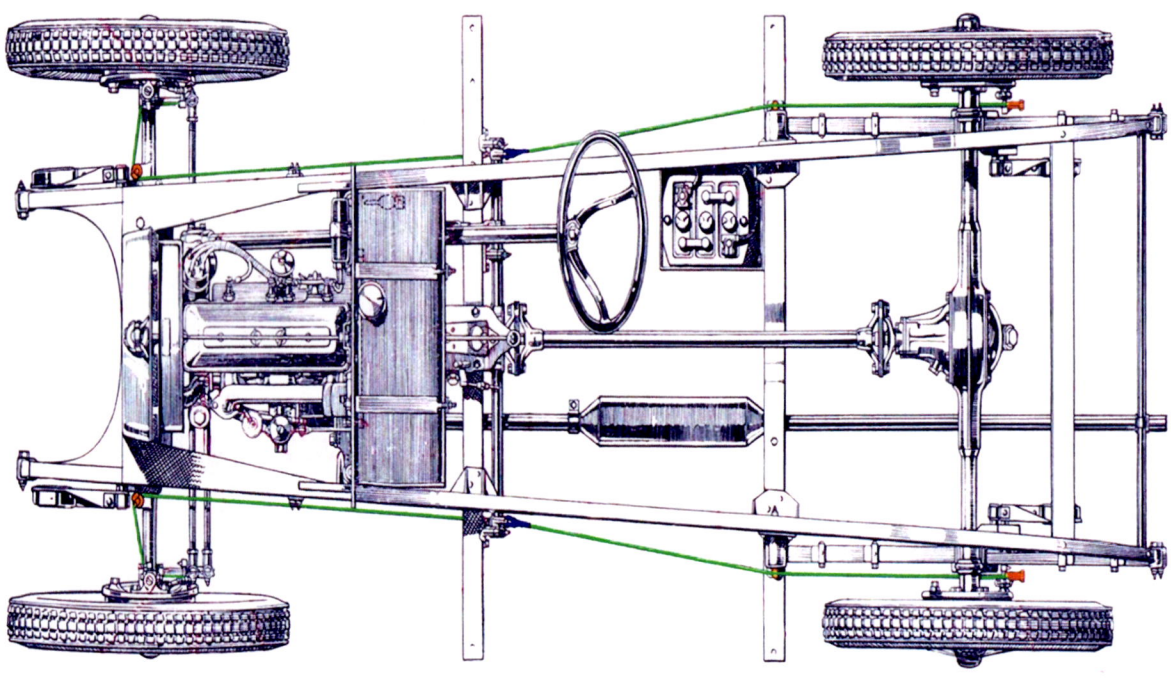

Fig.1: Morris Minor chassis and cable brakes layout

The brake cable arrangement (cable routes in green) (Fig.1) starts from the central pivot shaft near the front flexible fibre disc of the propshaft. The front brake cables go around two pairs of pulleys to the drum-actuating levers. The rear brake cable routing is simpler, direct from the pivot lever to each drum lever.

Variables in the Morris Minor Braking System

While most braking systems have much in common, with cable brakes there are additional factors that need attention. Wear of all the elements reduces the efficiency of the brakes from the foot pedal to the brake shoes. The main issues are:

1. The early foot brake pedal length, after the main pivot, was found to be about 25mm shorter than it should be, hence offering less leverage. If possible, fit the longer type found in later models.
2. Minimise any wear or looseness from pedal through to the adjusting turnbuckle to the main pivot cross shaft.
3. The original turnbuckle from pedal to main brake cross shaft is not very robust. Excellent stainless-steel replacements are available from marine suppliers.
4. A worn main actuating cross shaft bronze bush will add to an imbalance of braking between wheels.
5. The cables to the wheels should not be frayed; sooner or later they will fail.
6. The length of brake cables is specific to various models
7. The cable trunnions (pins) in the respective clevis must move freely.
8. Ensure that the four brake cable bronze pulleys on the front run freely and are well lubricated.
9. The brake arms on the brake drums are offset and handed.
10. A worn brake drum lever pivot arm bronze bush will affect brake shoe contact.
11. The brake shoe camshaft position can cause the brake shoe springs to rub against the axle. If the drum countersunk fixing screws are too long, they may touch the springs.
12. The brake shoes have a 1.5mm steel slipper secured to the aluminium shoe. The slipper is under huge pressure and becomes plastically deformed or worn after time (Fig.2). Wear results in loss of adjustment. Grinding the wear flat simply increases the clearance between shoe and brake drum. Pay close attention to this important factor.

Specifications for Morris Models 1929–33

Brake Drums
The early types of drum were thin steel pressings that distorted under braking pressure from the shoes. These were replaced with heavier, more rigid cast drums but the exact chassis number is unknown.

Brake Cam Levers
On cars up to chassis M9248, all four brake cam levers fitted to the cars were identical. From chassis M9249, handed levers were fitted to the front brake cams. You can identify these by looking along the line of the lever from the little end. Notice that there is a slight twist in the forging at the little (cable) end. The purpose of this twist is to ensure that the cable fork remains in line with the cable when under tension: this end of the cable is not parallel with the centre line of the car. From chassis M29528 onwards levers that were more angled were fitted. You can identify these by the definite "knuckle" or "shoulder" on the top edge of the lever. These angled levers provide more efficient braking, because they can be rotated further before they go over centre. The levers are completely interchangeable with the earlier levers. They were fitted to all side-valve Minors prior to the introduction of hydraulic brakes in late 1933. Note that all these levers were handed for the front brakes.

Cable Lengths
Front cables fitted to chassis from MM101 to M9248 should be slightly longer than those fitted to chassis M9249 to M29527, but only by ½" (47" and 46½" respectively). The reason for this small difference is that up to chassis M9248 the cable has to run slightly further because the kingpin pulley is not shackled.

Brake Shoe Slippers

The brake cam metal slippers on the ends of brake shoes were severely deformed (Fig.2). Therefore, I had them built up by low temperature TIG welding (Fig.3). Then I needed to grind them down to almost the original thickness (Fig.4). Ian Harris of Morris Supplies offers a trade-in shoe service for shoes with new slippers.

Fig.2: Worn slipper   Fig.3: Built up with TIG weld   Fig.4: Slippers ground down

Problem: Old Brake Drums

At the time of writing the early Morris Minors have brake drums that are 80 years old or more. Inevitably they will be worn to various degrees and cars that have stood for a long time will also have corrosion inside and outside the drums (Fig.5).

Fig.5: Wear and corrosion on the drums braking surface

The original brake drums on my car (chassis M10228) were significantly worn. My initial strategy was to take up the excessive clearance by shimming the brake shoe linings with 1.5mm aluminium strips. This took up the wear, bringing the shoes closer to the drum and improving the angle of the shoe actuating cam to about 45°. Balancing the braking load on all four wheels was tedious; a constant process of trial and error. During use I regularly checked the drum temperature indicative of binding or brake load on each drum.

The shim solution worked quite well but inspection of the brake shoe linings showed that there was no better than 50 percent contact with the drums, even after considerable use (6,000 miles). I believe that after increasing the overall diameter of the brake shoes (with shims under the lining) the profile will not match the radius of the drum exactly. See the brake shoes positioned in the drum (Fig.6) and the partial shoe contact with the brake drum (Fig.7).

Fig.6: Brake shoes in brake drum

Fig.7: Partial brake lining contact

There is a limit to the amount of brake drum wear. In the case of my car, despite only being used until 1953, the wear was so significant that the drums would not stand grinding to remove corrosion or ovality. The only answer was to have new brake drums manufactured.

Manufacturing New Brake Drums

The original Morris brake drums were cast steel with smooth outer rims (Fig.8). Over time with heat build-up and brake shoe pressure the drums became oval. To avoid repeating the design problem of the past I decided to have external ribs incorporated around the periphery: this provides greater rigidity and prevents drum distortion (Fig.9). An added bonus was that the ribs afford a degree of cooling and even reduce brake fade.

Fig.8: Original drum with smooth outer

Fig.9: New drum with outer rim ribs

I contacted BG Developments of Bromsgrove, specialists in braking systems for racing cars. They machined four bespoke replica brake drums out of EN-GJL-250 steel (plus heat treatment) for £105 each.

Fig.10: Brake drum in CNC machine

Fig.11: Brake drum with ribs prior to painting

The machining process required a CAD drawing measured from an original drum supplied to generate the associated programme data for the Computer Numerical Controlled (CNC) machining process (Fig.12).

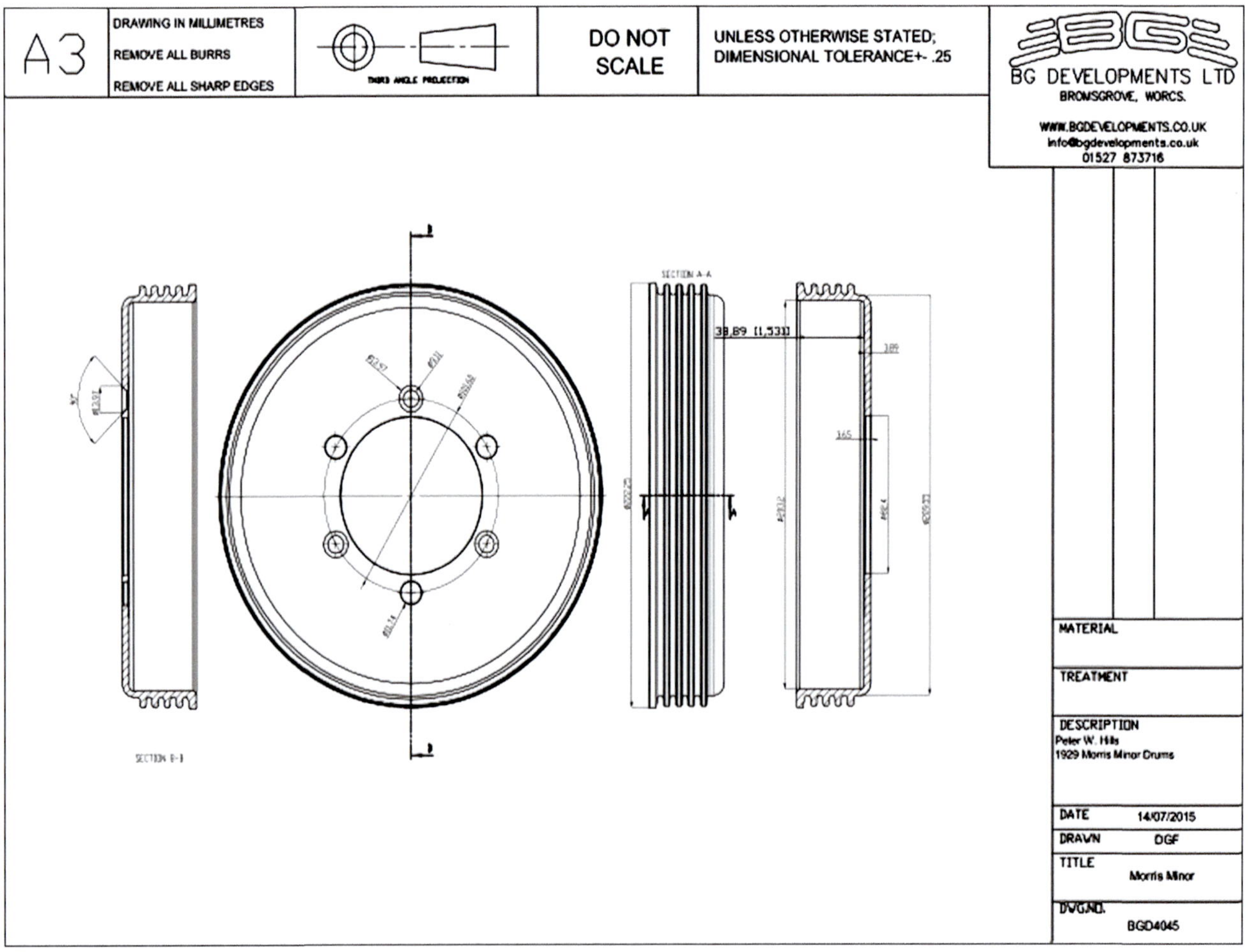

Fig.12: CAD drawing of the improved Morris Minor brake drum

The drums were machined from a billet, then stress relieved by heating to 580°C and holding at that temperature for one hour to ensure that the whole part reached temperature. The drums were then removed from the furnace and left to air cool before being checked for distortion.

BGD preferred to use an electrophoretic coating rather than powder-coating because the powder-coating would bubble at high temperature in service. This coating is used on a lot of AP racing's suspension components and brake calliper brackets. The cost was £25 per drum (Figs.13, 14) but I felt the investment was worth it.

Fig.13: New brake drum fitted

Fig.14: The rigidity and cooling fins

Incorporating the ribs/fins at the same diameter saved having to remove the excess metal during machining. The drums are slightly heavier than the originals but they look nice and are certainly not out of place. They should be good for the next 80 years!

Fitting the New Minor Braking System

The next phase was fitting the new brake drums. This proved more difficult than expected. Bear in mind that the original drums are 8 inch internal diameter and all associated elements have to be brought back to original specification.

Anyone who has had to remove and refit brake shoes will know how awkward this process can be. To remove and refit the brake shoe springs you need a simple tool and copious amounts of wire. Use a piece of wood with a hole to insert one end of the steel wire (piano wire is good) and thread the loose end through the spring loop. Then wrap it around the wood so that the wire does not slip out and lift the spring (Fig.15). Removing or fitting the springs is then quite easy (Fig.16). Sometimes long-nosed pliers are needed to push the spring hook over the shoe hoop.

Fig.15: Dowel with wire

Fig.16: Installing the shoe spring

While waiting for delivery of the new drums I decided to rivet new brake linings to the rear shoes (Fig.17) with reconditioned slippers. The linings available today no longer incorporate asbestos and are not quite as effective but there is no choice.

When I attempted to fit the new drums, I found that the diameter of the newly lined brake shoes was greater than 8 inches (Fig.18). I checked the thickness of the re-profiled shoe slippers, but it was obvious that the new brake linings were far too thick. I had an original new set of Morris linings still in the box and found that they were 2mm thinner than the modern MG-type linings supplied.

Fig.17: Riveting the brake linings

Fig.18: Dimensional check

Since most vintage braking systems have worn brake drums, the modern brake linings supplied are thicker to compensate. My choice was either to replace the new linings with the set of thinner originals or grind down the new linings to fit the standard drums.

Using the side of a large grindstone wheel to remove the excess lining material evenly I progressively shaped the brake linings (taking precaution against debris). Once they fitted the new drums I noticed a significant improvement in braking but still not what I wanted. We then did a 250 mile round trip to Prescott, for the VMR annual hill climb and on returning home a further inspection revealed only partial contact between the shoes on the rear drums (Fig.19).

The front wheels had the older type of lining material that exhibited localised polished areas indicating periodic contact all the time in motion. This marginal resistance would cause loss of much-needed power (Fig.20).

Fig.19: Partial lining contact linings

Fig.20: Polished areas from drum constantly rubbing on shoe lining

I realised that the linings were not shaped to match the drum profile when activated. I understand that there are companies that profile brake shoes to match but they require the complete brake drum back plate assembly to mount the shoes for grinding. As I was unwilling to disturb my earlier work, I tried a different approach.

Profiling the Braking Shoes

Taking one of the old worn brake drums, I glued some heavy-duty emery type cloth to the inside diameter to bring it close to the 8 inch original. Then, by rocking each shoe back and forth, checking the removal of the high spots (Fig.21) I progressively profiled the shoes. This process took some effort but seemed to be effective. Compare the pre- and post-profiling (Fig.22).

A subsequent road test proved that the Morris was braking more effectively. We attended the MOREG annual meet at Thoresby Hall, a 350 mile round trip from London. This bedded in the brakes further. After making small cable adjustments the Morris achieved something I never thought possible; I was able to produce a skid on a tarmac road, albeit on only one wheel (Fig.23).

Fig.21: Old drum sanding the shoe lining

Fig.22: Before and after sanding linings

Fig.23: Morris skidding on tarmac!

However, after the 350 mile trip I decided to inspect each wheel – only to find that contact was still partial. I decided to make my own shoe profiling system. Using one of the redundant brake drums I cut away a section and welded a trunnion with a plate adjustable to the tangent to the brake shoe (Figs.24, 25). The first version was ineffective: the heavy-duty emery paper stuck to the contact plate and soon blocked up. I then made a cutaway and fitted a flexible rasp blade that did the job very well. By positioning the rasp blade close to the brake shoe, I applied the brake cable while the brake drum was rotating. At the rear wheels this was easy. I jacked up one side of the car, started the engine and put it into third gear: the complete profile assembly then rotated. Applying slight pressure on the brake cable caused the rasp to remove any high spots, ensuring that the brake shoe lining was perfectly shaped to the brake drum profile. On the front wheels I fitted the complete wheel over the profiler; that made it easier to rotate and profile.

Fig.24: Brake shoe profiler rasp   Fig.25: Brake shoe profiler fitted to rear wheel

Fig.26: Shoe profiler on front wheel

Setting the Morris Brakes Objectively

I was not prepared to drive the Morris for 1,000 miles hoping to bed in the modern brake linings; I wanted effective brakes from the start. I believe the best way to achieve all-round shoe drum contact from the onset is profiling.

I have read many articles on how to set up the brakes on vintage Minors. The *Morris Handbook* gives the procedure that is probably best suited for a new vehicle without having to contend with all the variables previously listed. The well-used vintage car requires a lot of messing around to get each wheel braking evenly.

Some Morris drivers have given up and fitted Bowden cables or converted to hydraulic brakes. However, being a purist, I wish to retain the practical originality of my car while ensuring that the as-designed braking system is effective.

A popular method of setting the brakes is to check the temperature of each drum. This is a subjective way to establish if shoes are in partial contact (warm drums). Then on hard braking if hot drums are judged to be a similar temperature at each wheel you can assume that the braking is even. But this is still guessing. To measure each wheel-braking load objectively you need to take the car to an MOT road-testing station and place the car on the brake dynamometer.

Now that the MOT is no longer law in the UK for vintage and classic cars, it is not possible to obtain a braking value for each wheel, unless you can convince your local MOT station to give you 15 minutes of machine time. The modest charge is worth it!

When my Minor had its first MOT in 1992, the readings on the dynamometer were between 30 and 40 – hardly a pass. With the new drums fitted the front brakes were 70 and 90 and the rear 50 and 60. I was then able to tweak each brake cable to get all wheels around 90. After more running in since profiling the linings, a further test would probably indicate improved readings.

Closing Comments

The bottom line is that after years of some hairy close-call moments on the road, I can now confidently stop the car in emergencies and other demanding situations. In the past I would ensure a decent gap between me and the next car to give me time to brake, usually the car behind would overtake and then suddenly brake! This gave me little distance to slow down before shunting it! I can now manage that situation so much better.

I hope this article is of some assistance to those who have struggled to get their vehicles braking effectively.

I do not feel that investing in a new set of brake drums is excessive. Bear in mind that this is all about road safety. The new drums on my Morris should ensure that DS9936 is suitable for road use for many years to come.

[*VMR comments: As for the content of this article, this is yet more proof that Minor brakes of the original 180° cable variety can be made to work very efficiently provided that they are set up correctly and worn parts are replaced with items of standard specification. It should perhaps also be noted that Peter bases his car in Putney, London, where it is his only vehicle, so having poor brakes in that neck of the woods is not exactly an option! IG-2015*]

TG04: Propshaft Alignment Made Perfect

Introduction and Background

Experience counts. After overhauling the gearbox, the Morris Minor's propshaft with fibre discs has to be disconnected and reset. The accepted method of aligning the propshaft is to loosen the bolts at the front and rear spiders to the fibre discs. Jack up the rear wheels onto axle stands, then run the engine in top gear. Lean a stout plank of wood against the spinning propshaft and chassis to apply pressure and reduce any run out. This approach can achieve optimal alignment. After stopping the engine, tighten up the spider bolts: be careful not to compress the fibre disc excessively. Check that the dynamic alignment is running true. At high revs there should be no apparent vibration from the propshaft.

A perfectly aligned propshaft minimises any stress on the gearbox and differential and ensures a longer life for the fibre discs – it may even increase horsepower.

The function of the fibre disc is not to correct system alignment inaccuracies but to allow the vertical movement of the rear axle relative to the gearbox. Remember that, like a three-legged stool, the spiders will always appear to fit level. Yet how can you be sure that the machined faces are square to the central axis?

As part of the preparation for my drive around Zimbabwe and Zambia in 2023, I decided to replace both fibre discs and check the complete propshaft system alignment in considerable detail. This technical article reports my method, findings, corrective actions and results.

Propshaft Spider Alignment

The first step was to remove the propshaft and brake drum spider at the gearbox. I made up a basic rig with V knife edges from scrap metal (Fig.1) for initial assessment of the propshaft. By ensuring that it was level and the vees were vertical and rotating the propshaft spider against a fixed reference point, I was able to determine alignment and variations of each spider arm contact surface.

The rig revealed that, while both propshaft spider securing holes were 120° apart, none of their faces was at right angles to the shaft centre line. An error of 2mm was detected at one spider arm and no faces were square.

1929 Morris Minor 4 Seat Tourer - M10228

Fig.1: Simple shaft alignment check rig

The irregular spider bolt hole faces against the fibre disc would cause slight distortion of the flexible disc. The fibre disc would absorb the spider's mechanical errors but cause it to distort. These accumulative errors would absorb precious energy and create undesirable vibration and consequent wear.

The only way to correct the spider's machined faces accurately was to set up the propshaft on a long-bed lathe and machine or face off the contact areas.

The brake drum spider is easily removed from the gearbox. When mounted on the test rig the spider arm faces to the fibre disc were found to be at various angles to the centre line (Fig.2). They also needed facing off on the lathe to be square.

The next check was to establish whether all the spider bolt holes were consistent. I had a spare spider that was also faced off (Fig.3) that I used as a master to check the alignment of all the spider bolt holes. This enabled me to check the spider on the differential *in situ*. Fortunately, it was found to be perfect in all respects.

Fig.2: Brake drum spider

Fig.3: Spare master spider

Using the master spider and $5/16$" engineered bolts, I could fit each spider together and ensure that there was no resistance or play (Fig.4). I used the master to confirm the position of the matching holes of each fibre drive disc (Fig.5).

Fig.4: Master spider checks

Fig.5: Fibre drive disc

In my case all bolt holes matched with the master spider except those of the brake drum spider. In the brake drum each spider arm hole was offset radially by 1.5mm. This explains why in the past I struggled (forced) to install the securing bolts in the fibre disc and why the propshaft never ran true. The error in my system must have been present since the car left Cowley in 1929!

To correct the offset hole error, I used a round file to elongate each hole carefully, bit by bit, until they perfectly matched the master spider and fibre discs.

Preparing to Install the Propshaft System

The original spider's castellated nuts with split pins make tightening a very tedious job. I decided to fit new engineered bolts (smooth shank) with $5/16$" BSF Nylock nuts. These would enable me to nip up the nuts easily (if needed) as part of any future service routine.

The fibre discs (Fig.5) are supplied with relatively thin metal plates to distribute the load of the spider and the securing nuts. Experience had revealed that the thin plates easily distort. I made up heavy-duty washers with grooves ground to slot between the plate rivets (Figs.6, 7). This more robust approach distributes the load on the soft fibre disc better and I think it should increase its useable life. Time will tell.

Fig.6: Fibre disc nut washer and bolt

Fig.7: Heavy-duty shaped washer

Before assembly I found it beneficial to run a $5/16$" inch drill through the new fibre disc bolt holes to clear out any remaining rubber debris.

Installing the Propshaft

Note that for various Morris models there are as many as seven different lengths of propshaft, depending on chassis type and gearbox and with or without the handbrake drum fitting.

The installed propshaft should be a firm fit but it should not distort the fibre discs by compression or extension. Initially, only run up the nuts but do not tighten. I have found the best order of assembly is as follows:

1. First install the brake drum spider with large castellated nut and split pin (Fig.8).
2. Secure the fibre disc to the brake drum spider, setting the nuts facing to the rear.
3. Position the propshaft through the chassis in the most convenient position to connect to the rear spider on the differential.
4. Connect the propshaft to the front fibre disc, with nuts and large washers facing the rear (to make easier access for tightening).
5. Fit a fibre disc to the rear spider on the differential, with nuts and large washers facing to the front.
6. Slide the rear propshaft spider across the rear fibre disc. It should slip into position by rotation. A large screwdriver or tyre lever can help lever the spider into position. A quarter inch tommy bar or punch can help align the spider and fibre disc bolt holes. When fitting bolts, again have the nuts facing front but not tightened.
7. Because the rear wheels will be on axle stands, rotate one wheel while observing any ovality of the propshaft. In my case it was just perfect. The dial gauge hardly flickered.
8. Start the engine and in third gear gradually increase the speed to 50 mph on the speedometer. After stopping the engine and re-checking the propshaft alignment manually I found it to be perfect. Then nip up the spider's Nylock nuts and repeat the engine run. Not a hint of vibration at top speed was felt.

Closing Comments

As most vintage car owners will know, attention to detail pays huge dividends. For years I have known that my propshaft system could be improved. In a previous article I mentioned the application of a plank of wood against the rotating shaft to obtain alignment.

In this article I have shown that this rough method does not correct underlying alignment faults that will ultimately lead to premature wear and degradation. The home-made alignment rig helped identify distortion of the propshaft spider arms (Fig.9).

Fig.8: Propshaft fitted at gearbox

Fig.9: Alignment rig and chassis M10228

The checks on a lathe were simple and not time consuming. The effort is well worth the result for a long-term benefit – incremental improvement for a long-service Morris Minor.

TG05: The Dynamo – Making it Charge

Introduction and Background

Owners of vintage cars often complain that their car's battery-charging system is virtually nonexistent. Most Morris Minor owners I have met reckon that their car's dynamo output is so poor that they have to rely on a fully charged battery for short runs. If forced to drive the car at night, battery drain soon brings the car to a halt – especially if traditional tungsten lights are fitted. Some owners have converted their cars to alternators, but this is a drastic departure from the original.

During the initial restoration of my OHC Morris in 1990, I cleaned the dynamo's commutator, the brushes seemed lapped in and I re-connected the wiring. I washed the windings with thinners to remove the oil that had seeped in over the years. The bearings seemed fine; so I packed them with grease. Later I regretted this. I should have replaced them with sealed bearings but even this decision was questionable.

Despite this work, the dynamo output was never greater than 2 amps. Experienced owners informed me that any attempt at improving the charge rate was not worth the effort or cost. Some had replaced their dynamo's windings and achieved marginal improvement, but I felt their systems may have had other shortcomings or the job was poorly done.

After covering 4,300 miles in my Morris the cylinder-head gasket blew. During the repair I noticed that the dynamo was in very poor condition. I decided to return the dynamo to the standard in which it left Cowley in 1929. If it was effective then, surely a renovated unit should perform better today?

This article discusses the theory, operation and reconditioning of the three-brush dynamo, converting to a two-brush system, improved battery management and reliable motoring, and future maintenance of the dynamo.

How the Three-Brush Dynamo Works

The three-brush dynamo functions in reverse to an electric motor. Two carbon brushes are in contact with the commutator that collects the battery-charging current. The third brush has an adjustable position on the commutator that varies the power to the field windings (Fig.1). The field windings produce the essential magnetic field or flux that determines the dynamo's output. The greater the magnetic flux, the higher the output achieved. To charge the battery the dynamo must generate a voltage higher than the residual 6 volt battery level or the current flow will reverse. The cut-out is essential as its contacts close when the engine is not running.

The output terminals of the dynamo are connected to the positive and negative sides of the battery. The faster you drive, the greater the charge to the battery. However, if the charge exceeds the battery charge capacity, overheating of both the dynamo and battery takes place and causes progressive damage to these systems. Overheating the windings causes the insulation to degrade.

Many vintage and pre-war vehicles – especially the Morris Minors – are fitted with a summer and winter motoring switch. In the Northern hemisphere summers have long daylight hours and headlights are seldom needed. Thus a lower dynamo output to the battery is required. To prevent overcharging, a resistor was introduced to the circuit to dissipate the excess power (effectively a mini toaster in the car). The half-charge resistor (Fig.2) is located in the dynamo or associated with the instrument panel's dash switch. The resistor is reported to be 1.5 ohms (30 watts). A ceramic type is recommended. Reasons for low or zero charge can be attributed to an open circuit resistor, a breakdown in field winding insulation, worn brushes and/or damaged commutator. The summer switch was a crude solution as drivers seldom paid attention to it.

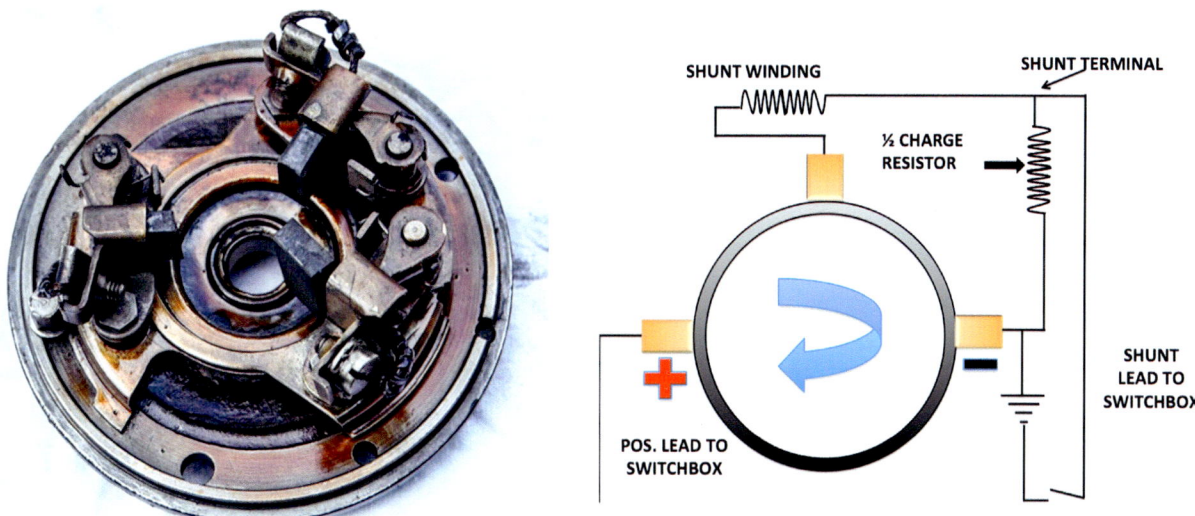

Fig.1: The dynamo's three brushes   Fig.2: Schematic shows half-charge resistor

Benefits and Disadvantages of the Three-Brush Dynamo

As the three-brush dynamo was developed before the advent of the multi-coil voltage regulator, a single cut-out relay was in common use – ignore the heavy fuse wire (Fig.3). This single relay cut-out is designed to prevent the battery discharging through the electrical circuit when the ignition is switched on. When the engine is running above idling speed and the cut-out contacts close, the ignition light turns off and the battery starts charging.

At the time the Morris was launched the cut-out was the best economic solution. However, if it is defective the consequences can be disastrous. Should the contacts fuse, the battery would drain back though the wiring, eventually melting the insulation and possibly starting a fire. This would be exacerbated if there was any petrol nearby. Many cars have burnt out due to this. Early Minors (like mine) have petrol tanks under the dashboard and your knees. Always a concern!

If a battery is constantly overcharged, it will have a reduced life and damage the dynamo. According to the *Morris Minor 1929 Illustrated List of Spare Parts* the battery cost £3/9/-, the crankshaft was £2/11/- and a complete chassis frame was only £5. The Minor Tourer's selling price was £125. The battery was 2.6 percent of the total cost of the vehicle compared to less than 0.2 percent on today's cars (not electric vehicles). I am confident that early motorists took great care of the acid-based accumulator unlike today where the sealed gel cell battery is generally ignored.

Fig.3: Cut-out with single relay

Fig.4: Burnt commutator & dry joints

The Dynamo OHC Drive System

Much is expected of the dynamo assembly: it doubles as the drive from the crankshaft to the camshaft and provides the charge for the battery. The dynamo is mounted over the crankshaft with a bevel drive. On early OHC Minors, the cylinder head driveshaft to the dynamo was crudely sealed with a felt washer. When the car was stationary, oil would gravitate down the drive shaft into the dynamo below, then into the recess around the seal and contaminate the commutator brushes, field windings and rotor. This OHC engine came to be known for its "oil- cooled" dynamo! Apart from the dynamo overheating, the oil could contaminate the brushes and insulate them from making effective electrical contact with the commutator, resulting in spark erosion of the copper surface (Fig.4). High heat would melt the soldered connections and fling it away due to the centrifugal forces resulting in dry joints and a reduced output.

At the top end is a flexible disc between the dynamo drive yoke and the OHC yoke that allows for any minor alignment differences between the bottom and top. This assembly is crucial to the operation of the OHC engine (Fig.5). It relies on small keys and a secure fit of the yokes to drive the camshaft. Any slippage within the drive system stops the engine function because it determines the timing system.

The fitting of an improved oil seal in the camshaft drive largely overcomes the original design issue – item 35 (Fig.6). This modification has proved quite effective.

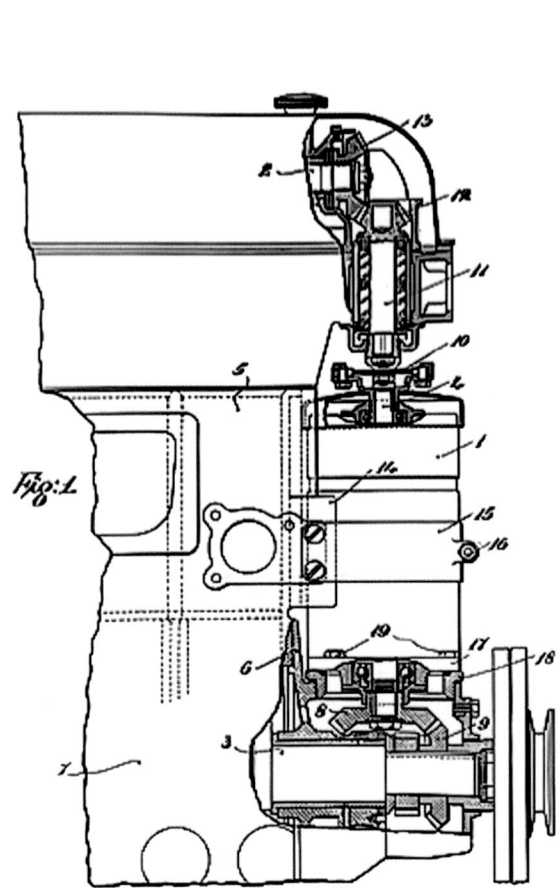

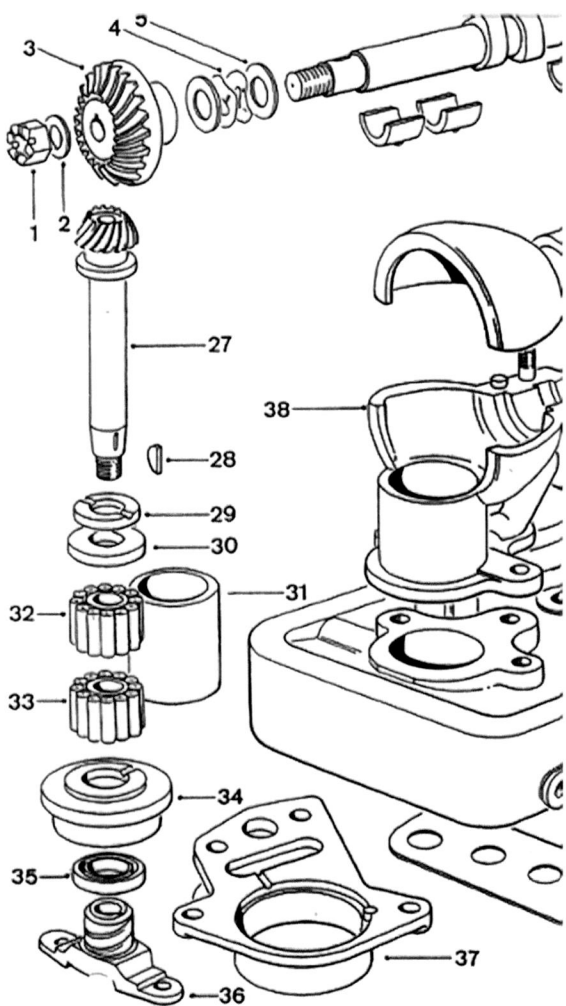

Fig.5: View of dynamo crankshaft to OHC   Fig.6: Oil seal at OHC to dynamo yoke

Reconditioning the Dynamo Rotor

In 2004 during an overhaul to replace a blown cylinder-head gasket I needed to disconnect the dynamo from the OHC drive. I noticed that there was excessive play in the dynamo rotor shaft. After removing the top cover, I seemed to have discovered gold. Sadly, not! It was the 70 percent remains of the top ball bearings (Figs.7, 8) amazingly held in place by the flexible drive coupling.

Fig.7: Bearing debris on dynamo cover   Fig.8: Collapsed top bearing

During the initial restoration of my Morris engine I had not paid sufficient attention to the dynamo: the bearings seemed fine but required lubricating. Since oil was no longer leaking to the dynamo – in fact, the top bearing had run dry and virtually collapsed. My father had an amusing saying that certain oil leaks were "a good fault". The remark was applicable in this case: if it had leaked, the open bearing would have been lubricated automatically. Of course, I should have lubricated it regularly as part of the usual service routine but this is not a simple task as it has limited access.

After removing the dynamo's rotor, I found consequential damage from the effects of overheating – probably caused by excess charging despite an indicated low output. The rotor laminations were displaced: the collapsed bearing had resulted in the rotor rubbing against the field magnets. The commutator was in a shocking condition: due to overheating the winding connections to the commutator copper bars were devoid of solder and some commutator slots were fused together with plastically deformed copper (Figs.9, 10). Not a pretty sight!

Fig.9 Distorted laminations on rotor   Fig.10: Dry joints commutator to windings

Despite its poor condition the dynamo continued to deliver some output <2 amps.

Urgent attention was required to return the dynamo rotor to an acceptable condition. The following reconditioning work was done:

- Align the rotor laminations (taking care not to impact the winding insulation).
- Re-sweat (solder) the windings to the commutator bars.
- Skim the commutator.
- Undercut the commutator slots (ensure no electrical shorts between bars).
- Secure the windings above the commutator slots with suitable binding cord.
- Varnish the rotor assembly and bake to ensure that varnish is hard.
- Fit new quality sealed bearings to both ends of the rotor.

Figures 11 and 12 illustrate the unit after careful renovation. Fortunately, I had the experience and the equipment to undertake the repairs. After skimming, the commutator's slots have to be undercut. Use a junior hacksaw blade with the fine teeth ground off on each side to ensure that the slots are separated from each other.

After undercutting the commutator, it was polished with 600-grade paper to ensure that it was smooth and then brushed free of any residual metal debris. A continuity check with a multi-meter confirmed that there were no shorts, earthing or dry (high resistance) joints.

Fig.11: Skimming the commutator

Fig.12: Commutator slots undercut

Before assembly I de-greased the old field windings and ensured that the connecting cables were properly insulated (Fig.13). Once the dynamo was assembled, I tested it by running it like a motor, powered from the car battery (Fig.14). It spun at a relatively low speed, confirming that the carbon brushes were making good contact. After adjusting the third brush the speed increased.

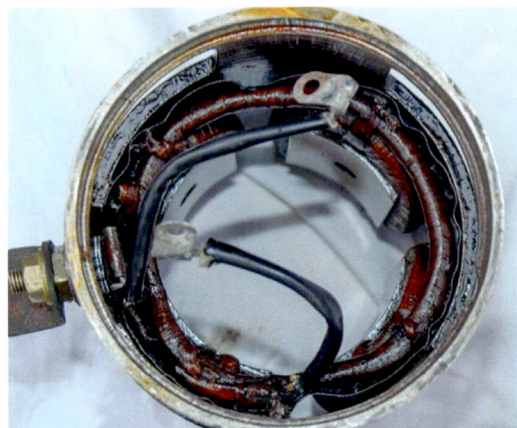

Fig.13: Dynamo's field connections

Fig.14: Testing the dynamo as an electric motor

Installing the Dynamo and Engine Timing

The next stage is to return the dynamo to the engine. Ensure that the meshing between the dynamo bottom bevel drive and the crankshaft is correct, along with the timing. If undertaking a total engine overhaul these steps in assembly are crucial. Assuming that the distributor and oil pump have been removed, the process to get the timing accurate is as follows:

1. Set piston number 1 to top dead centre (TDC). Remove the cover plate on the bell housing to ensure that the flywheel is in the correct position (mark 1-4). (Fig.15). Use white paint to mark the reference for using a strobe timing light.
2. Fit the distributor so that its rotor arm faces number 1 cylinder.
3. Fit the oil pump so that its offset drive to the distributor matches without affecting the rotor arm position facing the number 1 cylinder. Bolt the oil pump in place.
4. Place the dynamo drive (Fig.16) over the crankshaft drive (Fig.17), ensuring that the dynamo yoke is in line with the engine. Once it is screwed down there should be a slight click when rotating the top yoke to check the gear meshing clearance. If clearance is too much, use a thinner shim at the base. If it is too tight, try a thicker shim. Press the clutch in during these checks so that the crankshaft is in its foremost position. Rotate the crankshaft to different positions and check that the "click" is consistent. Then return the crankshaft to TDC.
5. Next fit the cylinder head and torque it down.
6. Fit the flexible coupling from the dynamo to the camshaft drive. Maintain number 1 cylinder at the TDC position; the cam bevel gears will have a matching X stamped on the mesh (Fig.18). Cams 1 and 2 will be at 45° and the top yoke at a right angle to the engine. This is tricky as the cam springs tend to nudge the alignment one way or the other.
7. Place the flexible drive between the yokes. It should be a neat fit. If the gap is too great, you will need washers. Fit the two customised bolts with nuts partially secured, then rotate the crankshaft so that all four bolts are fitted.
8. It should now be possible to use the starter motor to swing the engine (without spark plugs) for several revolutions and centralise the drive disc. Then tighten the nuts.

Fig.15: Flywheel TDC timing mark

Fig.16: Dynamo bevel to crankshaft

Because tightening the dynamo bolts is awkward and uncertain, I decided to replace them with BSF Allen screws. Using both long and short Allen keys I confidently removed and secured the dynamo.

Fig.17: Crankshaft bevel gear

Fig.18: Dynamo drive to camshaft

New Dynamo Field Windings

When the car was back on the road it was disappointing to find only a marginal improvement in charge output. The detailed reconditioning of the rotor and associated wiring seemed to have had little effect.

I hoped that the 85-year-old oil impregnated field windings would still be effective after degreasing. Clearly, this was not the case. It was difficult to undertake field winding wire insulation tests. I thought that the insulation must have broken down and reduced the magnetic flux essential for electrical generation.

These findings made me decide to make my Morris a far more effective vehicle without seriously detracting from its originality: I wanted the dynamo field coils to be rewound.

I had sourced several LED light bulbs from Peter Jury of Classic Dynamo & Regulator Conversions Ltd based in the UK (www.dynamoregulatorconversions.com). Peter is well versed in vintage cars and their electrical systems and provides an excellent advisory service. His company is dedicated to rebuilding and modifying vintage and classic dynamos, including electronic regulators and cut-out conversions. I contracted Peter to make up a new set of field windings (Fig.19) to replace the original 1929 coils.

The completed field windings fitted in the dynamo along with the magnet shoes that I had cleaned up (Fig.20). Peter assured me that the renovation I had done on the rotor was of sufficiently high standard that he could use it without any additional work.

Fig.19: New and old field coils

Fig.20: New field coils fitted

Prior to assembly I also asked to have the outer dynamo casing powder-coated as I am progressively coating items of my car to minimise chances of corrosion as well as making it easier to keep clean.

Conversion to a Two-Brush Dynamo

Peter Jury suggested that the unit's performance would improve significantly if converted to a two-brush system. As I am a bit of a purist for originality, it was quite a while before I accepted his recommendation. Finally, I agreed because this system would also function with a proper voltage regulator rather than the simple cut-out. Changing to a two-brush system is achieved by removing the third brush that is on a separate adjustable ring. The assembled and tested two-brush dynamo (Fig.21) was duly delivered and installed in my Morris.

To complete the system, Peter supplied an independent solid-state voltage regulator (6 volts, 11 amps, allowing 66 watts), available as an advanced dynamo regulator (ADR). It has an aluminium casing for heat dissipation but is no bigger than a matchbox (Fig.22). I placed it behind the dashboard. I left the existing cut-out in place for show – only you and I are aware of this!

Connecting the solid-state voltage regulator was straightforward as detailed wiring instructions were supplied. The unit comes with a modern fuse that has a built-in lamp to indicate when overloaded.

Once all was assembled and ready for the road, to my great delight the ammeter showed +8 to 10 amps charging on starting the engine. After driving for a few minutes I could see the ammeter needle progressively moving to the zero position, confirming that the battery is fully charged. What joy!

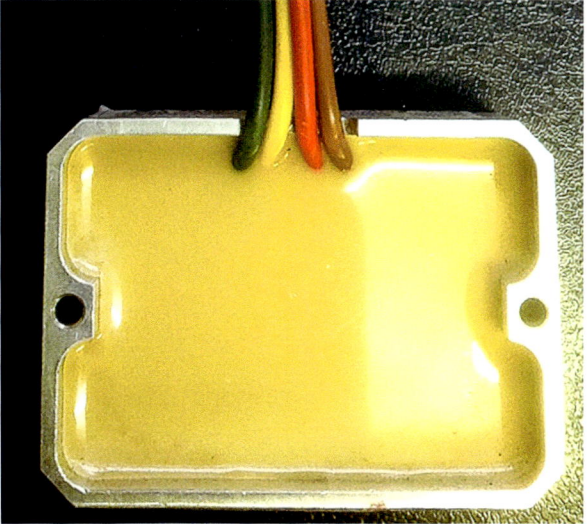

Fig.21: Assembled dynamo and yoke

Fig.22: Solid-state voltage regulator

Discussion

My attempts to restore the dynamo to specification so that it generates the designed level of current when the car left Cowley resulted in a massive improvement to the electrical performance of my 1929 Morris Minor. The LED lamps draw a fraction of current with all lights illuminated. My car is a much more effective and viable vehicle on the open road. Its LED lights enable me to drive at night should the need arise, but most vintage car drivers would agree that this is to be avoided.

The benefit of switching to the two-brush dynamo with voltage regulator is that it is not only efficient but safer. It prevents the chance of the battery discharging back through the wiring – that can melt and ignite the wiring with possible catastrophic consequences. My precious little car that I have owned for 54 years is now much safer and more reliable.

There is a considerable cost involved in renovating the dynamo system, but I feel the investment was fully justified. I can now enjoy many years of happy, fully charged and safe motoring.

Dynamo Fault after 12,800 miles

After taking my Morris on its safari around Zimbabwe and Zambia at its final destination (the place where I found it) the car decided: Enough! I first thought it was a major engine fault with almost no compression but later realised it was a timing issue.

To be clear, the dynamo was doing its job as a charging unit, but its other function to drive the overhead valves was the fault. The keyway securing the dynamo yoke had fractured; the yoke was loose and so lost the timing connection to the overhead camshaft and hence the valve opening sequence.

After removing the dynamo, the problem was obvious: the shaft was severely worn, the key slot distorted, and the bearing surface was worn (Fig.23). The top bearing was loose on the shaft and so was the yoke. It was a shock to find that the sealed bearing had seized. It had rotated against the dynamo shaft, causing severe wear. Was it a poor-quality bearing or is "sealed-for-life" no guarantee for longevity? Perhaps the working stress from the drive with any minor alignment added excessive load on the small bearing?

The final objective of the Back-to-Africa trip was to drive the Morris across the Victoria Falls Bridge: we needed a quick fix to achieve this. We fashioned a replacement key from tool steel and made a shim from a Red Bull can (giving the Morris wings!) to take up the wear of the drive yoke to the dynamo shaft (Fig.24). The temporary fix held well and might have functioned for quite some time but the bearing was in poor condition and would have to be replaced at the earliest opportunity.

Fig.23: Dynamo shaft wear and deformed key slot

Fig.24: Red Bull shim to fix seized worn yoke

Back in Cape Town, I had the worn dynamo shaft metal-sprayed with a low temperature system and then ground to size. A quality sealed bearing along with a new yoke and key was fitted to bring the system back to standard. But for how long?

My analysis is that the bearing's failure was responsible for the shaft starting to wobble. That progressively eroded the internal area of the yoke. Finally, the clearance was so great that the key no longer maintained its purpose: that put an end to camshaft synchronisation and resulted in engine failure.

Closing Comments

The question remains as to whether the sealed bearing's life is limited for this crucial application and duty. The dynamo is always working at temperature, being close to the engine block together with hot air from the radiator. An RS grade bearing has better sealing but one must allow for expansion to prevent any self-generated heat that will contribute to the tough working environment. This will inevitably cause the bearing's lubrication to leak and friction will reduce the bearing's life. Removing the top side of the sealed bearing might provide access to a more practical and regular lubrication but then contaminating the electrical system is a risk.

The dynamo is not in the easiest of locations or access to check regularly. Perhaps when the engine needs its 4,000 mile de-coke and the cylinder head has to be removed, it would then be practical to replace the dynamo's top bearing.v

TG06: Engine Decarbonising

Introduction and Background

To quote the *Morris Minor Handbook*: "The formation of carbon is unfortunately one of the troubles every internal combustion engine is heir to".

Decarbonising the Overhead Cam (OHC) engine fitted to the 1929 Morris Minor and later models (including the MG J-type and P-type) was a regular practice – perhaps every 5,000 miles. However, modern fuel and lubricants are much improved and most vintage cars are driven only occasionally: decarbonising or de-coking will be required only when the power falls off or a pinking noise is noticed under load.

"If it ain't broke don't fix it". A compression test will indicate the efficiency of the engine. Meddling for the sake of it can disturb a functioning engine. Of course, if you need to access the cylinder head for some other reason, take the opportunity to de-coke it.

The method of removing the cylinder head, decarbonising and grinding valves and then re-assembly is detailed in the handbooks of the Morris and other pre-war cars. My intention is not to reinvent the wheel but to describe my experience in undertaking such work pictorially. I hope that these illustrated notes will guide custodians of our special cars. When it comes to deciding when de-carbonisation is necessary the notes should apply to both OHC and side-valve engines.

Background

My "Cammy" 1929 Morris Minor 4 Seat Tourer (DS9936) had done 4,300 miles since restoration when it suddenly lost power: a compression test confirmed loss in number 1 and 2 cylinders, suggesting a blown head gasket.

I prepared the car for a top-end overhaul (Fig.1). After draining the radiator, removing the bonnet and horn, and protecting the wings, the car was ready for the main work. Disconnect the two oil pipes to the cylinder head as well as the drive yoke to the dynamo before attending to the cylinder head – a rather fiddly job.

Fig.1: Engine prepared for overhaul

Fig.2: Carburettor and manifold removed

Disconnect the carburettor and exhaust manifold from the cylinder head to allow better access to the head nuts (Fig.2). After progressively loosening the nuts it helps to be able to lift the cylinder head and place a 3mm plastic strip under it to remove all cylinder head nuts easily. If the head will not budge, a firm tap with a wooden mallet against the side of the head usually releases it.

Once the head was removed, I was surprised to find considerable carbon and oily deposits on the piston heads (Fig.3). The narrow gasket area between number 1 and 2 cylinders had indeed blown (Fig.4). The engine had not seemed poorly: it always started on the first attempt. There was no indication of smoke at the exhaust, nor did it use much oil.

Fig.3: Engine block, head removed   Fig.4: Gasket leak between cylinders 1 and 2

The carbon deposit (Fig.4) indicates that the engine had been running rather rich. The rust staining at the rear end (right) caused by water leakage suggests that the cylinder head was not tightened down evenly or – more serious – perhaps it was warped.

After the Morris had completed its Back-to-Africa tour and returned to the UK having covered 12,500 miles, I found that water had contaminated the sump oil. The cause was a leak from the (OS) rear stud sleeve that passed through the water jacket (Fig.5) that had rusted.

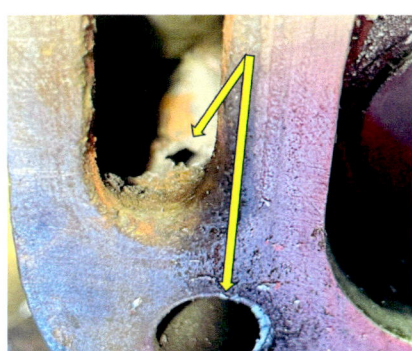

Fig.5: Insert rear OS of OHC   Fig.6: Water-jacket leak area   Fig.7: New MS insert

The sleeve had failed 94 years after manufacture (Fig.6) shows the corroded hole in the water jacket area. I was not even aware of the tube's presence. If yours has never been replaced, then I suggest you do so at the next de-coke. The old tube is easily bored out and replaced with a new 100mm steel tube (Fig.7). It is quite a straightforward fix and by using a water inhibitor in future it may last longer than the next 94 years!

The cylinder head after 4,300 miles (Fig.8) looked quite a mess. If I did not know any better, I would say that the stud tube leak was present earlier. However, it was the opposite stud hole that had the sleeve and appeared to be in order. Clearly, the mixture was not right and running very rich. This was early days in my experience with this engine.

Fig.8: Cylinder head showing considerable deposits and water leakage at rear

Decarbonising

The amount of carbon deposit after only 4,300 miles since restoration surprised me. I carefully removed as much surface carbon as possible, taking care not to scratch the valves, I collected samples from each section for comparison. There was more carbon on cylinders 1 and 2 (left) than on 3 and 4 (Fig.9). Was this caused by combustion or temperature?

Fig.9: Carbon collected from cylinder head

Fig.10: Carbon removed from pistons

I wondered whether the difference in deposits might be associated with the cooling gradient from the front to rear of the engine. Perhaps a bias in the inlet manifold so that the mixture is richer at one end of the engine. Removing the carbon from the heads of the pistons (Fig.10) was straightforward. I checked for any wear ridge at the top of each cylinder; fortunately, none was discernible. It was important to establish the straightness of both the engine block and cylinder head: not even the slightest distortion can be tolerated (Fig.11). If warping is detected, you need to get a professional engine restorer to attend to it.

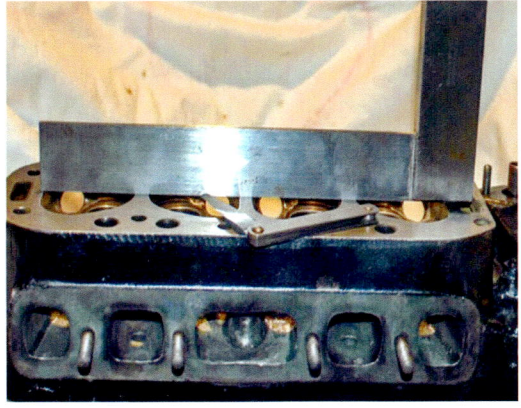

Fig.11: Checking engine block for distortion

Fig.12: Valves removed

Valve Grinding

When removing the valves take careful note of each location (Fig.12) as each valve is matched to a particular valve seat. Take a strip of wood, drill eight holes in a row, number them starting from the front of the engine and place the valve stems in the holes (Fig.13).

Store the valves in the wooden holder until needed. Ensure that you deal with only one valve at a time. Clean and inspect each valve and wash it in paraffin (including the cylinder head) before starting to grind the valves.

Fig.13: Grinding valve seats – wooden holder

Fig.14: Soft spring under valve

Obtain a valve grinding stick with rubber sucker (Fig.13) and fit a light spring (Fig.14) to the valve stem so that it lifts from time to time while grinding. This ensures that its position changes and avoids score marks. Depending on how severe the valve seat conditions are, some may need cutting by a professional engine restorer.

Obtain a two-part (coarse and fine) valve grinding paste available from most classic car parts suppliers – usually only the fine paste is needed to clean up valves. Rotate the valve in its matching seat with stick and rubber sucker adhered to the valve head. Rotate the valve back and forth between your hands (Fig.15) using slight downwards pressure. If necessary, start with a small dab of coarse paste between the two seat surfaces. Keep checking that you are not creating grind lines or score marks on the valve or seat. If any slight pitting remains, continue until the pitting is removed. Wash off the coarse paste with paraffin or a grease solvent, then use the fine paste. Repeat the twisting to establish a fine consistent grey-matt circle around the middle where the seat contacts the face (Fig.16). Achieve a finish at least one sixteenth of an inch (1.58mm) wide for the intake valve and one-third of an inch (3.17mm) for the exhaust valve.

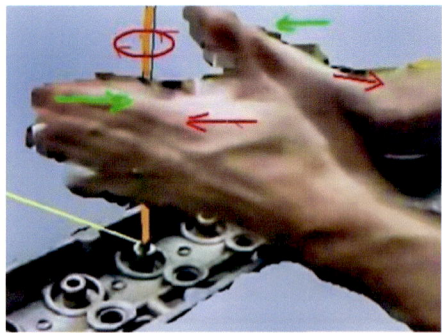
Fig.15: Rotate stick back and forth

Fig.16: Matt finish

Fig.17: Valve seats ground

After grinding, thoroughly wash the valve of grinding paste and return it to its position in the rack. Repeat for each valve, then wash away any trace of grinding paste on the cylinder head. Pay great attention to this.

While the cylinder head was on the bench, I decided to grind the as-cast surface of the inlet and exhaust ports and surrounding areas smooth – as best I could. This marginally improves gas flow (not quite a racing engine), but every little bit helps! After grinding and cleaning the valve seats are ready for assembly (Fig.17).

Valve Stem Straightness

In my engine I noticed a score mark on the stem of one valve (Fig.18). To ensure that it would not stick in the valve guide I carefully smoothed off the burr. I then checked the straightness of each valve on my lathe (Fig.19) with a dial gauge. Fortunately, all were true.

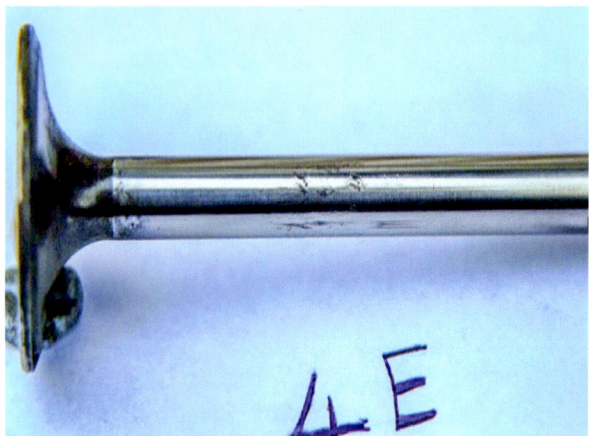
Fig.18: Burr on valve stem polished off

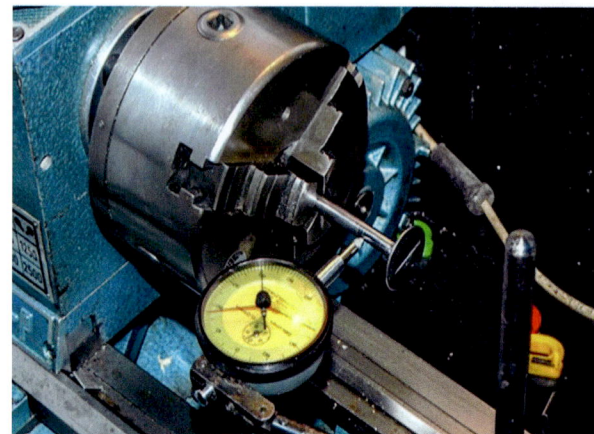
Fig.19: Checking valve stem straightness

Valve Seating Leak Test

To confirm the effectiveness of the ground valves I undertook a leak test. I fitted the spark plugs to the cylinder head and placed the valves in their respective positions but without their securing springs; they stayed in place by gravity. Placing the assembly in a tin bath and setting it downside up, I poured in blue paintbrush cleaner to each piston recess (Fig.20).

The test was left for 24 hours and to my delight not a drop of liquid came through the valves into the inlet and exhaust ports, proving that the valves were 100 percent sealed to their seats. (Fig.20).

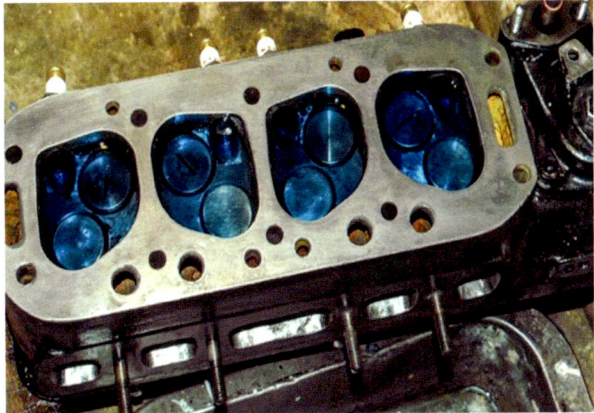

Fig.20: Valve seat leak test

Fig.21: Flooded valve leak test area

The next step was to fit the valves with their springs, assemble the camshaft and cam pivot shafts, and set the valve clearances as detailed in the *Morris Minor Manual*.

Fitting the Cylinder Head

In 1991 I had the cylinder head of my Minor restored by Sports & Vintage Motors Ltd of Shropshire. A sealed bearing fitted at the drive to the dynamo ended the perennial problem of oil dribbling down into the dynamo. S&V recommended a modification to secure the overhung cam pivot shafts at the rear of the engine better. They fitted a brass dual-bearing plummer block bolted down with longer cylinder head studs (Fig.22). The block secures the cam pivot shafts to prevent constant bending that over time develops fatigue cracks and failure. The plummer block also ensures that the valves at number 4 cylinder open fully.

Fig.22: Bronze plummer block at rear

Fig.23: Copper tube to position gasket

It is always best to fit a new cylinder-head gasket. I learned this method from my father: smooth axle grease over the engine block, then take great care to align the gasket over the various studs. More recently, the improved method is to spray the gasket with silver paint – two coats. Then a further coat just before assembly. When able to do so, run the engine for a short while to allow the gasket to seal and settle. To ensure that the gasket does not snag when fitting or get bent, use a length of half inch copper tube (Fig.23) to press it down gently, little by little, until it is in position. Place number 1 piston at top dead centre (TDC) with the distributor rotor arm facing number 1 cylinder. The dynamo yoke should be in line with the engine. Before fitting the cylinder head set the number 1 and number 2 cam lobes to 45°; the top yoke should now be at right angles to the head and the teeth on the drive gears should match the marks (Fig.24).

Connect the flexible drive disc to the dynamo yoke but do not tighten the nuts fully. Once the engine head is tightened down, remove the spark plugs and spin the engine to allow the flexible disc to find its natural position. Only then tighten the disc drive bolts.

Torqueing Down the Cylinder Head

One of the most awkward exercises is tightening the cylinder head of the OHC Morris Minor. The head bolts are under the camshafts and can only be tightened effectively with a flat spanner with the exhaust manifold removed (Fig.25). Even then, you can never be quite sure that the cylinder head is evenly tightened down. After running the engine hot, the standard procedure is to tighten each nut at least half a turn but access to the nuts is limited with the manifold in place. Using an open spanner held at around a 30° angle, your grip is limited. This often results in slippage and deformation of the head nuts.

Fig.24: Drive to dynamo gears meshed at "X"

Fig.25: Limited access to nuts unless manifold is removed

Fig.26: Crow-foot socket

I believe that the main reason for my head gasket leaking between cylinders – and where water was evident at the rear – was that the head gasket was not uniformly tight across the gasket.

When I originally commissioned the engine, I did a compression test. I found differences between cylinders that I assumed to be due to variations in the bore and rings although relatively new. Had I misinterpreted the data?

I decided to use a torque wrench: this eliminates the human variable by ensuring that all head studs bear an equal load. My problem was getting effective purchase on the head nuts inconveniently located under the cam-follower guide shafts. I solved this by modifying a crow-foot socket (Fig.26). I had to purchase a full set when I only needed the 13mm socket that fitted the 5/16" BSF nuts. Later I used the ⅜" equivalent for my MG J2 engine. The unit initially selected did not give access to all areas until I ground around the rear and sides of the crow-foot spanner so that it rotated freely.

With this tool, I can torque down the OHC cylinder head whether cold or hot. For a newly restored engine, do this after 250 miles, after 500 miles and onwards. When re-torqueing the head nuts, first loosen slightly to break the friction, then torque them down progressively from 18 lb ft (25 Nm), 20 lb ft (27 Nm), 22 lb ft (30Nm) as mileage builds up. Sports & Vintage Motors recommends a torque of 25 lb ft (33 Nm) when using new studs and nuts. Keep in mind that the crow-foot socket is 16mm off the centre line with the torque wrench – thus a torque setting of 22 lb ft would probably be around 23 lb ft. When no further tightening is needed beyond the set torque value, you can assume that the nuts are at their design load. I have read that the Morris side-valve engine can be torqued to 45 lb ft (60 Nm). Later models may have bigger studs but this seems doubtful: best stick to 25 lb ft. Cylinder head studs can stretch over time; when rebuilding an engine, it is advisable to replace them. Regular attention to the cylinder head tightness will ensure that the head gasket provides long and reliable service.

Compression Test Data

Why Test?

A compression gauge is helpful in diagnosing and locating the causes of lost compression; it is a quick way to establish if valve or gasket leaks are developing, if broken piston rings are present, or simply to track the engine wear over time.

Dry Test Conditions

Run the engine hot, then close the petrol supply until the carburettor empties. Tests should be done with all plugs removed and the engine at operating temperature. Lock the throttle open and check that the choke valve is wide open. Disconnect the coil to avoid any sparks or fire and reduce the ignition load. Crank the engine with the electric starter, noting maximum reading on the compression gauge for each cylinder.

Wet Test Conditions

Pour about 15 ml SAE40 engine oil (use a syringe) on top of the piston; ensure that the oil is kept clear of the valves. Take a further compression test as oil is added to each cylinder. If there is no appreciable increase in pressure, then the rings are tight. If there is a rise of 10lb or more over the first reading, there is some leakage past the rings due to wear.

Actual Test Data

The comparative graphs (Figs.27, 28) illustrate changes – the mileage has doubled between each test.

Since restoration in 1992 and for a variety of reasons, including living abroad for 9 years, my car had not done a lot of mileage. Hence the intervals between successive compression tests.

However, conventional wisdom is that compression tests may be relevant for new and rebuilt engines only after they have done at least 5,000 miles. My next test will be done at 10,000 miles.

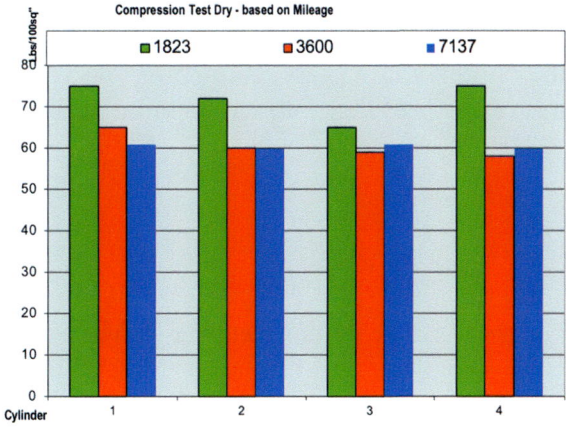

Fig.27: Dry – Consistent data

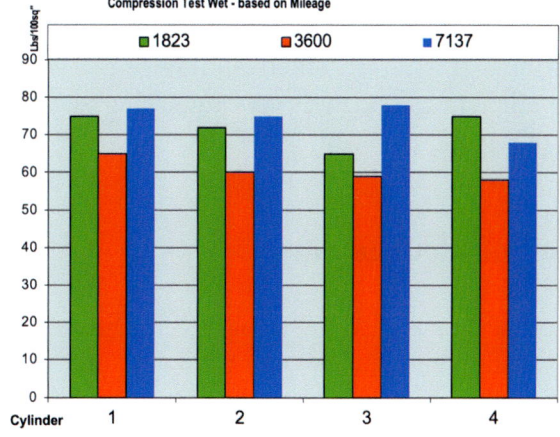

Fig.28: Wet – Increased leakage past pistons

Despite ensuring that the cylinder head is fully torqued and using a recently calibrated wrench, I still wonder why the compression reduces progressively from number 1 to number 4.

The wet test can be quite variable unless conditions are exactly the same, particularly in the measured amount of oil added. Bear in mind that the engine cools rather quickly and a temperature gradient could also influence the data. I have created a spreadsheet to calculate the bore and valve and gasket losses that I would be happy to share on request.

Closing Comments

An owner new to vintage cars who has not been exposed to engineering may find the task of decarbonising the engine rather daunting. The first requirement is a set of the basic tools: good-quality spanners and a socket set will come in useful for many years to come. The step-by-step procedures detailed in the *Owner's Manual* are generally easy to follow. So have a go.

Invest in a torque wrench; it will pay dividends for other jobs as well as the cylinder head; I opted for a new low-range unit as I was not confident that those I had inherited had remained in calibration.

If you suspect that the cylinder-head gasket is damaged in any way, I recommend fitting a new one. Your choice is between a traditional composite gasket or an annealed solid copper one that can be used multiple times. Our engines are too precious to compromise and I prefer the composite.

Testing the valve sealing for leaks was a very valuable exercise because it confirmed that the valve grinding was effective.

Torqueing down the cylinder head is easily achieved if the camshaft and guide shafts are removed when the engine is cold. Remember that the cylinder-head gasket will compress over time and further tightening will be needed in the future. This is best done when the engine is hot. The crow-foot socket makes subsequent torqueing practical without having to dismantle the camshaft assembly – especially while the engine cools.

Undertaking compression tests is an objective measure of the condition of the engine and its wear over time. It gives you confidence that the engine's compression is reasonably balanced across all cylinders and has acceptable leakage via the pistons and valves.

Take photographs at every stage – not just to remember how to re-assemble, but to keep a condition record for future reference.

Since putting my Morris back on the road at 7,000 miles, the engine is running better and leaner and has a consumption of around 30+ miles per gallon.

Undertaking the decarbonising and valve grinding is an experience that will give the new car enthusiast a better understanding of the workings of the engine and its care. Returning the vehicle to efficient motoring is very satisfying and can result in greater confidence to tackle more advanced repair work.

Acknowledgement

Peer review and suggestions by Tim Stevens a member of the Vintage Minor Register (VMR).

TG07: Clutch Overhaul

Introduction and Background

When the need arises to remove the gearbox on the 1929 Morris Minor and later versions, it is a good time to check the clutch not only for wear but looseness of the clutch plate and central boss, as well as lining rivets. A useful guide is the clutch and bell housing schematic, an exploded view of all the elements (Fig.1).

An area of wear that is often ignored is the clutch and brake shaft (P26) with its associated bushes that exert undesirable bending stresses on the spigot shaft. Often both the shaft and bronze bushes are worn. The shaft will need building up and machining to size and new bushes will have to be machined. When I renovated these elements, the improvement in clutch action was noticeable.

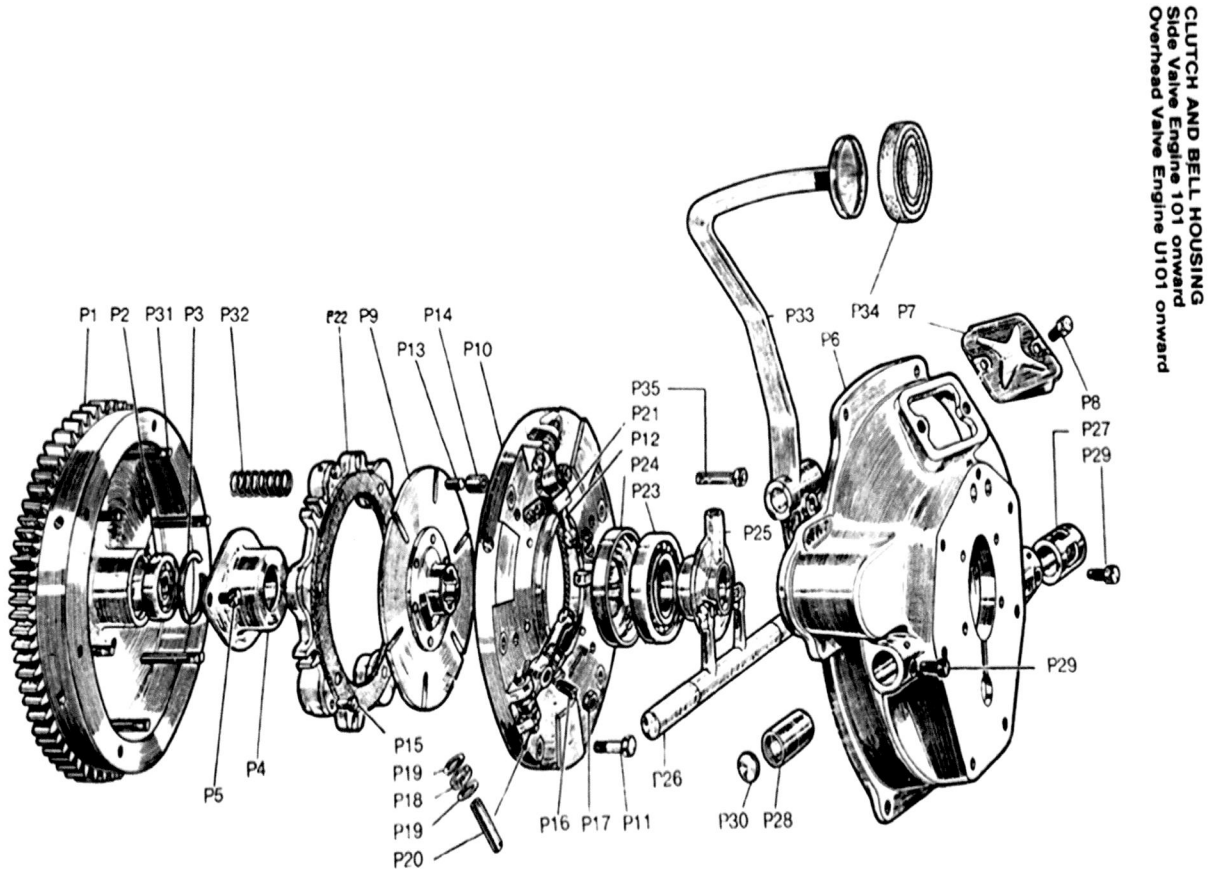

Fig.1: Parts diagram showing key elements: Spigot bearing (P2), pressure plate (P22), clutch plate (P9), thrust or release bearing (P23).

All the elements of the clutch assembly must function in unison. If you experience some jerking when setting off in the car, several issues could be the cause: a loose or worn propshaft flexible drive, backlash from differential to half-shafts, poor foot action on the clutch, a clutch plate's rivets loose in the boss (Fig.2). In my case, it was the last mentioned as well as a burnt clutch lining.

Fig.2: Rivets deformed, elongated slots

Fig.3: Rivet anvil in vice

After obtaining a new clutch plate from Ian Harris Morris Spares Ltd I proceeded to rivet the assembly using the existing splined boss. Later in preparation for my 1,509 mile trip around Zimbabwe and Zambia and aware that the irreplaceable spigot shaft splines were worn I decided to fit a completely new clutch plate with splined boss that improved the fitting and backlash.

As I did not have a riveting kit I decided to make a tool. Using a large bolt, I drilled a $5/16$" recess in the head (Fig.3) and secured it in the bench vice as an anvil for retaining the shape of the round head end of the rivet (Fig.4).

Once positioned, the next step was using a four pound hammer to impact the rivet's parallel end to provide sufficient metal to secure the plate. This seemed quite effective.

After fitting all six rivets I used a small ballpeen hammer to peen each rivet, improving their appearance (Fig.5) and introducing surface compressive stresses to reduce the onset of metal fatigue.

Fig.4: Rivet anvil and clutch plate

Fig.5: Clutch plate riveted and peened

Prior to fitting the whole clutch assembly (Fig.6), it is advisable to replace the spigot bearing in the flywheel with a new sealed unit (RS type seals reduce oil leaks). There is an oilway through the spigot shaft that is supposed to lubricate the splines as well as the bearing in the flywheel. Each time I have had to remove the gearbox I have found the bearing dry and sometimes partially seized. This is another area that does an important job and is often ignored.

Before mounting the main plate (P10) on the flywheel ensure that all bolts are identical in weight. Even the smallest amount of unbalance contributes to excess vibration and causes lost power, wear and possible fatigue. Unbalance increases at the speed by the square of the distance from the central axis due to centrifugal forces – so every bit counts.

Once all items are ready to secure the clutch assembly to the flywheel, fit the balanced high-tensile engineered bolts tightly enough to hold the assembly together. Now for the most important step: aligning the clutch plate with the spigot shaft bearing in the flywheel. There are mandrels available for this but the best approach is to use an actual spigot shaft. If you can make use of a spare spigot shaft, it will slot into the clutch plate splines and centre the plate perfectly to the bearing in the flywheel. Fitting the gearbox and removing it in future is made much easier since it avoids plasticly deforming the gearbox spigot end shaft that can seize when forced. The spigot bearing is easily damaged from the start of its life.

Next, progressively tighten the plate securing bolts and torque to 15 lb ft. Assuming that the contact faces of the clutch withdrawal release fingers are smooth and of equal weight, lubricate with SAE140 oil prior to fitting the gearbox. This is also a service interval requirement.

Check that the clutch release (or thrust bearing) is in good order. A modern sealed bearing is recommended (Fig.7). It is much cheaper than trying to source an original (priced at £180 the last time I checked). You can source a relatively modern sealed thrust bearing for around £50, although they are becoming scarce.

Fig.6: Clutch assembled – note fingers

Fig.7: Clutch thrust bearing fitted

You will find that the installation becomes easier after the first time. It is helpful to use two or three long rods to align the main casing securing the bolt holes and ensure that the gearbox is in neutral. Then, using a jack or some wooden blocks to support the gearbox, refitting should prove straightforward.

Some bolts have nuts on the engine side and others on the gearbox side. If the nut is against steel, it requires a spring locking washer. Nuts against aluminium do not need a spring washer as the aluminium surface is self-locking. After tightening up the bolts evenly, the next step is to connect all the peripherals: hand brake linkage, propshaft, foot and clutch pedal, accelerator, speedometer cable and power cable to the starter switch.

Finally, set the clearance of the clutch fingers to the thrust or release bearing. This can be an awkward operation through the gearbox top access and breather plate. It is made easier by making a shaped 3/32" feeler gauge (Figs.8, 9).

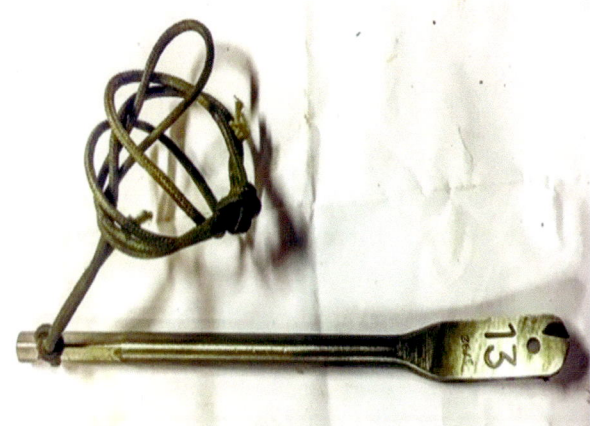
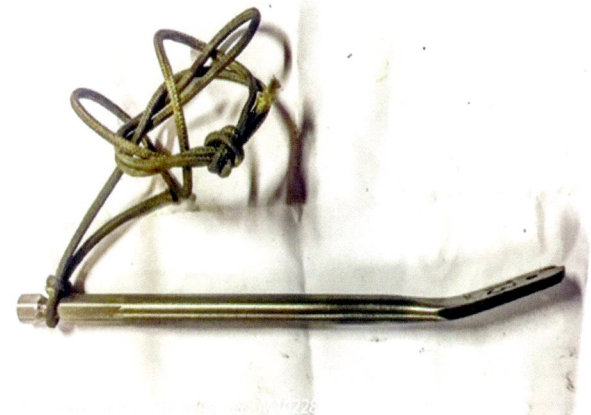

Fig.8: Clutch finger feeler gauge   Fig.9: Clutch finger feeler gauge – side view

It is important to have a securing string – the last thing you want is to drop it into the bell housing! I used a surplus wood drill that proved to be perfect for the application. After grinding away its drill section I brought it to size and then (with heat) set the angle to ease access. It is a very effective tool for setting the clutch finger gap.

Fig.10: Gearbox installed and connected

Once the gearbox is installed (Fig.10) and the floorboards and seats are fitted, the car is ready for a road test. Once settled in after 50 miles or so, check the clutch finger clearances. Then at every 1,000 miles again check and adjust the clearances.

Closing Comments

As most car owners will be aware, the wearing surfaces of the clutch are a consumable item and if stressed on climbing a hill from a standing start they can slip and "burn". If the clutch continues to "slip" or even squeal, then the linings need replacement.

I trust that this article will guide Morris Minor owners and future custodians in overhauling the clutch with confidence that their vehicles will always give reliable use.

References

Anon – *Gearbox and Clutch Removal. (1930/31 OHC Minor Saloon)* 201908
Peter Hills – *Fixing a 1929 Minor 3-Speed Gearbox Jumping Out of Gear*
VMR M-171 – 201910
Anon – *Gearbox 3-Speed Morris Minor* 201801
Anon – *Morris Gearbox Dismantling*
MG 1936 Manual. <https://www.triplemregister.org/uploads>

TG08: Three-speed Gearbox Overhaul

Introduction and Background

Many owners are reluctant to tackle the overhaul of a gearbox: "There are so many moving parts." Actually, it is more forgiving than you would think – much easier than rebuilding an engine. Having overhauled the gearbox several times on my 1929 Morris Minor and had many discussions with Morris and MG owners, the VMR and Pre-War Forum as well as other published material, I decided to record our collective experiences.

"Do not reinvent the wheel." This old saying certainly applies and making good use of the experience of others has enabled me to compile a list of contributors to help others to tackle a gearbox overhaul with confidence. I have incorporated elements of Joe Rayner's comprehensive guide (Ref.1) in this article that emphasise what not to do – based on mistakes I have made.

Background

In 1970 on finding my Morris and starting restoration, I inherited a very rusty noisy gearbox. The second gear layshaft was severely worn and I had one made locally in Zambia. After my car was returned to the road in the UK 1992 first and second gears whined excessively until getting into third when all was relatively smooth. This will come as no surprise to many: spur gears are inherently noisy. Surely they can be set to mesh better? This became an obsession in my attempts to achieve a smooth running and sounding gearbox.

First Overhaul (6,885 miles)

This was done primarily to replace a noisy original clutch release bearing and to determine the condition of the gears. I found the gear teeth and the thrust washers heavily corroded and pitted. Without spares I simply reassembled the gearbox while I searched for replacement first and second gear clusters and thrust washers.

Second Overhaul (7,195 miles)

Having sourced and fitted some replacement gears and new bearings, there was modest improvement, but this work was short-lived.

Third Overhaul (7,324 miles)

This followed a catastrophic gearbox failure. I had made the mistake of selecting a short layshaft locking bolt that ultimately did not serve its purpose (Fig.1). Driving from London to Bath I noticed an oil leak from the bell housing that I attributed to expansion of the hot oil. In fact, the layshaft had moved away from its front support, providing an open port for the gearbox oil to leak into the bell housing (Fig.2). Failure analysis revealed that the second gear cluster layshaft was only supported by the casing's cast trunnion. When I selected reverse on a steep hill the layshaft displaced with a loud "Bang"! The twisting of the shaft created excess stress and caused a gear tooth to shear, as well as fracturing the cast aluminium rear support trunnion in the casing (Figs.3, 4). I missed getting the

Morris to Prescott and had to transport it back to London. This was the first time the car had failed me, but it was all my fault.

Fig.1: Ensure layshaft lock bolts are fitted correctly

Fig.2: Retracted second gear layshaft caused oil to flow into bell housing

This self-induced failure was an easy mistake to make when you are selecting from lots of bits and pieces in a bucket. Repairing the aluminium cast casing would be a major challenge; there were several casings available to me, so I replaced it.

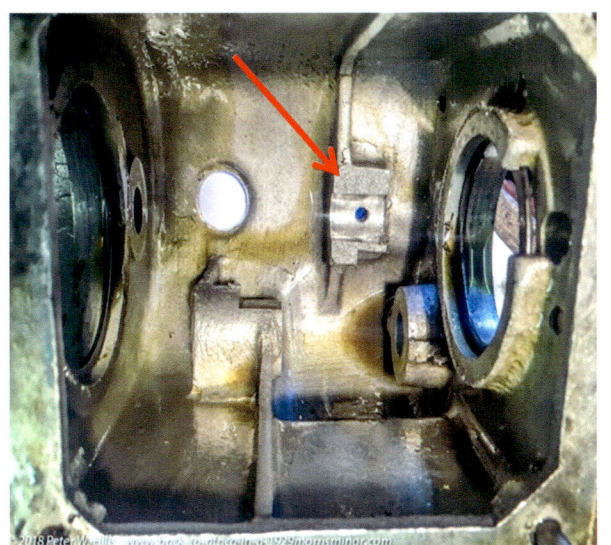

Fig.3: Fractured layshaft trunnion

Fig.4: Fractured cover of trunnion

The Morris fraternity rallied round and I obtained a complete set of gear clusters and gear casing. This time I made sure to use the correct length layshaft locking bolts.

I had committed to attend the 2018 Morris Register National Rally and as an interim fix decided to assemble the "new" gear with mixed gears. The gearbox was functional: a little less noisy in first gear and resonating sporadically in second. It was always a relief to get into the quieter third gear, basically a direct drive. In 2019 after we attended the Chateau Impney and Prescott rallies, the car was shipped to Cape Town, South Africa for the planned Back-to-Africa safari.

Fourth Overhaul (8,629 miles)

Covid-19 postponed my tour to Central Africa. This allowed me more time to attend to the car's reliability in Cape Town. The car took part in several local rallies and tours around the mountainous Cape. I was still concerned that the gearbox was not meshing as well as it should. I had a range of better spare first and second gears and new phosphor bronze bushes and layshafts. I was determined to further reduce the gearbox noise. I was fortunate to have readily available engineering services as well as expertise from members of the Crankhandle Club of Cape Town. Attending to every detail, I expected that this overhaul would be the most sustainable. Sadly, there was little noticeable improvement.

Fifth Overhaul (10,157) miles

After some 1,500 miles the number 1 big-end bearing failed and the engine had to be removed. This created yet another opportunity to check the gearbox. To my surprise I found that the second gear bush had seized on its layshaft and was turning in the gear. My error had been that in trying to achieve a perfect fit I overlooked the fact that the bronze bush has a higher coefficient of expansion and requires appropriate clearance: the rule of thumb is two thou. per inch diameter. After some reaming and refitting I made sure that this error was not repeated. I also noticed that the first and second gear cluster mesh was offset. By changing the thrust washer thickness, I was able to align the gears better. Back on the road first gear was smooth but in second there was still that intermediate speed rattle that receded as the car went faster. The noise seemed to reduce as the gears started to bed in during the 1,500 mile tour of Zimbabwe and Zambia.

Gearbox Internals

To commence an overhaul, I made constant reference to the schematic and parts list from Morris Motors (1926) Limited with the elements set out more clearly (Fig.5).

Fig.5: Three-speed gear box schematic

Tools Needed

- Wheel stands (4) or wooden blocks and a hydraulic jack to provide comfortable space to work under the car.
- The usual spanners and sockets, pliers, screwdrivers, brass drift, copper hammer.
- A hot air gun (recommended by Joe Rayner) proved very beneficial. The modest cost of around £26 (Fig.6) pays dividends and it is useful for many other jobs (especially electrical for shrink sleeving). By warming the aluminium gear box casing, it rapidly expands so that interference fittings (bearings and shafts) are easily removed and re-fitted. Forcing items in and out of the gearbox casing causes wear and stress.

Fig.6: Hot air gun

- Gasket material and jointing compound are essential: Hylomar or Wellseal do a better job than the traditional paper gasket. However, I made new gaskets using a small ballpeen hammer to shape them to fit. I was careful to ensure that no oilways were blocked by gasket material.

Safety

Disconnect the battery before working on the vehicle. Jack up the car, place it on stands or wooden blocks making sure it is very stable.

Access

Remove both front seats, lift the floorboards and foot board support brackets, choke and slow running controls, accelerator and hand and foot brake levers (Fig.2).

Disconnect the starter switch and remove the gear stick, the speedo cable at the gearbox, the spider from the gearbox to the propshaft flexible disc.

Removing the Gearbox

Place a bottle jack with wooden block under the gearbox to take the weight off so that it will not hang on the spigot shaft. Alternatively, use a plank and rope to secure the gearbox (Fig.7). Once the bell housing bolts have been removed, place two or three 100mm (4") rods through the bolt holes for support. This will make it easier to separate the gearbox from the engine.

In an ideal situation simply pressing the clutch pedal will separate the gearbox from the engine flywheel housing. If there is insufficient clutch movement, try placing a large spanner between the clutch and the release bearing (Fig.8). This helps to separate the gearbox. Take care not to overload the clutch fingers as they could get distorted.

Fig.7: Remove load off the input shaft

Fig.8: Separate gearbox from engine

In some cases, separation may not be easy because of previous poor assembly. Do *not* attempt to separate the gearbox by wedging tyre levers or screwdrivers between the aluminium bell housing and the steel engine housing. You will fracture the aluminium casting (Figs.9, 10) as happened in my car's previous life with inevitable results. This earlier cracked aluminium bell housing was welded in Zambia.

Fig.9: Bell housing weld repair

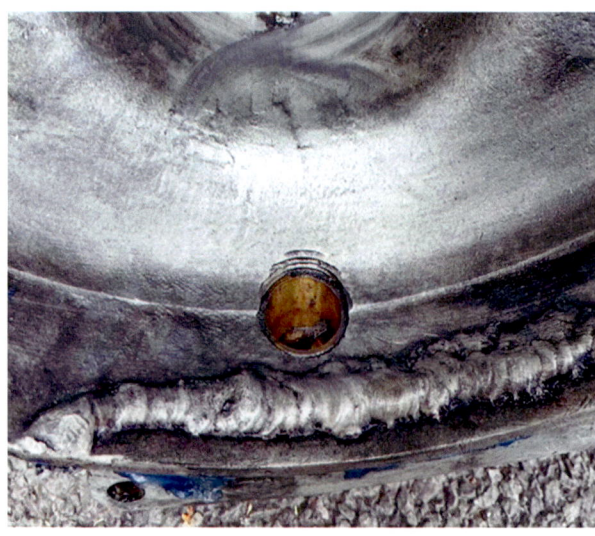

Fig.10: Bell housing weld repair

The main reason a gearbox holds tightly to the engine is that the spigot shaft (drive gear) has seized in the spigot bearing in the flywheel that was also bereft of lubrication (it was replaced with a sealed type). When fitting the clutch plate, you need to use a mandrel to centre the clutch plate but this is not always precise enough. If not perfectly centred when trying to insert the gearbox, the spigot shaft end will jam against the edge of the spigot bearing (Fig.11) resulting in plastic deformation of the shaft end. This is then jammed and makes removal very difficult.

I was fortunate to have two spare spigot shafts but found that the ends of both were oval. I corrected the distortion by light grinding in a lathe (Fig.12). The shafts then fitted easily in a new sealed spigot bearing. When fitting the clutch plate, I used the spare spigot shaft to centre the clutch plate. This made fitting the gearbox and subsequent removal much easier.

Fig.11: Spigot bearing in flywheel (dry)

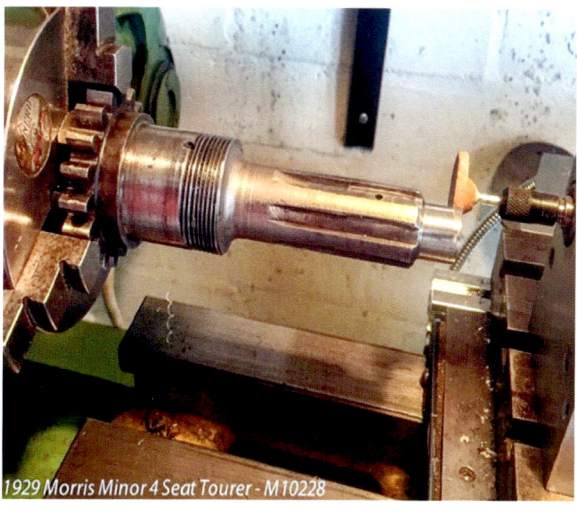

Fig.12: Spigot shaft ground to size

The 1929 photograph (Fig.13) taken at the Morris factory illustrates how easy it should be to fit the gearbox to the engine. If a spare spigot shaft is not available, an alternative approach before tightening up the clutch plate is to test fit the gearbox with its spigot. Then gently remove the gearbox, tighten up the clutch and check again. If the gearbox does not slip in and out easily, the clutch is not aligned.

Using a hot air gun to remove the gear trains and bearings from the gearbox housing makes the process easier. A brass drift is also helpful to ease out the bearings. Remember: prevent damage to the balls and their contact surfaces by impacting on the bearing's outer race only. The circlips in the housing can usually remain in place. When stripping, make note of the gears' brass shims and their

Fig.13: Morris Assembly Line – Easy Fitting

locations. The shims are there to prevent the inner race of the anti-friction bearings from rubbing against the housing. I use a camera to record everything step by step as my memory is not always guaranteed.

Rebuilding the Gearbox

The first check is to ensure that all the studs and associated threads in the casing are effective. Over 90 years it should be no surprise that some will be stripped or very worn. I fitted BSF Helicoils where needed. The threads for the studs securing the selector cover needed restoring and the three threads that secure the gear stick cover plate also needed attention. It was easier to tap a new thread one size up. The side locking pin that prevents the gear stick from rotating is often loose; this needs to be made secure.

Next, clean the replacement gearbox case inside and out. I used a high-pressure water washer to ensure that all detritus and stains were removed. It is advisable to use a lint-free cloth to avoid leaving any fibres: however small, they could block the oilways.

Recognising that our cars' gearboxes are some 90 years old, any replacement gears obtained will be used and matched to a different gear train. Mixing and matching gears will never be perfect. Selecting the best combination is a compromise that you hope will bed in over time.

One approach is the careful application of valve grinding paste to the spur gears and by some arrangement rotating them to accelerate the bedding-in. This involves huge care and absolute cleaning to remove every trace of the grit. I did not use this method.

The variables are reduced wear, meshing gear teeth and thrust washer clearances: attention to detail pays dividends. I had the first and second gear layshafts hard-chromed and ground to size. I had pressed a new set of phosphor bronze bushes into the gear clusters for an interference fit. As a result, they became so compressed that the layshafts would not fit. I needed to have the bushes reamed to accept the matching layshaft with sufficient clearance. Applying oil to the assembly gives a feel for a good fit. When I was undertaking the fifth overhaul I found that one bush had seized on the layshaft and was rotating in the first gear. Sufficient clearance should allow for some expansion as the gearbox warms up. This is important.

When replacing the anti-friction bearings with sealed bearings, I retained the seal only on the outer side to reduce external oil seepage. The open-sided inner bearings would of course enjoy effective gearbox lubrication.

One of the sets of first and second gear clusters I acquired had the bush the wrong way around (Fig.14). The concave end should be to the outer face. The bushes have spiral oil grooves and in this reversed case the oil would have worked against itself.

Fig.14: Left gear bush upside down – must show chamfer

Fig.15: Second gear cluster, layshaft flat and thrust washers

The layshafts are smooth but have a flat face ground along the centre (Fig.15). This acts like a pump enabling the oil to flow in and out of the lube hole (Fig.16).

The first and second gear clusters have a hole that accommodates an aluminium locking pin. This is peened to further secure the gear clusters that have an interference fit (Fig.17).

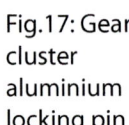

Fig.16: Gear cluster lube hole

Fig.17: Gear cluster aluminium locking pin

My car's spur gears were in fairly good condition with hardly any noticeable wear – although there was some rounding where the gears engage.

I had accumulated a collection of thrust washers (Fig.15) of various thicknesses that enabled me to achieve optimum clearances on either side of the gear clusters. Fitting the first and second gear clusters is a fiddly job, especially placing the thrust washers in position and securing them with the layshafts. A tommy bar can help to position the washers but I have found that the secret is to turn the gearbox to the vertical and use gravity to hold the elements in place. Fit the first gear and then the second gear. Then check the alignment of the gears to each other (Figs.18, 19). Select thrust washers of different thickness to achieve this but allow slight axial movement.

Using the hot air gun on the casing made fitting the gear clusters much easier. The layshafts slipped into place and they were nicely secure when the case cooled. So as not to repeat an earlier mistake, I was careful to fit the longer locking dowel bolt to the layshaft correctly.

Fig.18: Gear meshing offset

Fig.19: Washer aligned gears

Once the first and second gear clusters were in place (Fig.20) I needed to assemble the main drive shaft with gears and spigot shaft (drive gear) as well as make new gaskets.

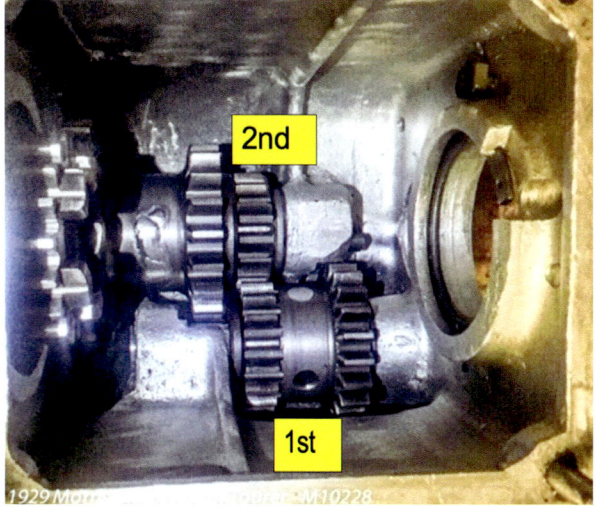
Fig.20: First and second gear clusters fitted

Fig.21: Spigot bearing gear locating clip

Notice that there is a small hole above the larger layshaft position (Fig.21). This is a return lubrication hole for the gearbox input bearing with a matching cup in the cover (Fig.22). Take care not to block this oil return duct. However, on the Outer Cover of some spigot shaft bearing there is a "mystery" hole (Fig.22, 23). Its purpose is illogical. Perhaps it was a modification to lubricate the clutch.

Fig.22: Outer spigot bearing cover with open oil drain hole

Fig.23: Inner spigot bearing cover with oil drain hole now blocked

I used a metal epoxy material to block this hole (Fig.23) as it serves no obvious purpose. I understand that some gearboxes do not have such a hole.

There is also an internal lubricating duct in the spigot shaft that is intended to lubricate the splines where the clutch plate moves back and forth and perhaps also lubricates the spigot bearing. Check that this lube duct is clear: it should not be blocked.

To assemble the spigot shaft and avoid excess load on the gear and dog teeth, secure the unit in a wooden block in a vice. I could not do much to correct the plastic deformation of the splines that fit into the clutch plate boss but there was slight sloping wear on the dog teeth. With a Dremel, I carefully and lightly squared up the mating surfaces, removing only a few microns. I hoped this would have the effect of improving the locking contact of the dogs and perhaps reduce the chance of dropping out of gear.

The spigot shaft assembly and all elements are shown (Figs.24,25). It is important to get the order correct: the oil slinger dished washer is often turned the wrong way around. The dish must face away from the bearing. If fitting sealed bearings, remember to remove the cover facing the gearbox so that is constantly lubricated. It is secured with a left-hand thread unit. This is locked in position with a spring wire (Fig.25) – bottom far right. Warm the gearbox casing with the heat gun so that the spigot bearing slips into place without unnecessary pressure.

Fig.24: Spigot shaft bearing assembly

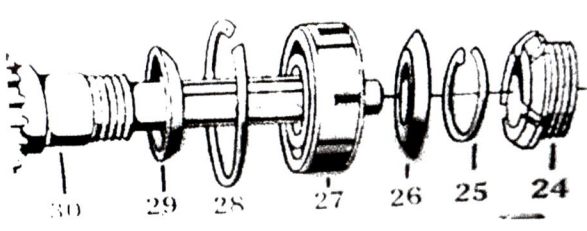

Fig.25: Spigot shaft assembly order

The next step is fitting the main drive shaft assembly (Fig.26). The needle bearings of the main drive shaft that fit inside the spigot shaft are seldom so worn as to require replacement.

Fig.26: Drive gear, main drive shaft assembly to brake and propshaft spider

Fig.27: Note position of oil throwback cupped washer

Once the main drive shaft and gears are fitted in the casing and married to the spigot drive shaft you can position the oil slinger and outward facing dish washer (Fig.27). The drive spider washer and castle nut must be fully secure and then fixed with a split pin.

Think back to the situation described earlier, where the layshaft was not secure and oil leaked profusely into the bell housing leading to the subsequent catastrophic failure (Fig.3). In "normal" conditions a common source of an oil seep into the bell housing is where the layshaft protrudes. I had covered the end of the layshaft with Hylomar sealant prior to fitting but without much success. The permanent solution is either to use a glue gun to secure a small pad over the shaft exit hole to the bell housing (Fig.28) or drill three small holes and tap and fit a cover plate to ensure a more permanent fix. I prefer the latter option. I was subsequently sent a copy of the schematic in the *MG 1936 Service Manual* that mentions this same fix (Fig.29).

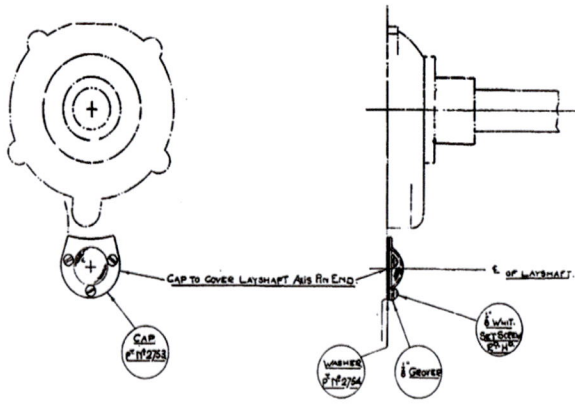

Fig.28: Layshaft hole where oil seeps into the bell housing

Fig.29: MG 1936 Service Manual – recommended cover plate

Next, fitting the speedo drive. Use PTFE tape on the threads to ensure that oil does not leak in this area: a copper washer is a must. Although the rear bearing is the main source of oil to the speedo drive, I have left the outer side bearing seal in place to reduce rear leakage. Time will tell how effective this is.

I do not consider this an issue as there is a lube duct to the speedo drive gearing and sufficient flow to that area. However, make sure that this lube duct is not blocked when making the end casing gasket.

Before fitting the speedo drive, turn the gearbox on its side and pump oil into the entry hole. Then fit the drive gearing. Ensure that the correct three-speed speedo and matching drive is a 14/8 (Fig.30). The 17/6 is for the four-speed box, but I have found that there is hardly any difference in actual speed or odometer indication if interchanged.

I have always fitted rare earth magnets in the main oil collection points. This can be done using epoxy resin to the brass oil sump plug. The effectiveness is clear to see: the debris collected was the result after the third overhaul (Fig.31). The magnet stops the iron filings from contaminating moving elements. I advise the use of magnets in the gearbox and differential as well as the engine oil filter basket. Once the gearbox is married to the engine, fill it with SAE140 oil to the filler level.

Fig.30: Speedo Drive, 14 vs 17 ratio

Fig.31: Oil sump magnetic debris plug

Closing Comments

Undertaking the overhaul of the transmission system is not for the faint-hearted but neither should it be seen as too complex or difficult. I could not risk my car breaking down during my tour of Zimbabwe and Zambia. So I had to ensure that no stone was unturned. I have repeated much of the mechanical restoration over the past 54 years of ownership as I gained knowledge of the car and experience, along with car forums and advice from other enthusiasts (see below).

I am neither a perfectionist nor pedantic but I believe that William Morris made a car that was capable and reliable: so there is no reason why a fully restored car cannot be made to perform as it did when it left the factory (Fig.32). The car's reliability was demonstrated by Cameron Gilg and Walter Kay in their epic journey in a 1933 Morris Minor from Liverpool to Cape Town in the same year. Despite suspension problems, the side-valve engine, gearbox and differential were fault free.

I hope that this article will help other Morris Minor owners and future custodians in overhauling and reconditioning their gearboxes. Take care, never force any component, use copper or fibre hammers where appropriate. Cleanliness will ensure that the gearbox will have a long life. The sump plug magnet for debris collection is a must.

Fig.32: The Morris's three-speed gearbox assembly

Acknowledgements

My thanks go to all who have assisted and guided me. I have drawn several points from John Emmet and Rick Osborne in particular of the UK and members of the Crankhandle Club in Cape Town, South Africa.

References

Joe Rayner – "A guide to rebuilding the Minor Three-speed gearbox" v2 201803

Morris Minor Data Sheet MM/14 – Stiff Gear Change.pdf 192909

R. Lucke – "Gearbox Input Shaft" 200510

John Emmett – *Vintage Morris Register* M158 – "The Morris Minor/MG MMM 3-Speed Gearbox" 201606

Rick Osborne – "Minor Three Speed Gearbox Dismantling & Thrust Washer" 201601

Peter Hills – *Vintage Morris Register* M167 – "Gearbox & Clutch Failure Analysis" 201810

Anon – "Gearbox and Clutch Removal" (1930/31 OHC Minor Saloon) 201908

Peter Hills – *Vintage Morris Register* M171 – "Fixing a 1929 Minor 3-Speed Gearbox Jumping Out of Gear" 201910

Anon – "Gearbox 3 Speed Morris Minor" 201801

Anon – Phosphor Bronze Bearings for Layshaft and Reverse Gear Clusters – Dimensions

Anon – Morris Gearbox Dismantling

MG 1936 Service Manual <www.triple-mregister.org/uploads/retro/service>

TG09: Gearbox Jumping Out of Gear

Introduction and Background

Many Morris owners are known to have their left leg somewhat distorted from pushing against a gear lever: it is prone to jumping out of gear at random or when hitting a bump. Having overhauled my gearbox so many times, mixing and matching "used spares", I was surprised when my gear lever suddenly started to jump out, usually when in third. I needed to investigate the cause and fix it.

After consulting users on the Vintage Minor and Pre-War Minor forums, the consensus was that the springs in the gear selector system were the probable cause. (Figs.1, 2).

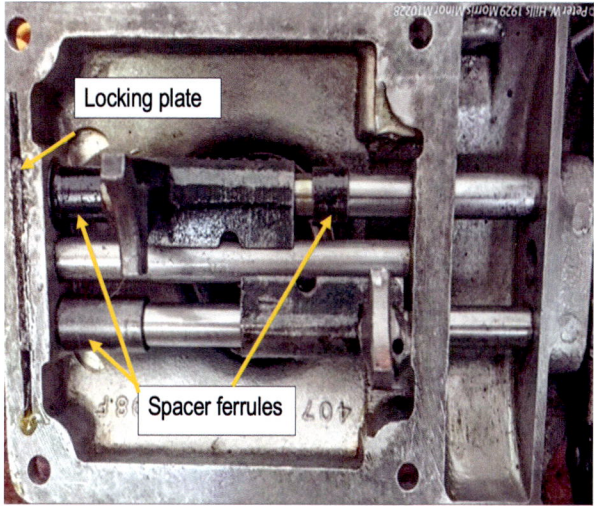

Fig.1: Gear selector rods and spacers

Fig.2: Selectors, springs and balls

Gearbox Selector and Stick

After lifting the gearbox top cover to remove the selector actuators you first need to ease up the end locking plate (Fig.1). Once stripped, I found that the locating ball springs were different lengths (Fig.2) due to poor assembly: part of the spring had been sliced off when the actuator shafts were fitted (an easy thing to do). I obtained replacement springs (OD ¼", open length 1⅛", wire 18 gauge). The strength of the springs is important for smooth gear changes: too weak and it will jump out of gear on the over-run, too strong and it will be notchy, leading to crunchier changes than normal.

Spring protruding, awaiting the locking ball. Easy to slice off!

Fig.3: Spring proud of its supporting recess

Some owners believe that their selector problems were caused by worn selector balls (quarter inch diameter). After measuring all the spares in my stock, I have yet to find a severely worn or distorted ball – I discount this as a reason for the lever jumping out.

After looking at the whole mechanism in detail it was clear that the gear selector castings were worn – as was the gear lever itself (addressed later). Fortunately, I had spare selector units and I could pair up the least worn. It is possible to have the worn faces built up and ground to size, but I was satisfied that my units were fairly good.

The challenge was to assemble the balls and springs back into the selectors. After struggling to do this and failing to find any references, I had a cup of tea and a think. How did the Morris Factory do this under the pressure of production?

They would have pre-assembled units ready for the selectors to be presented. To achieve this, they would have fitted a dummy dowel to retain the ball and its spring in the selector casting temporarily. The kit I used to do this is illustrated (Fig.4).

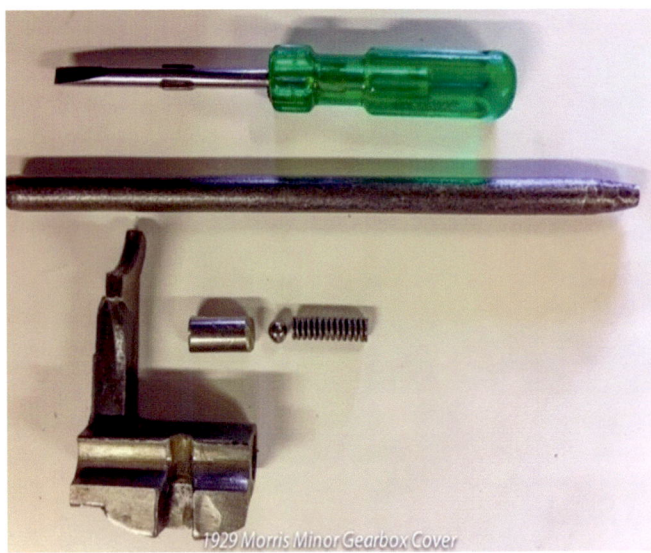

Fig.4: Tools and dummy dowel with selector

I made a dummy dowel slightly smaller in diameter than the selector shaft (about ¾" in length) and slightly chamfered at the end that faces the ball to prevent it impacting the spring.

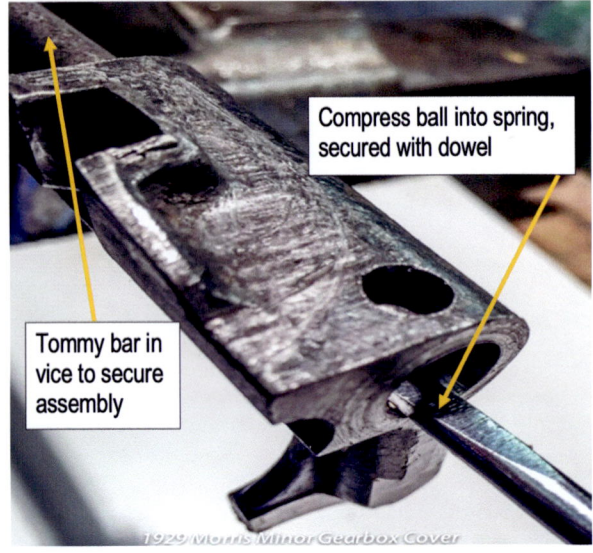

Fig.5: Tommy bar in a vice

Fig.6: Dowel securing the ball and actuator

The assembly process is as follows:

1. The dummy dowel is to retain the ball and the spring in its slot temporarily until ready for ultimate assembly. Use a tommy bar that fits in the selector orifice: secure it in a vice when fitting the ball and spring. The tommy bar positions the dummy dowel and ball up to the spring slot in the selector hole.
2. Depress the spring with the small screwdriver; this assists in placing the ball on top of it. Then press the ball down on the spring (Fig.5) while gradually positioning the dummy dowel over it (Fig.6) and secure in place.
3. Remove the tommy bar, place it at the opposite end of the selector housing and partially through the selector arm to just touch the dummy dowel. Gently insert the selector shaft, complete with spacer ferrules (Fig.1) from the other end to displace the dummy dowel (Fig.7) to secure the ball and spring permanently in position.
4. Press home the actuator shaft and then the gear selector will have a ball in one of its position grooves.
5. Repeat the process for the second actuator.
6. Then fit the actuator shaft locking plate. This may need a slight peen to prevent it from coming out before the cover is on the gearbox.

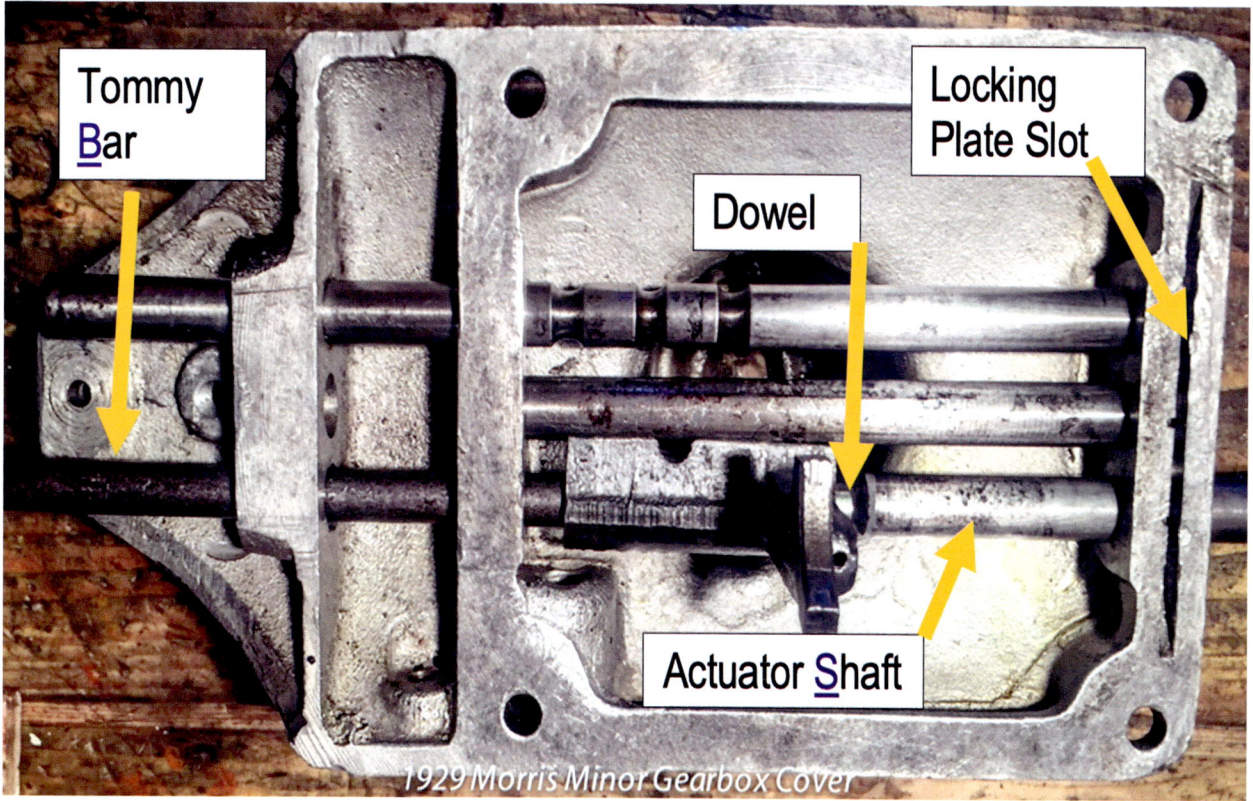

Fig.7: Tommy bar and actuator bar positioning the dowel

Gear Positions of the Gearbox

Before fitting the top gear selector cover I recorded the positions of the gears (Figs.8–11) in their respective positions: reverse, first, second and third. A seldom seen view.

Fig.8: Reverse gear

Fig.9: First gear – actuator slots

Notice the slots for the gear lever actuators: the first gear cluster is always rotating as it meshes with the spigot shaft. I suspect that the pervasive second gear transition noise may be caused by excess thrust washer clearances nudging the first gear cluster.

Fig.10: Second gear

Fig.11: Third gear

Reconditioning the Gear Lever

The gear lever should fit neatly in the selector slot – mine had minimal wear. However, when matching the tip of the gear lever to the selector slot I found that it had excessive play – the "square end" was virtually round (Fig.12) and it was a sloppy fit in the slot. The groove in the pivot ball area was also significantly worn on either side of the centre section. This is retained in contact position by a dowel bolt stem gear housing. It prevents the gear lever from twisting. Clearly, this was the main reason for dropping out of gear in my case and renovation was essential.

Fig.12: Lever tip worn   Fig.13: Ball TIG repaired   Fig.14: Tip welded for shaping

I had the tip and ball slot built up by TIG welding (Figs.13, 14). After re-shaping the unit to become a snug fit in the selector slot I took the opportunity to have the complete lever electroplated in nickel. Since a bare metal shaft rusts, I decided that electroplating was the long-term solution (Figs.15, 16).

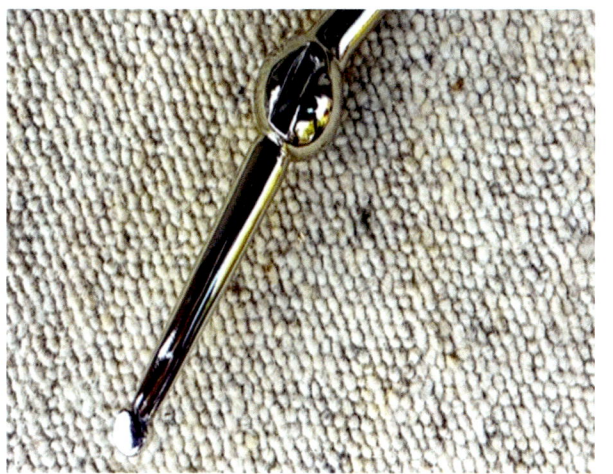

Fig.15: Gear tip and ball slot rebuilt

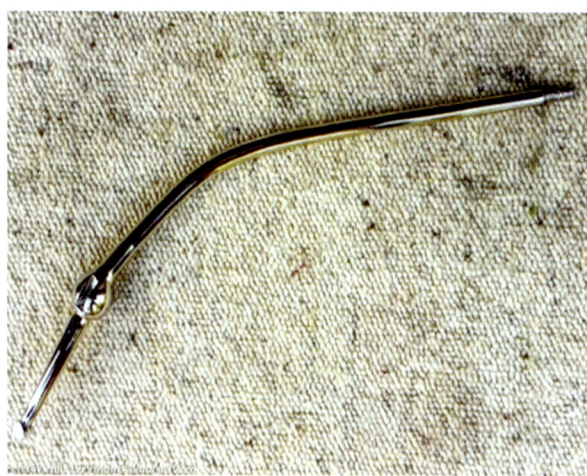

Fig.16: Gear stick after nickel plating

The outcome was a very smart-looking gear lever. When installed the extra layer of copper and nickel electroplating made the gear change quite stiff – almost like running in a new car but it soon loosened up and has since been trouble free.

When fitting the gearbox selector cover, position the gears to the neutral position. Then, before bolting the cover down, carefully fit the gear lever so that the gear actuator legs are in their respective slots (Fig.9). Check that the gears work by using the crank handle. Before fully tightening the gear cover check again that the gears change correctly. Position the gear selector with a stout screwdriver from the gear lever hole so that the lever is slotted correctly.

Fig.17: Overhauled Morris Minor OHC engine 9668 assembled and ready to be installed

Closing Comments

My subsequent tour of Zimbabwe and Zambia was not without problems but the gearbox covered 1,509 miles without a hitch. Most people expected that the suspension and tyres would be stressed the most but, like the gearbox, they all performed perfectly. In fact, the earlier rather noisy second gear after the long trip was noticeably less as it is "bedding-in". It still has an occasional rattle but the improved meshing was worth the attention to detail.

TG10: Upgrading Lamps, Indicators and Brake Lights to LEDs

Introduction and Background

Probably the most significant advance in lighting since Edison and Swan developed incandescent bulbs is the light emitting diode or LED. Vehicles have used variations of filament bulbs, with their effectiveness depending on the quality and size of the lamp's reflector. Our older cars often needed to have their reflectors re-silvered. Their shape is designed to concentrate the beam. While the introduction of quartz halogen lamps gave more light at the cost of more energy, few were practical for vintage and classic cars due to their rate of discharge.

In 1907 Captain Henry Joseph Round of Marconi Labs in England discovered the phenomenon of electroluminescence that enabled the Russian scientist and inventor Oleg Losev to create the first LED 20 years later. By 1962 the LEDs launched by Texas Instruments in the United States were expensive, miniscule and had limited applications.

However, in the twenty-first century LEDs are everywhere. The low cost, reliability and high-power output (over 1,000 lumens) of the LED is progressively replacing the traditional tungsten light bulb.

The main advantages of LEDs are lower energy consumption, longer life, robustness and multiple roles from a single source. They are used in applications as diverse as aviation, automotive industry, domestic lighting, traffic signals, displays and camera flashes They have an operating life from 25,000 to 100,000 hours and present fewer environmental concerns.

While the 6 volt, 5 watt filament bulb uses 0.85 amps (nearly 1 amp), the equivalent LED uses only 0.025 amps. In the case of a 6 volt, 21 watt filament bulb that consumes 3.5 amps, the LED equivalent uses 0.17 amps.

Early LED headlamps were constructed with side-mounted LEDs to take advantage of the car's reflector (Fig.1). Although they used less energy, they did not significantly improve brightness due to the quality of the reflectors. After a few iterations the construction now employs a single front-facing LED set behind a dome like a magnifying glass (Fig.2). This arrangement produces a superior piercing beam independent of the lamp reflector that enables the lighting of our older cars to come closer to the modern vehicles.

Fig.1: Headlamp reflector type

Fig.2: Single LED headlamp 2022

Replacing tungsten car bulbs with LEDs

Any owner of a vintage or classic car with an ammeter will be aware that with the engine switched off and all lights on, the ammeter will be probably read hard negative. In the case of my 1929 Morris Minor (OHC) –16 amps was the norm. If the dynamo is not charging, driving any distance with the lights on would be limited by the battery's charge level.

In September 2014 I attended the Beaulieu International Auto Jumble where I met Peter Jury of Classic Dynamo & Regulator Conversions Ltd of the UK. His company specialises in restoring vintage dynamos and designing and supplying solid-state voltage regulators and LED bulbs. I have found him to be most knowledgeable and helpful at all times. It was after consulting Peter that I decided to replace all the light bulbs on my Morris with LEDs. Costing less than £100, the fitting of the LEDs was straightforward: the positive result is that my ammeter hardly flutters with all lights on.

Selecting the rear LED lamps was an interesting learning curve. A single enclosure with an LED can perform multiple duties. The latest generation includes indicators with side lights, red, white and orange illumination. In 2017 I fitted a dual LED bulb 6 volt negative earth (Fig.3). This consists of LEDs around the circumference (yellow) that produce the white light (for the number plate) while the 6 LEDs at the end produce red for the tail light. The dual illuminating LEDs are earthed at one of the terminals. Replacing the old bulbs was no problem. The smaller front side lights are single illumination (Fig.4) but today dual white and orange LEDs for indicators are available. I have fitted these to my MG J2.

Fig.3: Dual – rear LED

Fig.4: Early side light LED

Since writing my original article on this subject I have replaced the headlamp bulbs on my Morris for a unique design reason. The headlamps are fitted on the wings but, unlike most vehicles, they are rotated almost 90° to the vertical (Fig.5). The earlier LEDs were intended for the upright reflective lamp holder (Fig.1) and the light would spread across the road. When fitted to the Morris the beam was up and down. My current bulbs were fitted in 2022 (Fig.2): the beam focus is direct and ignores the reflectors and the orientation of the lamps.

The car's dynamo charge rate used to be less than an amp due to deterioration of the 85-year-old field winding insulation and aggravated by oil leaking down from the OHC drive shaft. The leak has been solved and Peter Jury has replaced the field windings; the output is now around 8 amps. The dynamo renovation is the subject of a separate article.

Installing LED Indicators and Brake Light

I installed indicators and brake lights on my Morris Minor to make it safer for me and other road users. Few motorists today recognise arm signals and, when driving in bad weather or at night, it is even more dangerous. A brake light is an important indicator in traffic today and was installed. A further reason is that for my planned Back-to-Africa tour around Zimbabwe and Zambia the car needed to meet most modern regulations when confronted with police roadblocks and vehicle checks that are common in those countries.

In 2017 I purchased a Morris 8 indicator, horn and dip control arm that fits on the steering column and provides these facilities. For the indicator lights I secured units supported on rubber stalks that I bolted onto the bumpers. The LEDs are very visible day and night. I also installed a solid-state 6 volt flasher unit and mini speaker. The flasher unit activates a panel light in sync with the flashing indicators.

Fig.5: Angled headlamps, orange indicators mounted on bumper

Fig.6: Control arm, indicator, horn and main beam flasher

I had to decide how and where to mount the brake light switch. There are several approaches to activating the brake lights – such as detecting a change in tension of the brake cable or the rotation of a common pivot shaft. The location would have to be relatively free from contamination or damage from external elements when on the road. The Morris has simple cable brakes. So, the most practical solution was to mount a switch in direct contact with the brake pedal. I fitted a micro switch with sprung blade and nylon rollers to the underside of the driver's side angled floorboard. It plugged into the cable so that removal when working on the gearbox is easy. My solution (Figs.7, 8) has functioned flawlessly for 8 years despite being disconnected and lifted several times for working on the engine. I fitted an extra bracket from the floorboard to the firewall to prevent any movement that might defeat the action of the micro switch.

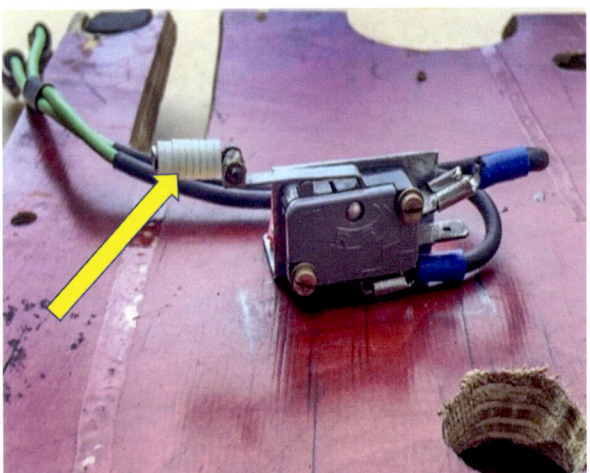

Fig.7: Brake microswitch sprung contact arm with nylon riders

Fig.8: Microswitch blade against brake pedal

When my car was first returned to the road in 1992 I wired it with individual strands, following the traditional routing. All the cables came up the engine side of the firewall and in through an entry slot above the petrol tank. Not surprisingly, after 25 years the cable insulation had hardened and degraded, due to the heat of the engine.

I decided to rewire and change the cable routing away from the engine to be more accessible and sustainable. The cable routing diagram (Fig.9) shows the routing I made for the front headlamps, side lights, indicators, and rear and brake lights.

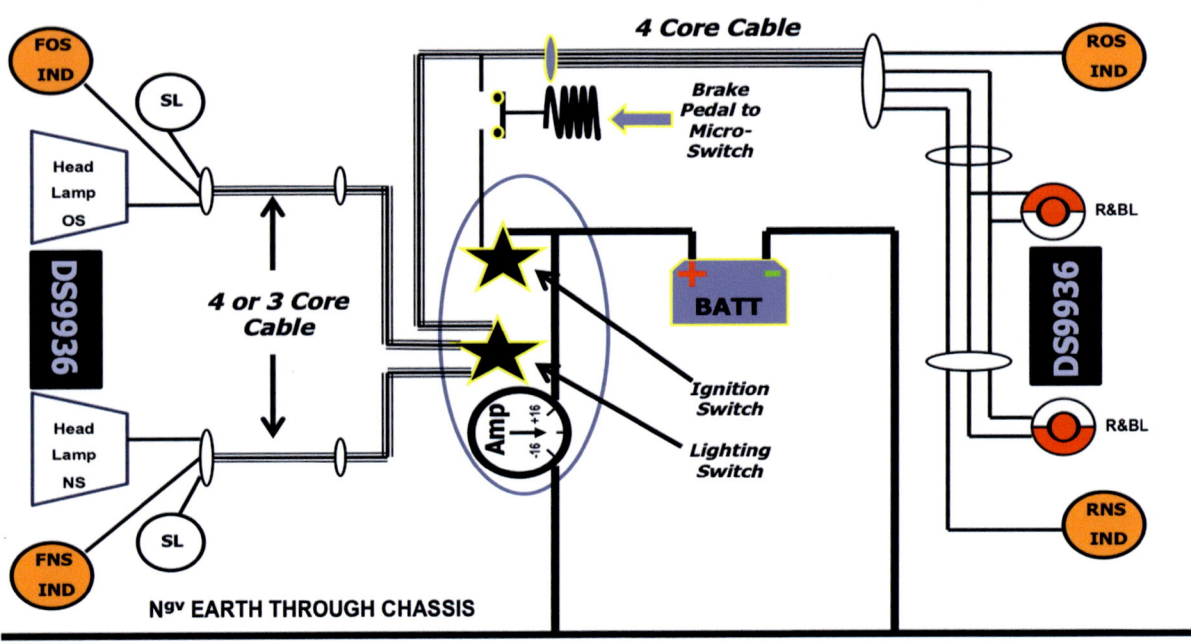

Fig.9: Cable distribution schematic – all lights

I could achieve all the functions and connections by using a single four-core cable and then terminating it at the central instrument panel (Fig.11).

I selected industrial grade Cabtyre cable – you need to shop around as the typical High Street or DIY shop seldom carries this quality. I only needed 15 metres to complete the wiring, a modest investment. My selection was based on the view that Cabtyre internal strands are individually insulated and then covered with heavy-duty black rubber outer insulation, providing significant mechanical protection. A single cable was easy to secure along the chassis channel – neat and invisible. Since the cable to the front main and side lights runs inside the mud guards and is exposed to impacts of stone, the heavy-duty outer coating is further protection.

Some may argue that, having switched to LED lamps where the electrical current drawn is minimal, there is no need for a heavy-duty cable. That is not the point: the cables on our old cars are often exposed and my approach is sustainability. I was able to route the cables neatly along the chassis up the inside of the firewall. (Figs.10, 11).

Fig.10: Cable routing – OS firewall

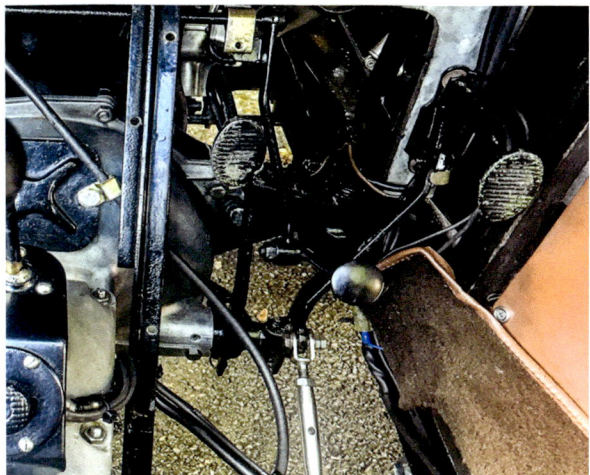

Fig.11: Cable routing – NS firewall

One four-core cable was all that was needed to supply rear lights, the number plate light, brake lights and indicators. Separate cables supplied the front side lights, headlamps and indicators. The individual wires to all the lights were covered with additional protective shrink sleeving. The indicator's cabling was positioned behind the bumpers and secured with small clamps; the route to the instrument panel was along the inside of the firewall (Figs.10, 11) to protect it from damage.

All wire strands were twisted tight and sweated with lead-free solder before being connected to clip-on connectors. This is particularly beneficial at the dashboard switch terminations as the securing screws can easily cut into the wire's strands and reduce cable efficiency and lead to potential failure. Modern connectors were used with shrink sleeving at every opportunity so that the wiring is electrically safe and eliminates contamination. The wiring should last for many years without degradation from heat and vibration.

Since I have modernised the lighting system on my Morris, I have created a simple schematic (Fig.12) that is specific to my lighting system as a guide to others.

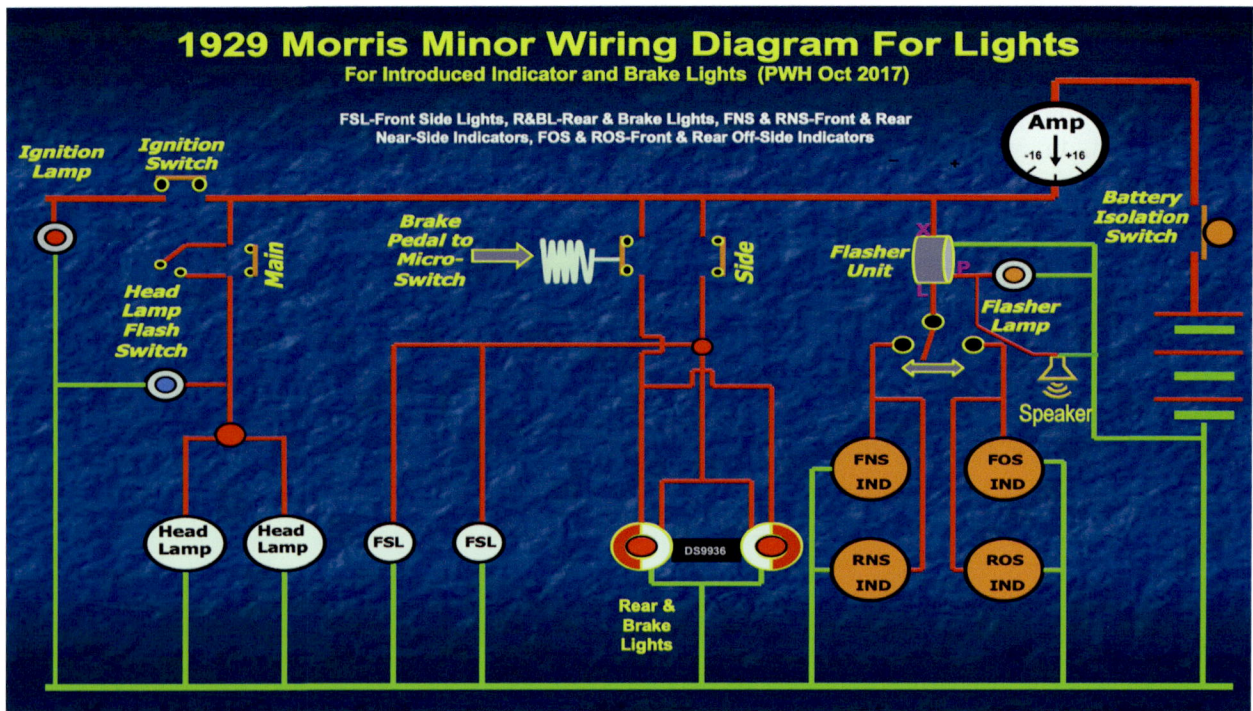

Fig.12: Lighting – functional electrical circuit

I fitted panel lights in the dashboard on either side of the steering column for easy viewing (Fig.13): Orange for the indicators and Blue for the headlights. Since the indicator arm does not switch off automatically after turning, I included a mini speaker that bleeps in sync with the flasher unit – a bit annoying but it does the job!

Fig.13: Panel lamps

Fig.14: Rear lights and indicators

The available mini LEDs were too long for my panel light fitting. I tried a 6 volt bulb but it was too bright; so I replaced it with a 12 volt bulb which is dimmer and less distracting.

Against the black mudguard, when the rear lights and the offside indicator are switched on, they are quite noticeable. Despite its diminutive size the car is visible from 30 metres during daylight and certainly very noticeable after sunset. The number plate is also adequately illuminated from the dual output LEDs (Fig.14).

The indicators were working perfectly but when I ran the engine they began to flutter at a high rate. This interference from the spark plugs was solved by fitting suppressors. Since installation 7 years ago and having travelled some 7,000 miles in rather hostile environments, there have been no electrical faults. The LED lights have been superb.

Closing Comments

Installing the LEDs was a fairly simple operation but it made a significant improvement to battery drain as well as superior light output. Fitting the indicators and brake lights took some planning but the decision to install a single multi-core cable rather than attempting to add extra wires for the new functions has produced a superior result.

I can now drive around London and elsewhere with confidence, knowing that my turning signals are more noticeable than my hand. These improvements were yet another important step in my advance planning for the Back-to-Africa tour.

Reference

www.dynamoregulatorconversions.com

TG11: Radiator – Keeping It Cool

Fig.1: The Morris Thermal Syphon Radiator

Introduction and Background

A vintage car is not only "cool" – it needs to stay cool! An engine's radiator with efficient water ways is one of the most import elements to maintain the car's reliability and performance. Often ignored, a poorly maintained cooling system is the cause of most engine failures. When a vintage or classic car runs hot and then hotter, whether under load or in heavy traffic, a key indicator is the oil pressure gauge. The oil pressure varies according to the temperature that determines the viscosity: the viscosity and oil pressure will be lower when an engine overheats. Apart from driving conditions there may be issues with the cooling system that incrementally cause it to become less efficient.

My 1929 Morris Minor (Fig.1) was restored and on the road in 1992 and had completed 7,200 miles. Prior to shipping the car to South Africa I started a range of checks as part of my preparation. Returning my car to Zambia in 2023 where I found it in 1970 meant the car had to be in tip top condition for its arduous 1,500-mile journey in a hot climate. I acquired a range of spares to continue the preparation in Cape Town. This article discusses my focus on the radiator, water jackets and the cooling fan.

The Cooling System

All early veteran and vintage cars engines depended on the thermal syphon water circulation system. Simply, the hot water in the engine block rises to the radiator header tank then dribbles through the honeycomb radiator tubes that, with air flowing on the outside, cools it sufficiently to return to the engine, cooling it down while pushing out the hotter liquid back to the radiator header tank. Key to this self-pumping process is air efficiently passing through the radiator.

The more modern vehicles had water pumps to increase the cooling rate and then systems were pressurised to prevent water evaporation. Water expands when hot so if an unpressurised system is overfilled then it is quite common to lose half a litre or a pint of water in just a few miles of motoring.

Many pressurised systems have an overflow or expansion tank so that water on expansion is piped to a small separate tank and then on cooling it syphons itself back to the main radiator header tank.

Radiator

In preparation for my car's trip to Africa I decided to use a flushing additive to de-scale the radiator because the London water is particularly hard. Preparation is important – ensure that a hose pipe or bucket of water is to hand. Undertake the work out in the open, and wear rubber gloves and protective glasses. Warm the engine but make sure that the radiator is not too full because when adding the de-scaler, the chemical tends to react vigorously and generate gas and bubbles that may overflow onto the paintwork. If it does, immediately wash it off any paintwork because it can discolour it.

After letting the de-scaler do its work for about an hour, open the radiator drain tap and lower the radiator hose. It is best to drain the liquid into a tray or directly to a drain and then dilute it with the hose while washing it away. Thoroughly flush the engine block and radiator with fresh water. I use a pressure washer.

When refilling the radiator of my Morris water spewed out of the bottom radiator hose. On inspection I found that the outlet pipe was corroded through (Fig.2). What is amazing is that the residue and debris must have blocked the pipe for ages. I wondered how long I had been living on borrowed time with this. It is just as well that the cooling system on the OHC Minor is not pressurised; otherwise it surely would have leaked a long time ago. What surprised me was that a steel pipe and not a brass pipe had been soldered into the brass radiator.

Back in Zambia in 1972 a motor racing friend, Derek Dutton, pitched up at my home with a 1933 Morris radiator suitable for the side-valve engine that I found in the wreck I had recovered from the jungle. By 1991 I had the radiator re-cored giving specific instructions that the lower outlet pipe should be positioned on the left and not the right of the radiator's bottom tank. When the renovated radiator was delivered the pipe had not been moved to the left side; so I returned it to be corrected and thought nothing more of it.

Fig.2: Radiator's lower outlet corroded

Fig.3: Radiator pipe severely corroded

It took 26 years for the pipe to fail but on closer inspection it appeared that a cheap mild steel exhaust pipe had been used. Soldering steel to brass is always quite a challenge but clearly the radiator restorer managed this to save costs! Once the pipe was removed the extent of the severe corrosion was obvious (Fig.3). It is remarkable that it lasted so long.

Repairing the Radiator

To repair the radiator, I managed to obtain a heavy-duty piece of brass pipe, probably from a fire hose. It required light machining to create a flange suitable for increased purchase to the radiator opening. Due to the importance of the radiator with respect to temperature control and potential effect on the whole assembly I had the soldering done by a professional. I used a pull-along suitcase to take the radiator on the bus to a specialist repair company near the Crystal Palace Football Ground in London (Fig.4). They agreed to do the job while I waited and the result was excellent (Fig.5). After 13,800 miles, it continues to serve its purpose.

Fig.4: Aaron Radiator Co. Ltd, London

Fig.5: Outlet pipe soldered to radiator

Once the radiator was installed in the car, hoses fitted and filled with water I was confident that this major repair would last a very long time. The lesson learned is that all radiator pipes must be non-ferrous: brass or copper is recommended.

Radiator Stay

I always thought that the radiator support rod to the firewall was a poorly engineered system (Fig.6). It consisted of a top nut soldered to the top of the thin brass radiator tank where the steel rod is screwed in and bolted to the firewall. Is its purpose to provide support for the radiator or simply to secure the Sparton horn?

The steel nut is really not conducive to soldering but its small diameter would also stress or fatigue the brass radiator in a concentrated area. In the past the soldered nut constantly came adrift: I decided to have a brass disc machined that would spread the load over a larger surface area (Fig.7) and make a properly fused soldered joint to the radiator.

Fig.6: Stay supports Sparton horn

Fig.7: Sparton horn stay in brass disc

The brass disc was only partially threaded for the stay rod and then a lock nut. It proved to be a superior solution (Fig.8) without distributing the load onto the header tank.

Fig.8: Improved radiator stay support

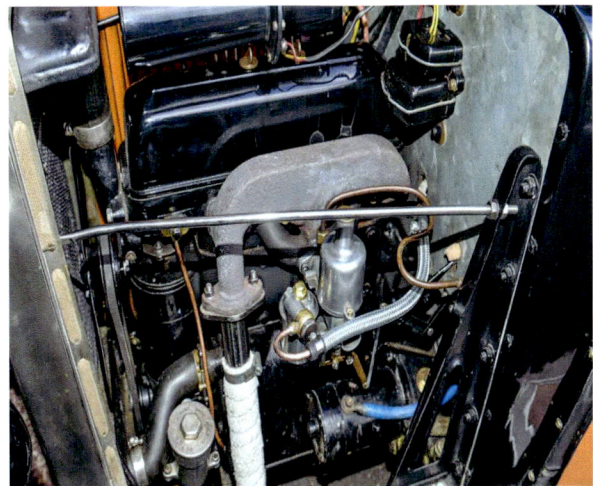

Fig.9: Radiator stay rods to firewall

I could not agree that the Sparton horn stay was designed to steady or support the radiator; so I added stainless rods secured either side of the radiator shell to the firewall brackets (Fig.9). These take the load away from the centre stay but have the benefit of positioning the radiator left and right enabling alignment of the bonnet more accurately.

Water Jackets

In 1991 before I fitted the existing mild steel water jackets I had them powder-coated. During the installation I found that several threads in the cast engine block were highly corroded. The threaded cast-iron section is only 3/16 inch thick and there is limited thread for sufficient bolt purchase; it is also subject to corrosion. With the original steel bolts protruding past the casting, the ends would corrode and swell with debris. When being withdrawn the corroded bolt damaged the delicate threads in the casting. Somehow, I managed to secure the water jackets with gaskets.

After using my Morris for almost 28 years I noticed the presence of a brown stain down the side of the engine block from one water jacket. I was not too concerned as I assumed it was just weep from the relatively lose securing bolts. RadWeld would probably fix it.

Since I had obtained stainless-steel water jacket plates with rubber gaskets I needed to give the engine block a complete pressure washing. When the old plates (Figs.10, 11) were removed, I realised how lucky I had been – a "get out of jail" card for failure avoidance! I found that the water seepage was only held back by a gossamer-thin layer of powder-coating paint. The most severe corrosion on each water jacket was at the bottom where most debris had accumulated. I was curious about this, wondering why so much debris had settled there since I regularly flushed the engine block. The amount of accumulated debris from the entry and exit pipes was astonishing and disturbing. Was it dirt in the water or corrosion debris? I was sure it was the latter.

Fig.10: Water jacket outer – holes corroded through

Fig.11: Water jacket inner – corroded hole, screwdriver poking through

I then overlaid the old and new rubber gaskets (Fig.12) and saw that the old gasket (curly) was too broad and had created a pocket against the engine block where deposits could accumulate. When I fitted the new rubber gaskets I trimmed the inner area so only the part that is against the engine block is present. I hope this prevents accumulation in future.

Fig.12: Water jacket inner – new rubber gasket overlaying the old (orange)

Regardless of the radiator thermal water flow, one would think it would carry all deposits to the radiator base tank and deposits should be easily flushed from there. These deposits could also create a mild electrolytic effect that would exacerbate corrosion in a localised area.

Before replacing the water jackets, much preparation and renovation work was needed. I used a pressure water jet to clear out all debris in the engine block interstices (Fig.13). Then I used a rotary wire brush on a drill to remove stubborn nodules on the casting (Fig.14). The red marks were my reminder of where bolt hole threads were stripped and needed correction.

Fig.13: Pressure washing the jackets

Fig.14: Jacket threads (red) to be fixed

The water jacket area of the cast-iron engine block is quite delicate: it is thin and yet the water jacket plates need to be sufficiently tightened to it without stripping the threads. As many threads were either damaged or loose they were no longer fit for purpose.

The solution to correcting the situation involved using Helicoils. However, fitting Helicoils was new to me – another learning curve. I had previously needed a Helicoil to be fitted to fix an oil leak on another part of the car. I contracted a mobile Helicoil service and I watched very closely how it was done. For those, like me, who wish to understand the system this is my observation.

Helicoil Thread Restoration

Original stripped threads can be tapped out with the next BSF size up; sometimes this is not viable but mostly we wish to stick to originality. To retain the thread size, the first step is to acquire the appropriate Helicoil Kit (Fig.15). These are available in specific BSF sizes such as ¼ inch and 5/16 inch. Brands such as Helicoil or V-Coil consist of similar elements: a drill, tap, installation tool and pushing rod. The associated coils are included in the kit but it is recommended to buy extra coils from specialist nut and bolt suppliers.

The next step is to run the specialised drill through the old thread hole to clear debris and set the size. The special tap creates the thread to the required depth. Cutting fluid is recommended. Where the thread depth is longer than the Helicoil this is not an issue. In the case of the Morris's 3/16" wide water jacket, because the Helicoil comes in lengths of quarter inch or 6.5mm, it would extend beyond the casting. This must be addressed; otherwise you will be unable to fracture the coil's "tang" after insertion (Fig.16). First measure the depth of the actual thread length then trim off one or two coils with piano-wire cutters. This will ensure that the coil does not protrude. If it does and you try to push against the tang to fracture it, the coil will spring out the other side. This is not a recoverable situation: you will need to remove the coil and start again with a shortened coil. If you don't have piano-wire cutters the corner of an electric bench grindstone will trim the coil. Insert the thread with the tang end first. There is a slotted tool that fits the tang to enable you to screw the coil in to the last internal thread depth. You need to take absolute care doing this. Then push firmly against the tang (Fig.16) or use a light hammer with a punch action. If the coil is inserted properly the tang will fracture off. The associated bolt can then be inserted, making a very secure fitting.

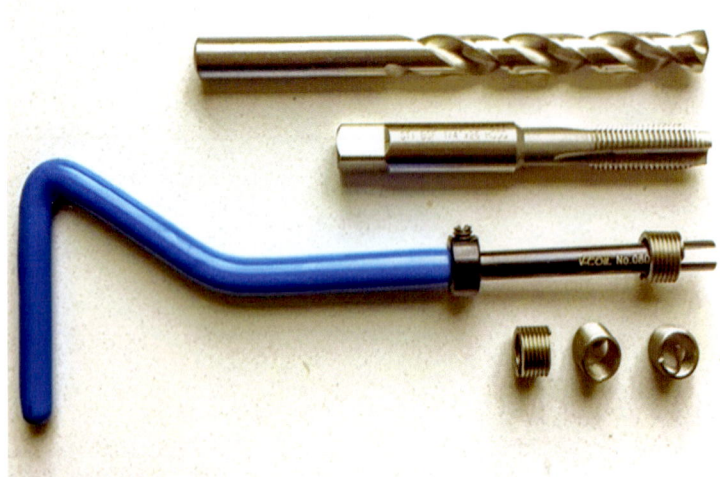 

Fig.15: Helicoil kit: drill, tap, installation tool, pushing rod   Fig.16: Helicoil tang – see fracture nick

In total I fitted 14 Helicoils with ¼ inch long stainless-steel BSF bolts. I expect the use of stainless-steel bolts and Helicoils will finally resolve an inherent weakness in the water jacket system for many years to come.

Before fitting the water jackets, I trimmed the internal rubber gasket so that it matched the profile of the engine block rather than providing a catchment area for the debris as found earlier. I applied a jointing compound to the gasket as well as to the threads of each bolt to prevent any possible leakage via the bolt's threads (Fig.17).

Fig.17: Water jacket – stainless-steel with SS bolts

It would seem that 28 years for thin mild steel water jackets to last is pretty good. However, putting the car on the road in 1992 and later hibernating it for 9 years and again using and hibernating on and off for several years may have exacerbated the problem. At the time I did not use an inhibiter in the water but now I do: I believe that it not only halts internal corrosion but that it also improves heat conduction and transfer. Later when I needed to remove the engine and I drained the water, it came out crystal clear, which was most pleasing. No longer do I see brown water caused by corrosion of the cast-iron engine. A pity I did not do this back in 1992 but, coming from sunny Zambia, who would be aware of an engine block freezing and cracking in winter?

I have also learned not to fill the radiator to the top because when the engine warms up the water expands and at least a pint will be discharged through the overflow pipe. That includes the coolant that needs to be added regularly. When filling the radiator to check the water level, a simple test is to place your index finger in the filler: it needs to just touch the coolant – then the radiator is full enough.

Radiator Fan

An experienced member of the Crankhandle Club in Cape Town made the observation that my Morris's cooling fan was too far away from the radiator (1¾ inches) and would not provide effective cooling. The only solution was to move the fan closer to the radiator.

Fig.18: Radiator fan – spacer   Fig.19: Radiator fan – assembled

After removing the radiator then the fan, I had a 1" (25mm) block machined in aluminium with outer grooves positioned on either side of longer studs (Fig.18). The fan was then bolted on securely (Fig.19) after taking into consideration the fan protrusion. I also replaced the original (worn and noisy) needle roller bearing with two sealed ball bearings. It now runs smoothly and quietly.

After fitting the radiator and ensuring the distance of the fan from the core (Fig.20) I carried out a simple check of the amount of suction. With the engine running at 1,000 rpm and placing a piece of paper at the front of the radiator, it sticks firmly against the core. Previously, before the fan was moved, the paper would slip off. This test confirmed that the fan is now working more effectively.

© Peter W. Hills 1929 Morris Minor M10228

Fig.20: Radiator fan – spacer moved fan blade closer to the core

Closing Comments

Regular attention to a car's cooling system will always pay dividends. The radiator, hoses, water ways in the engine block, and the fan are all interdependent. Coolant management and regular inspection of these elements will extend the life of your precious vehicle.

With all this work completed, I feel confident that my 1929 Morris Minor is now as "cool" as it is going to get! These improvements gave the car its best chance to manage the hotter environment of Central Africa. Nevertheless, I continue to keep a beady eye on that oil pressure gauge and always store a litre of top-up water in the back seat.

TG12: Speedometer Upgrade

Introduction and Background

In this article I describe how to service and upgrade the standard Smiths Speedometer (Fig.1) fitted to the 1929 Morris Minor and many other similar vehicles of the period. I hope that these notes, accompanied with photos, will be helpful to enthusiasts who wish to undertake such service and improvement work.

Fig.1: Smiths speedometer calibrated in mph andkm/h

Background

In 1970 when I rescued my 1929 Morris Minor 4 Seat Tourer (M10228) from the Zambian jungle there were no instruments in the wreck. I acquired lots of bits and pieces at a car jumble in the UK and, after doing some work, I installed them in the restored vehicle in 1992. The speedo needle always had a jerky movement that I attributed to a defective or poorly routed drive cable. However, the unit started to make a *tuk-tuk* noise that seemed more serious and needed urgent investigation.

Principle of Operation

Working with delicate instruments is second nature to me but when I opened up the Smiths speedometer I was surprised at the simplicity and genius of design. The speedo must have had its DNA from governors used in steam engines and similar speed control systems in underground mine winders. When I was headhunted to the UK from Zambia, some of my mining colleagues reckoned that, as I was a local lad educated and trained in Africa, I must have "golden balls" for getting a senior appointment in England and they presented me with a mine winder governor, *c.* 1940 (Fig.2)! The similarity with the Smiths speedo spindle (Fig.3) of the period is remarkable. Of course, readers of this book are quite familiar with these clanging "golden" balls!

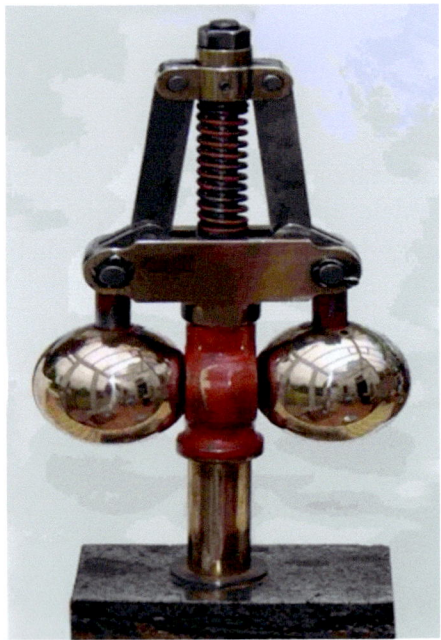

Fig.2: Mine winding speed governor   Fig.3: Smiths speedo spindle

As the spindle rotates, centrifugal force causes the lead weights to move outwards against a helical control spring. The horizontal movement levers a rod up and down the central shaft of the spindle relative to the rotational speed. It pivots a gear train to the speedo's indicating needle. The main helical spring returns the governor to zero and the needle hair spring provides a stable damped movement.

Elements of the Original Assembly

It is always useful to take photographs both before dismantling a small item and during the process. Prepare your work area. I find it best to spread out a large towel on the bench to retain any bits that jump out and provide a soft base for more fragile items.

If the speedometer is to be returned to a vehicle, make a note of the odometer reading. There are three screws at the rear casing and three around the bezel holding the glass. Carefully remove the mechanism from the casing. Lay out the main elements of the speedometer (Fig.4). It helps to have a needle puller and jeweller's screwdrivers when undertaking this work.

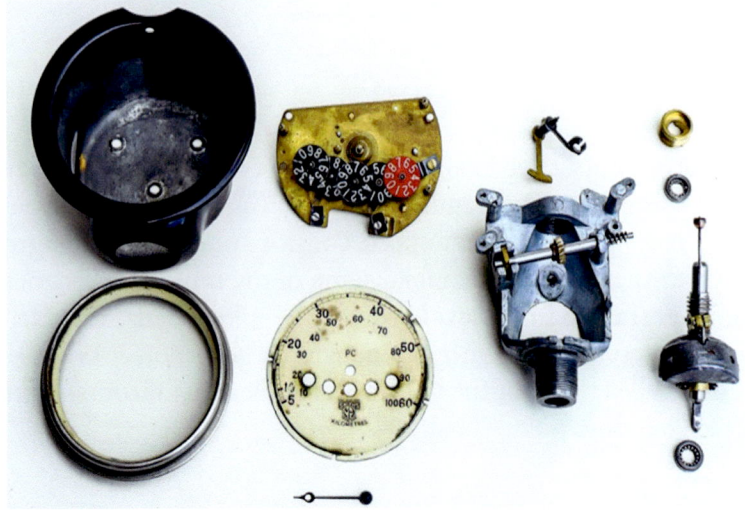

Fig.4: Elements of the Smiths speedometer

The first step is to clean all the elements thoroughly in paraffin or similar de-greaser. Ensure that no cloth fibres adhere to the mechanisms. Soaking brass items overnight in tomato sauce usually cleans them well.

Internal Inspection

When I dismantled this speedometer, lots of tiny balls fell out onto the bench. Luckily the towel was there to retain them. Clearly, the rotor was no longer supported by the open ball-bearing system – hence the *tuk-tuk* noise. The fix seemed simple but the cause was not obvious. The balls are located in an open race (Figs.5, 6). A threaded adjustable cup at the top of the spindle support frame holds them in position by applying slight pressure on the spindle taper (Fig.7). This was the culprit: the adjustment cup had worked loose and released the ball bearings – hence the noise.

Fig.5: Balls in upper race

Fig.6: Balls in open lower race

Fig.7: Spindle showing top and bottom bearing contact area

Fitting the tiny ball bearings in their respective races is a fiddly job and it is essential to use some light grease to position them. The top threaded adjustment cup needs careful setting to ensure that the spindle rotates freely while retaining the tiny balls. The assembly shows the top bearing with its threaded adjustment cup and the lower bearing. It is important to ensure that the spindle is properly centred so that its gearing meshes with the angled drive shaft to the odometer (Fig.8).

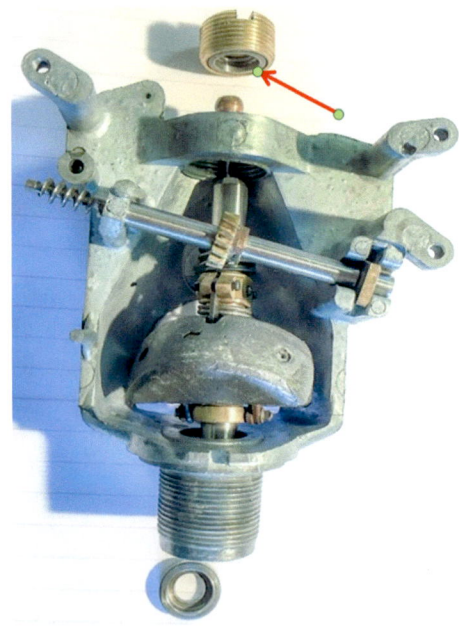

Fig.8: Threaded adjustment cup (top)   Fig.9: Side view showing threaded cup locking screw

Once the threaded cup is fitted, there is a cup locking screw on the die-cast zinc frame (Fig.9). On further examination, I found that the original locking screw thread had never been drilled sufficiently or threaded into the casting for it to lock the bearing cap. This meant that it had not been effective since manufacture!

With the threaded bearing cup working loose over time and finally releasing the ball bearings out of the race, the spindle was knocking the casing. It is surprising that no damage was done to the mechanism.

Upgrading the Speedometer Design

After studying the open ball-bearing design I realised that a simple modification would greatly improve the performance and life of the speedometer. I managed to source miniature sealed ball-bearing races that fitted the shaft and existing zinc frame without having to change the original dimensions. The spindle with sealed-for-life ball races positioned top and bottom has upgraded this 94-year-old speedometer.

Fig.10: Bearing races in position   Fig.11: Bearing race fits top cap

The spindle tapers partially fit the internal bore of the ball bearings, enabling sufficient friction grip (Fig.10) and are in perfect alignment with the upper and lower bearing races in position. The top threaded bearing cup accepted the sealed bearing race perfectly (Fig.11) but I had to mill the zinc base slightly to accept the depth of the ball race so that the spindle aligned with the angle drive to the odometer (Fig.12).

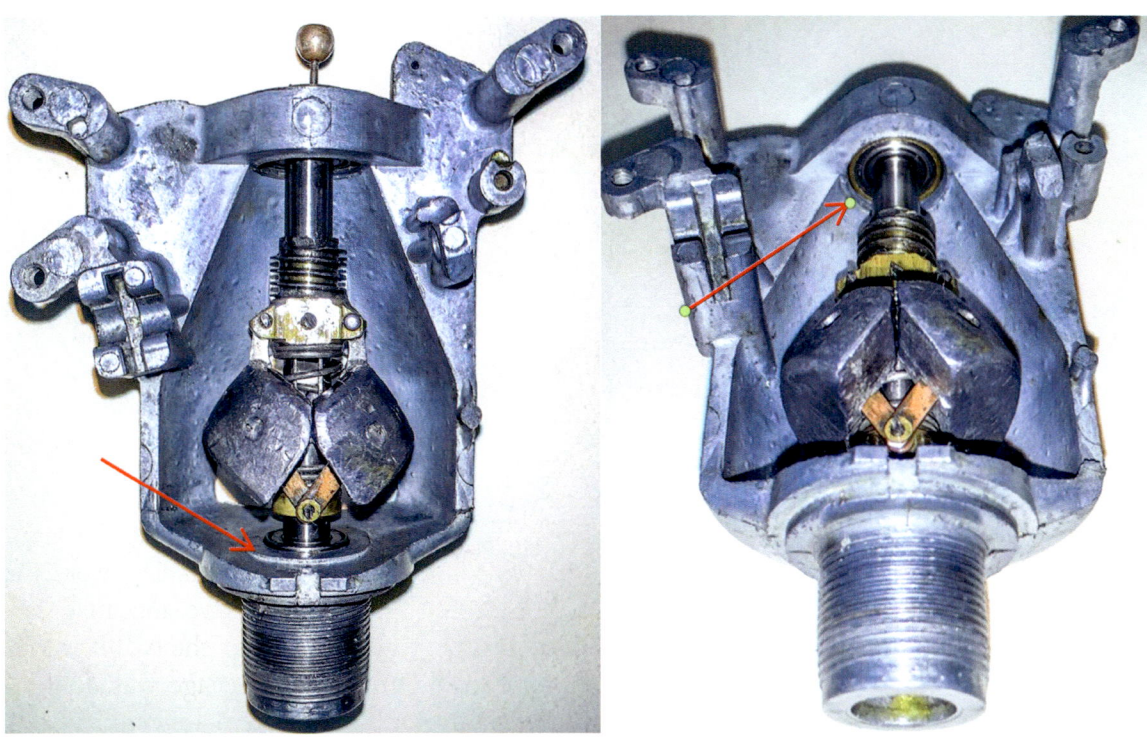

Fig.12: The lower and upper bearing races in position

Assembling the Speedometer

When assembled, it is essential that the spindle runs freely. The spindle alignment, meshed with the inclined shaft (Fig.13) is retained with a brass keep plate (left).

Fig.13: Odometer gear drive meshed with main spindle and shaft keep plate

Fig.14: Plan view of top bearing and needle indicator cup

During fitting of the odometer plate and mechanism, gently place the spindle rod's spherical securing ball (top) into the needle gear cup (Fig.14).

The rear plate with needle actuating gear and odometer dial numbers are shown (Fig.15). Notice the indicating needle gear (top) and cup for positioning the spherical ball from the main spindle assembly.

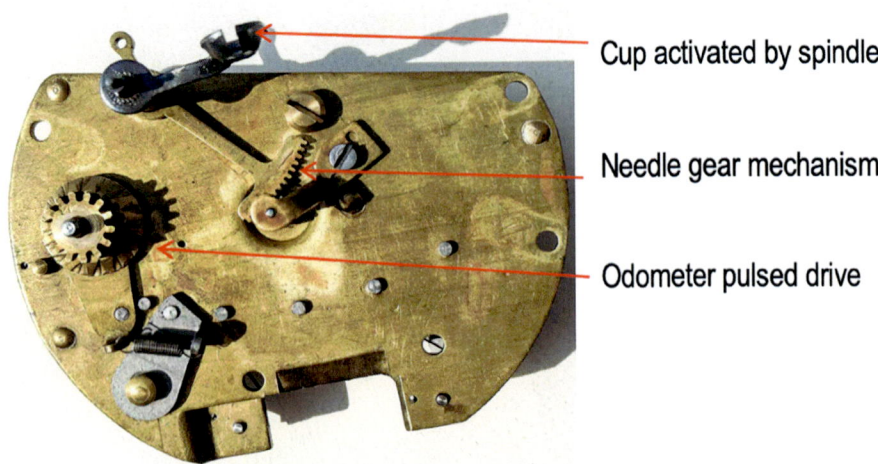

Fig.15: Rear of odometer plate – needle drive and odometer

The odometer pulsed drive has a concentric plate under the gear with a spring actuator that needs to be properly fitted. It has a logical position: the front of the odometer with numerical discs for indicating distance (Fig.16) that seldom need touching apart from cleaning. Remember that brass is a self-lubricating material and little or no oil is needed. If you have jewellers' oil available you can apply it lightly to any steel to brass pivot contact areas, using a sewing needle to apply the minimal amount of oil. Take care not to distort or damage the delicate needle return hairspring.

Fig.16: Front of odometer and needle return hairspring

Installation into the Instrument Panel

Once assembled mount the unit in the vertical position and fit the speed indicating needle. Do not do this lying flat as the spindle weights must be in their normal operating position. Gravity sets it at zero.

Before placing the mechanism into the unit housing, test it with a slow speed electric drill or screwdriver in the clockwise direction. This is best done by connecting a speedo drive cable with the drill at the other end. Start turning slowly and if assembled correctly the speedo should have a smooth indication throughout its speed range.

Ensure that the mileage on the dials is set as desired or at the mileage shown when you started. Then insert the mechanism into the main housing.

The key to achieving an efficient speedo is a good drive cable that has generous bends from the gearbox to the speedometer (the routing is not always easy). Pay considerable attention to this.

When on the road check against a modern car what your actual speed is and if necessary adjust the needle position. This will require removal of the instrument.

Service Checklist
1. Note the odometer reading before dismantling.
2. Lay a large cloth or old towel on your working area.
3. Remove the speedo from the instrument panel and from its casing.
4. Any loose balls or parts will be captured on the cloth.
5. Take photos from all angles.
6. Remove the indicating needle and main dial.
7. Wash the whole instrument in paraffin or similar cleaning fluid.
8. Remove main spindle and ball bearings.
9. Fit new miniature sealed bearing races or original balls.
10. When assembling lightly grease the bearings to hold their position.
11. Lightly lubricate any steel pivots to brass bearings: use a needle to do this.
12. Reset the spindle so that top and bottom bearings are retained and secured.
13. Lock the top threaded cup that sets the spindle clearances.
14. Assemble the odometer when vertical, fit the indicating needle at 5mph (0).
15. Test speedo with a slow electric drill and suitable cable.
16. Reset the odometer reading to original value and install in instrument panel.
17. Check the main drive cable and replace if needed.

Closing Comments

The fitting of sealed ball races to my speedo has certainly improved its operation and 7,000 miles later it continues to function well. I expect that the miniature sealed-for-life bearings will ensure that it runs for a very long time quietly and efficiently. However, the original loose ball design can be effective as long as it is serviced from time to time: the top and bottom bearings will need modest grease lubrication despite the awkward process.

There are many variations of the Smiths speedometer and other makes of the period but they all operate by the same basic principle and can be maintained with a little care.

Appendices

Appendix I

List of Tables

Appendix II

Scheduled Morris Stops

ZIMBABWE

Date	Morris Test Run From	To	Morris Miles
31/3/2023	Paddocks (Bvuma, Mutare)	Leopard Rock Hotel	16
02/04/2023	Leopard Rock Hotel	Paddocks (Bvuma, Mutare)	14
	BTA Tour Starts From	**To**	**Morris Miles**
03/04/2023	Mutare, Hillside Golf Club	Birchenough Bridge Hotel – overnight	87
03/04/2023	Birchenough Bridge	Birchenough	3
04/04/2023	Birchenough	Masvingo	108
04/04/2023	Masvingo	Great Zimbabwe	20
04/04/2023	Great Zimbabwe	Zvishavane – overnight	84
05/04/2023	Zvishavane	Bulawayo – Granite Lodge – 5 nights	115
06/04/2023	Bulawayo	Matopos and return	70
06/04/2023	Bulawayo	Bulawayo	20
08/04/2023	Bulawayo	Gweru – Bradley Garden Experience	121
09/04/2023	Gweru	Harare – Pangoula Farm – 4 nights	185
13/04/2023	Harare	Chinhoyi – Zebras Dazzle – overnight	97
14/04/2023	Chinhoyi	Makuti Lodge – overnight	95
15/04/2023	Makuti	Kariba Safari Lodge, Siavonga – 3 nights	66

ZAMBIA

Date		To	Morris Miles
18/04/2023	Siavonga	Chirundu	62
18/04/2023	Chirundu	Lusaka – Cummins – 2 nights	96
21/04/2023	Lusaka	Kabwe – Safari Lodge – overnight	95
21/04/2023	Kabwe	Kapiri Mposhi	125
21/04/2023	Kapiri Mposhi	Ndola – Protea Marriott Hotel – 2 nights	70
23/04/2023	Kitwe, Itimpi	Kitwe Kamushi Farm – 3 nights	30
26/04/2023	Kalulushi	Kalulushi	15
	Return with BMW	**Morris in the Box Trailer**	
27/04/2023	Kitwe	Lusaka, Sandra's Creations Cecily's Fund Dinner	
28/04/2023	Lusaka	Kafue, Lusaka – Hans Sportel – 2 nights	6
30/04/2023	Lusaka	Choma, Masuku – 3 nights (photos)	7
03/05/2023	Masuku (photo shoot)	Livingstone – 3 nights	
04/05/2023	Livingstone (photo shoot)	Victoria Falls (Morris across and back)	23

Total Morris Miles			**1,509**

Appendix III

Travel Stats

Fuel Consumption and Costs

Morris Minor – first 523 miles 24.76 miles per gallon petrol
– next 986 miles 35.91 miles per gallon petrol
– total 46.57 gallons for 1,509 averaging 32.39 MPG
Total fuel cost US$335.87 (ZAR6,213)

BMW X5 and Trailer – 9,767km, 2,909 litres. ZAR 33,780

Road Tolls – ZAR 2,664 (£117), 1 percent of all costs

Exchange rates March 2023:

GB£1=ZAR22.7, GB£1=ZWD460, GB£1=ZMW 26,
US$1= ZAR18.5, US$1=ZWD362, US$1=ZMW 21.5

Appendix IV

The Boy Scouts of Rhodesia

Graham Pringle and I loved scouting from joining as young Cubs and progressing to Senior Scouts. The culmination of consistent effort was being awarded the highest accolade in scouting, the Queen's Scout Certificate in Southern and Northern Rhodesia, respectively (Figs.1, 2). Figure 3 shows Graham receiving his certificate from the Mayor of Bulawayo. I was not so honoured as by the time my badge was confirmed there was an exodus from Northern Rhodesia: the prospect of Independence loomed and the scouting association had virtually collapsed for the time being. Only years later, after an application to Gilwell Headquarters, was my certificate issued.

Later in life I attended a business conference in Ohio, USA where each delegate was invited to summarise their background and mention any notable achievements. When I said that I was a Queen's Scout, some wag popped up saying "in California that has a different meaning." Yes, it brought the house down with laughter. Not everything translates borders (in the States they have Eagle Scouts as our equivalent).

Fig.1: 1961 Graham D. Pringle – Queen's Scout Certificate

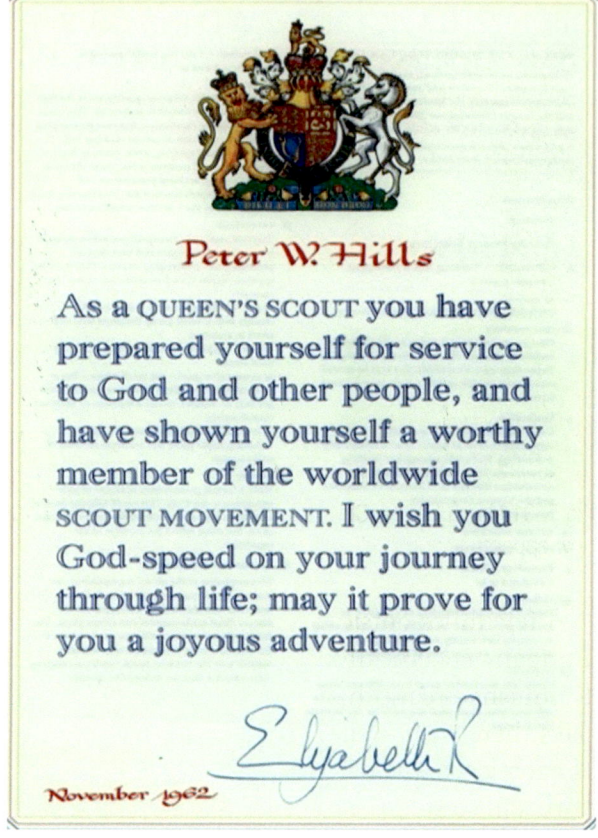

Fig.2: 1962 Peter W. Hills – Queen's Scout Certificate

Fig.3: 1961 Graham receiving his Queen's Scout Certificate from the Mayor, Bulawayo Southern Rhodesia

Fig.4: 1962 Sir Charles McLean Commonwealth Chief Scout visited Kitwe where I had the honour to brief him

Figure 4 was reported in the Northern Newspaper when the Commonwealth Chief Scout, Sir Charles McLean visited Kitwe and I had to take time off work to meet him.

Scouting was such an enjoyable life journey: camping, learning bush crafts, sports, first-aid, leadership and more. Graham and I are relatively new friends but with so much in common we realised we have lived almost parallel lives. During our Back-to-Africa trip we made a point of visiting and, where possible, stopping at scout camp sites: Chinziwa Boy Scout Park, Bvumba, Mutare then Gordon Park Matopos near Bulawayo (Figs.5, 6).

Fig.5: 31 March 2023 – Chinziwa Boy Scout Park, Bvumba now appears abandoned

Fig.6: 5 April 2023 Boy Scout's Gordon Park Matopos where Graham enjoyed many camps

A few miles outside Kitwe was the memorable Tinkers Claim site donated by the Rhokana mining company specifically for the scout movement. It was defined by a string of *koppies* rising above the Kalulushi stream that was ice-cold and crystal clear; there were indigenous trees everywhere. In those days there was no such thing as a Portaloo. At camp we had to dig latrines as well as wet and dry pits at each kitchen area. These had to be sufficiently deep and at the end of camp they would be covered with soil so that the monkeys and other creatures would not dig up the biodegradable detritus. Sadly, soon after Zambia's independence, UNIP (United National Independence Party) held a youth camp there but did not provide tents; so the youngsters simply chopped down all the trees to make basic shelters for their weekend camp. The stream was subsequently polluted and the area became an environmental disaster. Google maps indicate that the whole area is a maze of uncontrolled settlements in what was once pristine land for all humanity – such is progress! One of the prime disciplines instilled into all scouts is "always leave the camp site cleaner than you found it and never cut down or mark any trees." If not the UNIP youth, then the charcoal burners may well have caused the same destruction which is endemic wherever we toured in the Morris.

During our tour of Kitwe, I was quite upset to see that the "new Scout Hall" was now a supermarket (Fig.380). How can a public-subscribed building be acquired for commerce? Where do Zambia's Cubs, Brownies, Girl Guides and Boy Scouts of Kitwe meet now?

The scouting movement started in Southern Rhodesia in 1909 when three boys acquired a copy of Baden Powell's *Scouting for Boys* and decided to form a group called the 1st Bulawayo (Pioneer) Scouts. By 1910 it began to take shape under the leadership of the Rev. T.O. Beattie who later attended the 1959 Central African Jamboree at Ruwa Park (Fig.12). (Ref.18: *The Rhodesian Study Circle*).

Graham Pringle joined Bulawayo's 20th Scout Troop, indicative of the growing interest in Scouting there. It was the same in Kitwe: most of my school pals joined the Scouts as it was a type of freedom and show of independence. You had to work as a team and join in all sorts of activities including competitive bridge building. At camp, as a junior, I was often assigned to scrubbing pots – the juniors get the dirty work! Later as Troop Leader things were different, although I did enjoy being the camp cook.

Scouting grew rapidly and by 1924 the Rhodesias and Nyasaland sent a large contingent to the second World Scout Jamboree in Ermelunden, Denmark. The logistics for this adventure are mind boggling – an 8000 mile train and boat journey 100 years ago. The popularity of the scouting movement in Rhodesia was largely due to its outdoor programme: hiking, camping, cooking and pioneering in the wild bush. The training and progressive badge system was about achieving a range of skills targeted towards helping others and leading to responsible citizenship. When I started my training at the local copper mine, we all had to undertake and pass a first-aid course; for me it was no pressure having been involved in first-aid competitions at scouts – I came top of the class.

Around 1900 most of the indigenous population of Northern Rhodesia had never seen white people and knew nothing of their ways. Today young Africans in Zambia throw themselves heart and soul into the Pathfinder Scout movement. People respect a uniform that gives identity and recognition. Scouting was started at the Lubwa Mission by the Church of Scotland in 1930 and continues to this day. In 1964 during the Alice Lenshina Lumpa conflict I visited Lubwa Mission where, sadly, and shockingly, I saw a victim of smallpox in an isolated hospital room gazing at me through the glass – an awful experience.

In Kitwe I was a Cub (Fig.6) and over some 14 years rose to Senior Scout Troop Leader. In 1960 Frank Bosco our Seniors Master took 5 of us to Livingstone to undertake the Venturer's badge that involves a minimum 25 mile hike. My assignment was to map out the gorges below the Victoria Falls. It was very hot and baboons kept following us; sleeping under the stars was a little nerve-wracking. We only had a stave and sheath knife for protection! Since we had driven 835km down from the Copperbelt, the Livingstone Province held a special meeting in our honour (Fig.7). I am the short fellow second from the front!'

While still at school I ran an African Cub Pack in Wusikili Compound that was an 8 mile cycle ride from home. I used to get a lot of ragging from some of the rougher racist types at school but I ignored them. Years later young Zambians, then grown men, would meet me in the town saying "Hello Hathi", my Cub Instructor's name.

Fig.7: 1953 Cub Peter Hills tries his hand at the Scout Fête shooting gallery – I won a Port decanter

Fig.8: 1960 The 1st Nkana–Kitwe Senior Scouts trip to Livingstone to map out the gorges of Victoria Falls

The 1959 Central Africa Jamboree was held at Ruwa Park, in Southern Rhodesia. The camp was divided into four sectors: Victoria Falls, Matopos, Zimbabwe and Kariba. Scouts came from as far as Kenya and the Belgian Congo and of many ethnic and religious persuasions. It was an enlightening time for us to meet and exchange badges from scouts of different countries. For years I had a pen friend in Arusha of Tanganyika (Tanzania).

Graham was assigned to Matopos Camp (Fig.9) while I being from Northern Rhodesia was at Victoria Falls Camp (Fig.10). Unfortunately, we never met at that memorable gathering. I shared a tent with my lifelong pal David Bromfield. On our arrival I remember him whispering to me that hidden in his sleeping bag was a new family-size Coca-Cola bottle: we had never seen such a huge thing before – how were we going to drink it all?

The Jamboree brochure detailed all events (Fig.11): the iconic balancing rocks depicted on the cover were the Jamboree logo. I carved my woggle from vegetable ivory that is common in Livingstone with the same motif for my NR and Kitwe Scout scarves (Fig.11). In 2019 I donated all my scouting attire – shirt, badges, scarves, documents – to the Scouting Headquarters at Gilwell Park in England who were delighted to add them to their museum.

At Ruwa, we were treated to day trips: visiting the ancient cave paintings in Domboshawa and at Lake McIlwaine where we saw many crocodiles. There was an inter-camp football match that Dave Bromfield played in for our Camp. At the opening ceremony the RRAF did a flyover in a Canberra jet bomber that made a huge noise: it was all new and very exciting to us boys from the north.

As usual I had my trusty Kodak Brownie box camera. I snapped the first scout master Cannon T. O. Beattie meeting Lord Rowallan, the Commonwealth Chief Scout (Fig.12). Like most youngsters those days we collected postage stamps – I mailed home the first-day cover stamps (Fig.13). Much to my Mum's chagrin, I never enclosed a letter! I thought one day these stamps would be valuable. On the journey home we swung by Kariba Dam (Fig.273) to see the progress of the construction of this massive hydroelectric scheme that would create a 114 mile lake, the largest in the world at that time. In 1960 the Queen Mother officially opened the Dam. The Jamboree was a memorable learning experience, never forgotten.

Fig.9: Matopos camp entrance – my photo

Fig.10: Victoria Falls camp entrance – my photo

Fig.11: 1959 Central African Jamboree – Ruwa Park, Brochure and NR scarf and vegetable ivory woggle (balancing rocks was the event logo)

Fig.12: 1959 Central African Jamboree – Ruwa Park Salisbury, Rev. T.O. Beattie first scout master and Lord Rowallan Commonwealth Chief Scout

Fig.13: 4 May 1959 First-day cover stamps – they are all I could afford from my pocket money!

Appendix V

Politics: Zimbabwe and Zambia

The Federation of Rhodesia and Nyasaland was established on 1 August 1953 and was a mirror of today's European Union. Power was centralised in Salisbury (Harare) that became the Federal Capital, thus attracting new investment to establish the administration centre of ministries (agriculture, mining, defence, health) of the Federation. New embassies from around the world added to the wealth of the city. The University of Rhodesia was an important development. Much of the revenue from Northern Rhodesia's world-class copper mining industry contributed to the growth of Salisbury from what was a regional town to a vibrant city with high-rise offices and hotels. Northern Rhodesia and Nyasaland were the "poor relations" that felt the impact post-independence. We called Southern Rhodesia the *bamba zonke* (take all) country.

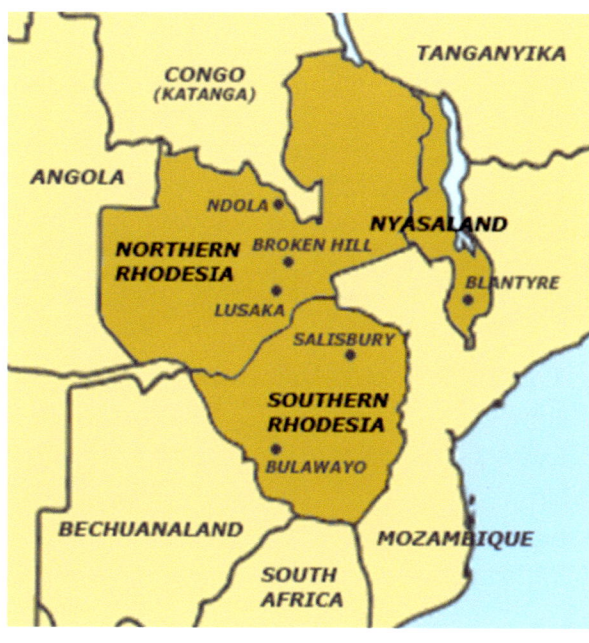

During the twentieth century the British Empire progressively dismantled itself and after the Second World War this process was accelerated. By 1964 the Protectorate of Northern Rhodesia became Zambia, the Protectorate of Nyasaland became Malawi and, after a bitter conflict, the Colony of Southern Rhodesia evolved to Rhodesia after Ian Smith's Unilateral Declaration of Independence and finally became Zimbabwe in 1980.

Zambia did not have a good start at independence: the headquarters of the main ministries were in the South and it inherited the regional administrative offices. Apart from several short-sighted political decisions, the country had little chance of early success, with only a handful of Zambian graduates who had qualified mostly in political science and law.

Prior to independence all road and rail communications were first class. A combination of factors subsequently resulted in the deterioration of the infrastructure, particularly the road network: corruption, neglect, lack of maintenance, a massive increase in road traffic and the rail network being abandoned. Huge intercontinental trucks with as many as 26 wheels plough the highways to destruction. Potholes have become an accepted way of life, not only on main highways; town and city roads are not maintained, resulting in more rubble than tar. This background of a collapsed road network in both Zimbabwe and Zambia made the trip in a small 94 year-old car quite challenging. Initially the political situation was a concern but it eased considerably after Covid-19 and proved irrelevant by the time we started the tour. The preparation, the BTA Team and our confidence were certainly the key to success.

Appendix VI

Names and Places – New and Old

NEW TOWN NAMES Zimbabwe
Mutare
Mazvingo
Zvishavane
Gweru
Harare
Chinhoyi
Kwekwe
Hwange

OLD TOWN Southern Rhodesia
Umtali
Fort Victoria
Shabani
Gwelo
Salisbury
Sinoia
Que
Wankie

NEW TOWN NAMES Zambia
Kabwe
Kitwe – Garneton
Mansa
Chipata
Chililabombwe

OLD TOWN NAMES Northern Rhodesia
Broken Hill
Kitwe – Itimpi
Fort Rosebury
Fort Jameson
Bancroft

NEW ROAD NAMES (Kitwe) Zambia

Matuka Avenue
Obote Avenue
Oxford Road
Iseni Avenue
Chibote Avenue
Lilongwe Street
Kuomboka Drive
Unity Way

OLD ROAD NAMES (Kitwe) Northern Rhodesia
Regent Street
Strand Avenue
Oxford Street
Cornwall Avenue
Galway Avenue
Stanley Street
Salisbury Drive
Yorkminster Way

Appendix VII

Colloquial Expressions

Bamba zonke	Take all
Braai	Barbeque
Bundu	Bush or jungle
Boerewors	Farmer's spicy sausage (South Africa)
Clobber	Clothing
Dop / Toot	Tot of liquor or a drink
Flicks	Cinema or the Pictures
Koppies	Small hills or rocky outcrop
Kraal	Cattle enclosure
Loadshedding	Scheduled electricity power outages
Mombe	Cattle
Tatenda	Be thankful (Thank you)
Tjorrie	African name for a donkey cart or motor car
Tom	Money
Tsotsis	Bandits, street wise scammers
Sadza	Maize porridge or mealie meal
Stoep	Veranda

Appendix VIII

Cross References

Bibliography

Ref.1   Cockcroft, Barry, *Turn Left – The Riffs Have Risen* (London: the RAC, 1981)

Ref.2   The Cecily's Fund – *Educating Zambians for a better future* – 16 Sept. 2023

Ref.3   Edwards, Harry, *Morris Motor Car* 1913–1983 (London: Moorland Publishing, 1983)

Ref.4   *Classic & Sports Car Magazine*, 'Out of Africa', 1 September 1993

Ref.5   Caldecott, A. C. E., *The Tanganda Tea Co.: Origins and Development*, 1997

Ref.6   Salt, Beryl, *A Pride of Eagles* (Solihull: Helion & Co., 2015)

Ref.7   Smith, Ian Douglas, *The Great Betrayal* (London: Blake Publishing, 1997)

Ref.8   Stuart-Findlay, Derek, *Our Intrepid Cape Motoring Pioneers* (Cape Town: Tandem Press, 2015)

Ref.9   Johnston, Bob, *Early Motoring in South Africa* (Cape Town: C. Struik Publishers (Pty) Ltd, 1975)

Ref.10 *Crankhandle Club Chronicle*, June 2023, July 2023 (Cape Town, 2023)

Ref.11 *Vintage Minor Register* Magazine M186, Summer 2023. BTA Report

Ref.12 *Vintage Minor Register* Magazine M187, Autumn 2023. BTA Report

Ref.13 Nagle, John D. Nagle and Edwards, Harry, *The Complete Morris Minor* (Hunckley: The Morris Register, 2012)

Ref.14 Peter W. Hills – www.World.BirdPhotos.com – birding web site

Ref.15 McIntyre, Chris and Susan, *Bradt's Zambia Safari Guide*, 7th edition (Chalfont St Peter: Bradt Guides, 2023)

Ref.16 *Morris Register Monthly* Magazine, December 2023, BTA Report

Ref.17 *Classic & Sports Car* Magazine, "Africa Queen" June 2024

Ref.18 *Origins of the Boy Scouts Association* (Salisbury: The Rhodesian Study Circle, 1979)

About the author
Peter William Hills

Dipl. Man, FBINDT, MBA

Demobbed after the end of WW2, Peter's uncle and father went to work in the former protectorate of Northern Rhodesia now Zambia. In 1950 the family moved from Essex in the UK to Kitwe where Peter did all his schooling. He was recruited by Anglo American Corp and trained as a measurement and process control engineer. From 1965 to 1980 the land-locked country was surrounded by warring nations that affected imported supplies and services. To overcome some of the industry's many challenges Peter developed and introduced a range of technologies by creating teams of forensic engineers to support both the copper mining and private sector. Peter is proud that several Zambians were developed to sustain these specialist support services that continue to this day.

During 1970 he rescued a 1929 Morris Minor tourer from the jungle outside Kitwe. By 1984 he was head hunted to the UK so he took the Morris chassis as part of his personal effects to Chester England. Researching the Morris's history was as exciting as its restoration identifying all its ten owners and some of their history. He subsequently worked around the world while undertaking an honours degree and then an MBA. By 1992 the Morris was restored to Concours condition but in 2004 Peter and Sandy relocated to Mumbai India to turn-around an ailing industrial electronics company. With the job done, by late 2013 they returned to the UK and now follow the sun spending time in London and Cape Town South Africa. This enabled the realisation of a dream to return the Morris to Itimpi outside Kitwe. In 2023 despite huge challenges the car was driven 1,509 miles from its initial place of registration in Zimbabwe via the addresses of all listed owners back to where the car was rescued 53 years ago. While there was a perceived risk in this audacious adventure, Peter's determination, focus and project management has resulted in a lifetime achievement that rewarded not only Peter but also those of his team, Graham, David, Wayne and many friends associated with Tracing My African Routes.

In addition to Peters' vintage car hobby, together with Sandra, they undertake bird photography wherever it takes them. His photo collection is published in www.worldbirdphotos.com, often rated 70/1000 of the best bird web sites in the world with images in a variety of publications and bird books. Amongst Peter's passion are vintage cars and bird photography:

Fig.530: My 1933 MG J2 – son of Chilupala – Restored 2024

www.worldbirdphotos.com